MW00638893

PARENTS OF THE SAINTS

PARENTS

OF THE

SAINTS

THE HIDDEN HEROES BEHIND
OUR FAVORITE SAINTS

PATRICK O'HEARN

TAN BOOKS
GASTONIA, NORTH CAROLINA

© 2020 Patrick O'Hearn

All rights reserved. With the exception of short excerpts used in critical review, no part of this work may be reproduced, transmitted, or stored in any form whatsoever, without the prior written permission of the publisher.

Unless otherwise noted, Scripture quotations are from Revised Standard Version of the Bible—Second Catholic Edition (Ignatius Edition) Copyright © 2006 National Council of the Church of Christ in the United States of America. Used by permission. All rights reserved worldwide.

Excerpts from the English translation of the *Catechism of the Catholic Church*, Second Edition, ©1994, 1997, 2000 by Libreria Editrice Vaticana, United States Catholic Conference, Washington, D.C. All rights reserved.

Cover Design by Devin Schadt.
Interior layout by Michael Fontecchio.
Edited by Jane Cavolina and Jeffrey Cole.

ISBN: 978-1-5051-2131-5
Kindle ISBN: 978-1-5051-2132-2
ePUB ISBN: 978-1-5051-2133-9

Published in the United States by
TAN Books
PO Box 269
Gastonia, NC 28053
www.TANBooks.com

Printed in the United States of America

This book is lovingly dedicated
to
Our Lady, the Queen of all Saints
and to
my parents.

Contents

PREFACE

While walking with my wife one December evening in 2014 as the sun was setting, the Holy Spirit unexpectantly laid this book on my heart. At the time, I was thirty years old, recently married, and had never written a book. And, truthfully, I had always dreaded writing. But somehow Our Lord, Who also began His public ministry at the age of thirty, had prepared me for this daunting project long before. Yes, everything in my life up to this point, especially my disappointments, desires, joys, and sufferings, had culminated in the *Parents of the Saints*, which took me over three years to write, including many late nights. This book was written to inspire other married couples to holiness while reminding us that our most important task as parents is to form saints.

As a young child, I devoured the lives of the saints and still do. Like many of the parents of the saints, the goal of my young life involved discovering my vocation. I remember many nights pondering what it was that God wanted of me and then pleading for Our Lord and Our Lady's guidance. Inspired by Sts. Francis of Assisi, Martin de Porres, and Thérèse of Lisieux and their love for the Holy Eucharist, humility, and hiddenness, I began making several discernment trips to the Benedictines, Carmelites, Franciscans, and Trappists in college before joining the Benedictines for a few years as an aspiring monk. Reading these books on the lives of the saints enkindled my desire to be a religious brother, and I thought God was calling me to spend my brief time on this earth hidden from the world in a monastery interceding and adoring Him. But God had other plans.

Through some painful circumstances, God changed the course of my vocation and the desires of my heart. Eventually, He led me to the path of marriage and introduced me to the parents of St.

Thérèse of Lisieux, Sts. Louis and Zélie Martin, who changed my
life forever. When God called me to marriage, I realized Louis and
Zélie were two people with similar desires. Like me, they both
longed for religious life, but, eventually, God led them to marriage.
Ironically, every night before retiring in religious life, I knelt before
a statue of St. Thérèse, which was next to my monastic cell. Looking
back, I think the words of the Gospel, "He who has seen me has seen
the Father" (Jn 14:9), also applies to most of the saints. Specifically,
he who sees the saints unknowingly sees the hidden virtues of their
parents shining through them.

Prior to encountering Louis and Zélie, I struggled for some
time relating to the barefooted friar who slept on the floor or the
nun who levitated in the choir loft. Many of our saints books depict
such holy men and women. I still remained devoted to them, but I
needed other saintly exemplars who experienced the challenges of
the married vocation and, with God's grace and Our Lady's help,
lived heroic lives. As a husband and father, I yearned to read stories
on holy married couples and how they formed their children, but
those books were scarce. What were their secrets to sanctity? Were
their children born saints, or did they also live extraordinary lives
like their children? This quest led me to research fifty saints from
the distant past to the present day, specifically with an emphasis on
learning about their parents and what set them apart from others.
In order to become the parents God is calling us to be, we ought to
learn from those who have heroically accomplished this task. And
what better guide than the over one hundred parents of the saints
presented in this book.

I never intended to write a lengthy book. But, as this book
progressed, I felt more and more saints whisper to me in prayer,
"Tell my parents' story. The world needs to know about our unsung
heroes, who laid the foundation for our spiritual lives." These parents
have been hidden like a light under a bushel basket for centuries,
and now God and their saintly children want them to shine in the
present time, which is one of the darkest hours for our Church and
our world (see Mk 4:21). God has the answer for our troubled times:
He wants parents to cooperate with Him to raise up extraordinary

souls. Our Church needs new saints more than ever—saints who will set the world on fire with the love of God and help save souls from the fires of Hell.

While discerning with the Franciscan Friars of the Renewal in New York City, it was said that one has everything there to become a saint, referring to their rich prayer life, religious vows, and love for the poor. Hence, part of my writing this book was to remind couples that you also have everything you need in the Sacrament of Holy Matrimony to live a saintly life and to raise saints. We must look no further than the godly parents of the saints. Their virtuous lives provide a sure pathway to sanctity by their heroic response to the graces of their wedding vows—graces that flow unceasingly from the pierced hearts of Jesus and Mary to generous couples. And, while each of us must listen to the Holy Spirit's unique promptings in our own lives, these devout parents have set an example for all married couples by challenging us to live entirely for God, our family, and others.

This book is neither an exhaustive list of every holy parent of a saint, nor does it capture every virtue exhibited by these hidden heroes. Also, the dearth of writings pertaining to the parents of the saints, especially those living before the last three centuries, makes it difficult to do justice to their lives. Moreover, there are many past and future holy parents whose children will never become saints due to their children's free will. The Rule of St. Benedict tells us that the abbot will one day give an account for all his children. And, if the abbot has done everything in his power to win them to Christ by his teaching and example and they still stray, only then is the abbot "acquitted at the Lord's Judgment." The same could be said of holy parents, who will not lose any of their merit, even if their children sadly stray or fall short of becoming saints, provided these parents cooperated with God's grace to instill virtue in their children and prayed for their salvation.

With the holy family as the model for raising a family, this book is written to shed light on the parents of the saints so that individuals, regardless of their vocation, will be inspired not only to strive to be saints, but, if God calls them to the married vocation, will desire more than anything to raise their children to become saints. Yes, a father and mother who embrace the Gospel message, like the saintly parents featured in this book, can transform the world one diaper at a time, one prayer at a time, and one conversation at a time because the domestic church is the first school of the saints.

It is my prayer that you will be inspired by these holy parents and fall more deeply in love with God and His Church, and be convinced that holiness is found in the home as much as in the cloister.

ACKNOWLEDGMENTS

I would like to express my deepest gratitude to those who helped make this book possible—some by loaning me books, others by proofreading, and still others, most of all, by their prayers:

Fr. Jacinto Chapin, FFI, Fr. Justin Kerber, CP, Fr. Lester Knoll, OFM Cap., Fr. Lawrence Kutz, Luke Zemlick, and my family.

I would like to thank Jane Cavolina and Jeffrey Cole for their outstanding editorial assistance, and Mike Fontecchio for his amazing interior layout. I also wish to express my appreciation for Devin Schadt, in particular, for his cover design and mentorship. I must also thank my wife, Amanda, for her edits, support, and patience with me during this endeavor! I would like to thank my father-in-law, Jeff, and my mother-in-law, Sonia, for their strong faith and openness to life. I would like to thank my parents, Steve and Maureen, for their heroic witness and for passing on to me the greatest treasure, the Catholic Faith.

Finally, I give thanks to God for the gift of the holy parents of the saints and their splendid witness to the married vocation.

Has not the one God made and sustained for us the spirit of life? And what does he desire? Godly offspring. So take heed to yourselves, and let none be faithless to the wife of his youth.

—*Malachi 2:15*

INTRODUCTION

June 24, 1950, marked the first time in the Church's history that a mother would attend the canonization of her own daughter, the eleven-year-old Italian martyr, St. Maria Goretti. With God's grace, Assunta Goretti had achieved a feat that every devout mother dreams of—to raise her child to become a saint. September 25, 2010, marked the first time in the Church's history that both a father and mother would attend the beatification of their own daughter, Bl. Chiara Luce Badano. Unlike Maria Goretti, who was stabbed to death, Chiara suffered from a lengthy bout of terminal cancer that ended her life at only eighteen. Just as the widowed Assunta Goretti remained by her daughter Maria in her dying moments, Chiara's parents watched vigilantly at their only child's bedside

What a trial for these parents to witness the death of their daughters, both teenagers. No human pain can compare to the loss of one's child, yet no human joy can compare to the reality that one's own child would become a saint by keeping the Faith to her last breaths, fighting the good fight, and so enter into the Father's house for all eternity.

October 18, 2015, marked the first time in the Church's history that a husband and wife were canonized together: Sts. Louis and Zélie Martin. This holy couple is not as widely known as their daughter, St. Thérèse of Lisieux, who is one of the Church's greatest saints and one of only four female Doctors of the Church. Perhaps as impressive as having their beloved child become a saint was the opening of the cause for beatification and canonization for their third daughter, Léonie Martin, which occurred on July 2, 2015, in the Visitation Monastery chapel in Caen, France. Unlike Thérèse, Léonie was Louis and Zélie's most difficult child. In fact, Zélie once wrote, "It's her future that worries me the most. I say to myself, 'What will become of her if I'm no longer here?' I don't dare think about it."[1] Léonie, who became Sr. Françoise-Thérèse, a Visitation nun, could one day join her sister Thérèse and her parents among the canonized saints—oh, to be in that number! Louis and Zélie are among many holy parents of the saints whose virtues and whose secrets to raising saintly children can no longer be hidden from the world.

Few and far between are the books written on the parents of the saints, the churches named after them, and the feast days commemorating their virtues. Their mission was simple: to impart the Faith to their children and raise them to be saints. As spelled out by Pope Ven. Pius XII below, parents are the first teachers and primary educators of their children, and they are entrusted with the "solemn duty laid upon them"[2] to protect their children in their shell of virtuous living from the snares of Satan and to form God's adopted sons and daughters into the pearl of heroic virtue by leading them to the pearl of great price—Jesus Himself, hidden in the Holy Eucharist.

During his homily at St. Maria Goretti's canonization on June 24, 1950, Pope Ven. Pius XII spoke these powerful words to all parents. His Holiness stated:

> You fathers and mothers, tell me—in the presence of this vast multitude, and before the image of this young virgin who by her inviolate candor has stolen your hearts . . . in the presence of her mother who educated her to martyrdom and who, as much as she felt the bitterness of the outrage, is now moved with emotion as she invokes her—tell me, are you ready to assume the solemn duty laid upon you to watch, as far as in you lies, over your sons and daughters, to preserve and defend them against so many dangers that surround them, and to keep them

---

[1]   Sts. Louis Martin and Zelie Martin, *A Call to a Deeper Love* (Staten Island, NY: St. Paul's, 2011), 274.

[2]   Margaret Breiling, "A Saint to Emulate," EWTN, ewtn.com/library/MARY/GORETTI.htm.

always far away from places where they might learn the practices of impiety and of moral perversion?[3]

Assunta and Luigi Goretti heeded this solemn duty when they came to the altar of God to pronounce their marriage vows. After Luigi's sudden and tragic death from malaria, Assunta provided Maria with an example of heroic sacrifice as she tended to the spiritual and bodily needs of her seven children. There is no question that Assunta "educated her to martyrdom," as exemplified by Assunta's cooperation with God's grace despite, at the young age of thirty-five, losing her husband and having to raise her many children alone. More importantly, Assunta sought to protect her children from the evils that tear at the very fiber of family life by engraving morals and virtues in her children's hearts. In our present world, where the evils of atheism, egocentrism, materialism, relativism, and sexual immorality have infested our culture, parents like Assunta and Luigi Goretti are needed to raise children who would rather die than offend God. The Church needs parents who are willing to raise not just good people, but children who want to live totally for Christ during their short earthly pilgrimage so that they can live forever with Him in Eternity.

Hence, behind every holy card, image, and statue of the saints lies the story of a person who came from a father and mother. It is within this school of love, this domestic church, where most saints learned to pray, love, and receive the mustard seed of faith, which, in time, developed into heroic virtue. Fr. Stéphane-Joseph Piat, OFM, a twentieth-century French priest and an expert on St. Thérèse's family, reiterated this notion:

> In order to cause a peak of sanctity to emerge, God works at and raises up a whole series of generations. Giants of holiness who rise up in isolation and detached, as it were, from the family territory, are rare. Alexis, "the saint under the staircase," who ran away on his wedding night; Francis of Assisi, whom his father cursed and disinherited; Jane de Chantal, who stepped over the body of her own

---

[3] Ibid.

son to reach the convent, remain exceptional cases.
Normally, the saint receives his early fashioning in the
home circle.[4]

Unfortunately, not every saint was blessed to come from godly
parents. For example, St. Hilary of Poitiers, a fourth-century bishop,
was born to wealthy, polytheistic pagans. In the seventh century,
the fifteen-year-old St. Dymphna was murdered by her own father
because he wanted to marry her after his own wife died. In the
tenth century, St. Romuald witnessed his aristocratic father murder
a relative in a duel over property. Romuald atoned for his father's
crime by undertaking forty days of penance, and eventually became a
Benedictine monk. A few centuries later, Landulf of Aquino and his
wife, Theodora, aided by their children, held their son, St. Thomas
Aquinas, hostage for a year as they attempted to thwart his vocation
by offering him a prostitute, whom he heroically rejected. Theodora
attempted to save her family's name by allowing Thomas to escape
at night so that he might follow his vocation to the Dominicans.

In the eighteenth century, St. Eugène de Mazenod grew up
in a very unstable home environment stemming from his parents'
tumultuous relationship over their finances and living situation.
Despite Eugène's best attempts to keep his parents together, they
divorced, which was extremely rare at the time. Many families
would do well to remember him and seek his intercession as the
patron saint of dysfunctional families. In the nineteenth century,
St. Maria Bertilla Boscardin was raised by an abusive and alcoholic
father, and the twentieth century witnessed the birth of Bl. Pier
Giorgio to Alfredo and Adelaide Frassati. Sadly, Alfredo was a
pronounced agnostic, and his wife a lapsed Catholic. Neither parent
realized their own son was dying of poliomyelitis, which ended his
life at twenty-four. Despite their indifference to the Faith and their
negligence during his final days—thinking his illness was merely
rheumatic pains and sadness due to his grandmother's death—Pier
Giorgio greatly loved his parents. Pier recalled with fondness how

---

4   Stéphane-Joseph Piat, OFM, *The Story of a Family: The Home of St.
    Thérèse of Lisieux* (Rockford, IL: TAN Books, 1994), ix–x.

he inherited his love for Tuscan cigars from his mother. He wrote, "My mother smoked over me when I was being fed at the breast."[5]

While no parents are perfect, many saints and blesseds have arisen, due to the grace of God, in spite of having godless parents. Yet many of the Church's greatest and lesser-known saints, blesseds, venerables, and servants of God were the beneficiaries of holy parents who laid their home's foundation on solid rock, which is Our Lord and his blessed parents, St. Joseph and the Blessed Mother.

Luigi and Assunta Goretti are one of many godly parents of the saints whose mission was to raise holy children without any fanfare or recognition, save God's glory. And their lives and virtues must be brought to light so that all might be inspired to do God's will more faithfully and zealously. Throughout the centuries, the parents of the saints have gone unnoticed, hidden like a shell at the bottom of the ocean, covered with sand, yet protecting and forming the pearl inside, which is God's precious saints who live on. But, unlike a pearl, forming and raising a saint takes a lifetime of hard work with God's grace. In fact, a lady who knew St. Louis Martin from his childhood wrote: "The grandmother, Madame Martin, lived next door to us; her son, Louis Martin, was the friend of my brothers. When he returned from Mount St. Bernard, I can distinctly recall him, and hear his happy mother exclaiming: 'Ah! my Louis, my dearest Louis, he is a real pearl!' She was right; and my brothers used to say to us: 'Louis Martin is a saint.'"[6]

Numerous parents of the saints displayed many virtues, and each parent was unique. Yet, based on my research, I discovered seven hallmarks that permeated their lives and even the lives of their children. These hallmarks include a devotion to the sacramental life, surrender, sacrificial love, suffering, simplicity, solitude, and the sacredness of life. And each chapter in this book centers on how these hallmarks were profoundly present in the interactions between these parents and their saintly children. Most of these devout parents lived

---

[5] Luciana Frassati, *A Man of the Beatitudes: Pier Giorgio Frassati* (San Francisco: Ignatius Press, 2001), 68.

[6] Céline Martin, *The Father of the Little Flower: Louis Martin, 1823–1894* (Rockford, IL: TAN Books, 2005), 3.

very unassuming lives, so much so that the world and the Church rarely took notice. Yet, as will be revealed in the following pages, these parents were the hidden heroes behind the lives of the saints.

HALLMARK ONE (PART I)

Sacramental Life

Only this I beg of you, that wherever you may be, you will continue
to remember me at the altar of the Lord.[1]—St. Monica

When meeting the parents of a famous artist, musician, scientist,
war hero, or writer, certain individuals, especially parents, might
want to know out of curiosity: How did you raise such a gifted son
or daughter? Had we lived at the same time and were fortunate
enough to meet the parents of Michelangelo, Mozart, Einstein, St.
Joan of Arc, or J.R.R. Tolkien, we might have asked: How did you,
Ludovido and Francesca Simoni, inspire your son, Michelangelo,
to sculpt and paint the most breathtaking works, including David,
the Pietà, and the Sistine Chapel? How did you, Leopold and Anna
Maria Mozart, teach your son, baptized as Johannes Chrysostomus
Wolfgangus Theophilus Mozart, yet known to the world as Mozart,
to compose such angelic symphonies? How did you, Hermann and
Pauline Einstein, teach your son Albert to develop groundbreaking
scientific theories like the general theory of relativity? How did
you, Jacques and Isabelle d'Arc, raise such a courageous daughter
in St. Joan of Arc, who at the age of seventeen led several victories
over the English army and became a martyr for the Faith? How did
you, Arthur and Mabel Tolkien, ignite your son John Ronald Reuel
Tolkien's vivid imagination and uncanny prose to pen *The Lord of
the Rings* and *The Hobbit*? Above all, we might like to know from
these parents the answer to the question: How did you cultivate

---

[1] St. Augustine, *The Confessions of St. Augustine* (Totowa, NJ: Catholic
Book Publishing Corp., 1997), 255.

your children's talents? Did you teach them yourselves or utilize the world's finest tutors? Where did your sons and daughters acquire their talent?

After all, the following question was first posed to Jesus in His own country by His own kinsmen when they asked, "Where did this man get this wisdom, and these mighty works? Is not this the carpenter's son? Is not his mother called Mary?" (Mt 13:54–55). While Jesus is the only person in the history of the world who could say that His talents and virtues originated in Himself because He is God, the saints mentioned throughout this book were not only the recipients of God's gifts, but they used these gifts exceptionally for "building up the body of Christ" (Eph 4:12). What made the holy parents of the saints different from most parents is that they made sure their son's or daughter's talents were not buried, or used for their own glory, but instead honed them: "He who had received the five talents went at once and traded with them; and he made five talents more" (Mt 25:16). And what separated the devout parents of the saints from most parents is that they allowed their greatest love, Our Eucharistic Lord, to become their children's greatest love.

In Catholic circles, we ponder similar questions that were asked of the Lord when we meet the parents of a priest or religious sister. Many of us secretly want to know: What did you do to raise such a holy child? Was it the family Rosary? What spiritual books did your children read? Did you pray that your son or daughter might have a religious vocation? Did a holy priest or nun greatly impact your child's vocation? What can we do to raise our children to have a vocation to the priesthood or consecrated life, or at the very least lead a good life, and even more so remain Catholic for the rest of their lives? Most importantly, what can we do to raise our children to be saints? The late spiritual author and speaker Fr. Thomas Dubay, SM, conveyed the notion of human excellences that every parent hopes for in their children:

> There are two kinds of human excellence, the first of which is on the level of natural talents, gifts, accomplishments. These occur in many areas and to differing degrees: intelligence, scholarship, literature,

music, art, sports. The second and higher type lies on the level of personal goodness, integrity, virtue, sanctity. Here we find the beauties of selfless love, humility, honesty, patience, chastity, fidelity, generosity.

It is immediately obvious that someone can be eminent in the first area of talents and accomplishments and yet a moral wretch in the second. There are few who excel on both levels: Augustine, Thomas Aquinas, Catherine of Siena, Teresa of Avila. It should be obvious to a consistent theist that to be a saint is immeasurably more important than to be a world class scholar, violinist or an Olympic gold medalist.[2]

THE HOLY EUCHARIST

The holy parents of the saints were clearly concerned with both kinds of human excellence: natural talents, gifts, and accomplishments as well as personal goodness, integrity, virtue, and sanctity. For instance, St. Zélie once wrote to her daughter Pauline, "If you knew how happy your being on the Honor Roll made me! But if you can't be on it again, don't feel bad about it; I won't be sad at all."[3] On the other hand, her husband, St. Louis, "showed that he was not quite pleased"[4] when his daughters earned average reports for their classes. In the words of his daughter Céline, who would later become Sr. Geneviève of the Holy Face, "We were mortified on seeing his displeasure."[5]

Yet, for these parents, raising another Thomas Aquinas or Catherine of Siena was far more important than raising another Einstein or Mozart. While the world tells parents to raise their children to be successful no matter the cost, the parents of the saints remind us that our chief priority in life is to get to Heaven by following the Lord's command, "If anyone would be first, he must be last of all and servant of all" (Mk 9:35). The parents of the saints

---

[2] Thomas Dubay, SM, *Deep Conversion, Deep Prayer* (San Francisco: Ignatius Press, 2006), 15.

[3] Martin and Martin, *A Call to a Deeper Love*, 199.

[4] Martin, *The Father of the Little Flower*, 50.

[5] Ibid.

were content with last place on a secular and perhaps even spiritual level, for they did not take a cursory glance at the Gospel like most; rather, they pondered the Word of God day and night, especially Christ's words, "The last shall be first." Let's face it: last place carries negative connotations. Who wants to be last? Even the Pharisees had a strong aversion to last place because their pride wanted them to be preferred. According to Our Lord, "They love the place of honor at feasts and the best seats in the synagogues" (Mt 23:6).

On the contrary, last place does not mean that the parents of the saints put little effort into their vocations and occupations while expecting great results—this would be far from the truth. In truth, the parents of the saints aimed to give their very best because God expects a perfect effort, though, to teach us humility, the results can be far from perfect. Rather, last place meant that these godly parents let others chase after the things of this world—money, pleasure, power, and prestige—while they pursued the one true prize: Jesus Christ, present in the Holy Eucharist, Who transforms us. The saints knew that last place in this life meant first place in Heaven. Specifically, St. Zélie declared, "Only in Heaven will the poor be able to have the best, on earth one mustn't think of it."[6] St. Thérèse understood this well from her own father, who could have been even more financially well off, but chose to keep Sunday holy by not working. When it came to Eucharistic Adoration, Louis also sought the last place by sacrificing his comfort for others, as Céline noted:

> This devotion to Our Lord in the Tabernacle manifested itself also by his exemplary fidelity to Nocturnal Adoration. He was one of the first to arrive at the appointed hour; and when free to choose he selected the most inconvenient hours, and gladly changed with someone else if a more favorable hour fell to his lot. At Lisieux, where this pious practice had not been established, he persuaded our uncle, M. Guérin, who belonged to the Board of Consultors of the Cathedral, to introduce it there.[7]

---

[6]   Martin and Martin, *A Call to a Deeper Love*, 305.
[7]   Martin, *The Father of the Little Flower*, 6.

On June 7, 1897, less than four months before her death, St. Thérèse told her biological sister, Sr. Geneviève:

> The only thing that is not *envied* is the last place; there is, then, only this *last place* which is not vanity and affliction of spirit. . . . However, "the way of man is not within his power," and we surprise ourselves at times by desiring what sparkles. So let us line up humbly among the imperfect, let us esteem ourselves as *little souls* whom God must sustain at each moment. When He sees we are very much convinced of our nothingness, He extends His hand to us. . . . Yes, it suffices to humble oneself, to bear with one's imperfections. That is real sanctity! Let us take each other by the hand, dear little sister, and let us run to the last place . . . no one will come to dispute with us over it.[8]

While Thérèse longed to be a martyr and to suffer more for Jesus, she finally realized that Our Lord had it right when he declared, "The last will be first, and the first last" (Mt 20:16). Like most of us, Thérèse's revelation of real sanctity did not happen overnight. From an early age, she relied on her parents' example, her own struggles, and much prayer to realize how she could fulfill Our Lord's words. Most notably, Louis and Zélie reveal that those who wish to be great must strive to be the smallest, the simplest, and the least noticed in the eyes of the world. In doing so, they follow the example of Our Eucharistic Lord, Who willingly chose last place by becoming man, and Who gave us the Holy Eucharist as the greatest example of His self-effacement. Their lives will also reflect the actions of the Holy Spirit, Who acts unassumingly and unseen, but nevertheless mightily and powerfully. With God's grace, the parents of the saints and their children were able to do the ordinary with extraordinary love and without pomp and circumstance.

---

8   St. Thérèse of Lisieux, *General Correspondence Vol II* (Washington, D.C.: ICS Publications, 1988), 1121–1122.

St. Monica

As she lay dying in Ostia, near Rome, in the year 387, St. Monica, in her humility, made one final request to her son, St. Augustine, who is one of the Church's greatest saints and prodigal sons, and, above all, the greatest pearl in his mother's necklace of virtue. "Only this I beg of you, that wherever you may be, you will continue to remember me at the altar of the Lord,"[9] she pleaded. For most of her fifty-six years of existence, Monica poured out her fervent prayers and tears at Mass, resulting in her two greatest converts, namely her pagan husband, Patricius, and her son, Augustine, who had renounced the Catholic Faith for fifteen years and fathered a child out of wedlock before his conversion. A paradoxical shift had begun with Monica's request. Instead of beseeching God at each Mass for her beloved son's conversion, Monica would now implore Augustine to intercede for her soul so that she might be delivered from Purgatory and thus enjoy eternal bliss with the Blessed Trinity. A look into Monica's final request to Augustine also sheds light on the quote from Tertullian, an early Church Father, who famously penned, "The blood of the martyrs is the seed of the Church."[10] One could argue that the prayers, sighs, and tears of a holy mother are the seeds of saintly children. Or, better yet, a father and mother's love for the Holy Eucharist is the seed of future saints. At one point, when Monica's hope for her son's conversion began to fade, a holy bishop reassured her with these words: "Go now, it is not possible that the son of so many tears should perish."[11] These bishop's consoling words ought to echo in the hearts of devout parents until the end of time, especially those who pray for their wayward children's return to the Faith.

Sts. Louis and Zélie Martin and Pierre Martin

In a small, northern French village lived a holy couple, Sts. Louis and Zélie Martin, whose lives will be discussed in greater detail than any

---

[9]   St. Augustine, *The Confessions of St. Augustine,* 255.

[10]   Tertullian, *"Apologeticum,"* tertullian.org/works/apologeticum.htm.

[11]   Joan Carroll Cruz, *Secular Saints* (Rockford, IL: TAN Books, 1989), 537.

other parents of the saints because their daughters documented their remarkable lives. Louis and Zélie, who lived in the mid-nineteenth century, are exemplars for raising saintly children. In addition to all five daughters entering religious life, and one of them, St. Thérèse, considered one of the greatest modern-day saints, the Martins themselves were canonized on October 18, 2015. Ironically, they never founded a religious order or died a martyr's death, but lived the little way—a life of doing little things for Jesus in their ordinary day, a practice that they passed on to their daughter Thérèse. The Martins' little way involved not only following "the way," which is Christ, but receiving Him Who is "the way" (Jn 14:6) in Holy Communion as often as possible. For instance, Céline Martin, St. Thérèse's older sister, who was the last daughter to enter the Carmelites, and who would take the name Sr. Geneviève of the Holy Face, provided a glimpse into her parent's rich sacramental life when she declared, "Mother lived a life of deep piety. Every morning she assisted with my father at the 5:30 Mass; both of them went to Holy Communion as often as the custom of that time permitted. In addition to that, on Sundays they assisted at the Solemn High Mass, and at Vespers."[12]

In fact, Zélie was so in love with the Holy Eucharist that, five weeks before her death, weakened by cancer, she still attended Mass. Throughout their lives, Louis and Zélie were ardent devotees of the First Friday Devotions. Only two centuries earlier, Our Lord had communicated to St. Margaret Mary Alacoque His great desire that the First Friday of every month be devoted to honoring His Sacred Heart by attending Holy Mass, and that His image be placed prominently in every home as a means of offering reparation for the sins committed against Him, especially in the Holy Eucharist. Responding to Our Lord's request, Zélie wrote, "I never miss, nor does Marie and, naturally, nor does Louis, receiving Communion every First Friday of the month, no matter what difficulties we foresee that day. We change the time of the Mass we usually go to,

---

[12] Céline Martin, *The Mother of the Little Flower. Celine Martin, 1831–1877* (Rockford, IL: TAN Books, 2005), 46.

and that's all that's needed."[13] Zelie was so devoted to the First Friday Devotions that not even stage IV cancer could hinder her zeal. Her daughter Marie recalled in her August 9, 1877, letter to her aunt and uncle, only a few weeks before her mother's death: "Last Friday morning she went to seven o'clock Mass, because it was the First Friday of the month. Papa helped her along, for, without him, she could not have gone at all. On arriving at the church, she admitted that if someone were not with her, she would never have been able to push open the door of the church!"[14]

During the Mass, the body language of the parents of the saints reflected the gravity of the unmerited gift of Christ's Passion, Death, and Resurrection, which are made present to us on the altar. Specifically, Thérèse wrote, "When the preacher spoke about St. Teresa, Papa leaned over and whispered: 'Listen carefully, little Queen, he's talking about your Patroness.' I did listen carefully, but I looked more frequently at Papa than at the preacher, for his *handsome* face said so much to me! His eyes, at times, were filled with tears which he tried in vain to stop; he seemed no longer held by earth, so much did his soul love to lose itself in the eternal truths."[15]

What an example Louis gave to his future saint by listening attentively to the priest's homily. Such is the wisdom of the parents of the saints who recognized that the time spent at Mass comprised the greatest moments of their lives because it is here that Heaven and earth collide. In fact, Sunday Mass was the highlight of the Martin's week, as Thérèse once said:

> I return once more to my Sundays. This *joyous* day, passing all too quickly, had its tinge of *melancholy*. I remember how my happiness was unmixed until Compline. During this prayer, I would begin thinking that the day of *rest* was coming to an end, that the morrow would bring with it the necessity of beginning life over again, we would have to go back to work, to learning lessons, etc.,

---

[13] Martin and Martin, *A Call to a Deeper Love*, 190.
[14] Martin, *The Mother of the Little Flower*, 105.
[15] St. Thérèse of Lisieux, *Story of a Soul* (Washington, D.C.: ICS Publications, 1996), 42.

and my heart felt the *exile* of this earth. I longed for the everlasting repose of heaven, that never-ending *Sunday* of the *Fatherland!*[16]

Besides attending daily Mass, Louis made annual pilgrimages to France's most stunning churches, such as Notre Dame, Our Lady of Victories, and Chartres. While there, he offered the greatest sacrifice for his family by attending Holy Mass devoutly and interceding for them as the high priest of the Martin family.

When they were first married, Louis and Zélie made evening visits together to the Most Blessed Sacrament. After Zélie passed away, Louis continued to make daily visits to the Blessed Sacrament with Thérèse, who fondly recalled, "Each afternoon I took a walk with Papa. We made our visit to the Blessed Sacrament together, going to a different church each day, and it was in this way we entered the Carmelite chapel for the first time. Papa showed me the choir grille and told me there were nuns behind it. I was far from thinking at that time that nine years later I would be in their midst!"[17]

Louis was madly in love with Our Eucharistic Lord. He would often accompany the local priest carrying Viaticum to a dying soul by holding a lighted candle in the middle of the night. In addition, Louis's daughter Céline commented that "he always raised his hat . . . irrespective of the company with whom he was walking,"[18] when he passed a Catholic church. He once donated two thousand dollars for the Lisieux cathedral's new high altar. Louis's reverence for the Eucharist ought to inspire us today to at the very least make the Sign of the Cross when passing a Catholic church to show our unwavering belief in the Real Presence.

To understand Louis's love for the Eucharist, we must look no further than the example of his father, Captain Pierre Martin. As the spiritual leader of his family, Pierre was unabashed about his Eucharistic devotion. In fact, his own regiment chided him for praying on his knees long after Mass concluded as he savored the sweetness of the Lord whom he had just received. The captain

---

[16] Ibid.
[17] Ibid., 36.
[18] Martin, *The Father of the Little Flower*, 6.

responded to one of his naysayers, who questioned him about his extended thanksgiving, "Tell them that it is because I believe!"[19] That is why many of the parents of the saints and their children, including Pierre, believed that nothing on earth could compare with receiving or visiting the Most Blessed Sacrament. Thanks be to God, the love that many of the grandparents and parents of the saints had for the Holy Eucharist trickled down from generation to generation just as a waterfall trickles down the same rocks century upon century, smoothing the rocks over time while giving life to the surrounding vegetation, including a little flower like St. Thérèse. For those souls who are disposed to receive Our Lord in Holy Communion, no praise or worship song, Scripture verse, or inspiring sermon can compare to the reality of "the Word," Who became flesh in the womb of a young virgin, and Who becomes present in the appearances of bread and wine in the Holy Sacrifice of the Mass. And that is why Pierre was filled with prolonged gratitude in the depths of his heart well after Mass concluded, for to receive the Holy Eucharist is to receive all of Heaven, and the greater the gift, the greater our gratitude ought to be.

Pierre taught his son, Louis, never to let human respect curb his zeal toward the Eucharist. Had Pierre merely gone through the motions, his soldiers might have questioned whether or not he actually believed that the Eucharist was Jesus' Body, Blood, Soul, and Divinity, or a mere symbol. Rather, the demeanor of Pierre and his son, Louis, suggested that they were not only receiving God, but even standing in front of the Beatific Vision—veiled, that is. In fact, when Pierre prayed the Our Father, many were moved by his devout recitation. And, just like those who were edified by Pierre's devotion to Mass and recitation of the Our Father, so too was Thérèse moved by the great devotion of her father, Louis, at Mass, which sometimes included tears. What an example that Pierre provides to grandparents and parents alike by his fervent reverence for the Mass and Our Lord's Prayer, which inspired those around him, but more importantly led his son and granddaughters to become true

---

[19] Piat, *The Story of a Family: The Home of St. Thérèse of Lisieux*, 10.

worshippers of God. After all, do not children and grandchildren seek to model their parents' and grandparents' behavior?

Because the Holy Sacrifice of the Mass was everything to the parents of the saints, it was essential that Sunday, the Lord's Day, maintained its solemnity as the principal day for the celebration of the Eucharist because it is the day of the Resurrection. Despite ridicule from his friends, Louis remained steadfast in keeping his watchmaking store closed on Sundays due to his strict adherence to the commandments, especially the Third Commandment. Despite lucrative sales from country folk who came to Alençon on Sundays to buy goods, Louis sacrificed money for obedience to God's commandments. Further, Louis refused to purchase anything on Sunday. According to Céline, "Once having noticed for sale on the passing cart of a hawker a grindstone that he wanted, he asked the man to hold it for him until the following day."[20] The Martin children were known to have eaten stale bread that was bought the day before rather than buy fresh bread on Sunday. The family rarely traveled anywhere on Sunday, with the exception of church, as they did not want to undertake anything that forced others to work. Zélie communicated Louis's love for keeping Sunday holy and how God blessed those who keep this day holy when she penned, "Here's a man who never tried to make a fortune. When he set up his business, his confessor told him to open his jewelry store on Sunday until noon. He didn't want to accept permission to do so, preferring to pass up good sales. And, nevertheless, he's rich. I can't attribute the affluence he enjoys to anything other than a special blessing, the fruit of his faithful observance of Sunday."[21]

Louis's devotion to Sunday is a reminder to parents to curtail all unnecessary work in favor of a day of prayer and relaxation with family and friends versus society's need for constant productivity and consumerism.

---

[20]   Martin, *The Father of the Little Flower*, 11–12.
[21]   Martin and Martin, *A Call to a Deeper Love*, 189.

Henry and Aurelia Galgani

Living at the same time as Sts. Louis and Zélie Martin, Henry and
Aurelia Galgani shared the same mission, that is, to raise saints. In
fact, St. Gemma, who was Henry and Aurelia's fourth child and
oldest daughter, was born only five years after St. Thérèse. Shortly
after her birth on March 12, 1878, Henry moved the family to
the town of Lucca, in Tuscany, Italy. In this land of saints, Henry
wanted to provide a better education for his children. In fact, he
was a direct descendant of St. John Leonardi. Henry and Aurelia's
love for their children, especially Gemma, was undeniable. Henry
frequently went on walks with his children and paid close attention
to their growth "in virtue and learning."[22] Besides love, Aurelia also
passed on her intense Eucharistic devotion to her children. Their
son, Gino, who died while studying for the priesthood, was inspired
by his parents and by Gemma's love for God. Gemma's spiritual
director, Ven. Fr. Germanus, described Aurelia as:

> Not only a good Christian, but a saint and a most perfect
> model to all Catholic mothers. Her prayer was continual.
> Every morning she partook of the Bread of Life with
> sentiments of vivid faith, allowing no obstacle to prevent
> her going to church, even when suffering from fever.
> From this divine Food she drew strength and spirit for
> the perfect fulfillment of her duties. She loved all her
> children, but above all Gemma, in whom she, better than
> anyone else, was able to recognize the gifts of God.[23]

Well before Gemma could partake of the Holy Eucharist, her
mother took her to Mass and to make visits to the Most Blessed
Sacrament. Ven. Fr. Germanus said, "Her mother, a saint indeed,
had instilled into her a knowledge and foretaste of its sweetness; and,
in order to excite within her more and more a craving for the Bread
of Life, she very often took her before the Tabernacle, whence Our

---

[22] Ven. Fr. Germanus, CP, *The Life of St. Gemma Galgani* (Charlotte, NC:
     TAN Books, 2012), 3.
[23] Ibid., 4–5.

Savior continually sends His divine rays into the hearts that long for Him, and more particularly, into guileless souls."[24]

Because of her holy mother's example, which implanted an intense desire to receive Holy Communion, Gemma begged her father, her confessor, and the religious sisters to allow her to receive First Holy Communion earlier than was then the custom, a request to which they eventually acquiesced. Ven. Fr. Germanus once stated:

> Hence her mother, well aware of her own duty and far from indulging in useless demonstrations of affection, set herself with the utmost care to cultivate in her child's soul those precious germs of all virtues. Here we see a mother becoming the spiritual directress of her daughter, and Gemma, in her turn, full of gratitude to Our Lord for having given her such a mother, was ever mindful of the assiduous and unceasing care thus lavished on her. She used to declare that it was her mother that she owed her knowledge of God and her love of virtue.[25]

Sadly, Aurelia battled tuberculosis for five years and eventually lost the fight at the age of thirty-nine, when Gemma was only eight years old. Interestingly, Gemma desired to hear her mother's last words, but her father wanted to protect Gemma from further emotional distress as she was already shedding many tears. As a result, Henry sent Gemma to stay with her aunt. Filled with spiritual foresight, and not wanting his wife's invaluable lessons to have been for naught, Henry sent Gemma to a half-boarding school run by devout nuns, the Sisters of St. Zita. The sisters' impact on Gemma was strong, as she declared, "I was in Paradise!"[26] Gemma's father died at the age of fifty-seven from throat cancer, which left the nineteen-year-old Gemma and her siblings not only orphans, but also without money, as many people had maliciously taken advantage of Henry's generous heart as a chemist-pharmacist. Gemma's spiritual director summed up her situation best: "Thus, O my God, dost Thou will

---

[24] Ibid., 12.
[25] Ibid., 5.
[26] Ibid., 11.

to try souls most dear to Thee, even in their tenderest years."[27] This is true of many of the saints' lives, especially those who lost parents when they were very young.

Although Aurelia died young, her children certainly knew, before she departed, the source and strength behind her virtue: the Holy Eucharist. Gemma inherited her mother's great love for the Holy Eucharist and longing for Eternity. Nine months after her mother died, Gemma would make her First Communion—a day her mother would have dreamt to witness. On June 19, 1887, the eve of her First Communion, nine-year-old Gemma wrote these beautiful words to her father:

> Dear Papa:
>
> Today is the vigil of the day of my First Communion, a day for me of infinite contentment. I write these lines only to assure you of my love and to move you to pray to Jesus in order that the first time He comes to dwell with me, He may find me disposed to receive all the graces He has prepared for me. I beg your pardon for all my disobedience and all the pain I have ever given you, and I beg of you this evening to forget them all. I ask you to bless me.
>
> Your most loving daughter, Gemma[28]

Besides conveying her deep love for her earthly father, Gemma's words reveal her desire to be a pure tabernacle for the Lord. At the same time, her letter highlights the necessity of every father and mother to pray fervently for their children, especially as they are about to receive the various sacraments for the first time. Throughout her life, Gemma, like her mother, went to daily Mass. Gemma also said, "It was indeed my Mother who from my earliest years instilled into me this longing for Heaven."[29] Though Gemma would often ask Our Lord to take her to Heaven during her intense sufferings, she came to realize through her own mother's example that the

---

27 Ibid., 9.
28 Ibid., 14.
29 Ibid., 6.

Eucharist offers a foretaste of Heaven. This stirred in her heart a longing to one day behold Our Lord in Eternity, where He will be truly unveiled before our eyes in His full glory. The Holy Eucharist was Aurelia's only true consolation amidst her sorrows, particularly her life-ending illness, for only Jesus can give us true peace when everything around us, including ourselves, is falling apart. Perhaps this is why Gemma once made the following resolution while on retreat: "I will often visit Jesus in the Most Blessed Sacrament, particularly when afflicted."[30]

Grazio and Maria Forgione

While one future saint emerged under the Tuscan sun, one of Italy's most recognized saints was acquiring the seeds of faith from his devout parents, Grazio and Maria Forgione, in their small, southern country town of Pietrelcina. Grazio and Maria were known in their town for their great piety, which included attending daily Mass, praying the nightly Rosary, and abstaining from meat three times a week in honor of Our Lady of Mount Carmel. Grazio and Maria instilled in their seven children, two of whom died as infants, their great love for the Holy Eucharist and Our Lady. Grazio and Maria's rich sacramental life was embraced by most of their children, but especially their second-oldest boy, Francesco, born on May 25, 1887, who later became St. Padre Pio. So in love was he with the Holy Sacrifice of the Mass that Padre Pio, a Capuchin priest, spent several hours in preparation and often shed tears during Mass because he understood its mystery and richness. It is likely that as a child, Pio witnessed his holy parents shed not only tears of sorrow at Mass over the loss of their two children, but, more importantly, tears of gratitude because his parents understood God's radical love: to die for man and to humble Himself by becoming present in the appearance of bread.

Certainly, Grazio and Maria's devotion to the Holy Eucharist inspired Padre Pio to become one of the twentieth-century's greatest mystics: a priest conformed to the Crucified Christ by literally bearing the wounds of Christ, and whose reverence for Mass was

---

[30] Ibid., 15.

so profound that his Masses would sometimes last three hours. Despite Grazio and Maria's solid faith and saintly son, this family also experienced a great trial, as their daughter Pellegrina led an immoral life. Another daughter, Grazia, was a Brigantine nun known as Sr. Pia, who, following the Second Vatican Council, left the convent after forty-three years. Padre Pio suffered from both of these trials brought on by his sisters and prayed for them daily. Though we are not sure whether Pellegrina ever returned to the Faith, what a cross Pio's parents faced to know that the greatest treasure they tried to instill in their children, namely the Holy Eucharist, had been rejected by their prodigal daughter, who sought the bread that perishes. Like Grazio and Maria, God sends each person trials to deepen their love for Him and to detach them further from the world. Unfortunately, sometimes our greatest trials come from those nearest and dearest to us. Grazio and Maria witness to the fact that even if parents are living saints, their grown children have free will and can choose to follow another path. Most parents tend to blame themselves, but it is not always their fault. All Grazio and Maria could do now was increase their prayers for their daughter, especially at Mass, keep the doors of communication open, and hope for the best. To quote the words of the bishop who advised St. Monica when her frequent admonitions to Augustine fell on deaf ears, "Speak less to Augustine about God and more to God about Augustine."[31] Adding to his parents' sufferings, Padre Pio was restricted by the Holy See from celebrating Mass publicly for several years, and the Vatican released a public statement expressing doubt about the supernatural nature of his stigmata—the wounds of Christ present on his hands and feet.

From the years 1909 to 1916, Padre Pio's superior sent him home to recover from an illness. It was there at home that he finished his last year of seminary, maintained his Capuchin vocation, was ordained, and began his priestly mission. After his ordination on August 10, 1910, which occurred before the required age of twenty-

---

[31] Patrick Madrid, *Search and Rescue: How to Bring Your Family and Friends into or Back into the Catholic Church* (Manchester, NH: Sophia Institute Press, 2001), 9.

four due to fears over his impending death, Pio celebrated Mass at
the local parish and taught at the local school. He lived in his own
home near his parents' house, which was purchased as a result of his
father's hard work. As Pio began to heal, we can only imagine his
family's prayer life, especially their daily Rosary as well as their holy
conversations, now that Pio could share the spiritual lessons from his
seminary and religious formation. At the same time, what a cross and
joy for Grazio and Maria—the cross being that their son was sick,
and perhaps the fear that he might never rejoin his order, mixed with
the joy of being able to attend their son's Masses regularly. What a
dream come true for saintly parents like Grazio and Maria Forgione.

Five years after recovering from his illness, Padre Pio was
assigned to the Capuchin friary in San Giovanni Rotondo, where
he would spend the remainder of his earthly life. Not being able
to see Padre Pio whenever they wanted was one of the greatest
offerings that his parents, and all parents of religious, can give
to the Lord. In fact, Padre Pio often commented that leaving his
parents for religious life "felt like his very bones were crushed."[32]
His mother said at the time of his departure, "My son, do not think
of your mother's sadness at this moment. My heart is bleeding, but
St. Francis has called you and you must go."[33] Despite San Giovanni
Rotondo being over one hundred miles from his parents' home in
Pietrelcina, the family maintained strong communications through
letters and visits, and above all through prayer and the Holy Sacrifice
of the Mass. On her last visit to see Pio, the seventy-year-old Maria
knelt down to kiss her son's hands for each of the family members,
a sign of reverence to her priestly son and his consecrated hands.
As she was about to kiss his hands for herself, "Padre Pio raised his
arm saying: 'Never! The son should kiss the hand of the mamma,
not the mamma the hand of the son!'"[34] Such was the devotion and
humility of Padre Pio, who recognized that without his mother's
love for the Eucharist as well as his father's sacrifices, as will be seen

---

[32] Frank Rega, *Padre Pio and America* (Rockford, IL: TAN Books, 2005),
11.

[33] Ibid.

[34] Ibid., 95.

later, he may never have become a priest. In fact, Pio's father moved to San Giovanni Rotondo after his wife passed away around 1938 to be near his son and would spend the last eight years of his life living with one of Pio's spiritual daughters, American-born Mary Pyle, who cared for him. Grazio loved to attend his son's morning Mass each day, so much so that, as he aged and the climb to the monastery became difficult, he rode on a donkey.

Stanislaus and Marianna Kowalska

Living around the same time period as the Forgione parents was another pious couple named Stanislaus and Marianna Kowalska. Their third daughter, Helen, was born at eight o'clock in the morning on August 25, 1905, in Głogowiec, Poland. She would become St. Maria Faustina of the Most Blessed Sacrament. Helen's religious name offers a glimpse into her parents' love for this august sacrament. Our Lord once beautifully revealed to Faustina in the last year of her life something so many of us take for granted: "But I want to tell you that eternal life must begin already here on earth through Holy Communion. Each Holy Communion makes you more capable of communing with God throughout eternity."[35] Long before Helen became Faustina, she witnessed her parents' great love and fidelity for the Blessed Sacrament. Faustina inherited her devotion to the Holy Eucharist from her father, especially by spiritually uniting herself to the Mass when, on rare occasions as a young girl, she could not attend due to sickness or poverty—the sisters had only one dress, which they shared among themselves. Sr. Sophia Michaelenko best described Stanislaus's devotion as follows:

> These practices were characteristic of Stanislaus' personal faith—simple but deep. He himself would never miss Mass on Sunday and the feasts of the Church; and, as was the custom then, he would receive Holy Communion on the feasts of Easter and Christmas and perhaps some other major feast days. Later, when age would keep him from going to church, he would hang a watch over his bed so

35 St. Maria Faustina Kowalska, *Diary: Divine Mercy in My Soul* (Stockbridge, MA: Marian Press, 2011), 640.

that, in spirit, he could participate in the Sunday Mass that was being celebrated in the church. Stanislaus likewise managed his household according to the commandments of God and of the Church, an age-old Polish heritage. One of his sons, who was later the organist of the parish church stated, "As to religion, Father was very demanding of us and of Helen, for which we are now very grateful."[36]

José and Dolores Escrivá

Another holy couple, José and Dolores Escrivá, lived at the beginning of the twentieth century in Barbastro, Spain. On September 19, 1898, they were united in the Sacrament of Matrimony in a side chapel at the Cathedral of Saint Mary of the Assumption. As parents, they handed on their great love for the Holy Sacrifice of the Mass to their six children, María del Carmen, José María, María Asunción, María de los Dolores, María del Rosario, and Santiago, who would inherit their great love for the sacrament of love, as it is commonly called. One in particular would stand out among them, José María, who would become St. Josemaría Escrivá. Note: He later combined his first two names due to his great love for St. Joseph and Our Lady. In 1928, he founded Opus Dei, which is Latin for "the Work of God," whose mission is to help lay people sanctify the ordinary, especially their homes and their work. The seeds of Opus Dei were planted by the holy example of Josemaría's parents. He once reflected upon his blessed youth, "My mother, my father, my sisters, and I always went together to Mass. My father gave us alms that we happily brought to the disabled man who leaned against the wall of the bishop's house. After that, I went on ahead to get holy water to give to my family. Then, Holy Mass. Afterward, every Sunday, in the chapel of the Christ of the Miracles, we prayed the Creed."[37]

---

[36] Sr. Sophia Michalenko, CMGT, *The Life of Faustina Kowalska: The Authorized Biography* (Ann Arbor, MI: Servant Publications, 1987), 15.

[37] Andrés Vázquez de Prada, *The Founder of Opus Dei: The Life of Josemaria Escrvia, Volume I: The Early Years* (Princeton, NJ: Scepter Publishing, 2001), 34.

In addition to Sunday Mass with his family, Josemaría's father would arrive punctually at weekday Mass every morning around seven at the nearby Church of St. James, when they lived in their Logroño apartment. Like his father, Josemaría become an ardent lover of the Eucharist, especially during seminary, when he was noted for frequently visiting the Most Blessed Sacrament during his free periods and sometimes spending the entire night before the Eucharistic King as he sought God's light and grace. In fact, Josemaría once wrote, "I like to call the Tabernacle a prison—a prison of Love. For twenty centuries He has been waiting there, willingly locked up, for me and for everyone."[38]

Alberto and Maria Beretta

While many of the parents of the saints raised children who would become religious priests and nuns, they also bore saintly children who were "secular saints," i.e., lay saints who were either married or single. Alberto and Maria Beretta, a holy Italian couple, were preparing the Church for one of her greatest lay saints in their daughter, St. Gianna Beretta Molla, when they exchanged vows only six years after the birth of St. Josemaría Escrivá. The Berettas' love for God was so profound that the late Cardinal Martini, archbishop of Milan, wrote, "A family like that is a model for today's families."[39] Their eleventh son, Giuseppe, who was born directly before the saint and later became a priest, wrote these words about his parents' rich sacramental life, which sheds light on how Gianna became St. Gianna:

> Mamma was really the valiant woman of the Scriptures. Her day began early, at 5:00, when Papa awoke to go to early Mass and begin his day's work before the Lord and in the Lord's name. He went alone, because Mamma stayed home to prepare breakfast and, in a small lunch box, his midday meal. When Papa left for work in Milan,

---

[38]   St. Josemaría Escrivá, *The Way, Furrow, The Forge* (New York: Scepter, 2013), 778.

[39]   Pietro Molla and Elio Guerriero, *Saint Gianna Molla: Wife, Mother, Doctor* (San Francisco: Ignatius Press, 2004), 23.

> Mamma passed through our bedrooms to awaken us, caressing our faces. We knew that shortly she would go to church to assist at Holy Mass, and we dressed quickly to go with her, happy to kneel beside her to prepare ourselves to receive Jesus in Holy Communion and to make our thanksgiving with her. What marvelous words she would suggest we tell Jesus! Then we would return home, have breakfast, and be off to school.[40]

It is no coincidence that Jesus tells us: "Truly, truly, I say to you, unless a grain of wheat falls into the earth and dies, it remains alone; but if it dies, it bears much fruit" (Jn 12:24). Were not Alberto and Maria's "little deaths" to sleeping in each morning like the grain of wheat? Instead of sleeping in, the Berettas gave God the first fruits of their day by attending Mass. This couple witnessed to their thirteen children that the Holy Sacrifice of the Mass is the greatest prayer of the Church and the best way to start the day. Even mental prayer, fasting, and good works are all secondary, since they flow from the graces received at Mass. The Berettas heeded the words of St. Peter Eymard, who lived less than fifty years before their time, when he so beautifully declared, "In order to comprehend the value of the Holy Mass, you must remember that this sublime act is in itself greater than all the good works, virtues, and merits of all the saints together, the Blessed Virgin Mary not excepted, from the beginning until the end of time. For each Mass [makes present] the sacrifice of the God-Man Who, dying as man and, as God, raising His death to the dignity of a divine action, gives it thereby an infinite worth."[41]

The Berettas recognized that in order for them to live their vocations heroically and give themselves throughout the day to their spouse, their children, their coworkers, and their neighbors and work in a virtuous manner, they must first give themselves to Jesus, Who in turn gives Himself totally to each communicant, allowing them to radiate His fragrance to others. For Our Lord's fragrance,

---

[40] Ibid., 24.

[41] St. Peter Julian Eymard, *Holy Communion* (New York: Sentinel Press, 1940), 29.

composed of sacrifice and sweetness, can only exude from souls who seek first to put on Christ and to be consumed by Him.

Antonio and Maria Rosa dos Santos

While France and Italy have no shortage of saints, and some would argue that both countries have the most canonized saints, one country emerged on the world's stage near the end of World War I due to Our Lady's apparition in the tiny village of Fatima, Portugal, where Antonio and Maria Rosa dos Santos passed on the Faith to their children. Both parents were noted for their fidelity to the Church's laws and feast days. Maria Rosa taught catechesis at the local church and ensured that her family prayed the Rosary together. Antonio and Maria Rosa's love for the Eucharist was communicated to all of their seven children, but especially their youngest child, Servant of God Sr. Lucia dos Santos, whose cause for beatification was opened in 2008 by Pope Benedict XVI.

In Fatima, in 1917, the Blessed Mother appeared to Lucia along with her cousins Jacinta and Francisco Marto, who were recently canonized on May 14, 2017, by Pope Francis. Four years before Our Lady appeared to Lucia and her cousins, Lucia received her first Holy Communion in 1913 at the age of six, right around the time Pope St. Pius X issued the decree *Quam Singulari*, which lowered the age of communion from twelve to seven, the age of discretion. While at home, Maria Rosa taught the catechism to Lucia to prepare her for Holy Communion, and also sent her to the local church for further instruction. By thoroughly preparing their daughter for her First Communion, Antonio and Maria Rosa were taking their responsibilities seriously rather than simply going through the motions. Lucia's words on the day of her First Communion echo the sentiments of her parents and her great love for the Holy Eucharist. She wrote, "I felt as though transformed in God. It was almost one o'clock before the ceremonies were over. . . . My mother came looking for me, quite distressed, thinking I might faint from weakness [due to the Communion fast from midnight at that time].

But I, filled to overflowing with the Bread of Angels, found it impossible to take any food whatsoever."[42]

Antonio and Maria Rosa remind all parents that their primary duty is to educate their sons and daughters in the Faith and, most of all, to provide a witness that the Eucharist is the greatest treasure in this life. Many parents send their children to religious education classes or Catholic schools hoping that this will keep them in the Faith. However, even if these institutions and their faculty are faithful to the teachings of the Church, which should be the expectation of every parent, a father and mother can never shirk their primary duty to make sure that their children know the why of their existence, which is "to know Him, to love Him, and to serve Him in this world, and to be happy with Him forever in Heaven."[43]

Karol Wojtyła Sr.

Three years after Our Lady of Fatima appeared in Portugal in 1917, one of her favorite devotees, Pope St. John Paul II, who credited his survival from an assassination attempt to the intercession of Our Lady of Fatima, was born in Poland. After John Paul II's mother died, he and his father attended Mass every day before he attended school and prayed with the scriptures in the evening.[44] Karol Wojtyła Sr. fostered his son's great love for the Holy Eucharist through daily Mass. While many fathers enjoy priceless quality time with their sons fishing, hunting, or attending a sporting event, Karol Sr. communicated to John Paul II that the manliest thing a father and son can do together is attend the Holy Sacrifice of the Mass. By his very prayer life and devotion to the Most Blessed Sacrament, Karol Sr. manifested Isaiah's words, "The father makes known to the children your faithfulness" (38:19).

---

[42] Andrew Apostoli, *Fatima for Today: The Urgent Marian Message of Hope* (San Francisco: Ignatius Press, 2010), 16.

[43] Fr. Bennett Kelley, *The New Joseph Baltimore Catechism, Official Revised Edition, No.2* (Totowa, NJ: Catholic Book Publishing, 2011), 9.

[44] See Jason Evert, *Saint John Paul the Great: His Five Loves* (Lakewood, CO: Totus Tuus Press, 2014), 4.

Karol Sr. represents one of the many holy parents who revealed the splendor of the Holy Eucharist to their children by his own faithfulness. As seen in this section, others like Sts. Louis and Zélie Martin were of the same mindset. As the personal family acquaintance and biographer of the Martin family, Fr. Piat, described, the Eucharistic devotion and virtue of Louis and Zélie left a sort of indelible mark on their children. His words personify not only the Martins, but serve as a summary of every devout parent in this chapter:

> Their parents lived only for God, with the sole intention of accomplishing his will. They understood authority to mean service, which consisted in directing the souls confided to them toward the good. By example, more than by words, they instilled virtue and piety, knowing how to correct faults, inspire generosity, and make the most austere lessons attractive. Young children, observers and imitators that they essentially are, cannot be indifferent when they see those whom they cherish most attend daily Mass, observe strictly the abstinences and fasts stipulated by Church law, sanctify Sundays with inviolable fidelity, supernaturalize the duties of their state, venerate priests, take an active part in parish affairs and preside over the different rituals of the family liturgies: morning and evening prayer, grace before and after meals, and Marian devotions during the month of May.[45]

Make no mistake, the holy parents of the saints were convinced that the Holy Sacrifice of the Mass is the most powerful and most important prayer in the world. And, therefore, these parents realized that the best way to teach their children to love the Mass was to esteem it above everything, as seen throughout this chapter.

At the same time, these devout parents show us that there is no greater gift a parent can pass on to their sons and daughters than the Holy Eucharist. Other gifts will never satisfy or last—toys will be

---

[45] Stéphane-Joseph Piat, OFM, *Celine: Sister Genevieve of the Holy Face: Sister and Witness of Saint Thérèse of the Child Jesus* (San Francisco, CA: Ignatius Press, 1997), 17–18.

abandoned, clothes will be outgrown, cars will break down, and sports teams will disappoint, but the Holy Eucharist is the gift that never stops giving and always satisfies. Above all, the Holy Eucharist transformed the children of godly parents into saints destined to bask forever in the beatific rays of the most Holy Trinity.

BAPTISM

Before these holy parents could feed their children with the Bread from Heaven and the real manna in the desert from Holy Mother Church, they wanted to ensure that their sons and daughters were members of God's family through Baptism and consecrated them to the service of God.

Most parents are filled with awe and gratitude toward God when they behold their child for the first time. Some parents immediately begin to survey their new baby to see whose physical features he or she possesses. Some may even think about the child's future, while others contemplate which name in the Canon of the Mass will be the most fashionable for their child: Cyprian or Felicity? Some may even go one step further to ponder what order their child might join: the Benedictines, Carmelites, Dominicans, or Franciscans. The possibilities are endless for their child. No parent knows what the future holds, but simply knowing that God holds the future is enough to quell any anxieties.

Only one mother in the history of the world knew her Son's fate, and she is the Blessed Mother. Our Lady's eyes were the first and last eyes that Jesus saw on this earth. Despite the indescribable joy to nurse God from her very breasts, Our Lady knew the prophecy: her Son was to die for the sins of many. She had to share Jesus with the entire world, just like every mother of a priest. Her child was not her own, but God's. Therefore, the parents of the saints revealed the importance of imitating Joseph and Mary by consecrating their children to God, just as Christ was presented in the Temple as prescribed by Jewish Law. As each child was born, St. Zélie Martin would say, "Lord, grant me the grace that this child may be consecrated to You, and that nothing may tarnish the purity of its soul. If ever it would be lost, I prefer that You should take it without delay."[46] So urgent was Louis and Zélie's desire to baptize their children that their children received the sacrament either the very day of their birth or the following day if the child was born at night. The same was also said of St. Maria Goretti's mother, Assunta, who sought to free her children from the bonds of Original Sin, which she loathed, by having her children baptized at the earliest opportunity, which was the day after their birth. These devout parents' zeal for Baptism reveals the solicitude parents should have for this sacrament, which forgives all sin and deifies the soul with the indwelling of the Blessed Trinity. Louis and Zélie recognized that their children were God's and not their own. Once their children were baptized, the Martins made sure their children carried out their baptismal promises by leading them in morning and evening prayers. Specifically, Zélie taught her children to recite the following prayer each morning: "My God, I give you my heart; please accept it that no creature, but You alone, my good Jesus, may possess it."[47]

Louis once remarked to the priest at the Baptism of his first child, Marie-Louise, "This is the first time that I have come here for a Baptismal Ceremony, but it will not be the last."[48] Contrast Louis's response with today's culture, in which many parents are quick to announce to friends and relatives after having two children, "We are done," as if they themselves are God and can determine when a child ought to be born. According to the Second Vatican Council document *Gaudium et Spes*, "Children are the supreme gift of marriage and contribute very substantially to the welfare of their parents."[49] The day after the birth of Marie-Françoise-Thérèse, now known to the world as St. Thérèse, the Little Flower, on January 3, 1873, Zélie wrote to her sister-in-law describing the birth and upcoming Baptism of this future great saint:

> My little girl was born last night, Thursday, at eleven-thirty. She's very strong and in very good health. They tell me she weighs eight pounds. Let's say six, which is still

---

[46] Martin, *The Mother of the Little Flower*, 7.
[47] Ibid., 10.
[48] Martin, *The Father of the Little Flower*, 36.
[49] Pope Paul VI, *Gaudium et Spes*, 50.

not bad. She seems very sweet. I'm very happy. However, at first, I was surprised I was so sure I was having a boy. I'd been imagining this for two months because I could feel she was much stronger than my other children. I barely suffered a half hour. What I felt before was practically nothing. She'll be baptized tomorrow, Saturday. The only thing missing to make the celebration complete is all of you. Marie is going to be the godmother, and a little boy close to her age will be the godfather.[50]

Thérèse's Baptism was delayed an extra day as they awaited the arrival of the godfather, Paul-Albert Boul, who was almost ten years old and whose father was Louis's friend. Thérèse was baptized by Louis's close friend, Fr. Dumaine, at their home parish, the Church of Notre-Dame. On a side note, Pauline, Zélie's second-oldest daughter, said Thérèse's delayed Baptism caused Zélie increased stress for she had already buried four children, and Zélie feared for this child's life.

Roughly eight years after St. Thérèse's death, St. Faustina's parents, Stanislaus and Marianna Kowalska, took their child, named Helen, to the baptismal font just two days after her birth. Standing in the center of their village in Swince Warckie, St. Casimir Church welcomed one of Poland's greatest saints. The Sacrament of Baptism was administered by the parish priest Fr. Joseph Chodynski. The baptismal certificate along with the baptismal font, which still stands, recall this glorious event:

On this day, August 27, 1905, at one o'clock in the afternoon, the following took place. Stanislaus Kowalksi,[51] farmer, aged 40 years of Glogowiec, having petitioned for Baptism in the presence of Francis Bednarek, aged 35 years, and Joseph Stasiak, aged 40 years, both farmers of Glogowiec, presented to us an infant of female sex, born of his wedded wife Marianna nee Babel, aged 30, at eight o'clock in the morning on August 25th of this year in

---

[50] Martin and Martin, *A Call to a Deeper Love*, 103–104.
[51] NB. In Polish, the last name "Kowalski" ends in "i" for male family members, while it ends in "a" for female family members.

the village of Glogowiec. The child received the name
Helen in Holy Baptism, which was administered on this
day, and the godparents were Constantine Bednarek and
Marianna Szewcyzk. The document has been signed by
ourselves, having been read to the petitioner and to the
unlettered witnesses.[52]

Interestingly enough, "by ourselves" referred to Fr.
Chodynski and Faustina's father, who signed the baptismal certificate with an
"X" as he did not know how to write his own name.

Five years after Faustina's birth, another future saint was born
in the small village of Skopje, Albania, on August 26, 1910. Her
name was Agnes, and her parents, Nikola and Dranafile Bojaxhiu,
had their third child baptized the very next day. Nikola called his
daughter his "little Gonxha," which means "flower bud," because
of his strong devotion to St. Thérèse of Lisieux, who was not even
canonized at the time, but whose holiness had already spread like a
wildfire across Europe. Peering into Agnes's eyes as the priest poured
the water over their daughter's head and baptized her "in the name of
the Father, and of the Son, and of the Holy Spirit," little did Nikola
and Dranafile know that their daughter would one day become St.
Teresa of Calcutta, taking the name of her father's favorite saint.

Almost ten years later, Karol and Emilia Wojtyła welcomed
their third child and second son, Karol Jr., on May 18, 1920. He was
baptized by the military chaplain, Fr. Franciszek Zak, a month later
at St. Mary's Church on June 20, 1920, and was given the name of
Karol Jozef. As his parents hovered over the baptismal font as the
priest baptized Karol Jr., did they have any idea that their son would
someday become Pope St. John Paul II, one of the greatest popes in
the history of the Church? Probably not. But did John Paul II think his
parents were saints? Certainly yes. In fact, Cardinal Stanislaw Dziwisz,
the saint's closest friend and long-time secretary, who attended the
opening cause for Karol and Emilia's beatification on May 7, 2020,
nearly 100 years to the day of the pope's Baptism at the same church,

[52] Ewa K. Czaczkowska, *Faustina: The Mystic and her Message* (Stockbridge, MA: Marian Press, 2014), 33.

declared, "I heard from him many times that he had holy parents."[53] Holiness often comes full circle because "saints are born of saints."[54]

Of the many splendid churches and monuments throughout the world, some are overlooked because of their simplicity. In Assisi's historic Cathedral of San Rufino, a marble baptismal font located in the back corner would forever link three parents and three saints. Most tourists pass by without noticing it or appreciating its significance— the same thing can be said about the Sacrament of Baptism. Baptism is something lost to many in our Church because of its invisible effects, but not to the parents of the saints. In the late twelfth century, St. Francis of Assisi's mother, Pica, took him to the cathedral's baptismal font and gave him the baptismal name Giovanni. Roughly thirteen years later, Bl. Ortolana and Favorino Sciffi brought their daughter Clare to this same baptismal font. Besides St. Clare of Assisi, this couple raised another saint in Agnes of Assisi, Clare's youngest sister.

While Favorino greatly opposed his daughters' vocations, Ortolana later followed them to the convent after her husband's death. Prior to her marriage, Bl. Ortolana laid the foundation for a holy marriage and saintly children by a life of deep prayer, which included a pilgrimage to the Holy Land. She is buried in the same church as her holy daughters, which hearkens back to the words from the funeral rite: "In the waters of baptism, (name of deceased) died with Christ and rose with him to new life. May he/she now share with him eternal glory."[55]

Seven centuries later, St. Gabriel of Our Lady of Sorrows, whose baptismal name was Francesco, was baptized on the day of

---

[53] "St. John Paul II's parents' sainthood cause has officially opened," Catholic News Agency (May 7, 2020), catholicnewsagency.com/news/st-john-paul-iis-parents-sainthood-cause-has-officially-opened-69386.

[54] Fr. Sławomir Oder, postulator for the cause of canonization of John Paul II, as quoted in the Catholic News Agency's article "St. John Paul II's parents' sainthood cause has officially opened" (May 7, 2020), catholicnewsagency.com/news/st-john-paul-iis-parents-sainthood-cause-has-officially-opened-69386.

[55] Kenneth Doyle, "Funeral Mass for Non-Baptized. When to Call a Priest?" CatholicHerald.org, catholicherald.org/web-extras/question-corner/funeral-mass-for-non-baptized-when-to-call-a-priest.

his birth at the same font as his patron, St. Francis. It is very likely that Gabriel's parents implored God and, in a special way, St. Francis during the Litany of Saints that precedes the Rite of Baptism to help their son become a great saint.

While ensuring that their children had food, clothing, and shelter, the parents of the saints desired above all that their children were filled with sanctifying grace, which flowed from their Baptism. These parents gave their children natural life by way of the Holy Spirit, "the author and giver of life," but now the Church would give their children supernatural life through the sacraments. It is important to remember that Baptism is only the beginning of the Christian life, for it ought to lead us to the other sacraments, as will be seen in the next chapter. And, just as every human being begins the size of a mustard seed, so does our faith. We all start small, and we must all start somewhere, but we are all called to continue to grow in our physical bodies and in our faith. And one day, with God's grace and daily perseverance, we will have faith the size of a towering tree.

HALLMARK ONE (PART II)

Sacramental Life and Our Lady

Don't worry, I offered you to our Lady, and she
will take care of you.[1] —Dolores Escrivá

CONFIRMATION

Without the Sacraments of Baptism and the Holy Eucharist, parents and their children would be deprived of the greatest spiritual grace necessary to get to Heaven, which is sanctifying grace. We need God's life in us, or we will never overcome temptation or enter into union with the Blessed Trinity. Just as the parents of the saints recognized the power of these two sacraments and made sure they and their children were adequately prepared to receive them, so also with the Sacrament of Confirmation. In fact, many of the parents of the saints and their children were fully aware of how amazing this unheralded sacrament truly is, which led them to seriously prepare themselves like the Apostles and Our Lady did at Pentecost. Is not preparing our children for the sacraments one of the greatest privileges and responsibilities of being a parent? Unfortunately, St. Zélie was not given this privilege with St. Thérèse because she died young. As a result, St. Louis and Léonie (Thérèse's godmother) helped prepare the future saint's heart for a new outpouring of the Holy Spirit. Thérèse did not take this sacrament lightly, as she once recalled:

---

[1]   Andrés Vázquez de Prada, *The Founder of Opus Dei, Volume I*, 52. Cited by Francisco Botello in *Sum.* 5609.

Like the Apostles, I awaited the Holy Spirit's visit with
great happiness in my soul. I rejoiced at the thought of
soon being a perfect Christian and especially at that of
having eternally on my forehead the mysterious cross the
Bishop marks when conferring this sacrament. Finally,
the happy moment arrived, and I did not experience an
impetus wind at the moment of the Holy Spirit's descent
but rather this *light breeze* which the prophet Elias heard
on Mount Horeb. On that day, I received the strength to
suffer, for soon afterward the martyrdom of my soul was
about to commence.[2]

Furthermore, Léonie described the wonderful impression
Thérèse's confirmation made on her:

I followed my little sister Therese to the altar and placed
my hand on her shoulder at the moment when the Bishop
confirmed Therese. She was only eleven years old (1884)
but she seemed fully aware of the great mystery, which
was taking place in her soul. I was at that time twenty-
one years old, and I could see that my little sister Therese
was an unusual child in her spiritual maturity. I was not
able to contain my emotion in accompanying my blessed
little sister to the altar that day.[3]

While we are not afforded the details of how Louis and Léonie
instructed Thérèse for the Sacrament of Confirmation, the most
important thing is that it was done with the greatest care. Perhaps,
like the Apostles in the Upper Room, Thérèse and her family offered
intense supplication for the coming of the Holy Spirit! For the greater
the gift, the greater our preparation ought to be. Thérèse prepared
herself with the greatest care because she understood Whom she
would be receiving: God himself—the Third Person of the Blessed
Trinity, the Holy Spirit—by means of a special outpouring along
with His manifold gifts, thereby conforming her even more to
Christ and His Church. And, like the Sacraments of Baptism and

---

[2] St. Thérèse of Lisieux, *Story of a Soul,* 80.
[3] Louis Wust and Marjorie Wust, *Zelie Martin: Mother of St. Thérèse*
    (Boston, MA: Daughters of St. Paul, 1969), 196.

Holy Orders, Thérèse knew we can only receive this sacrament once, making it that much more special, since it leaves an indelible mark on our souls.

Besides Zélie, another saintly mother, Aurelia Galgani, was unable to fully prepare her daughter, St. Gemma, for Confirmation due to her terminal illness. As a result, Aurelia once said, "I cannot do better than entrust this dear child to the Holy Ghost before I die; when the last hour is near, I shall know to whom I have left."[4] Gemma's spiritual director added, "Gemma meanwhile had been preparing herself to worthily receive this Sacrament; and not content with that, she brought a Mistress of Christian Doctrine to the house every evening in order to add greater perfection to her own work."[5]

This religious sister helped Gemma prepare herself to receive the Sacrament of Confirmation, which occurred on May 26, 1885, sixteen months before her mother's death. Following her Confirmation, Gemma desired to immediately attend another Mass in thanksgiving. During the Mass, Gemma received her first locution. She declared, "I heard Holy Mass as well as I could, praying for Mamma, when all of a sudden, a voice at my heart said to me: 'Wilt though give Me Mamma?' 'Yes,' I answered, 'but provided Thou takest me also.' 'No,' replied the voice, 'give Me unreservedly thy mother. For the present thou hast to wait with thy father. I will take thee to Heaven later.'"[6]

It was at this moment that the Holy Spirit gave Gemma a little taste of what it means to be entrusted to the Holy Spirit, as her mother had prayed. The Holy Spirit told Gemma her mother's mission on earth was coming to a close while hers was just beginning. At the same time, Aurelia offers a great lesson for all parents to imitate, which involves entrusting our children to the Holy Spirit. Our Lord entrusted the Holy Spirit to the Apostles and each one of us when He declared, "These things I have spoken to you, while I am still with you. But the Counselor, the Holy Spirit, whom the Father will send in my name, he will teach you all things, and bring to your

---

4   Germanus, *The Life of St. Gemma Galgani*, 7.
5   Ibid.
6   Ibid., 8.

remembrance all that I have said to you" (Jn 14:25–26). Parents will not always be around to watch their children grow up, to encourage them, or to reprimand them when they stray because God never intended that we live forever on earth. And, therefore, parents must surrender not only their lives to the Holy Spirit, but most of all their children to the hidden God, Who can do far more good than we can ever imagine. Without the Holy Spirit, these devout parents and their children could never have lived holy lives.

HOLY ORDERS

Having been empowered with the gifts of the Holy Spirit at their Confirmation, the parents of the saints and their children received the graces not just to survive in their vocations, but to thrive. Each sacrament mirrors elements of our biological life, such as Baptism and birth, the Holy Eucharist and nourishment, Confirmation and strengthening, and the Anointing of the Sick and death. Each sacrament is interdependent upon the others, specifically the Holy Eucharist and Holy Orders. Without the priesthood, there is no Eucharist. And without the Eucharist, there is no priesthood. The parents of the saints wanted their home to become the first seminary for their children by disposing them to God's will and by providing the Church with vocations. For example, Sts. Louis and Zélie Martin begged God to give them a son who would become a priest. According to Céline, "Our devout parents had each of them wished to enter Religious Life, and God had decided otherwise, but they wished at least to offer a priest to the Lord, a missionary priest."[7] Unfortunately, Louis and Zélie's two sons, both named Joseph, died as infants. Céline once described her parents' desire for religious vocations in these words: "Disappointed with regard to the priesthood, our mother then desired to see all her daughters consecrated in the Religious Life. She died prematurely, and it was our good father who carried out the offering, as he generously accepted the vocation of all five of them. Certainly, our environment,

---

[7] Martin, *The Father of the Little Flower*, 57.

which was profoundly Christian, lent itself to this religious appeal. But our parents never influenced us in that direction."[8]

In fact, the idea of a religious vocation was at one point frightening for the Martin daughters. Céline once recalled, "The Carmelite Monastery of Lisieux inspired us rather with fear, with its grilles and the mortuary urns that ornament the front doors."[9] Though wanting their children to enter religious life, Louis and Zélie believed most of their daughters would choose marriage, the natural vocation, with the exception of Pauline, their second-oldest daughter. That is why Zélie maintained her lace business even after marrying Louis, to ensure her daughters' future dowries. How beautiful it is that Louis and Zélie "never influenced [them] in that direction," referring to their daughters' religious vocations; instead, they gave their children the freedom to follow the Spirit's promptings, even if it meant getting married. All five daughters eventually became nuns, and the youngest, St. Thérèse, became the patron of the missions and today is well beloved by many priests.

While Louis and Zélie never had any biological children who became priests, they have many spiritual sons by way of Thérèse's continual intercession for them while on earth and even more so in Heaven. Ironically, Thérèse wanted to be a missionary while on earth; however, instead of impacting one country, her mission field spans the entire globe from Heaven. No one should doubt that Thérèse is the secret weapon for many dioceses' vocations—just ask any vocation director. The reason for this is explained by Thérèse, who wrote, "For a very long time, I had a desire which appeared totally unrealizable to me, that of having a *brother as a priest*. I often thought that had my little brothers not flown away to heaven, I would have had the happiness of seeing them mount the altar; but since God chose to make little angels of them, I could not hope to see my dream realized."[10]

To Thérèse's surprise, one day her Mother Superior showed her a letter of a young seminarian, Maurice Bellière, who had contacted

---

[8] Ibid., 58.

[9] Ibid.

[10] St. Thérèse of Lisieux, *Story of a Soul*, 250–51.

the convent requesting that a cloistered sister pray for him to one day become a successful missionary priest in exchange for remembering that sister at the Holy Sacrifice of the Mass. Thérèse gladly accepted and wrote her spiritual brother on May 9, 1897, "If, as I believe, my father and mother are in Heaven, they must be looking at and blessing the brother whom Jesus has given me. They had so much wanted a missionary son! . . . I have been told that before my birth my parents were hoping their prayer was finally going to be realized."[11]

The parents of the saints, specifically the Martin family, possessed an angelic admiration for the priesthood of Jesus Christ. Céline once wrote about her father, Louis, "His respect for priests was so great that I never saw anything like it. I remember when I was a little child I imagined from what I heard that priests were like gods; I was so accustomed to have them placed above the common level."[12] Céline further recalled that her father never spoke any ill of the clergy or their sermons. In fact, Louis had a regular confessor, Abbé Lepelletier, the cathedral assistant, and a spiritual director, Fr. Pynchon, SJ, whom Louis referred to as the spiritual director for the entire family. Louis's love for the priesthood was clearly passed on to Thérèse, who corresponded throughout her life with Maurice. Thanks in part to Thérèse's intercession, Maurice eventually became a missionary priest. Before her vows, Thérèse declared her reason for becoming a Carmelite nun: "I came to save souls and especially to pray for priests."[13] In her autobiography *Story of a Soul*, Thérèse wrote, "I feel in me the *vocation* of the PRIEST. With what love, O Jesus, I would carry You in my hands when, at my voice, You would come down from heaven. And with what love would I give You to souls! But alas! while desiring to be a *Priest*, I admire and envy the humility of St. Francis of Assisi and I feel the *vocation* of imitating him in refusing the sublime dignity of the *Priesthood*."[14]

Thérèse was in no way advocating for the woman presbyter; rather, she was reaffirming her respect for the priesthood's sublime

---

[11]   St. Thérèse of Lisieux, *General Correspondence Vol. II*, 1094.
[12]   Martin, *The Father of Little Flower*, 13.
[13]   St. Thérèse of Lisieux, *Story of a Soul*, 149.
[14]   Ibid., 192.

calling, something of which even Francis of Assisi felt unworthy. Above all, Thérèse fully embraced the notion that the last shall be first by being totally resigned to her vocation as a religious sister and not seeking anything beyond that, especially the priesthood. The Letter to the Hebrews tells us that "one does not take the honor upon himself, but he is called by God, just as Aaron was" (5:4). Just like Our Lady, who would have been the most qualified priest, Thérèse and many religious female saints knew that the priesthood is not something to be grasped at; rather, those who are the least in this life—those who remain hidden, bear their imperfections, and embrace God's calling for their lives—will be the greatest in Heaven.

Like Sts. Louis and Zélie Martin, many other parents of the saints prayed that God would bless their family with a vocation to the priesthood. Specifically, the parents of Sts. Maximilian Kolbe, Padre Pio, Ven. Fulton Sheen, and countless others believed that having a son raised to the altar was the greatest honor God could bestow upon them in this life.

And, while the Church prays daily for vocations to the priesthood and religious life during Mass, we must not forget to pray for holy marriages, for from them come holy priests and holy nuns. This brings us to the Sacrament of Matrimony in the life of the parents of the saints.

HOLY MATRIMONY

Just as God calls certain souls to the priesthood and religious life with a specific mission—some to live a hidden life by offering sacrifice and intercession for the world from behind monastic walls, and others to be humble parish priests or to shepherd the flock as bishops—so too does God call the majority of humanity to continue His mission of co-creating new life for the Kingdom of God. The married vocation is in fact the ordinary vocation, but God's call to marriage is truly supernatural because God delights in marriage and all of Heaven awaits a new soul, not so much for the potential of the soul, what will become of it, but for who it is: a child of God.

Since God loves holy marriages and rejoices in new life, He must bring spouses together. If God wanted St. Thérèse of Lisieux to come into existence, He had to first bring her parents together. On the Bridge of St. Leonard in Alençon, France, around 1858, the Divine Matchmaker brought together two future saints, who would raise up one of the Church's greatest saints. Or, as best put by Fr. Stéphane-Joseph Piat, OFM, "Providence, which was preparing from afar the cradle of Thérèse, guided Zélie Guérin to Louis Martin by subjecting both to the same preliminary experience of aspiring after the complete detachment from the world."[15] Providence had other plans, and it was trust alone that would lead Louis and Zélie and their children to Love Himself. Yet, before this holy marriage could happen, God needed to bring Louis and Zélie Martin into existence.

Pierre and Marie-Anne Martin

Pierre and Marie-Anne Martin hold one of the greatest distinctions in the Church's history, achieved only by a select few couples, which is to be both the parents and grandparents of saints, in their son, Louis Martin, and their granddaughter, Thérèse of Lisieux. Their holy union says it all. When Captain Pierre Martin became engaged to Marie-Anne Fanie-Boureau, a daughter of a captain, a dowry was obligatory as an officer's daughter. Unfortunately, due to family misfortunes, Marie-Anne lacked the necessary funds for marriage. Pierre did not let his bride's financial difficulties preclude him from marrying the woman he loved, and so he supplemented the required sum himself. He married out of true love and not wealth, or in spite of the lack thereof. They were wed on April 7, 1818, in the Church of St. Martin-d'Ainay in Lyon, France. Church records show that Pierre was a few days shy of his forty-first birthday when he married his eighteen-year-old bride. He was friends with Marie-Anne's father, Nicholas Boureau, who also served in the military and was a virtuous man. Pierre's military career, which included stints in Belgium, France, and Poland, likely delayed his vocation. However, Pierre trusted that God would not only provide for his family, but also protect him body and soul during the Napoleonic Wars.

Pierre and Marie-Anne had five children, Louis being their only surviving child. Their oldest son, Pierre, died in a shipwreck.

---

15 Piat, *The Story of a Family*, 21.

They also lost three daughters, Sophie, Marie, and Fanny, at the ages of nine, twenty-six, and twenty-seven respectively from unknown causes. Pierre died on June 26, 1865, at the age of eighty-eight. Still, he was blessed to meet four of his nine grandchildren in Marie-Louise, Marie-Pauline, Marie-Léonie, and Hélène. On the other hand, Marie-Anne was able to get to know all of her nine grandchildren, including St. Thérèse, who was ten years old when her grandmother died. Zélie's admiration for her mother-in-law was no secret. She once described Marie-Anne as having "an extraordinary courage and very fine qualities."[16] Pierre and Marie-Anne witnessed to the splendor of the Holy Sacrament of Matrimony by their fidelity to God, each other, and their children, which inevitably drew Louis to follow in their footsteps as a husband and father. At the same time, Pierre and Marie-Anne neither steered Louis to pursue a military career nor to become a religious priest, but simply allowed God's grace to unfold by being faithful to their own marriage vows and praying fervently for his vocation. Marie-Anne's love for her son Louis could not be expressed more beautifully than in the following words, which she wrote to him on August 23, 1843, the day after he turned twenty. She wrote, "Dear son, you are the subject of my dreams by night and the chief charm of my memories. How often I think of you when my soul, upraised to God, follows my heart's longing, and soars to the foot of His throne! There I pray with all the fervor of my love that God may pour upon all my children the happiness and peace which we need in this stormy world. . . . Be ever humble, my dear my son."[17]

Isidore and Louise-Jeanne Guérin

Ten years after the holy marriage of Pierre and Marie-Anne Martin, another couple, Isidore and Louise-Jeanne Guérin, exchanged their marriage vows. The Martins' and the Guérins' lives would be forever intertwined when their son and daughter married, which resulted in the birth of their granddaughter, St. Thérèse. On September 5, 1828, Isidore Guérin married Louise-Jeanne Macé. Together they had three children: Marie-Louise, who became a nun, and St. Zélie and Isidore, who both entered Holy Matrimony. All three children remained practicing Catholics until their deaths and progressed in virtue thanks to their parents' zeal for the Faith. On top of this, six of their granddaughters became nuns (five of Zélie's daughters and one of Isidore's). Despite the fact that Louise-Jeanne died a few months before her first grandchild was born, she probably never imagined that one of her own daughters and granddaughters would someday be canonized. And, though Zélie was the only one of her siblings to be canonized, she always thought her sister to be a saint. Zélie once wrote to her daughter, "Good-bye, my dear Pauline. Tell your aunt that I pray for her every day. However, I find it quite peculiar to pray for a saint, I who am covered in weakness."[18]

And while we uphold Isidore and Louise-Jeanne for being the parents and grandparents of saints and models of faith, they also fell short in a few areas, which should be addressed to prevent future couples from repeating their mistakes. There is no doubt that Zélie experienced her father's love and surely looked for his qualities, especially his great faith, in her future husband, Louis. On the other hand, Zélie's mother caused her immense suffering, especially due to Zélie's sensitive nature. In his book *Story of a Family*, Fr. Stéphane-Joseph Piat, OFM, who collaborated with Céline on many of the details of their family life and heritage, provided some great insights into Zélie's mother. He said, "Madame Guérin was endowed with the faith that moves mountains, but she was wholly lacking in the sense of psychology essential for the training of young people, and this want of the educative sense led her—and that notwithstanding real motherly affection—to mishandle seriously an exceptionally sensitive character. To some extent, the child seems to have been deprived of a mother's caresses."[19]

Zélie once confided to her younger brother, whom she deemed spoiled, "My childhood, my youth, was as sad as a shroud because, if my mother spoiled you, as you know, she was too strict with me. She, though so good, didn't know how to treat me, so my

---

[18] Martin and Martin, *A Call to a Deeper Love*, 252.
[19] Piat, *The Story of a Family*, 18–19.

heart suffered greatly."[20] As will be noted in a future chapter, Zélie would not raise her daughters like she was raised, save her father's affection. At the same time, Zélie would not let the wounds her mother inflicted on her to be passed on to her children. Favoritism, spoiling, lack of affection, and severity without gentleness would have no place in her parenting style.

Despite Louise-Jeanne's failures as a mother, she and her husband did do several things right. Specifically, they sacrificed their finances by sending Marie-Louise and Zélie as day boarders to a school run by the religious sisters of the Sacred Hearts of the Picpus Congregation, who also had a convent devoted to perpetual adoration. Due to the sisters' influence, Marie-Louise and Zélie received a solid education grounded in virtue, but, even more importantly, they "took away from this convent of teaching nuns the spirit of faith and the thorough religious instruction of which Zélie would give such ample proof when presiding over her home. At one time, thanks to her contact with this fervent community, she even conceived the hope of consecrating herself to God in the religious life."[21]

So grateful for her own formation by the sisters, Zélie would one day send her two oldest daughters to a similar school run by nuns. And, while these religious sisters renounced their biological motherhood, they can often be, as seen in Zélie's case, the only example of motherhood and love that some will experience in this life due to the failures of their own parents. Zélie's mother, though devout, perhaps unknowingly refused her daughter what she needed most: love, gentleness, and the ability to adapt to her temperament. Little did Zélie know that God was about to send the perfect man for her, someone who understood her sensitive nature. That being said, Louis's love would begin the healing process, though only God could fully heal the scars she inherited from her mother.

Sts. Louis and Zélie Martin

As Zélie Guérin was crossing the Bridge of St. Leonard in Alençon, France, on what seemed like an ordinary day, she heard an interior

---

[20] Martin and Martin, *A Call to A Deeper Love,* 18.
[21] Piat, *The Story of a Family,* 21.

voice say, "*That is he whom I have prepared for you*"[22] as she passed the brawny, noble-faced, and contemplative-mannered Louis Martin. The twenty-seven-year-old Zélie's heart began to beat with excitement upon seeing Louis, even though no words were exchanged. After this brief encounter, Zélie longed to see him again. Although he was a comfortable bachelor at the age of thirty-five, Louis noticed something special about the dark-eyed brunette. Louis confided to his mother that he wanted to formally meet her and not just gaze at her from a distance. There was a mutual attraction, which, according to Pope St. John Paul II, "is of the essence of love and in some sense is indeed love, although love is not merely attraction."[23] Unbeknownst to Louis, his mother had met Zélie a few times before at a lace-making class and was so impressed by Zélie that she had secretly prayed that Louis would someday marry her.

On July 14, 1864, Zélie wrote this letter to her younger brother, Isidore, to encourage him to find a devout bride. Her words might be one of the greatest pieces of marriage advice for any man:

> It seems you're still thinking of Mademoiselle X? I think you're foolish. . . . I can't stop thinking about it. You're going to hurt yourself, either with her or with someone else, because you only consider the superficial things, beauty and wealth, without worrying about the qualities that make a husband happy or the faults that cause him grief and ruin. You know all that glitters is not gold. The main thing is to look for a good woman whose interests center on the home, who is not afraid of dirtying her hands with work, who devotes time to her appearance only as much as she has to, and who knows how to raise children to work and be holy. A woman like that would scare you; she would not be brilliant enough in the eyes of world. But sensible people would love her better even if she had nothing, rather than another woman with a

---

[22]   Martin, *The Mother of the Little Flower*, 3.

[23]   Karl Wojtyła, *Love and Responsibility* (San Francisco: Ignatius Press, 1993), 76.

dowry of fifty thousand francs and who lacked these qualities.[24]

Louis and Zélie did not allow physical attraction or money to be the most important things they each looked for in their future spouse. Rather, virtue was the greatest magnet of their love because they knew their spouse could never bring them perfect happiness—only God Himself could do that. Mrs. Martin's prayers came true when Louis and Zélie married on July 13, 1858, at midnight (the custom of the day) at the Church of Notre-Dame in Alençon. This church became very dear to the Martin family not only as their parish, but the house of God where all their children would later be baptized and Zélie's funeral Mass would be celebrated.

Without Louis's mother praying for him and encouraging him to pursue Zélie, he might have remained a bachelor for the rest of his life. In effect, Louis's mother witnesses to the powerful role parents have in nurturing their child's vocation, especially praying in a special way for their future son-in-law or daughter-in-law that, like their own child, they might be holy and without blemish on their wedding day. Interestingly enough, the Church commemorates Sts. Louis and Zélie Martin's feast day on July 12, the eve of their nuptials.

On July 13, as the clock struck midnight, the Martins would witness to the splendor of this sacrament as they exchanged their vows in the silence and darkness of the night before their Eucharistic Bridegroom, Who once told St. Faustina, "Now you shall consider my Love in the Blessed Sacrament. Here, I am entirely yours, soul, body, and divinity, as your Bridegroom. You know what love demands: one thing only, reciprocity . . ."[25] Having professed their love and fidelity to each other before the Most Blessed Sacrament, Whom they sought to receive and visit daily, the Martins had the supreme exemplar of married love before their eyes. For the Eucharistic Bridegroom keeps nothing for Himself, but is poured out totally for His Bride, the Church. While a few family members and friends were present at this holy marriage, including Louis's

---

[24]　Martin and Martin, *A Call to a Deeper Love*, 11.

[25]　St. Faustina, *Diary: Divine Mercy in My Soul*, 628.

mother, whose prayers doubtless helped bring this holy couple
together, the Martins were now equipped with sacramental graces
as they embarked on their married journey together—a journey that
testifies to Louis and Zélie's unshakable trust in God and each other.
There is a reason marriage is a sacrament, for without these graces
the Martins would never have become saints or raised a daughter
(and possibly another one) to become a saint.

After their wedding day, Louis and Zélie settled at rue Pont
Neuf in Alençon, where Louis operated his own watchmaking/
jewelry shop. Their daughter Céline talked about her mother and
father's initial desire to live as brother and sister—also known as a
Josephite marriage in honor of St. Joseph and Our Lady, who lived as
celibates. Céline once wrote about her mother Zélie. Specifically, she
declared, "In her letters mother has stated that before marriage she
was ignorant of the mysteries of life, and that when she learned them
she was troubled, even to tears. Father profited by this circumstance
to propose to her his own project of their living together as brother
and sister. She agreed to this, in spite of her former desire to have
children. But God had other plans for them."[26]

After ten months of celibacy, a priest encouraged Louis and
Zélie to have children, and they wasted no time. They had nine
children in a span of thirteen years, from 1860 to 1873, three of
whom sadly died in infancy and one at the age of five. Fifteen years
after their marriage vows, Louis and Zélie's love was even stronger, as
evidenced by Zélie's words, which she wrote to Louis while visiting
her brother in Lisieux accompanied by a few of her daughters: "I'm
longing to be near you, my dear Louis. I love you with all my heart,
and I feel my affection so much more when you're not here with me.
It would be impossible for me to live apart from you."[27]

Francis and Emma Drexel

The presence of Our Lord and Our Lady at the wedding feast of
Cana in St. John's Gospel reveals that marriage has a special place
in their hearts. After all, Jesus changing six stone jars of water into

---

26 Martin, *The Mother of the Little Flower*, 4.
27 Martin and Martin, *A Call to a Deeper Love*, 135.

wine was much more than what meets the eye. He indeed changed water into wine and thus gave the wedding guests the greatest wine in the history of the world, but, in doing so, He also took His place as the Messianic Bridegroom—and we are His bride. Every couple hopes for a lasting marriage blessed with children, and one with more joys than sorrows. In the midst of these vows is the reality that God has permission to do whatever He wants—namely, to allow suffering to bring about a greater good. No one can escape the Cross. When Francis Drexel was united in the Sacrament of Matrimony to Hannah Langstroth, a Quaker, in 1854 (the year that the Dogma of the Immaculate Conception was proclaimed by Pope Pius IX), he had no idea that four years later he would be a widower at the young age of thirty-four. A month after their second child was born on November 26, 1858, the child who would become St. Katharine Drexel, Francis's beloved wife Hannah died suddenly. A wealthy banker, Francis immediately sought his brother's help in raising his two daughters, Elizabeth and Katharine. Not losing confidence in God, Francis remarried two years later to Emma Bouvier, a devout Catholic, who bore him his third daughter, Louise, in 1863.

Unlike the fairy tales, there was no wickedness in their stepmother Emma, rather, the opposite was true—goodness prevailed. Emma responded to the graces of the sacrament by raising her two stepdaughters and her own daughter, Louise, to become saintly children by attending Mass each morning. Emma loved all her daughters equally and prepared them for their future vocations by teaching them how to cook and sew, as well as ensuring they had the best education possible. Later, Francis asked his teenage daughters to teach Sunday school to his farmworkers' children at their large, country home dedicated to St. Michael the Archangel. Francis made sure his daughters were pursued only by men of virtue and not men who were only after their inheritance.

Francis and Emma realized everything was a gift from God, including their children and their money. Because their money belonged to God, they desired to help those less fortunate. Upon his death, Francis gave $1.5 million to various charitable organizations, such as orphanages, hospitals, and institutions to help the poor.

Initially resisting her vocation, Katharine once wrote, "I do not know how I could bear the privations and poverty of the religious life. I have never been deprived of luxuries."[28] Eventually, Our Lady and Pope Leo XIII called Katharine to renounce everything for Christ and follow the example of her father and mother's generosity. Rather than waste her large inheritance on herself, Katharine devoted her life to educating the Native American and African American populations. None of this would have been possible without the example and graces that flowed from Francis and Emma's nuptials; generosity, sacrifice, responsibility, and a love for the Most Blessed Sacrament were the pillars of their marriage. When suffering and loss came through the death of his first wife, Hannah, God never abandoned the Drexel family. The graces from Francis and Emma's sacramental marriage allowed this devout couple to prepare their three daughters for their future vocations, two as holy married women and mothers, and another, St. Katharine, as a religious sister.

Regardless of their vocations, each Drexel sister used their inheritance to start a school for African American children. The Drexel sisters continued their parents' legacy as they sought to spread the Gospel to the poor. In doing so, Katharine, Elizabeth, and Louise kept the torch of the Holy Spirit alive, passed on from their parents, and eventually spread the Gospel to over thirteen states, forty mission centers, and twenty-three rural schools, along with $11 million used to help educate African American children. As seen in the Drexel family, one holy marriage is so powerful that it can change the cultural tides, leading countless souls to Heaven, just as one unholy marriage can lead countless souls off the narrow path.

Alberto and Maria Beretta

Alberto Beretta and Maria De Micheli were married on October 12, 1908, in Milan, Italy. Alberto was nineteen and Maria twenty-one, and they desired to have a holy marriage with lots of children. Long before that time, Maria had helped raise her siblings while seriously discerning religious life, like so many of the parents of the

---

28 Anne Ball, *Modern Saints*, Book Two (Rockford, IL: TAN Books, 1983), 458.

saints. However, at the advice of her confessor, Maria embraced the call to marriage. Alberto and Maria's surrender bore great fruit—namely thirteen children. Their tenth child would become known to the world as St. Gianna Beretta Molla. Besides Gianna, this holy marriage generated two sons who became priests and one daughter who became a nun. All of their surviving children earned academic degrees, which was quite a feat at that time. In a large family like theirs, the children had more responsibility. For example, Gianna's eldest sister, Amalia, helped prepare Gianna for her First Holy Communion, which occurred on April 14, 1928. The sacramental graces from Alberto and Maria's marriage saturated their children. Gianna once wrote about her devout parents: "My parents knew about love, they taught us and showed us. Mamma died in April 1942. Father passed away five months after her."[29] It is no surprise then that Gianna's parents, who loved each more than their own lives, died months apart, for they were truly of one flesh and one heart. When one elderly spouse dies, it is not uncommon for the other to follow shortly, especially when the wife dies first. There is such a thing as dying of a broken heart, but perhaps Alberto and Maria's love was so strong that even death could not separate them from each other, and so Alberto longed to be reunited with his wife to praise God for all eternity.

RECONCILIATION

In the previous chapter, Servant of God Sr. Lucia's parents were noted for their great love of the Eucharist and the Rosary, which they passed on to their seven children, especially their little pearl, Lucia, who later became a Carmelite nun. Paradoxically, Sr. Lucia's greatest suffering came at the hands of her mother. After she was interrogated over the credibility of Our Lady's apparition at Fatima by the police and local authorities, Sr. Lucia's mother still doubted her visions. In fact, Maria Rosa dos Santos tried gentleness, threats, and beatings to convince Sr. Lucia that she was lying. In her writings, Sr. Lucia wrote, "What hurt me most was the indifference shown

---

[29] *Love is a Choice*, DVD. Ignatius Press, 2005.

me by my parents,"[30] as they did not welcome her home after she
returned from a cruel investigation by the authorities; instead, Lucia
was sent out to pasture the sheep. Unlike Sr. Lucia's parents, her
uncle, Ti Marto, the father of Sts. Jacinta and Francesco, believed
his children's testimony.

Despite her own failures, narrow-mindedness, and profound
suffering that she caused her daughter, Maria Rosa somewhat
vindicated herself by encouraging Lucia to go to Confession with
her. Maria Rosa seriously thought this would be their last Confession
if the Blessed Mother failed to perform her promised miracle because
they might be killed by the cruel mob. Echoing sentiments that may
have penetrated our Mother of Sorrows' heart at Calvary, Maria
Rosa declared, "If my child is going to die, I want to die with her!"[31]
Even though Our Lady fulfilled her promise, and Sr. Lucia did not
become a martyr, Maria Rosa reveals that godly parents make sure
their children are prepared for Heaven by personally partaking of
Confession on a regular basis and encouraging their children to
follow suit.

St. Louis Martin and many of the parents of the saints recognized
how desperately they needed the Divine Physician's mercy and
healing in order to be a merciful spouse, father, or mother. As a result,
many of these devout parents went frequently to the Sacrament of
Reconciliation. Louis and Zélie did not coerce their children to
receive this sacrament of humility; rather, the children became firm
believers in the efficacy of the Sacrament of Reconciliation as a result
of their parents' example, which in turn fostered their love for this
amazing sacrament. Specifically, Céline, Zélie's second-youngest
daughter, recalled, "Mother used to take me on her knees to help me
to prepare for confession."[32] Moreover, Céline said that her "mother
had regular recourse to the parish priest of Montsort for confession
and direction. She attended all the meetings of the Third Order of

---

30 Lucia dos Santos, *Fatima in Lucia's Own Words: Sister Lucia's Memoirs,*
   Volume II, Third Ed. (Fatima, Portugal: Secretariado dos Pastorinhos,
   2004), 72.
31 John de Marchi I.M.C, *Fatima: From the Beginning* (Fatima: Edicóes
   Missóes Consolata, 2006), 133.
32 Martin, *The Mother of the Little Flower,* 12.

St. Francis, of which she was a member, at the Poor Clares Convent. She visited these nuns, recommending herself to their prayers in her problems and sufferings."[33]

Aurelia Galgani also prepared her children, especially St. Gemma, for the Sacrament of Reconciliation. Every Saturday, she took her children to church to receive God's forgiveness, which at the same time helped her children to be reconciled to God and their family members. When Aurelia was unable to accompany her children, either due to her sickness or for another reason, she enlisted help. She knew the absolute necessity of this sacrament for growing in virtue not only for herself, but for her entire family. Aurelia reveals the importance of making Confession a scheduled, family event and not an afterthought on our deathbeds. According to Ven. Fr. Germanus, "She herself prepared them for it (confession), and when it was Gemma's turn, this devout mother used to weep on seeing her gravity and attention and the great sorrow she displayed for her little faults."[34] Aurelia clearly helped Gemma and her siblings discover how rich and incomprehensive God's mercy is and how much even the slightest sin wounds Our Lord. Aurelia frequently showed Gemma an image of Our Lord's Crucifixion and would say to her, "Look, Gemma, how this dear Jesus died on the Cross for us."[35] This devout mother wanted her daughter never to forget that we must not only shed tears of sorrow for our sins, which crucified Our Lord, but also tears of love for Him, Who willingly died for us. Gemma also reminds us with this most beautiful resolution never to take for granted or abuse God's grace and mercy: "I will confess my sins and receive Holy Communion each time as if it were to be the last."[36]

Like St. Gemma, St. Josemaría was also moved by his mother's example, but especially the following words, which left a profound impression on him for the rest of his life. "José Maria, you should

---

[33] Ibid., 48.

[34] Germanus, *The Life of St. Gemma Galgani*, 6.

[35] Ibid., 5.

[36] Ibid., 15.

be ashamed only to sin,"[37] declared his mother, Dolores, when he was embarrassed to kiss his friend's mother or disliked wearing new clothes. At the same time, the parents of the saints reveal that no parent is perfect. Mistakes and sin will come, "but where sin increased, grace abounded all the more" (Rm 5:20). Though the most important and most difficult task in life for the parents of the saints was to get themselves and their children to Heaven, their mission did not stop there; rather, the Holy Spirit inspired these men and women to be heralds of the Gospel in their community, parish, and work. In fact, Sts. Louis and Zélie Martin were very much concerned for the salvation of souls. Céline wrote: "They prayed and had prayers said for sinners; especially when in the neighborhood any one of them was in danger of death, they tried to arrange that he should receive the Last Sacraments."[38] In a letter written to their eldest daughter, Pauline, while she was a boarding student at the Visitation Convent at Le Mans, Zélie wrote, "I commend to your prayers, and, above all, to those of your aunt and good Sister Marie-Gertrude, whom I like, a poor man who's going to die. It's been forty years since he's been to confession. Your father is doing all he can to persuade him to convert, but the man thinks he's a saint. Like Saint Paul, he thinks that nothing more remains for him than to receive the crown of justice!"[39]

These holy parents desired to bring all souls to Christ's Church, and, above all, to Heaven. In order to do that, they realized that the greatest conversion must occur daily, beginning with themselves.

THE ANOINTING OF THE SICK

One of the most beautiful stories in the lives of the saints occurred in the year 1856. As Margaret Bosco, the mother of St. John Bosco, was near death from pneumonia, she called her priestly son to administer the Last Rites. Margaret said to her son, "There was a time I helped you receive the sacraments. Now it's your turn to help me. Let's

---

[37] John F. Coverdale, *Uncommon Faith: The Early Years of Opus Dei, 1928–1943* (New York: Scepter Press, 2002), 18.
[38] Martin, *The Father of the Little Flower*, 14.
[39] Martin and Martin, *A Call to Deeper Love*, 230.

recite the prayers for the dying together."[40] John fulfilled his mother's wishes. After he prepared his mother to meet her Maker, she had one final request. Specifically, Margaret said, "I'm asking you this one favor. It's the last I'll ever ask of you. Leave me. When you suffer, you only double my pain. Leave me and pray for me. That's all I ask. Good-bye, John."[41] John obeyed his mother, but returned to comfort her later. Those were indeed Margaret's last words to her son, who said a Mass for his mother's soul shortly after her death.

Even saints like John Bosco had difficulty saying goodbye to their parents despite believing their loved ones were with Jesus. Clearly, it is always more difficult for those left behind to detach themselves from their departed loved ones. Christ wept upon hearing the news of his friend Lazarus's death and certainly lamented the passing of His beloved foster father, St. Joseph, though this incident was not recorded in Scripture. It seems as though a part of us dies along with them. Far from being stoics who never show any emotion, or people who are happy at every moment, the parents of the saints and their children shared in Christ's tears during His agony in the garden, for suffering is unavoidable. In fact, suffering and resignation to the will of God are attitudes often portrayed in the biographies of the saints. It is only natural to want to hold on to loved ones. Surely, John Bosco did not want to be separated from his mother, who beautifully instilled in him virtue and discipline.

Margaret also passed on her great love for the Holy Eucharist and Our Lady to her son. Moreover, she inspired John's vocation and modeled what every mother ought to be—the most important woman in a priest's life outside of Our Lady, for she is the woman who reflects the maternity and gentleness of God. Margaret did not raise her son to keep holding on to her, but to move forward with faith in the Resurrection. Margaret was at the same time a woman of the Cross and a woman of the Resurrection, who had the amazing privilege that most mothers can only dream of, i.e., to have her son prepare her to meet Our Lord through the Sacrament of the Anointing of the Sick,

---

[40]   W. Leifeld, *Mothers of the Saints* (Ann Arbor, MI: Servant Publications, 1991), 167.

[41]   Ibid.

the "sacrament of those departing," which "completes our conformity to the death and Resurrection of Christ, just as Baptism began it."[42] And, if Margaret was fortunate to have made her last Confession to her son, which we do not know, what penance could he have given to his holy mother, who had given him such a heroic example of sanctity? One of the most difficult moments in life is seeing our loved ones suffer and die. There is no pain so great, no sorrow so deep. On August 26, 1877, St. Louis Martin, who had so often procured a priest for his dying neighbors, sought a priest to give his wife the Last Rites two days before her death. In doing so, Louis had fulfilled the final obligation to his wedding vows that he made nineteen years earlier: to make sure his wife was properly prepared to meet Jesus. St. Thérèse recalled witnessing this sacrament years later, "The touching ceremony of the last anointing is also deeply impressed on my mind. I can still see the spot where I was by Céline's side. All five of us were lined up according to age, and Papa was there too, sobbing."[43] Zélie's death also had a tremendous influence on Céline. She recalled her mother's calmness in the throes of death:

> As for our mother, she remained calm and self-possessed. She was to die thus in a truly saintly way, giving us, to the very end, the example of complete self-forgetfulness and most lively faith.
>
> In the moments of anguish during her malady, her sorrowful plea would rise to Heaven: "Oh! Thou Who hast created me, have mercy on me!" And God had pity on her by hastening the progress of her disease; for, at that time, there were not, as now, sedatives to relieve the pains of poor sufferers.
>
> It was on Tuesday, August 28, 1877, half an hour after midnight, that our admirable mother was taken from us. She was only forty-five years and eight months old.[44]

Zélie learned to die gracefully partly from witnessing the heroic final moments of her father-in-law, Captain Pierre Martin, and her

42 CCC, 1523.
43 St. Thérèse of Lisieux, *Story of a Soul*, 33.
44 Martin and Martin, *The Mother of the Little Flower*, 110.

own father, Isidore Guérin. Zélie recounted the holy deaths of these two men, whose son and daughter would become saints. To her brother Isidore, she wrote on June 27, 1865:

> My father-in-law died yesterday at one o'clock in the afternoon. He received the sacraments last Thursday. He died like a saint, as he lived, he died. I would never have believed that this could have such an effect on me. I'm shattered. . . .
>
> I confess, death terrifies me. I just came from seeing my father-in-law. His arms so stiff and his face so cold! And to think that I will see my family like that or that they will see me! . . . You may be accustomed to seeing death, for me, I'd never seen it so close.[45]

To her sister-in-law, Céline Guérin, she wrote on September 3, 1868, concerning her father:

> My heart was broken in sorrow and, at the same time, full of heavenly consolation. If you knew, my dear sister, with what holiness he prepared for death. At three o'clock, he made the sign of the cross. I have the hope and even conviction, that our dear father was well received by God. I want my death to be like his. We've already had three Masses said for him. We intend to request a great number of them so, if he has anything to atone for, he'll quickly be delivered from Purgatory.[46]

Although she was frightened by death, Zélie was not terrified of suffering. Two months later on November 1, 1868, she told her brother, "My good father was not used to suffering. As for me, I'm not afraid of going to Purgatory; suffering seems completely natural to me. If God wanted it, I would immediately make a deal to do my father's penance in Purgatory as well as mine. I would be so content to know that he was happy!"[47]

---

[45]   Martin and Martin, *A Call to a Deeper Love*, 16.

[46]   Ibid., 42.

[47]   Ibid., 47.

The greatest unknown for us is death. We don't know how or when it will come to us, and this causes anxiety for many. While some tend to ignore it out of fear, most saints stared death in the face, or at least that's what their biographers said. More realistic are the words of Zélie when she declared to her brother, "Death terrifies me." Zélie's brutal honesty about death resonates with many of us. Despite her fear of death, Zélie, her husband, her father, and her father-in-law proved that the best recipe for a holy death is a holy life.

The parents of the saints, especially Louis and Zélie Martin, were devoted to having Masses said for the departed souls. According to Zélie, "I intend to request one hundred and fifty Masses right away for my father and mother."[48] Zélie also made it a habit to walk to the cemetery each Sunday. But she did not stop there. "My father follows me everywhere; I seem to see him suffering. I offered up all the sacrifices I could make during my life and all my sufferings for him. I even made the 'heroic vow' for his benefit. As for me, when I'm in Purgatory, I'll serve my time."[49] The "heroic vow" referred to those who offer all their merits and works for the souls in Purgatory.

Like St. Zélie Martin, St. Padre Pio also mourned the loss of his dear parents. As his mother, Maria, journeyed to spend Christmas with her son at San Giovanni Rotondo, she became seriously ill and was diagnosed with double pneumonia. Her husband and other children were quickly summoned. Padre Pio, who had worked so many miracles in his life—such as bilocating, prophesying, reading people's souls, and appearing in the sky to American forces to prevent his monastery from being bombed—could not work a miracle for the most near and dear to him and heal his mother. In response to her illness, Padre Pio responded, "God's Will be done."[50] Maria Forgione passed away peacefully while kissing the crucifix on January 3, 1929, as the forty-two-year-old Padre Pio administered his most memorable and painful Last Rites as a priest.

---

[48] Ibid., 43.
[49] Ibid., 44.
[50] Rega, *Padre Pio and America*, 96; Bonaventura Massa, *Mary Pyle: She Lived Doing Good to All* (San Giovanni Rotondo, Our Lady of Grace Capuchin Friary, 1986), 107.

Padre Pio was described as being "inconsolable and fainted."[51] Padre Pio eventually went into a room close by, where he was said to have shed copious tears, causing those near him to cry. Padre Pio told people, "These are precisely tears of love. Nothing but love."[52] He was so heartbroken over his mother's death that he could not bring himself to attend her funeral. Instead, he watched the funeral procession from a nearby home and cried out as his mother's coffin passed, "My mother, my beautiful mother!"[53] Many who knew Maria Forgione began to seek her intercession immediately, to which Padre Pio responded, "You have found the path to grace."[54] What would seem like the greatest blessing for Padre Pio—to anoint his mother—was also one of the most difficult things he would have to do. Unfortunately, Padre Pio would have to relive the pain when he anointed his father, Grazio, seventeen years later. After falling down some steep steps at the house where he lived near Pio's monastery, Grazio's condition became so severe that Pio was granted permission to remain at his father's bedside. Author Frank Rega described Grazio's final days: "Padre Pio spoon-fed Grazio, and Holy Communion was brought for both men from the Friary. Finally, the son administered the Last Rites to his father. Grazio died in his son's arms on the evening of October 7, 1946. Padre Pio's grief was intense, and it took a week after the funeral for him to recover fully and to return to his ministry. When some of the friars tried to comfort him, Padre Pio whispered, 'It is a father I have lost.'"[55]

In these words, Padre Pio conveyed the depths of his love for his human father, who, along with his mother, he loved more than anyone else because his parents loved him unconditionally and sacrificed so that he could become a priest. And, while we can have

---

[51] Rega, *Padre Pio and America*, 96.

[52] Gennaro Preziuso, *The Life of Padre Pio: Between the Altar and the Confessional* (New York: Alba House, 2002), 138.

[53] Rega, *Padre Pio and America,* 97.

[54] Geraldine Nolan, *A View of Padre Pio from Mary's House* (San Giovanni Rotondo, Italy: 1993), 95.

[55] Rega, *Padre Pio and America*, 215; Dorothy M. Gaudiose, *Mary's House. Mary Pile: Under the Spiritual Guidance of Padre Pio* (New York: Alba House, 1993), 121.

many spiritual fathers and mothers in our lives, we can have only one biological father and mother. No person can ever take the place of a father or mother, and no parent ought to doubt their influence on their children's lives. In God's providence, Grazio died on the feast day of Our Lady of the Rosary, as he loved to pray the Rosary with his family. It is clear from Padre Pio and so many saints that the more we love God, the greater is our love for our loved ones, especially when their time on earth draws near and they pass away. Padre Pio's life challenges the misconception that the saints were so detached from their parents and relatives that they easily carried on after their death with perfect resignation. Instead, Sts. John Bosco, Zélie Martin, and Padre Pio reveal that mourning our departed loved ones is not a sign of weakness; rather, it is a sign of how much we loved them and how much they loved us. At the same time, Our Lord reminds us that "blessed are those who mourn, for they shall be comforted" (Mt 5:4). Eventually God's healing grace dries up our fallen tears and restores us. Yet Padre Pio, who was blessed with the gift of tears and often shed copious amounts during prayer and after receiving Holy Communion, reminds us of the most important mourning, even more important than mourning our loved ones. When asked by his spiritual director the reason for his tears, Padre Pio humbly declared, "I cry for my sins and those of mankind."[56] It remains a mystery as to why God allowed St. Joseph to die before Jesus' Crucifixion, leaving Mary without her husband's support during the brutal death of their Son. Perhaps God wished to highlight the importance of motherhood while offering Mary to all of humanity as their mother.

St. Joseph and Our Lady

Though St. Joseph is not a parent of a saint, for his foster child was God Himself, he is a model for all parents and is looked upon as the "pillar of families," one of the many titles attributed to him in the Litany of St. Joseph. As the head of the Holy Family, Joseph was a

---

[56] Rega, *Padre Pio and America*, 15; Alessandro da Ripabottoni, *Guide to Padre Pio's Pietrelcina*, (San Giovanni Rotondo, Editions: Padre Pio of Pietrelcina, 1987), 41.

pillar of strength and virtue for his Son, Jesus, and his bride, Mary. Like a pillar, Joseph provided unfailing support for Jesus and Mary to lean on. The psalmist foreshadows Joseph when he says, "For the righteous will never be moved; he will be remembered for ever" (112:6). In Exodus, Moses took the bones of the Old Testament Joseph as God led him and the Israelites out of Egypt by a pillar of cloud by day and a pillar of fire by night (See 13:19–22). In the Gospels, St. Joseph became a pillar to his family, leading them to Egypt and throughout their days at Nazareth. Can you imagine a three-year-old Jesus being startled at night and seeking shelter in Joseph's arms? Joseph truly was the terror of demons, chosen by the Father from all eternity to be the pillar and protector for the Father's only begotton Son and His beloved Mother, but also for every family who invokes his aid, especially the parents of the saints. What an awesome and noble responsibility entrusted to Joseph! Joseph became an icon of the Eternal Father to Jesus.

But the head of the family, the husband, cannot live without a heart, his wife. And therefore Joseph frequently sought Mary's maternal gentleness, intuition, and wisdom when forming their Son. Joseph's mission was to ensure that his family followed God's will unreservedly. Joseph could be considered the patron of the parents of the saints because he loved Mary and Jesus more than any human spouse or father. Like Joseph, the parents of the saints sought to be madly in love with God while seeking to imitate his quiet and hidden strength. In the words of author Devin Schadt, "You, my brother, like Joseph, have the responsibility to use your fatherhood to raise your family heroically, without pomp or self-glory; protecting, feeding, and teaching them in the hiddenness of your family life, allowing your children to grow safe and hidden from the assailing evils of the world."[57] And, like Joseph, the parents of the saints were neither concerned with public nor the Church's recognition. At the same time, many of the parents of the saints sought to imitate Joseph

---

[57] Devin Schadt, *Joseph's Way: The Call to Fatherly Greatness Prayer of Faith: 80 Days to Unlocking Your Power as a Husband* (San Francisco: Ignatius Press, 2014), 67.

by being madly in love with their spouses by never ceasing to prove their love for their beloved.

While Joseph is totally silent in Scripture, his heart silently praised God his entire life, and his actions and strength provided an example for Jesus to imitate. Though not much can be found concerning devotion of the parents of saints to St. Joseph, his desire to be in the background and live an ordinary life was definitely imitated in their lives, and his powerful intercession was sought by many of these parents and their canonized children. For instance, Sts. Louis and Zélie Martin's devotion to this patriarch could be seen in naming their two sons after Joseph, one of whom they conceived after praying a novena to this saint. Zélie wrote to her brother:

> I hope good Saint Joseph will let me keep this one. It's enough that he already has one. He had the kindness to send me another son right after I gave him the first. Surely, I owe this last one only to his special intercession. Last year I made a novena during his month, and I finished it on his feast day. Nine months later, to the day, he answered me. As you see, he couldn't have done any better. Perhaps you'll laugh at what I've written, but I don't laugh at it, I take it literally.[58]

Tragically, Zélie and Louis would have to bury their two little Josephs in a span of sixteen months. The first, Marie-Joseph-Louis, died from erysipelas and enteritis on February 14, 1867, at only five months old. A month later, Zélie conceived her sixth child, Marie-Joseph-Jean Baptiste, who died on August 24, 1868, from enteritis and bronchitis at only eight months old.

Louis and Zélie also sought St. Joseph's intercession for the cure of St. Thérèse, who became gravely ill and almost died after her birth. Céline recounted:

> At one time they thought she was dead. Another nurse was hurriedly called in, who only shook her head on seeing the condition of the sick baby. It was then that mother went up to her room and beseeched St. Joseph

---

[58] Martin and Martin, *A Call to a Deeper Love*, 34.

to bring the child back to life; at the same time resigning herself to the divine will, if God wished to take her to Himself. Trembling with mortal anguish, she went downstairs, to the find that the dearest child was saved. One may well believe that the Church is indebted for St. Thérèse of the Child Jesus to the tears and prayers of her mother.[59]

How providential that the two-month-old Thérèse was cured during the month of March, which is dedicated to St. Joseph. No one should ever underestimate the prayers of a mother or the saints, especially St. Joseph, who though overshadowed by his bride, intercedes powerfully before the throne of God for his devotees. On a side note, some even commented that Zélie's husband, Louis, resembled St. Joseph in both his strong stature and quiet demeanor, but above all in his faith. Louis's daughter, Sr. Geneviève, wrote, "I remember that when he used to take me to the Benedictine School, my teachers, the nuns, used to say he reminded them of St. Joseph. Indeed, he was truly a *just man*, and when I wish to picture what St. Joseph was like, I just like to think of my father."[60]

Besides St. Joseph's intercession for their families, many of the parents of the saints sought Our Lady to guide them and their children through the storms of life to the shores of Heaven. She was the most perfect mother, lover, and follower of Christ, who stood by Him through His heroic suffering until His death. Our Lady played an inestimable role in the lives of both the parents of the saints and their children. Just as Mary ushered in her Son's hour and public ministry by asking Him for a miracle, so too did Mary help lead these devout parents to their future spouses. In turn, many of these holy couples honored Our Lady by being married in churches dedicated to her, singing hymns in her honor, and seeking her intercession to conceive children. Most importantly, these holy parents asked Our Lady to stay with them at every moment of their lives and in a special way to watch over their children. More than anything, Our Lady became the actual mother to several saints when

---

[59] Martin, *The Mother of the Little Flower*, 85.
[60] Ibid., 55.

their own mothers tragically died. One day Our Lady appeared to St. Bridget of Sweden, a mother of eight children, one of whom is St. Catherine of Sweden, and reminded her, "Take care that thy children are also my children."[61] Mary is the greatest mother, for her love for her children exceeds all the love of the saints and angels and earthly mothers combined.

One of the greatest fears of any father or mother, second only to losing a child, is dying young, which may increase the likelihood that their children could abandon the Faith due to their absence. Now add to this the possibility that one's son becomes a satanic priest. For parents who are either lukewarm or openly atheistic, having a son or daughter join the occult would come as no surprise. But this happened to the devout Catholic parents Dr. Bartolomeo and Antonina Longo, who prayed the Rosary together daily. Their son Bartolo, born February 10, 1841, to this wealthy family in the small town of Latiano, in southern Italy, would become the antithesis of the Roman Catholic priesthood as a satanic priest. Thanks be to God, Antonina was not alive when this happened, as she died when Bartolo was ten years old, or else she may have died from a broken heart. On the other hand, perhaps if Antonina had been alive, she could have steered Bartolo away from such influences, since her death became the catalyst for his weakened faith. After his mother's death, Bartolo became enamored with the occult while studying law at the University of Naples, where St. Thomas Aquinas once taught. Bartolo immersed himself in fortune-telling and communicating with spirits. Bartolo went so far as to be ordained a satanic priest, which caused him to become deeply tormented and physically ill. He began officiating at satanic rituals and preaching against his parents' cherished Faith, as he sought to win souls for the devil. Bartolo's family members, including his father, sought a miracle for his return to God. Following his father's death, Bartolo's surviving family members looked to Heaven for help, especially to Bartolo's father.

On one occasion, Bartolo appeared to hear his deceased father's voice begging him to return to God. A despairing Bartolo heard the

61 St. Alphonsus de Liguori, *The Glories of Mary* (Brooklyn, NY: Redemptorist Fathers, 1931), 614.

words "Return to God! Return to God!" Shocked by his father's voice and utterly miserable, Bartolo reached out to his friend Professor Pepe, who introduced him immediately to Fr. Alberto Radente, a Dominican priest. Fr. Alberto would hear Bartolo's confession and would guide him back to the Faith. While Bartolo experienced the freedom and joy of having his sins forgiven for the first time in many years, the great accuser, Satan, would not let him forget his terrible past, for Satan likes nothing better than for us to be miserable and doubt the mercy of God. As Bartolo walked near the chapel at Pompeii one evening, God's grace flooded the dark recesses of his soul and loosened the chains of lies. And so, what an earthly father and mother cannot do by their own efforts and prayers, Our Lady can do if parents trust in the power of the Rosary, as the Longos did their entire life.

Following his conversion, Bl. Bartolo Longo became a Third Order Dominican, devoting much of his life to promoting public devotion to the Rosary and other charitable works, such as providing for orphans and the children of prisoners. He was beatified on October 7, 2003, by Pope St. John Paul II, who referred to Bartolo as the "Apostle of the Rosary."

At the same time Our Lady was imploring her Beloved Son for Bartolo's conversion, she was also pleading another request, one dear to her heart since it came from a mother like herself. Hoping to bring another soul into this world, one that would glorify God for all eternity, St. Zélie Martin asked Our Lady to intercede for her that she might conceive another child on Our Lady's own conception feast day. Our Lady answered Zélie's prayers, and she attributed the conception of her second child, Pauline, to the Blessed Mother. Zélie wrote: "Nor have I forgotten December 8, 1860, the day I asked our Heavenly Mother to give me a little Pauline. But I can't think of it without laughing because I was exactly like a child asking her mother for a doll, and I went about it in the same way."[62] In reminiscing about Our Lady's "little Immaculate Conception" in Zélie's life, she wrote in 1875, then forty-six years old, "Again, this year, I'll go to find the Blessed Mother at daybreak, and I want to

---

[62] Martin and Martin, *A Call to a Deeper Love*, 205.

be the first to arrive. I'm going to light my candle to her as usual, but I won't ask her for any more little daughters."[63] Zélie had at this time five surviving children, all of whom were girls: Thérèse was three years old, and Zélie was nearing the end of her childbearing years. Zélie summed up the desire of the parents of the saints when she added, "I'm only going to ask her [Our Lady] that those she's given me all become saints and that I may follow them closely, but they must be much better than I am."[64] In doing so, Zélie offered the most beautiful prayer any mother can offer: praying that both she and her children become saints. Zélie did not pray that her children become famous, successful, get accepted into a prestigious university, or land an esteemed job, but that they might become saints. Somewhat humorous was Zélie's desire to have not only a holy child, but also an attractive one. She wrote, "First and foremost that she have a beautiful little soul, capable of becoming a saint, but I also wanted her to be very pretty. As for that, she's hardly pretty, but I find her beautiful, very beautiful, and she's as I wanted her to be!"[65] Even the parents of the saints struggled with vanity and knowing what was best for their children.

When Zélie's five-year-old daughter Hélène died, Zélie's oversensitive nature became disturbed because she recalls not encouraging Hélène to go to Confession after telling a fib. Louis advised his wife, "Go to Our Lady, dearest. Kneel before our statue of Our Lady, and pray to the Mother of God. She will help you to know that our little daughter is safe in Paradise."[66] Zélie seemed to hear Our Lady speak these words in her heart: "Helene is here with me."[67] When concerned about our children, especially their salvation, Our Lady reassures all parents to seek her intercession, for she will protect them at every instant of their lives because she loves our children more than any parent could ever love them.

---

[63] Ibid.
[64] Ibid., 205–206.
[65] Ibid., 205.
[66] Wust and Wust, *Zelie Martin*, 146.
[67] Ibid., 147.

Zélie was not shy about her devotion to Our Lady. Not only did she recommend Our Lady's intercession to her children and to all she met, Zélie clung to Our Lady until her final moments. Her daughter Marie wrote, "Her rosary beads never leave her fingers; she is praying constantly in spite of her sufferings. We all have great admiration for her; she has such courage and surpassing energy. Until two weeks ago she used to recite the five decades of her beads on her knees, before the Blessed Virgin, in my room, which she loves so much. Seeing her so ill, I wanted to have her sit down, but it was useless to ask her."[68]

Louis also had a singular devotion to Our Lady. As a bachelor, he once received a three-foot statue of Mary, which came to be called Our Lady of the Smile because it smiled one day upon his seriously ill ten-year-old daughter, St. Thérèse. Thérèse was cured on the Feast of Our Lady of the Blessed Sacrament, May 13, 1883, which is also the Feast of Our Lady of Fatima. Prior to his marriage, Louis kept this large statue outside. However, he and Zélie decided to move it into their living room to foster their children's Marian devotion. This statue became the focal point of their family prayer, especially the Rosary. Unfortunately, not every family member gravitated to the statue. Marie, Louis and Zélie's oldest daughter, felt the statue was too large and wanted a smaller and more suitable statue for their house. Prophetically, Zélie wrote, "When I am gone, child, you can do what you like, but as long as I live, this Blessed Virgin will not leave this place."[69] Though Zélie would physically leave her children after her death, their spiritual mother Mary watched over them. Additionally, Louis would periodically visit one of Our Lady's shrines to seek graces for either a sick child, or "to receive the graces our country needs so much in order to prove itself worthy of its past,"[70] as he wrote to his daughter Pauline.

One of the most fascinating stories about Sts. Louis and Zélie Martin occurred after their death—exactly one hundred years after their marriage on October 13, 1958, which testifies again to

---

[68] Martin, *The Mother of the Little Flower*, 102.
[69] Ibid., 92.
[70] Martin and Martin, *A Call to a Deeper Love*, 129.

Our Lady's powerful role. As Third Order Franciscans, Louis and Zélie desired to grow in holiness. One of the concrete ways they showed their love for Our Lady was by wearing the scapular of Mount Carmel. According to pious tradition, Our Lady promised St. Simon Stock that whoever dies wearing this scapular shall not suffer eternal fire, provided there is perseverance in virtue. These benefits were later extended to the laity, who, through investiture in the scapular of Our Lady of Mt. Carmel, unite themselves spiritually to the Carmelite Order, especially in their devotion to Mary, and who, through being faithful to the promises made at the time of their investiture, are assured of the prayers of Our Lady after death.

The importance of the scapular of Mount Carmel to Louis and Zélie was attested to by Fr. Piat, who related:

> On October 13, 1958 in the presence of the Bishop of Bayeux, of the Most Reverend Pioger, Auxiliary Bishop of Sees, and the Most Reverend Fallaize, former Vicar Apostolic of MacKenzie, the remains of M. and Mme. Martin were exhumed and transferred to the plateau of the Way of the Cross near the apse of the basilica. Sister Geneviève (Céline) was moved to learn that the only object found intact on each of the bodies, outside of a metal crucifix, was the Scapular of Our Lady of Mount Carmel.[71]

Even though this saintly couple's bodies were not incorrupt, how fitting it was that their scapulars were, since four of their five daughters were Carmelite nuns. Louis and Zélie's entire lives were interwoven with our Blessed Mother, as she appeared for the first time at Lourdes, France, on February 11, 1858, only five months before their wedding. In fact, both Louis and Zélie visited Lourdes separately. Louis visited Lourdes as part of a diocesan pilgrimage in October 1873, and Zélie would visit two months before her death in 1877. Zélie described Louis's visit:

[71] Stéphane-Joseph Piat, OFM, *Celine: Sister and Witness of St. Thérèse of the Child Jesus* (San Francisco: Ignatius Press, 1997), 149.

My husband went to Lourdes on a diocesan pilgrimage and brought us back two little stones broken off from a rock a few meters from the Grotto of the Apparition. There was a good woman hitting it with a hammer, but her hitting did no good, and nothing was happening. Louis took it from her and skillfully succeeded in getting a piece. Everyone gathered around him, wanting a piece of it!

However, a security guard threatened to get the police captain, and when he arrived, the fellow said to him while pointing to Louis, "It's that tall one there, Captain." But they didn't say anything to him.[72]

Thankfully, Louis was not arrested for stealing and vandalizing, which might have etched his legacy as the patron saint of relic collectors!

Living at the same time as the Martin family in the nineteenth century, yet miles across the Atlantic Ocean in the heart of the midwestern United States, were Bernard and Ellen Casey, whom God blessed with sixteen children, one of whom is the newly beatified Solanus Casey. In fact, Bl. Solanus Casey was born less than four years before St. Thérèse on November 25, 1870. The Rosary was also at the center of the Casey's family spirituality. Ellen led the Rosary every night, while their children would take turns leading a decade. Most importantly, Bernard and Ellen wanted their great devotion to remain with their children for the rest of their lives. In fact, their son Solanus would recite the Rosary every day of his life and often recommended it to those he counseled. It also did not hurt that Solanus would become a Capuchin priest and have a rosary literally attached to his habit, as is the custom of the friars. After Fr. Solanus's parents passed away, it was the Rosary that his parents taught him from his youth that linked them together. Just as the links of the rosary connect the beads to the cross, so too does the Rosary connect us not only with our Heavenly Mother Mary and God, but also with our living and departed relatives, who remain spiritually united to us when we pray.

---

[72] Martin and Martin, *A Call to a Deeper Love*, 136–137.

In the same year Bl. Solanus Casey was born, 1870, Maria
Dabrowska was born in Zdunksa Wola, and her husband, Julius
Kolbe, in 1871 in Henryka, Poland. The Kolbes were Third Order
Franciscans and possessed a tremendous devotion to Our Lady,
which was passed on to their three sons, but in a particular way to
St. Maximilian Kolbe—one of the greatest devotees of Our Lady in
the history of the Church and a cherished son of St. Francis. Where
did Maximilian acquire his Marian devotion? Throughout his life,
Maximilian's father would annually make the eleven-day walking
pilgrimage from Zdunska Wola to the famous Marian Shrine of Our
Lady of Częstochowa—a roughly sixty-six-mile journey. The Kolbe
household also had a small prayer corner, as was custom in many
Polish families, which was referred to as the "honorary corner." It
included a small icon of Our Lady where little Maximilian acquired
his great love for her and for the Rosary. At their parish, Julius was
a moderator for the living Rosary. Even as her children aged, Maria
never ceased to promote her love for Our Lady by assisting her two
sons, Franciscan priests Fr. Maximilian and Fr. Alphonse, to spread
their Marian magazine, *Knight of the Immaculate*, through word of
mouth and by handing copies to friends and strangers. Surprisingly,
this publication reached a circulation of eight hundred thousand
copies by 1938, one of the only worldwide, nonsecular magazines.
It provided meditations and authentic Catholic teachings, combating
the rise of Nazism and various heresies and ideologies that alienated
souls from God. What a witness Maria offers to mothers of priests
and religious that their vocation does not end after their son or
daughter answers the call, as if their mission is complete and they can
now sit back and admire what God has done through them. Make
no mistake, Maximilian Kolbe and all priests and religious can count
on two people praying for them: their mothers and their Heavenly
Mother Mary. Maria wrote to Fr. Maximilian seven years after his
priestly ordination, referencing her love for Our Lady with these
words, "May you receive from the Blessed Mother a holy wisdom
in saving souls. May you snatch them from the power of Satan . . .
and again, may you gain that hidden holiness, unknown to others,
unknown to yourself. Only in God will it be valued and loved. This

and all goodness from God and his Blessed Mother, along with the things that you yet cannot imagine. . . . I wish you with love, My Dearest Son."[73]

In addition to seeking Our Lady's wisdom and help, Maria preached a "hidden holiness, unknown to others, unknown to yourself," and desired to imitate her by reflecting Our Lady's humility to her sons. Like so many of the parents of the saints, Maria was rooted in the virtue of humility. As many people approached Maria after her son's heroic life was revealed—following his martyrdom at Auschwitz during World War II, when he offered his life so that another man, a husband and father, might live—to praise her for raising a saint, Maria humbly took no credit. Instead, Maria pointed to the real secret behind raising her saintly son. She said, "I felt my inadequacy and begged the Mother of God to substitute for me."[74] Maria asked Our Lady to guide her vocation as a wife and mother, confident that Our Lady would make up for her deficiencies and be their sons' true mother.

As the nineteenth century came to a close and one of its greatest saints, St. Thérèse, died in 1897, another saint's life was just beginning. Born on October 16, 1890, St. Maria Goretti was just seven years old when Thérèse died. One of the secrets behind Maria's holiness and purity from a young age was her family's prayer life, especially the Holy Rosary. As Assunta Goretti, Maria's mother, recalled:

> At home we would close the day by reciting the holy Rosary, except during summer when sometimes we couldn't manage it as there was so much work to do. Little Maria never missed it; and after her father's death, when we had already gone to bed, she would recite another five Mysteries for the repose of his soul. She did this in addition because she knew that I couldn't have Masses celebrated because I didn't have enough money.[75]

---

[73] Mary Felicitia Zdrojewski, CSSF, *To Weave a Garment: The Story of Maria Dabrowska Kolbe, Mother of Saint Maximilian Kolbe* (Enfield, CT: Felician Sisters, 1989), 94.

[74] Zdrojewski, *To Weave a Garment*, 148.

[75] Cruz, *Secular Saints*, 505.

In addition to Mass, the Holy Rosary was the favorite prayer of many of the parents of the saints and their children. It is a prayer that has divine power, as seen by the Gorettis. Each time Maria prayed the Rosary, she remembered her father's soul and prayed for the grace to suffer heroically in the face of death.

Two years after St. Maria Goretti's death in 1902, in a little town in Spain, a two-year-old boy named Josemaría contracted a life-threatening infection. Josemaría' s doctor, Dr. Campos, told his parents, José and Dolores Escrivá, that their child would not survive the night—the worst news any parent could hear. With their ardent faith, José and Dolores refused to accept the doctor's bleak sentence and immediately began a novena to Our Lady of the Sacred Heart. Further, Dolores promised Our Lady that if her son was cured, she would make a pilgrimage with him to the historic Torreciudad Chapel nestled on the foothills of the Pyrenees. Dr. Campos even had the audacity to call and see at what time their son had died. Our Lady miraculously interceded, as Josemaría was healed from his allegedly incurable illness—a testament to his parents' great faith. José and Dolores made the fourteen-mile pilgrimage on horseback through the rugged mountain terrain to thank Jesus and Mary for the recovery of Josemaría and, in a special way, to consecrate him to Our Lady. Later, seeing several of his siblings die from unexpected illnesses, Josemaría feared for his own life. For instance, in 1910, his youngest sister, Maria del Rosario, died at only nine months. Two years later, another sister, Maria de los Dolores, died at the age of five, and a year later Maria Asunción died at the age of eight. As a result, Josemaría told his mother, "Next year it's my turn."[76] In response, Dolores calmly declared, "Don't worry, I offered you to our Lady, and she will take care of you."[77] And Our Lady did just that, allowing St. Josemaría Escrivá to live a full life to the age of seventy-three, when he died on June 26, 1975. Marian piety was formed in this saint's heart from his infancy, as the Escrivás prayed

---

[76] Andrés Vázquez de Prada, *The Founder of Opus Dei, Volume I,* 52.
      Cited by Javier Echevarria in *Summarium (Sum. 1785)* of the Cause of
      beatification and canonization. *Positio super vita et virtutibus,* Rome, 1988.
[77] Ibid. Cited by Francisco Botello in *Sum.* 5609.

the family Rosary and attended Saturday Mass at St. Bartholomew's Oratory, where the family recited the Hail Holy Queen.

Like St. Josemaría' s parents, the father of Pope St. John Paul II, Karol Wojtyła Sr., passed on his deep Marian piety to his sons. The day after his beloved wife, Emilia, died on April 13, 1929, Karol Sr. went on a pilgrimage to an outdoor shrine of Our Lady, accompanied by his two sons—the nine-year-old Karol Jr., future Pope St. John Paul II, and twenty-one-year-old Edmund. Karol Sr. wanted to entrust his two sons to Our Lady and ask that she watch over them until the day when they would see their mother in Heaven.[78] When he became pope, John Paul II's own papal motto was *Totus Tuus*, embracing Our Lady with the words "Totally Yours." In his book *Crossing the Threshold of Hope*, he wrote, "At first, it had seemed to me that I should distance myself a bit from the Marian devotion of my childhood in order to focus more on Christ. Thanks to St. Louis de Montfort, I came to understand that *true devotion to the Mother of God is actually Christocentric, indeed, it is very profoundly rooted in the Mystery of the Blessed Trinity*, and the mysteries of the Incarnation and Redemption."[79]

Around the same time that John Paul II was growing up in Poland, the Berettas in Italy were reciting the Rosary each night. According to St. Gianna's brother, "Papa stood before the image of Our Lady with the older children while we younger ones were around Mamma, who helped us answer until we fell asleep leaning on her knees."[80] Gianna died of cancer on April 28, 1962, at the age of thirty-nine, just seven days after the birth of her fourth child, also named Gianna. She chose life over having an abortion. In God's providence, she would die on the same day as St. Louis de Montfort, who died in 1716, whose feast day she shares, and who also loved Our Lady with singular devotion.

Nine years after the death of St. Gianna, Ruggero Badano visited the Shrine of Our Lady of the Rocks in Ovada, Italy, to seek

---

[78] See Evert, *Saint John Paul the Great*, 4.

[79] Pope St. John Paul II, *Crossing the Threshold of Hope* (New York: Alfred A. Knopf, Inc., 1994), 213.

[80] Molla and Guerriero, *Saint Gianna Molla: Wife, Mother, Doctor*, 25.

Mary's help in conceiving a child. One month after his heartfelt visit, Ruggero's wife Maria Teresa became pregnant after being infertile for the first ten years of their marriage. Our Lady answered their prayers on October 29, 1971, with the birth of their daughter Bl. Chiara.

Our Lady is the unseen mother of every home. When several of the saints lost their earthly mothers at a young age, Our Lady's maternal presence reached heights that no one can fathom, especially in the lives of Teresa of Ávila, Catherine Labouré, Thérèse of Lisieux, John Paul II, and countless others. After the burial of her own mother, the nine-year-old Catherine Labouré climbed a chair in her parents' bedroom and threw her arms around the statue of Our Lady saying, "Now, dear blessed Mother, you will be my mother."[81] Teresa of Ávila, who lost her mother while an adolescent, declared, "I remember that, when my mother died, I was twelve years of age or a little less. When I began to realize what I had lost, I went in my distress to an image of Our Lady and with many tears besought her to be a mother to me."[82] Prior to her death, Teresa's mother had imparted her love for Mary onto her children. Teresa once wrote, "I tried to be alone when I said my prayers, and there were many such, in particular the rosary, to which my mother had a great devotion, and this made us devoted to them too."[83]

Though a mother can never be replaced, especially in a household of eleven or thirteen children, as was in the case of Catherine Labouré's and Teresa of Ávila's families, respectively, the Blessed Mother comforted them as she does each one of us with her maternal love and protection. The sacraments, along with the Rosary, were the most powerful spiritual weapons of the parents of the saints, which in turn became their children's. Within this family atmosphere of prayer, especially Holy Mass, Confession, and the daily Rosary, the parents of the saints equipped their children with

[81] Anne Ball, *Modern Saints*, Book Two (Rockford, IL: TAN Books, 1983), 133.
[82] St. Teresa of Ávila, *The Life of Teresa of Jesus: The Autobiography of Teresa of Ávila*, 67.
[83] Ibid., 67.

the spiritual weapons to become soldiers of Christ, converting the world by their radical love and not by violence. Maria Kolbe said it best when she declared, "It has been repeated often, that no one is capable of loving the Mother of God unless he first has a genuine love for his own mother."[84] God has bestowed upon each mother the stupendous task of becoming icons of Our Lady to their sons and daughters! It was these holy mothers of the saints that provided a glimpse into the Immaculate Heart of Mary, just as a loving father is meant to reveal God the Father's love, while at the same time the mutual love between spouses reveals the Holy Spirit—the love that proceeds from the Father and the Son.

---

[84] Zdrojewski, *To Weave a Garment*, vii.

HALLMARK TWO

Surrender

I am afraid of nothing; our Lord upholds me. The grace of each moment is sufficient, and I shall have that to the very end.[1]—*St. Zélie Martin*

Sts. Louis and Zélie Martin

Theologians, lay people, and even Pope St. Pius X have referred to St. Thérèse of Lisieux as "the greatest saint of modern times." She was born in 1873 and lived an obscure life as a Carmelite nun, dying from tuberculosis at the age of twenty-four in 1897. She never stepped foot out of France except for one trip to Rome, yet her zeal for souls made her the patron saint of the missions. Even one of Thérèse's religious sisters commented after her death that she did nothing special. On the surface, there was nothing spectacular about Thérèse: she did not start a religious order or even die a martyr's death. After she died, the Church recognized that while she was an ordinary soul, she loved extraordinarily. Thérèse taught the world what it means to be a child of God through her writings and personal autobiography, *Story of a Soul*, which continues to inspire millions, including many saints, to have an unshakable confidence in God through abandonment to His Divine Providence. Thérèse once wrote, "Jesus does not demand great actions from us but simply *surrender* and *gratitude*."[2] You might be asking yourself, what does Thérèse have to do with this book—after all, is this book not about the parents of the saints? In order to better understand one of the

---

[1] Martin, *The Mother of the Little Flower*, 91.
[2] St. Thérèse of Lisieux, *Story of a Soul*, 188.

79

greatest saints of modern times, St. Thérèse, and her spirituality, we must uncover the secrets behind her formation so that we can imitate her example. St. Zélie Martin relied on God's grace each moment by living in the present, though not without difficulty. Having lost a child two years before Thérèse, whose name was Mélanie-Thérèse, and whom Thérèse was named after, Zélie was terrified that God would take Thérèse to Heaven as he did with four of her previous eight children—especially when Thérèse lay sick with a fever. "I quickly went upstairs to my room. I knelt at the feet of Saint Joseph and asked him for mercy, that the little one be cured, resigning myself completely to the will of God if He wanted to take her. I don't cry often, but I cried while I was praying."[3] Four words sum up the greatest prayer of surrender, which came from the mouth of Our Lord and has passed generation upon generation from parents to their children: "Thy will be done" (Mt 26:42).

Thérèse once beautifully declared, "I'm suffering only for an instant. It's because we think of the past and the future that we become discouraged and fall into despair."[4] As the youngest of nine children, Thérèse had a special relationship with her father. Despite her oversensitive and childish nature, she found that the key to the spiritual life was to remain small. According to Thérèse, "Jesus deigned to show me the road that leads to this Divine Furnace, and this road is the *surrender* of the little child who sleeps without fear in its Father's arms."[5] Thérèse came to these profound spiritual insights precisely through her father and mother's example. During the winter months after Thérèse's mother died, the family would play card games followed by her two older sisters reading Dom Gueranger's *Liturgical Year* and other informative books. Thérèse wrote in her autobiography, "Ah! how I loved, after the *game of checkers* was over, to sit with Céline on Papa's knees. He used to sing, in his beautiful voice, airs that filled the soul with such profound thoughts,

---

3   Martin and Martin, *A Call to a Deeper Love*, 111.
4   St. Thérèse of Lisieux, *St. Thérèse of Lisieux: Her Last Conversations* (Washington, D.C.: ICS Publications, 1977), 155.
5   St. Thérèse of Lisieux, *Story of a Soul*, 188.

or else, rocking us gently, he recited poems that taught the eternal truths."[6] Thérèse's earthly father had unlocked the key that would become her own spirituality, i.e., the little way of self-surrender. Thérèse knew that unless we become like a child, we cannot enter the Kingdom of God. This, of course, means spiritually. Thérèse possessed a radical trust in God's grace in the present moment, along with total dependence on Him. Yet this great saint may never have been born without her parents first surrendering to Divine Providence.

From an early age, Zélie, along with her older sister, Marie-Louise, desired to be a nun. It was Marie-Louise, also known as Élise, who let her middle sister, Zélie, join the convent first, as she would take care of their parents until the appropriate time, if God willed. Zélie set off to join the Congregation of the Daughters of Charity at the General Hospital of Alençon in order to dedicate her entire life to God. This order housed some two hundred poor and sick residents. According to her daughter Céline, Zélie was dissuaded by the Mother Superior, perhaps on account of her health, as she suffered from frequent headaches. Although she grew up with a rich faith, her mother was very harsh with the oversensitive Zélie, to the point of not even letting her have a doll, which she always wanted. Yet Céline's explanation leaves the door open as to whether it was in fact her mother's health that kept her from entering religious life. Was there something else that prevented Zélie from becoming a nun? In their book *Zelie Martin: Mother of St. Thérèse*, Louis and Marjorie West provide a more detailed account of her visit to the convent. On her last day with the sisters, the Mother Superior asked Zélie to join her in a novena to the Holy Spirit. Zélie was then advised to return to the convent nine days later. After finishing their novena, the Mother Superior shared these hopeful words to Zélie, "All this time we have been praying earnestly to know God's holy Will, haven't we? You know, dear, that sincere prayers are always answered. But sometimes, God Who is our loving Father, and Who knows what is best for us, gives us the answer 'No.' This does not

---

6 Ibid., 43.

mean that our Father in Heaven does not love us, but only that He
can look into the future and can see what is best for us."[7]

In addition, the Mother Superior told Zélie that God was pleased
with her generous heart, but that He was not calling her to religious
life. A disheartened nineteen-year-old Zélie was reassured by the
Mother Superior that the Lord loved her more than ever because
she had wanted to offer her service to Him, and that God would
reward her a hundredfold not only here on earth, but in Eternity.
The Mother Superior attempted to lift Zélie's spirits by telling her
these words:

> We *need* married saints, and all kinds of saints in the
> world, you know. There is much good to be done in
> the world. Perhaps God has destined you, Zelie Guérin,
> to become the mother of a Saint! Who knows what the
> dear Lord in His divine Providence has planned for His
> Zelie! In fact, where would we get good nuns and priests
> and religious brothers if there were not good parents to
> bring up their children in a God-fearing way? Perhaps,
> you Zelie dear, may have several children who will enter
> religious life! Wouldn't you *then* consider that several
> vocations in the same family are worth more than just
> the one vocation which you now think you have?[8]

Though we do not know for certain whether the Mother
Superior actually said these beautiful words, as they were not
recorded by a primary source who actually knew Zélie, such as her
daughters or her parish priest, they reveal that God's plans were
better than Zélie's. While Zélie could not understand God's will at
first, in light of being rejected from religious life, which seemed to
be her only desire, God was working through the Mother Superior
by doing what was best for Zélie's eternal salvation along with that
of her future husband and future children.

Though Zélie had not yet met Louis when she had been rejected
by the religious order, perhaps the Mother Superior knew in her
heart that Zélie's great capacity for love was meant not only for God,

---

[7]   Wust and Wust, *Zelie Martin*, 24.
[8]   Ibid., 25.

but also for a man and children. And Zélie would later discover that far from loving God less, her saintly husband and children helped her to love God even more, for they were a constant reminder of God's sheer goodness.

A heartbroken Zélie immediately confided her unfortunate news to her older sister, Élise. Ironically, Élise would later become Sr. Mary Dorothy of the Visitation in the convent at Le Mans, France. Like Zélie, Élise suffered from severe health problems. And, like her niece St. Thérèse, the young Élise contracted tuberculosis and was given three months to live. Yet, thanks to a novena to Our Lady of La Salette, Élise obtained the grace to become a nun and to die a nun, even though she still battled her illness for the rest of her life. Rather than choosing to be envious that God had not called her to become a nun like her sister, Zélie penned these beautiful words: "My God, since I am not worthy to be Your Spouse like my sister, I shall enter the married state to accomplish your holy will. I beg you then, let me have many children, and may they all be consecrated to You, My God."[9]

While Zélie surrendered to God's will, she recognized an important lesson in the process: God sometimes changes our desires and our plans for His glory. Zélie, having longed for religious life, slowly resigned herself to the married vocation. Although a cliché, there is truth in the fact that when God closes one door, He opens another. God's plans are always better than ours. Hence, it leads me to surmise that Zélie's health was not the primary impediment behind her not being accepted to religious life, for her sister, who had just as severe if not greater health concerns, was accepted by the Visitation Sisters. God's providence was guiding Zélie one step at a time, the same way He guides you and me. In fact, Our Lady showed Zélie the next steps. Like her sister who made a novena to Our Lady for better health so she could become a nun, Zélie prayed a novena to ask Our Lady for guidance. Miraculously, Zélie heard an interior voice: lace making. It is contrary to the virtue of faith to seek locutions or visions, or to demand signs from God. Yet this is what was given to Zélie.

---

[9]   Martin, *The Mother of the Little Flower*, 2.

Even though Zélie's occupation was set, her vocation was still unfolding. She waited nearly eight years before God revealed her vocation, when Louis Martin knocked at the door of her heart. Zélie never compromised who she was. In fact, she was offered an opportunity to marry someone well to do, but turned down his offer. Had Zélie chosen to marry the unnamed wealthy bachelor, who certainly lacked the faith of Louis, she may never have become a saint, and there would never have been a St. Thérèse! And the world would never have known Thérèse's "little way." Surrender was never easy for Zélie, especially after God closed the door on her dreams for religious life. In fact, Zélie went to visit her sister at the Visitation Convent in Le Mans on the day of her wedding. She later recalled this incident to Pauline:

> I went to see her for the first time at the monastery on my wedding day. I can say that on that day I cried all my tears, more than I'd ever cried in my life, and more than I would never ever cry again. My poor sister didn't know how to console me.
>
> And yet it didn't make me sad to see her there. No, on the contrary, I would have liked to be there, too. I compared my life to hers, and I cried even harder. In short, for a very long time, my mind and my heart were only at the Visitation Monastery. I often went to see my sister, and there I breathed a calm and peace I can't express. When I went back, I felt so sad to be in the middle of the world. I would have liked to hide my life with hers.[10]

Zélie further explained her trial when she declared, "You who love your father so much, my Pauline, are you going to think that I was hurting him and that I'd ruined our wedding day for him? No, he understood me and consoled me as best he could because his inclinations were similar to mine. I even think our mutual affection grew from it. Our feelings were always in accord, and he was always a comfort and a support to me."[11]

---

[10] Martin and Martin, *A Call to a Deeper Love*, 288.
[11] Ibid.

Louis's emotional support for Zélie provides an example for all husbands to imitate. Notice Louis did not try to solve his wife's vocational regrets or take them personally, but simply became a rock for her to lean on and a shoulder to cry on.

Upon the birth of her children, Zélie became more confirmed in her vocation and experienced God's peace more fully. At times Zélie's heart was restless, for no matter how holy our spouse is, "You have made us for Yourself, and our hearts are restless until they rest in You,"[12] in the words of St. Augustine. As Zélie matured in age and faith, she surrendered more fully to God. Zélie wrote to her sister after the birth of her first daughter, Marie, "I cannot realize that I have the honor of being the mother of such a delightful little creature! Oh, indeed, I do not repent now of having married!"[13] At the beginning of her marriage, Zélie was reluctant to have children, as mentioned previously, not for selfish reasons, rather, she wanted to give everything, including her virginity, to God and remain celibate like St. Joseph and the Blessed Mother.

After losing four of her children, and eventually being diagnosed with breast cancer in her forties, Zélie realized that surrender is the only path to Christ. She was afraid that after the death of her two sons, her next child would experience the same fate, which became a "never-ending nightmare."[14] However, Zélie learned to surrender to the Heavenly Father. She wrote, "This morning, during Mass, I had such dark thoughts about this that I was very deeply moved. The best thing to do is to put everything in the hands of God and await the outcome in peace and abandonment to His will. That's what I'm going to try very hard to do."[15]

Zélie's life became one of constant surrender, especially as her cancer weakened her body. Prior to her pilgrimage to Lourdes, where she sought a cure through the miraculous waters, which was not given, she penned these incredible words of surrender to her sister-in-law on February 20, 1877:

---

[12] St. Augustine, *The Confessions of St. Augustine,* 19.
[13] Wust and Wust, *Zelie Martin,* 67.
[14] Martin and Martin *A Call to a Deeper Love,* 51.
[15] Ibid.

If God wants to cure me, I'll be very happy because, deep down, I want to live. It's hard for me to leave my husband and children, but, on the other hand, I say to myself, *if I'm not cured, perhaps it's because it will be more helpful for them if I go away*. . . . Meanwhile, I'm doing everything possible to obtain a miracle. I'm counting on the pilgrimage to Lourdes, but if I'm not cured, I'll try to sing on the return trip all the same.[16]

Zélie also wrote to her daughter Pauline in May of 1877, a month before their pilgrimage:

In the beginning, your father didn't approve of my taking all three of you, but now he wants me to, saying that no sacrifice is too great to obtain such a miracle. And even if I don't obtain it, I'll never regret having taken you there. We must be open to generously accepting God's will, whatever it may be, because it will always be what's best for us. In any case, my Pauline, we must prepare ourselves well for this pilgrimage.[17]

Zélie's letters reveal the essence of surrender, which is embracing God's will because He is the best author, painter, and sculptor there is. With each moment, the Spirit guides the chapters of our lives with the ink of Our Lord's Precious Blood, which forgives, heals, and ultimately seeks to conform us to the greatest love story—Jesus' Passion, Death, and Resurrection. With each moment, the Divine Artist paints us more and more into the very image and likeness of His Son, Jesus, if we but trust and love Him, even when words make no sense and He chisels the rough edges of our lives through suffering, trials, disappointments, and death. In the face of death, Zélie surrendered to the will of God as each person will be called to, for no one can escape the grave. What made Zélie such a woman of faith is described by her sister, Sr. Mary Dorothy, who wrote, "What reassures me concerning our dear Zélie is her spirit of faith and her truly incredible and prodigious courage. What a valiant woman our

16   Ibid., 284.
17   Ibid., 317.

sister Zélie is! She is neither cast down by adversity nor puffed up by prosperity. She is admirable."[18] Zélie's heroic embrace of her death was clearly passed on to her daughter Thérèse, who wanted to suffer even more for Jesus and for souls as she began to cough up blood at the young age of twenty-four.

Zélie was not the only parent of Thérèse whose life embraced surrender. Long before Louis took the hand of his beloved Zélie in marriage, he too learned the beauty of surrender. On the day of Louis's Baptism, which occurred immediately after his birth on August 22, 1823, in Bordeaux, France, in the Church of St. Eulalie, the Archbishop of Bordeaux, Monseigneur d'Aviau du Bois de Sanzay, told Louis's relatives, "Rejoice, this is a child of destiny!"[19] Tragically, all of Louis's siblings would die before the age of twenty-seven from various accidents and illnesses.

In his teenage years, Louis studied the art of clockmaking in Strasburg, Germany. Desiring to be a religious priest since his youth, he set off to discern with the Congregation Hospitaliere du Grand-St. Bernard in the Swiss Alps at the age of twenty-two. This contemplative order was renowned for their famous St. Bernard dogs, which helped rescue stranded travelers in the dangerous mountains. Louis treasured the solitude of the monastery in the breathtaking Alps. Unfortunately, he was declined entrance until he learned Latin, a requirement for the order. Louis began to wonder, "What next?" While studying Latin under his parish priest, Louis became ill, which ultimately led him to rethink his vocation. Though Louis's desire for the priesthood and religious life faded, much to his chagrin, he surrendered to the will of God knowing that He would lead him on the right path. As the prophet Isaiah splendidly wrote, "In paths that they have not known I will guide them. I will turn the darkness before them into light, the rough places into level ground. These are the things I will do, and I will not forsake them" (42:16).

Trusting in Divine Providence and not looking back on what could have been with the Congregation Hospitaliere du Grand-St.

---

[18] Wust and Wust, *Zelie Martin*, 141.
[19] Piat, *The Story of a Family*, 8.

Bernard, Louis, at age twenty-seven, opened his first clockmaking shop in Alençon. While living with his parents as a single man, which he thought was his vocation as he was not actively pursuing any woman, Louis enjoyed fishing and would frequently share his catch with the Poor Clares of Alençon. In fact, fishing was "his favorite pastime,"[20] according to Zélie. He was also a member of the Nocturnal Adoration Society and the Society of St. Vincent de Paul, and he remained a member even after their marriage. Louis was living like a monk, but in the world. He was fully content being single, despite his mother's prodding and prayers. Louis knew a secret that many men and women fail to accept about marriage and life in general: only God can bring perfect happiness, and not sexual pleasure, money, the largest house, the best job, or even the most well-behaved children. Louis understood the words of Pope St. John Paul II well before they were spoken, that "man becomes an image of God not so much in the moment of solitude as in the moment of communion."[21] It was not until Louis met Zélie that God changed his plans and placed on his heart a desire for communion with her. Although Louis and Zélie never spoke during their first encounter on the Bridge of St. Leonard, Louis asked a mutual friend to formally introduce him to Zélie, who had been living in the same town for eight years. Once the two had met, the rest was history. As a single man, Louis had it all: God, first and foremost, a profitable business, and recreation. Yet Louis was missing something: a wife and a family to love and serve. God had changed the desires of Louis's heart, and he responded by being the initiator. Inscribed in every man's body is the role of an initiator. Further, every man possesses the strength endowed by God to be a lover, protector, provider, and a warrior. Louis himself was the son of a French military officer who hailed from Normandy. Listening to the inspiration of the Holy Spirit and relying on the gift of fortitude, which he seemed to inherit from his father, Louis valiantly pursued his bride in person.

---

[20]   Martin and Martin, *A Call to a Deeper Love*, 131.
[21]   Pope St. John Paul II, *Man and Woman He Created Them: A Theology of the Body* (Boston: Pauline Books and Media, 2006), 163.

Prior to that time, Louis had surrendered to God's will by saying no to temptations. While living in Paris for three years with his relatives before meeting Zélie, Louis had come face-to-face with many temptations. Zélie later conveyed her concern to her brother Isidore, who was studying in Paris at the time. She penned, "He [Louis] told me what temptations he had and the courage he needed to overcome his struggles. If you only knew what ordeals he went through. . . . I beg you, my dear Isidore, do as he did; *pray* and you will not let yourself be carried away by the torrent. If you give in once, you're lost. On the path of evil as well as that of goodness, the first step is the hardest, and, after that first step, you'll be swept away by the current."[22]

While we do not know what exactly Louis encountered in Paris, his very handsome and strong physique made him the admiration of many women in Alençon. Like his wife, Zélie, Louis safeguarded his virginity through great courage and prayer as they waited with longing and patience for God's will to unfold. Thanks be to God, Louis and Zélie chose to wait for true love in God's timing.

Julius and Maria Kolbe

St. Zélie Martin was not the only mother of a saint who herself desired to enter religious life. Maria Kolbe, who was born on February 25, 1870, longed to be Our Lord's bride. Unfortunately, the Russians occupied her section of Poland, which precluded this possibility. Maria's longing for religious life never disappeared, and, in fact, she would live a quasi-religious life when she was older. However, at this time, seeking to marry a holy man with a great love for the Blessed Mother, like herself, Maria, at the age of twenty-one, married the twenty-two-year-old Julius Kolbe on October 5, 1891. She was drawn to Julius's joyful spirit and deep faith. God blessed Julius and Maria with five boys, though tragically their two youngest, Valentine and Anthony, died before their fourth birthdays. The world soon forgot Maria Kolbe, but the Church has never forgotten her second son, Raymond, born January 8, 1894, who was named after St. Raymond of Penyafort, whose feast day

---

[22] Martin and Martin, *A Call to A Deeper Love,* 2.

is January 7. Ironically, the Kolbes wanted their first son, Francis, to become a priest, and Raymond was destined to take over their weaving business. Thanks be to God, Our Lady had other plans for Raymond, who would join the Order of Friars Minor Conventual in 1910 and take the name Maximilian. Heaven always has a better plan than parents do for their children. Before St. Maximilian Kolbe became a martyr at Auschwitz during World War II, he learned from his parents how to surrender to God's will. One of the greatest challenges that many of the parents of the saints faced was financial difficulties. As the Industrial Revolution reached Eastern Europe, the Kolbes' job security became volatile as textile factories replaced weavers. The Kolbes also had great concerns about the city environment, which could expose their children to less than virtuous peers, as most parents worked full-time in factory positions and could not monitor their children's behavior. Consequently, they moved from the larger town of Łódź to the smaller town of Pabiance, where their new home became a store for selling food and house items to factory workers. According to Julius, the Kolbes left Łódź "so that the boys would have a decent environment to grow up in."[23]

The Kolbes knew they could not shield their boys from every religious, political, or social threat, while living under the oppressive Russian regime, but Julius and Maria would not let the government or unholy peers corrupt their children. For instance, they exposed their sons to their great Polish literary heritage, which was banned by the Russian government in certain regions for fear that the Poles might seek their independence. Because of these threats, Julius and Maria embraced their role as the primary educators and guardians over their children.

After making the move to Pabiance, the Kolbes thrived for some time. Yet war and economic depression eventually forced the family into bankruptcy. Tragically, their bankruptcy was hastened by a few of their cunning neighbors and friends, who borrowed money from their store while never intending to pay it back, which only added insult to injury. As a result, Julius and Maria started working in the

---

[23] Zdrojewski, *To Weave a Garment*, 15.

factory. Julius, who had been previously arrested during a strike, began to organize workers for Polish freedom. It must be noted that surrendering to poverty was nothing new to the Kolbe family. When they were first married, they "were careful not to amass money or to spend it foolishly,"[24] as they told their priest friend Fr. Cesar Baran years later. Surrendering to God through the death of their two young sons, bankruptcy, the betrayal of friends, and political and religious persecution tested Julius and Maria's marriage vows to a degree that most people will likely never experience. They learned through their trials that the greater the struggle, the greater the occasion to prove their love to God, and so become less attached to this world and concentrate entirely on reaching Heaven—the "world without end" (Eph 3:21, Douay-Rheims).

Through surrender, Julius and Maria were able to accept the vocations God had intended for their children and not the ones they wanted. As noted, Julius and Maria initially wanted their firstborn son, Francis, to become a priest, something Maria prayed for from the day of his birth. Raymond was to take over their weaving business to provide them with some financial security when they were too old to work. When Raymond announced his desire to enter the seminary and join his brother, Francis, Julius and Maria slowly and somewhat painfully accepted this news. Already stripped of their finances, they would have to possess a deeper trust in God now that He had accepted their offering of their first fruits: their two sons. Making sure her two sons prayed the Rosary as she embraced them one last time in tears, Maria knew that God had a reason for calling them, though on a human level no mother or father wants to be separated from their children in this life. Julius and Maria had already lost two infant sons and now God was asking them to surrender their two adult sons. Yet their surrender was just beginning—it was a work of a lifetime.

After the death of Valentine and Anthony, Julius and Maria agreed to take private vows of chastity. Maria's desire for the religious life had never waned, and this desire only intensified after their two eldest sons left for the seminary, and their youngest boy,

---

[24]　Ibid., 11.

Joseph, neared adolescence. To her children's surprise, Maria and Julius followed through on their vows of chastity after seventeen years of marriage, as Maria joined the Benedictine Sisters in Lvov. Julius gave his approval, but also struggled greatly with his wife's decision. Maria did not last too long with them, though. Eventually she became an associate to the Felician Sisters, where she lived and prayed. Although Maria could not profess final vows due to her age and marital status, she remained obedient to her superior. Though the workings of their relationship remain a mystery, Julius and Maria's marriage, because it was sacramental, that is, ratified and consummated, could never be declared null. The Church can allow spouses to agree to live separately and in total continence, thereby forsaking their marital rights, while one of them lives in religious life, but does not encourage this. However, if one of the spouses decides that he or she can no longer live separately and in total continence, then the other spouse might have to respect that wish and live together as before.

Maria's childhood dream to live like a nun in a convent was finally fulfilled, but it came at a great cost. According to Sr. Mary Felicita Zdrojewski, as postulants, Francis and Raymond experienced serious doubts concerning their Franciscan vocation. As a result, Francis and Raymond planned to inform their superior that they would be trading their breviaries for guns before receiving their habits as novices in hopes of following their father in another form of sacrifice. Yet Divine Providence had another plan. Due to Maria's unexpected visit, during which she informed her sons of her new calling, Francis and Raymond's meeting with their superior was postponed. Maria's news filled her sons with excitement, but also confusion. How could their parent's robust marriage end so abruptly? Had Maria left her three surviving boys and husband when her children were young, surely she would have been shirking her responsibilities and vocation! Yet, now that her sons were older, Maria's decision to enter the convent seemed more plausible. Still, no husband in his right mind, even the most virtuous husband like Julius, could fully accept such a life-altering decision from the woman he had loved for over seventeen years without God's grace and through holy surrender. Raymond accepted his mother's calling as a sign that he needed to persevere in his vocation. Shortly thereafter, on September 4, 1910, both young men became invested as Franciscan novices and given the names Valerian and Maximilian, after two Roman martyrs. In addition, Julius and Maria's third son, Joseph, would also be entering the seminary.

As shown throughout Church history, Julius and Maria's decision to permanently renounce sexual relations is very unusual. No matter how holy Julius was, he never seemed to fully surrender to his wife's earthly separation, and who could blame him? Julius seemed lost after his wife left him for the convent. At one point, he lived and worked as a handyman at his sons' monastery. Later, Julius moved to Częstochowa, where he was a sacristan. Later, he would fight in World War I, which would cost him his life. In a letter to his youngest son, whom he called Joey, Julius laments over his loneliness: "I do not know where to go or under what circumstances. I am thinking of finding a peaceful corner. True, here in Częstochowa, it would not be bad, but my loneliness does not allow me to stay long in one place. All the more when you, my children forget to write me. You have your friends, but I have none to whom I could open my heart; I must be a hermit among people."[25]

Above all, Julius desired his wife to be happy and knew that was what mattered most. Maria would repeat frequently in her letters, "I am very happy here." Her desire to spend hours before the Most Blessed Sacrament and intercede for her husband, children, and native land was thus fulfilled in the convent. Specifically, Maria penned in a letter to her son Joey before his investiture. She wrote, "I assure you, my Dear Son, I will never forget you before the Lord, for this is a mother's holiest of duties. I know that you remember us, but especially at that happy moment when you make of yourself a total sacrifice at the foot of the altar, do not forget your parents and your brothers. When we mutually support one another in prayer, then for sure we will attain our appointed goals, even if the way be most difficult, for nothing is impossible with God."[26]

---

[25] Ibid., 38.
[26] Ibid., 51.

Though painful, Julius slowly came to accept God's will over the course of his life, trusting that surrender takes a lifetime and not one day. With each holiday approaching, Julius reminisced about their Polish suppers and wafers and ardently wished to return to the past, when the family was together and the children were young. Surrender leads us to cherish the present without worrying about the future or longing to return to past—the latter of which can be difficult for those who are widowed or elderly. In fact, widowed and elderly people can identify with Julius, who always sought to be with his family, even after his children were grown and his wife left for the convent, especially during the Holy Days of Christmas and Easter. Julius provides a great lesson for all of us never to take our families for granted and to treasure every moment with them because life passes quickly and all that will endure is the love and the memories. His vocation was built on love and living in the present moment, despite his struggle to surrender at times to his new vocation. Julius battled loneliness and perhaps some depression, but surrender was his only option to go forward. Simply put, Julius's strong faith, his great love for God and his family, and his hope in the Resurrection were the sails on his voyage of surrender, disposing him to union with the Blessed Trinity while giving life to the moral virtues.

Maria too relied on the theological virtues of faith, hope, and charity, or she could not have survived bankruptcy, the death of two infant children, saying goodbye to three children as they left for the seminary, and leaving behind the man she loved most on earth—her husband. Further, Maria experienced the sheer tragedy of living through two of the worst wars recorded in human history, World Wars I and II. Yet, more so than any war, financial blow, or even living a celibate vocation, Maria's biggest surrender involved her son Francis's vocation. After the assassination of Archduke Franz Ferdinand of Austria, Br. Valerian left the monastery and joined the fight for Polish freedom like his father had. Maria's dreams for Francis were shattered. She immediately blamed herself for Francis abandoning his vocation, citing her negligence in prayer, as she once confided her grief to the Mother of Sorrows, praying that Francis would return to the monastery. In writing to Joseph, who took the name Alphonse after being accepted into the Franciscan Conventuals in September of 1915, Maria expressed her grief over Francis, but also her trust.

> I beg you, my Dear Son, to remember him in prayer because he needs many, many graces and help from God so that everything will be corrected! For with God nothing is impossible.
> Oh! How difficult it is for the person who pulls himself from the hand of God and desires to fly on his own wings. Oh! That all who wish to serve God faithfully would understand this, so they would not allow themselves to believe deceptive temptations. . . . In spite of what has happened, I deeply believe our future is in the hand of Him who rectifies everything. In spite of our unfaithfulness and imprudence, at least we sincerely desire to serve.[27]

Maria supported her children's vocation to the religious life to a degree matched by few parents. Her unfailing support is conveyed clearly to Alphonse:

> May the sweetest Child Jesus and His Mother Immaculate guide you in all your undertakings general and specific, external and internal. May they allow you to recognize the precious pearl, which the spirit of the world does not acknowledge or value, a deep love of the evangelical counsels, and in the end, grant you the joy and glory of heaven, that is, the place the Lord has prepared for those who faithfully persevere on this way to the end.[28]

With such ardent support for her sons' religious vocations, it comes as no surprise that Maria would feel a certain shock and disappointment when she received a wedding photograph of Francis in the mail. On June 18, 1917, the former seminarian had married his first love, Irene Triebling, after being discharged from the military. Maria was not disheartened that she did not get invited to her son's

---

[27] Ibid., 57.
[28] Ibid.

wedding, as most mothers would be, but that Francis and Irene's wedding came too soon, in her opinion. Above all, Maria faced her greatest surrender yet, for she had prayed daily for over two years that her son Francis would return to the seminary and become a priest. Most mothers today would be thrilled to have one of their children get married and have grandchildren. Maria had one son ordained a priest, St. Maximilian on April 28, 1918, and would eventually have a second, Fr. Alphonse; yet, in the depths of her heart, she had such a profound admiration for Holy Orders and religious life that anything less for her sons seemed not good enough. The hastened wedding with little family involvement only made matters worse. Would Maria will the good of her son as her husband Julius had done for her when she desired to become a nun, or would her bitterness block her trustful surrender to Divine Providence?

Maria visited Francis and her new daughter-in-law, Irene, immediately after their wedding. Though the details of this meeting are unknown, Maria shared her regret and disappointment to her son Fr. Alphonse. Irene could sense her mother-in-law's disapproval of their marriage, and there was clearly a strained relationship from the beginning, which would only get worse before it got better. Though Maria is being lauded for surrender in this chapter, she clearly struggled to surrender, as does every saint and parent of a saint. Maria's son took the high road through this relationship, remaining close to his brothers through letters and forgiving his mother for disapproving of his new vocation. In fact, Maria's visits to Francis and Irene were rare and done more out of routine than love. After the birth of her first and only grandchild, a girl named Aniela, Maria promptly visited, but only after she beckoned her two religious sons, Fr. Maximilian and Fr. Alphonse, with these words, "I need courage and prayers."[29]

Throughout his life, Francis Kolbe experienced the greatest cross, feeling that his vocation to marriage was never good enough for his mother. To make matters worse, Maria received angry letters from her daughter-in-law. Specifically, Maria wrote to Fr. Maximilian, "Irene writes obsessive and repulsive letters about

---

[29] Ibid., 79.

our Francis, herself, and Aniela. She seems to think we should all be concerned with her and satisfy all her needs. There have been times when I wanted to answer her with sharp reproaches, but again, something holds me back saying, 'it would be of no use, only scandalous.' I listen to this inner voice and I will not write. . . . I leave everything to the will of God and His holy mother."[30]

Irene may have sensed that her mother-in-law always wanted Francis to be a priest, and, henceforth, she would never be good enough for her son or Maria. Surrender and accepting others as they were was never easy for Maria. Rather, it took her much time and prayer before she could fully accept both Francis's vocation to marriage and his wife and daughter. To add to her disappointment, Francis and Irene had stopped receiving the sacraments at one point. A heartbroken Maria confided to Fr. Maximilian at the time, "I hoped they would receive the sacraments as a gift to me on my name day, but there was no talk of it."[31] Despite Maria's greatest fear, and perhaps any devout mother's greatest worry that a child of theirs has forsaken the sacraments and, henceforth, put his or her soul in jeopardy, Maria allowed her trust in God to overshadow her anxiety over her son's, daughter-in-law's, and granddaughter's salvation. Maria once composed the following beautiful words to Fr. Alphonse, which echoed her confidence in God and the intercession of Our Lady and St. Francis in bringing back her prodigal son.

> He will not be lost because our prayers are not said in vain. God will find ways to save him, ways which we are incapable of dreaming about. And the Virgin Mary, she will help. Besides, he was offered to our Holy Father Francis before he was born. For the love of St. Francis, he has his name. How could we think that he would not be saved? No, because of all his failures, we will all the more praise the mercy and unfathomable goodness of God.[32]

At one point, Francis's frequent marital problems led him to separate from his wife and daughter as he wandered in search of jobs

---

[30] Ibid., 98–99.
[31] Ibid., 80.
[32] Ibid.

while begging his two brothers for financial assistance—ironically, as both had taken vows of poverty as Franciscans. Maria painfully told her two sons that "they are not to extend any form of financial charity; this would only make his wandering life easier if he realizes he can depend on them."[33] Thanks to Maria's prayers and a stern admonition by his younger brother Maximilian, Francis returned to his wife and daughter, though Maria still blamed herself as the source of her son's wayward life.

In the midst of her sorrows and disappointments, Maria led a life of self-forgetfulness by running errands for the sisters while maintaining her deep prayer life. The latter, along with her rich sacramental life and fervent Marian devotion, would be the only things that could sustain her for what was to come. Maria prepared herself for the great storms in life by surrendering to God's will daily in the little things. Like the Blessed Mother's seven sorrows based on Simeon's prophecy, "a sword will pierce through your own soul" (Lk 2:35), so too did Maria Kolbe have seven similar swords pierce her heart. Thanks be to God, Maria remained standing like Mary at the foot of the Cross as she leaned on the grace of God while surrendering to His will. Maria's first and second swords were the loss of Anthony and Valentine. Maria's third sword came when her son Francis left the seminary and abandoned the sacraments for some time. The fourth sword to pierce Maria's heart occurred when her beloved husband Julius was captured by the Russians during World War I. Julius was an officer fighting for the Polish legions in late September and early October 1914 after Maria left for the convent. Unfortunately, Maria and her three sons never knew where Julius was and were not sure whether he was dead or alive until a witness eventually confirmed his death. Even though Julius and Maria were not living in the same house and had agreed to embrace celibacy, Maria loved her husband and greatly mourned his death. Even more tragic, Julius was only forty-three years old at the time of his death. The Church and the Kolbe family lost a heroic husband, father, and soldier, who was instrumental in passing on his tremendous Marian devotion and sacrificial spirit to his three sons.

---

[33] Ibid., 95.

Sixteen years later, on December 3, 1930, Maria's fifth sword came when her third son, Fr. Alphonse, died hours before his appendicitis surgery. He was only thirty-four years old and had been a priest for nine years. A shocked Maria could not believe the news, but praying the Magnificat she realized, "He died a priest."[34] His older, saintly brother, Fr. Maximilian Kolbe, wrote to his mother, "He lived, suffered, and sacrificed himself for the Immaculata." [35] Fr. Maximilian also wrote of his little brother, "Alphonse, the Immaculate has taken him. . . . May she be praised for everything."[36] Seeing her son in a casket is probably the most heart-wrenching sight for any mother of a priest who imagined it would be her son who would sprinkle her casket with Holy Water one last time before burying her. But not Maria, who came to realize with time and grace that Our Lady's plans for her son would only continue in Heaven.

Maria's sixth and greatest sword occurred on February 17, 1941, when Fr. Maximilian and four other priests were arrested by the Nazis and put in the Pawiak prison for four months. On May 28, Fr. Maximilian was transported to the Auschwitz concentration camp with three hundred prisoners. In the midst of his suffering and death, he penned one short letter to his mother on June 15, 1941, nearly two months before he would be martyred on August 14 at the age of forty-seven. He wrote in German, the only language allowed, to lift her spirits and increase her trust in God.

> At the end of May, I came with many others to the camp
> of Auschwitz. I am faring well. Be at peace Mother, and
> do not worry about me or my health. God is everywhere.
> He watches over all and everything with great love.
> Until you receive my next letter, it is better not to write,
> because I do not know how long I shall remain here.[37]

As she read her son's last letter, perhaps Maria's heart was in even greater agony than her son's, for such is a mother's love. Maria had the blessing to carry her little Raymond "Maximilian" in the

---

34   Ibid., 107.
35   Ibid., 108.
36   Ibid., 109.
37   Ibid., 138.

womb for nine months and then labor out of love so that he could be brought to life. In her letter to the Niepokalanów Monastery—called the City of the Immaculate Mother of God and founded by her son Maximilian—where the Franciscan friars resided, Maria expressed her tumult and yet surrender.

> There seems little hope of Father Maximilian's return, and an exhausting battle erupts inside of me. I want to accept the will of God, yet I am violently assaulted with temptations. How is it that others are answered and fulfilled in their prayers, while I experience the opposite? The more I pray, the bitter are the results.
>
> I was tempted to forsake my trust in the protection of the Immaculate Mother. I am tormented; my son was faithful to her and she does not help him . . . she does not save him. I am overcome with remorse. . . .
>
> Physical and spiritual agony engulfs me. If my son were to die in *Niepokalanów*, I would at least know where he is buried. Although with joy I would give my life for his ransom, I fear to pray impetuously for his release. I am inspired to pray for what is most important—his sanctification and the glory of God.
>
> Vehemently and with conviction, I begged, as a mother who really loves her children, for Maximilian the strong love of the martyrs. A love stronger than death—love that allows one to face death with joy. I listen with a torn heart to an inner voice that whispers, "above natural love, one must place the love of God, and the desire for eternal happiness for those we love."[38]

In writing the above letter, Maria Kolbe reveals that, like Zélie Martin, even the holiest parents struggle to surrender perfectly as does every follower of God. Though unbearable even with a strong faith, Maria eventually resigned herself to her son Maximilian's inevitable death in the concentration camp by praying to God "for what is most important—his sanctification and the glory of God" along with "the strong love of the martyrs." Has not every person at one point in his or her life felt the tension Maria faced when

---

[38] Ibid., 139.

she declared, "I want to accept the will of God, yet I am violently assaulted with temptations. How is it that others are answered and fulfilled in their prayers, while I experience the opposite?" Maria was even tempted to forsake her confidence in her patron saint and favorite intercessor, the Blessed Mother. When trials take place like the loss of a loved one from war, cancer, or martyrdom, as Maria experienced, she shows that we must pray for the "sanctification and the glory of God" for ourselves, our loved ones, and the entire world. In doing so, Maria proclaimed the essence of surrender: "Thy will be done" (Mt 26:42), for everything that happens to us, good or bad, is permitted by God for our salvation and His glory. Make no mistake, Maria's prayers gave her son the courage to become a martyr.

One of the most famous stories concerning Maximilian Kolbe, which sheds light on Maria's sixth sorrow, recounts the time Our Lady appeared to Raymond at a young age and offered him two crowns—a white crown of martyrdom for perseverance in chastity or a red crown for physical martyrdom. Raymond told Our Lady he wanted both. Yet, surprisingly, this incident occurred after Maria had reprimanded Raymond for his behavior and asked him "What will become of you?"[39] Raymond's mother noticed an immediate positive transformation in his behavior and sought to know the reason why. After prodding him and telling him that it was not right to keep anything from her, a teary-eyed Raymond informed his mother that he had begged Our Lady with the same question his mother had asked him: "What will become of me?" Our Lady appeared to him with the two crowns.

After the heroic martyrdom of Fr. Maximilian by lethal injection, the friars wanted to gather as much information about Maximilian's life, especially his childhood and youth, by interviewing Maria, most likely with hopes of advancing his cause for canonization. It was only after his death that Maria had slowly revealed her son's youthful encounter with the Immaculata. Maria mentioned that Maximilian certainly did not want his mother to relate this incident to anyone as "he did not want to call attention to himself."[40] Maria

---

[39] Ibid., 148.
[40] Ibid.

and Maximilian's humility were such that they never sought the praise of man. Surrender led to humility for the Kolbes because they trusted that God would manifest His glory working through Maximilian after his death, rather than his mother promoting his canonization while he was alive.

Further, Maria witnessed Maximilian's transformation following his encounter with Our Lady, as he became more devoted and recollected in prayer—he even had the gift of tears at an early age, which made it more plausible that Maximilian was no storyteller. Yet, as many children are prone to telling fibs, did Maria take her son's prophecy as truth? When looking at her young son, did Maria ever think he would die a martyr as he had revealed to her? This we will never know. As Maximilian was forcibly taken to Auschwitz, there was no doubt in Maria's mind that her son's vision as a child was coming to fruition, hence she prayed that he would have the courage of a martyr. While Maria would naturally want her son's life spared, as would any mother, Maria prayed above all that he would "endure until the end," i.e., profess the Faith even to death.

The seventh sword to pierce Maria's heart, or more fittingly, her final trial of surrender, involved her last surviving son, Francis. As seen earlier, Francis pierced Maria's heart when he left the seminary, but it must be noted that Maria loved all of her children equally regardless of their vocation. Francis's conversion appeared to be coming full circle when he wrote a consoling reply to Maria's letter following the death of Fr. Maximilian.

Francis's patriotism and bravery in the cause of his country's independence never left him as he fought with an underground movement during World War II. To Maria's dismay, he was captured on January 19, 1943, and immediately incarcerated in various concentration camps, including Auschwitz. During this trial, Maria became even closer to Irene and Aniela. Unfortunately, Francis never escaped the Sachsenhausen concentration camp in Oranienburg, Germany, as he died at fifty-two years old, only months before the camp's liberation on January 23, 1945. Francis's official cause of death was ruled as enterocolitis, inflammation of the digestive tract, which was the cause of death of many prisoners in the concentration camps as the disease was rampant. Maria could only pour out her tears before the Eucharistic Lord and somehow ask God for the grace to stay strong. Sadly, Francis would be the third family member deprived of a Christian burial along with his father and his brother, St. Maximilian.

Less than a year later, Maria mourned the loss of Irene. She had now experienced the death of her husband, her five sons, and her only daughter-in-law. She united her pain with Our Lady of Sorrows, who also lost those dearest to her, namely St. Joseph and Our Lord. Maria's only living relative was her granddaughter, Aniela Kolbe Szymanska, who would get married in the City of the Immaculate Mother of God—a joy for this grandmother, who never distanced herself from her daughter-in-law and granddaughter with her prayers and helped them when the opportunity arose.

Despite the reality that all of her sons were faithful to Christ, Maria worried that the future saint, Maximilian, died without the sacraments. Maria's greatest desire for her husband, her children, her daughter-in-law, her granddaughter, and every person she encountered was that they would love God until the last beat of their hearts. Her anxiety was calmed when Fr. Maximilian's Franciscan confrere, Br. Ferdynand Maria Kasz, who spent time with Fr. Maximilian at Auschwitz, wrote:

> I state with full certainty that in Auschwitz Father Maximilian went to confession frequently and received Holy Communion. His confessor is still living; he was transferred with me from Auschwitz to Dachau. He told me that Father Maximilian went to confession every week. He received Holy Communion, also, since every Sunday one of the Polish priests celebrated Mass secretly in an attic.[41]

What Br. Ferdynand says next is so beautiful:

> As for the Christian burial, this he did not have. In the camp no one was buried as a Christian; the bodies were burned in the crematory. . . . I believe that martyrs go

[41] Ibid., 162.

to heaven without a Catholic burial. So it is with our
Dear Father Maximilian, for certain he is in heaven, and
from the moment of his death enjoys the presence of God
face to face.[42]

Despite the numerous trials listed above, Maria never turned
her back on God, for the greatest faith emerges only through the
greatest trials. Anyone admiring Maria from a distance without
closely studying her life might desire to emulate her, especially in
raising a great saint. Yet, after reading more about her life, few
would be willing to walk in Maria's shoes! Only supernatural grace
could sustain a mother who mourned the loss of all five sons and her
husband, survived two world wars, and, despite not being allowed
to make final religious vows, was a nun at heart.

Only the Eucharist, which Maria received daily and spent hours
adoring, could provide the grace that enabled her to abandon herself
to the will of God. Her unshakable trust in God and abandonment
to His Divine Providence is the reason her Felician sisters could
declare about her virtue, "She had a certain courage, losing everyone
she loved; no doubt she suffered much, and did so alone."[43] Perhaps
Maria's ability to surrender was aided by the fact that she was a
human mother before she became a spiritual mother; for she had
learned that by putting others before herself, especially her family,
one has little time to fret about one's own problems.

Maria's last surrender was death itself. She died on the Feast
of St. Patrick, March 17, 1946, at the age of seventy-six. Maria
happened to be on the way to a Third Order Franciscan meeting
and Vespers when she collapsed. She received the Anointing of
the Sick and the Viaticum from Fr. Alojzy Wojnar, and her final
words were "My son! My son!"[44] Perhaps Maria's saintly son, Fr.
Maximilian, returned from Heaven to comfort his mother at her
last moments and would now introduce Maria to Jesus and His
Mother, the Immaculata. Her last request was to be buried in the
community vault with the sisters she loved. Following Maria's death,

---

[42]   Ibid.
[43]   Ibid., 170.
[44]   Ibid., 167.

her order discovered that she slept on rough planks. Remarkably, Maria never took any shortcuts in religious life despite not being a full member. She used to say, "As always, I rise at the same time, winter or summer. I never miss the six o'clock Mass, this is the time the Lord ascends his throne in our Church."[45] Many of her religious sisters viewed her as a saint. As Sr. Mary Praxeda Mika declared, "She was a saint in little things and small ways; I doubt there is a sister who will soon forget her."[46] The Reverend Henryk Werynski, who served the Felician Sisters for four decades, said it best:

> She was a woman without evangelical vows but understood their meaning and lived accordingly. Only now do we see her through the prism of her son, Maximilian. Hers was the quiet doing of truth. There was nothing striking, nothing extraordinary. No one came special to Smolensk Street to see her or to gain favor. From all outward appearances, this woman's life was insignificant. She was poor, obedient, and silent. However, anyone who has loved and is loved deserves to be remembered.[47]

While insignificant in the world's eyes and, perhaps, just another tombstone at the Felician Sisters convent to any passerby, Maria's silent surrender to the will of God in the face of tremendous suffering was the torch that was handed on to her son Maximilian and that contributed to his sanctity. Maria would have it no other way than being forgotten by the world, for she modeled her life after Our Lady and likewise wanted the attention pointed towards God.

Luigi and Assunta Goretti

In 1897, Luigi Goretti, a farmer, decided to move his family from their native town of Corinaldo, Italy, nestled in the mountains overlooking the Adriatic Sea, to the milder, coastal town of Ferriere. Traveling two hundred miles westward across the Apennine

---

45 Ibid., 171.
46 Ibid.
47 Ibid., 172.

Mountains in two weeks with his wife and their four children, all
ages nine and younger, Luigi wanted to provide a better living for his
children, especially his future saint, Maria Goretti. Before relocating,
Luigi could barely feed his family from his own plot of land. In
Ferriere, the Gorettis became sharecroppers of Count Mazzoleni.
Unfortunately, Luigi contracted malaria and was unable to harvest
the field by himself. The count hired Giovanni Serenelli and his son,
Alessandro, to live with the Gorettis and share half of their profits, to
which Luigi acquiesced. As Luigi's malaria worsened, the Gorettis
would kneel beside the family bed in prayer each night. On his
deathbed, author Ann Ball states that "Luigi begged Assunta to take
the children and return to Corinaldo."[48] Luigi also expressed some
regret over moving his family away from their relatives and native
land. Though wanting to return to the mountains and their support
system, Assunta lacked the wherewithal, and the long journey with
her young children was not prudent. Instead, the Gorettis were
forced to work for the heartless Giovanni.

On one occasion, Assunta had found Alessandro's stash of
pornographic books while cleaning his room, but she did not
reprimand him as she did not want to stir up trouble. Had Assunta
listened to her husband's advice to return to her native land despite
the obstacles, or perhaps even confronted Alessandro lovingly and
sought to get him help for his addiction, Maria's violent death
might have been prevented—this we will never know. Assunta,
who grew up as an orphan and was raised by nuns until the age of
five, tried her best to instill the Faith and virtue into her children,
despite not being able to read or write, and despite her own failings.
Assunta had very beautiful daughters, especially Maria, who was
noted for her chestnut hair. Assunta always made sure that she and
her daughters dressed modestly even in the summer heat. On one
occasion, Maria told her mother she had overheard a female friend
of hers flirting with a boy near the well and talking about sexual
topics. Maria quickly filled up her jug and returned home. Assunta
was disappointed that Maria listened to the conversation. "Why did

---

[48] Anne Ball, *Modern Saints,* Book One (Rockford, IL: TAN Books, 1983),
167.

you stay to listen? Let words like that go in one ear and out the other. You just make sure you never talk like that yourself."[49]

After Luigi's death, Assunta became the sole breadwinner, working the farm while Maria served as the domestic mother, cooking, cleaning, and helping raise her siblings. Following Maria's violent death, Assunta could not simultaneously work and tend to her children. Not being able to bear the grief over Maria's death without any extended family, she placed her five children up for adoption as she could no longer support them without Maria. According to her biographer, Fr. Carlos Martins, "Maria's two sisters were raised by Franciscan nuns and the three boys were sent to live in Rome."[50] Later on, Assunta's three boys, Angelo, Sandrino, and Mariano, immigrated to the United States. Sandrino died unexpectedly within a year of reaching America, while Angelo and Mariano were married and gifted America with descendants of their saintly sister. That being said, perhaps Luigi's insistence that Assunta and the children return to Corinaldo meant for them to return to the mountains after Maria's death; or maybe his prophecy was meant to prevent the violent murder of his eleven-year-old daughter? Like her husband, Assunta may have lived with a similar regret, wishing they had never left their native land, or wishing she had returned immediately after her husband's death. Also, Assunta may have regretted not better protecting her children, especially Maria, from evil companions, such as Alessandro. Everything is easier in retrospect.

While Alessandro's violent murder of St. Maria Goretti called for eternal punishment, one easily forgets that Alessandro was a child of God who may never have committed such acts had it not been for his deplorable upbringing. The youngest of eight children of Giovanni and Cecilia Serenelli, Alessandro was born on June 2, 1882, into a poor Catholic family, like Maria Goretti. Unfortunately,

[49] Leifeld, *Mothers of the Saints,* 209.
[50] Pronechen, "Body of St. Maria Goretti Arriving in the U.S," *National Catholic Register* (September 15, 2015), m.ncregister.com/blog/joseph-pronechen/the-body-of-st.-maria-goretti-will-soon-be-brought-to-the-u.s.-part-ii#.WjhfGkFOnYU.

Alessandro's own mother tried to drown him shortly after his birth. She died a few months later in a mental asylum. Also, one of his brothers committed suicide while studying in the seminary. His father, however, ensured that Alessandro received the sacraments, which he did regularly. He occasionally even prayed the family Rosary with the Gorettis. Sadly, Alessandro's father was a heavy drinker and grappled with providing for his family, as they moved several times so he could find better work as a laborer. On top of this, Giovanni's personality was very "stern and harsh."[51] Consequently, Alessandro never experienced unconditional love and the stable home environment that characterized many of the saints in this book. As he neared the end of his life, he wrote that he wished he had associated himself with "generous and devoted people,"[52] rather than be influenced by "print, mass-media and bad examples."[53]

While in prison, Alessandro experienced God's mercy and peace after confessing his sins to the bishop. After he served twenty-seven years in solitary confinement, he was released three years early due to his excellent conduct. Immediately after being released from prison, Alessandro sought Assunta's forgiveness on Christmas Eve of 1937. There are no words to describe Assunta's anguish. Besides losing her best friend and soulmate in her husband, Assunta also said goodbye to her eleven-year-old daughter as well as having to give away her other children, all within a few years. Yet Assunta's biggest test was still to come. With Alessandro to be released from prison, she would now face her most daunting challenge as Christ's follower: Could she forgive in person the man who killed her young daughter, or would she choose a lifetime of bitterness? Like her daughter Maria did twenty-seven years earlier, Assunta, by the grace of God, forgave Alessandro. The seventy-three-year-old mother told Alessandro, "If Maria forgives you, and God forgives you, how can I not also forgive you?"[54] Assunta even invited him into her home for dinner, and they

---

[51]   Ball, *Modern Saints,* Book One, 168.
[52]   "Alessandro Serenelli: A Miraculous Conversion," mariagoretti.org, mariagoretti.org/alessandrobio.htm.
[53]   Ibid.
[54]   Gretchen Filz, "A Story of Great Mercy: St. Maria Goretti & Alessandro Serenelli," Catholic Company, Catholiccompany.com.

later attended Midnight Mass together! No mother could possibly move on from their young daughter being brutally stabbed to death and at the same time forgive the murderer had she not been a woman of surrender, who believed that God's goodness always triumphs over Satan and man's misery.

Giovanni and Margarita Sarto

Less than two hundred miles away from St. Maria Goretti's hometown is the town of Riese, in northeastern Italy. Giuseppe Melchiorre Sarto, the second oldest of what would be ten children, was born on June 2, 1835, to Giovanni Battista and Margarita Sarto. While the name Giuseppe Sarto may not strike a chord, his papal name does—Pope St. Pius X, who served as pope from 1903 to 1914. Like the Goretti parents, Giovanni and Margarita Sarto were poor peasants. Giovanni worked as a postman, and Margarita worked as a seamstress. During seminary, which was funded through a scholarship obtained by his parish priest, Giuseppe requested a leave of absence to attend to his sixty-year-old dying father. After Giovanni's death, Giuseppe volunteered to leave the seminary indefinitely to help support his mother and siblings. Margarita courageously turned down Giuseppe's request. She once pointed to her wedding ring after her son was made a bishop and declared, "If I had not had this, you would not have had that,"[55] referring to his episcopal ring. On August 20, 1914, Pope St. Pius X ended his last private audience on his deathbed with the words, "I resign myself completely."[56]

Pope Pius X's parents provided the foundation for the virtue of surrender by allowing their son to pursue God's will at the cost of their continued financial hardship. As parents of ten children—something many people today would call irresponsible—they trusted God's providence and lived in poverty doing God's will rather than having one or two children and living more comfortably. Like his parents, Pius X embraced a life of poverty and would often give away his watch for money to be distributed to the poor. He once

[55]   Piat, *The Story of a Family,* ix.
[56]   Ball, *Modern Saints,* Book Two, 270.

rightfully declared, "I was born poor, I have lived in poverty, and I shall end my days a poor man."[57] Further, the pope learned from his parents that God provides both materially and spiritually if we but surrender to His will. God's providence never fails us. Contrary to popular opinion, surrender as seen in the life of the Sarto family, and most clearly in the life of Christ, does not guarantee prosperity or even financial security; rather, surrender often leads to a certain level of poverty, suffering, and sacrifice. Above all, surrender allowed the Sartos, and beckons us, to experience the "peace of God, which passes all understanding" (Phil 4:7), along with joy because God is with us.

St. Bridget of Sweden and Ulf Gudmar

St. Bridget of Sweden, not to be confused with St. Bridget of Ireland, was born in Skederik around 1303. Many today recite her fifteen prayers, which the Lord instructed her to pray daily for a year in order to console Him for the 5,480 bodily blows received during his sacred Passion. Birgitta, Swedish for Bridget, is often depicted in holy cards wearing her black nun's habit, but many Catholics forget that she was the mother of eight children. St. Bridget strove to impart virtue to her children, but not without difficulty. While some of them failed to respond to God's grace through their own stubbornness and lack of faith, one in particular, Catherine, followed her mother's footsteps and became canonized. Yet what makes Bridget special and a precursor to St. Zélie Martin was her desire to surrender to the will of God, even when things did not go as planned, and when her desire to serve God with an undivided heart as a consecrated virgin was impossible. Rather than allow his daughter to pursue her vocation as a religious sister, Birger Persson insisted Bridget marry Ulf Gudmar. Far from being antireligious, her father was very devout and was known to receive the Sacrament of Reconciliation every Friday, and also to make various pilgrimages, including one to the Holy Land. Out of obedience, Bridget succumbed to her father's wishes, though she would often tell her future saintly daughter, St. Catherine, that "she would have preferred then to die rather than to

---

57 Ibid., 269.

marry."[58] Ironically, Bridget ended up loving the man she initially didn't want to marry.

Both Ulf and Bridget became Third Order Franciscans and, despite spending their first year of marriage practicing continence, accepted their vocation to be "fruitful and multiply" (Gn 1:28). Bridget also surrendered to the will of God when her husband went on frequent business travels by practicing chastity and intense prayer. Moreover, they renounced sexual relations during Lent and on major feast days and Fridays. In terms of prayer, it is related that Bridget "revered Jesus Christ with her prayers and her tears, to such an extent that, when her husband was away, she would keep watch for the entire night, striving to discipline her body through many genuflections and mortifications."[59]

When her beloved husband, Ulf, fell deathly ill, Bridget took him to the monks of Alvastra Abbey, where he died and was buried. In the meantime, Bridget resided in a small house near the abbey, where she spent many hours praying by her deceased husband's grave as a young widow of forty-one. She was recorded as saying about Ulf that she "loved him like my own body."[60] In effect, Bridget's life echoed the words of St. Paul to the Ephesians, when he implored "husbands should love their wives as their own bodies. He who loves his wife loves himself" (5:28). Ulf and Bridget's love for each other was truly heroic, for it mirrored Christ's love for His Church. Without faith, losing a spouse can lead to never-ending depression and despair. Eventually, like St. Mary Magdalene at the tomb of Jesus, Bridget's tears surrendered to the hope of the Resurrection. And, also like St. Mary Magdalene, God was telling Bridget to quit holding on to what was, for His plans can make life come from death.

Shortly after Ulf's death, Our Lord called Bridget full circle to the vocation she once dreamed of—to be a religious sister. In

---

[58] Ferdinand Holbock, *Married Saints and Blesseds Through the Centuries* (San Francisco: Ignatius Press, 2002), 242.

[59] Holbock, *Married Saints and Blesseds Through the Centuries*, 245.

[60] "St. Bridget of Sweden," Catholic.org, catholic.org/saints/saint. php?saint_id=264.

doing so, the Holy Spirit inspired Bridget to establish a new religious order, primarily for women. Sadly, she died before the monastery was completed. Bridget's ability to surrender to God's will was never easy, especially when it came to her vocation. Yet she fully embraced the will of God despite its twists and turns, sorrows and joys. Her unshakable confidence in God despite her failures, fears, and sufferings is precisely the reason why she was canonized in 1391, only eighteen years after her death in 1373. Ironically, Bridget was denied both the privilege of growing old with her husband and of becoming a fully professed religious sister. Bridget's abandonment to Divine Providence was the bridge that enabled her children to cross from mediocrity to sanctity. Her daughter, St. Catherine of Sweden, decided to marry like her mother at her father's wishes, but observed total continence with her husband and was given permission to accompany Bridget to Rome for twenty-three years. One of Bridget's granddaughters from her first daughter, Marta, would become an abbess at a convent named after her saintly grandmother. A son, Bengt, died while in formation at a Cistercian monastery, and Bridget's seventh child, Ingeborg, became a Cistercian sister. The apple does not fall far from the tree, as the saying goes. Because of Ulf and St. Bridget's life of surrender, they were able to plant an orchard of holy men and women.

Throughout this chapter, the parents of the saints and their saintly children reveal the heart of surrender. They relied entirely on "the grace of each moment"[61] and resembled a little child in their Father's arms. These parents' trust in God was rooted in their steadfast belief that they were sons and daughters of the Heavenly Father. St. Zélie Martin once wrote to her little brother, "When I think of what God has done for me and my husband, God, in whom I've put all my trust and whose hands I've put the care of my whole life, I don't doubt that His Divine Providence watches over His children with special care."[62] It was Zélie's radical trust in God, or, as her daughter Céline so beautifully wrote, her "assurance

---

[61] Martin, *The Mother of the Little Flower*, 91.
[62] Martin and Martin, *A Call to a Deeper Love*, 1–2.

of invincible, even audacious, confidence, towards our Father in Heaven, that sustained her in her many trials."[63]

Since the Fall of Adam and Eve, Original Sin has disrupted our ability to trust God completely and has tragically caused many of us to fear Him more than love Him. The parents of the saints were put in this world to remind their children and each one of us that God is Our Father. In every generation and in every circumstance, no matter how dire, God only wills the best for us and will never leave us, even when He seems distant, when the road before us is uncertain, or when we experience terrible suffering such as losing a spouse or a child, or suffering a betrayal.

God never said that surrender would come easy, as seen in these heroic lives. Surrender frequently comes with a price because, like Job in the Old Testament, we give God permission to take everything as everything belongs to Him. Céline once echoed this truth as she described how the surrender of her mother, Zélie, was mixed with pain: "And indeed she well knew anguish in the illnesses of her children, and in the death of four of them. She accepted everything with admirable resignation, notwithstanding a very keen sensitivity, which caused her to suffer greatly from anxieties and separations."[64] And though surrender cannot remove our sufferings, the parents of the saints show us it is far better than the alternative, which is the constant struggle to control, to fear, and to worry. Surrender, which is a daily battle, is the only path to interior peace.

By virtue of their surrender, the parents of the saints were led to the heights of sacrificial love, for to surrender to God is to partake of the greatest surrender, which was Jesus' Death on the Cross. Or, as best put by St. Thérèse, who learned how to surrender from her parents' example, "It is confidence and nothing but confidence that must lead us to Love,"[65] which leads us to our next chapter.

[63] Martin, *The Mother of the Little Flower*, 75.
[64] Ibid.
[65] St. Thérèse of Lisieux, *General Correspondence: Volume II*, 1000.

HALLMARK THREE

Sacrificial Love

After God, I owe it to my mother; she was so good! Virtue passes readily from the heart of a mother into that of her children. A child that has the happiness of having a good mother should never look at her or think of her without tears.[1]—St. John Vianney

Matthieu and Marie Vianney

As the twenty-nine-year-old St. John Vianney received the Sacrament of Holy Orders from his bishop in 1815, we can only wonder what sentiments filled his heart, especially directed toward his holy parents, Matthieu and Marie Beluze Vianney, whose prayers and sacrifices helped bring his ordination to fruition. After disappointment, failure, and even being dismissed from the seminary because of his inadequate grasp of Latin, John Vianney persevered with God's grace, especially due to his mother's intercession, both while living and then from Heaven. Sadly, Marie would not physically witness the greatest day of her son's life, for she went to her eternal reward at fifty-eight years old. John Vianney confessed that after his mother's death, he no longer felt any attachment to this world. Marie was John Vianney's greatest advocate, as she supported his vocation more than any other person. His father had opposed his vocation because he did not want to lose a skilled laborer on their farm.

---

[1] Francis Trochu, *The Cure D'Ars* (Rockford, IL: TAN Books, 1977), 10.

Years before John Vianney became a priest, Marie attended daily
Mass with her eldest daughter, Catherine, whenever possible. Soon,
her fourth of six children, John, came along. John loved to watch
his mother pray. At the time of his birth, Marie led her son John to
the greatest sacrificial love by literally pointing to the crucifix and
various pious pictures throughout their home as well as teaching him
the Sign of the Cross. Maria even gave him a small, wooden statue
of Our Lady, which remained by his bedside for life.

Finding her four-year-old son missing one day, Marie searched
in anguish, thinking he might have drowned, but was surprised
to find him kneeling in prayer in their stable. Marie responded
lovingly, when most women might easily have yelled at their son for
running off without permission. She embraced little John with tears
and said, "Oh! My darling, you were here! Why hide yourself when
you want to pray? You know we all say all our prayers together."[2]
Besides his mother, John inherited his sacrificial nature from his
father, Matthieu. As a young boy, Matthieu's family sheltered and fed
the poor, one of whom happened to be St. Joseph Benedict Labre,
who had just discerned out of a Trappist monastery. A biographer
of John Vianney once beautifully recalled this meeting between
Joseph Benedict and the young Matthieu in these words: "Little did
[Matthieu] guess, as he contemplated this youthful mendicant, so
pale and so meek, who was telling his beads all the time, that one
day he himself would be the father of a saint."[3] Like his parents,
Matthieu and Marie gave food to the poor and sheltered the
homeless, which sometimes included over twenty guests who slept
in the barn or above the bakehouse, thus performing the corporal
works of mercy. Before retiring for the night, the young John would
lead his family and the guests in prayer. Specifically, John continued
his grandfather's and father's tradition of reciting the Our Father and
Hail Mary, especially for the Holy Souls in Purgatory.

Love is not true love until it is tested. Matthieu and Marie's
greatest trial came when their parish, where they entered into
sacramental union, and where several of their children were

---

2   Ibid., 9.
3   Ibid., 4.

baptized, closed due to the 1790 Civil Constitution of the Clergy, with which the French government tried to subordinate the Catholic Church. Tragically, the French government seized Church lands and made priests swear loyalty to their new constitution. Priests refusing to swear the oath were placed under arrest and risked execution without an appeal within twenty-four hours. Families found harboring priests faced deportation. On several occasions, Matthieu and Marie sheltered various faithful priests who had rejected the oath of loyalty to the new constitution and even had Mass celebrated at their house and organized clandestine Masses in the middle of the night at various barns and houses, despite the risk of being caught. The Vianneys were willing to be exiled from their homeland and face death before renouncing their allegiance to Christ's Church.

A true shepherd, albeit a priest or parents, like the Vianneys, lays down his life for his flock or family. John Vianney spent roughly sixteen hours each day hearing Confessions, which was the fruit of his parents risking their lives so that their children could receive the greatest gift in the world—the Holy Eucharist. John Vianney's words, "a child that has the happiness of having a good mother should never look at her or think of her without tears,"[4] testify to his mother's sacrificial legacy. Tears of joy and gratitude likely fell from John Vianney's eyes each time he offered the Holy Sacrifice of the Mass, for had his parents not first sacrificed themselves, even risking their very lives, he might not be on the altar.

Gonzalo and Catalina de Yepes

One century before Matthieu and Marie Vianney lived, a sixteenth-century couple from Fontiveros, Spain, raised one of the Church's greatest mystical writers and lovers of prayer. Their names were Gonzalo de Yepes and Catalina Álvarez. This heroic couple's love of the Cross became their son's love of the Cross, for they implanted the meaning of true love in their son's heart. As an orphan, Gonzalo resided in Toledo with his wealthy uncle, who worked with silk. While working for his uncle, Gonzalo fell in love with Catalina, a poor weaver, on a business trip to Medina del Campo. Gonzalo's

---

4   Trochu, *The Cure D'Ars*, 10.

family threatened to disown him if he married Catalina, who came from the lower class. Rather than let the fear of poverty and suffering prevent him from following his vocation, Gonzalo allowed sacrificial love to permeate his heart as he married Catalina in 1529. Gonzalo would have been his century's version of Prince Charming, with the exception that he took on the poverty of his wife. In essence, Gonzalo resembles the true Prince of Peace, Our Lord, Who left the glory of Heaven for the poverty of the manger by exchanging the riches of Heaven for the rags of earth. Without any family support or financial resources, Gonzalo learned to weave and earned a negligible income from the textile trade of Castile.

In 1530, Catalina gave birth to her firstborn, Francisco. He was followed by Luis, whose date of birth is unknown, and, finally, in 1542, by Juan, who was born on June 24, the Feast of the Nativity of St. John the Baptist. Juan would later become St. John of the Cross. In spite of their hard work, the household was wretchedly poor, and food was scarce. Yet God's love and joy overcame the material challenges. Two years after John's birth, Gonzalo fell prey to a pestilence that swept through Spain and died, leaving a young widow with three malnourished children.

After Gonzalo's death, Catalina attempted to obtain assistance from Gonzalo's family, appealing first to his brother-in-law, who was an archdeacon in Torrijos near Toledo. Unfortunately, the archdeacon made excuses and closed the door in the widow's face. Another brother, who was a doctor in nearby Gálvez, agreed to adopt Francisco. However, upon discovering that the doctor's wife had been abusing Francisco, Catalina immediately took him back. Tragically, Catalina's middle son, Luis, died, apparently of malnutrition. Because Catalina was convinced that she could never survive in the stagnant economy of Fontiveros, she moved her family first to Arévalo and then, in 1551, settled in Medina del Campo, a thriving market town. Catalina continued her weaving, assisted by Francisco. Though suffering will be mentioned in the next chapter, John of the Cross's parents manifest that sacrifice leads to suffering and authentic love.

John of the Cross had few if any memories of his father as he was two when he died. In a mysterious way, Gonzalo's virtues lived on in his son, who also sought to resemble His Crucified Lover, Who was naked and rejected. From Gonzalo's heroic witness, John of the Cross came to realize that union with God is the goal of man's existence, and that, like his father, living an authentic life where one does not compromise one's values comes with consequences. Just as Gonzalo was rejected by his own family for being true to himself and marrying a poor woman, so too was John of the Cross rejected and locked up in his own monastery for nine months by his own Carmelite brothers for trying to reform his order. John of the Cross was imprisoned in a tiny cell, six feet by ten feet, where he was beaten three times a week. Through this trial, which John would eventually escape, he learned that conformity to our Crucified Savior is the greatest treasure in this life. Appearing to John of the Cross with the crown of thorns on His head while carrying His Cross, Our Lord once said, "John, ask of me what though wilt?"[5]

"Lord," John said, "I desire to suffer and to be despised for Thy sake."[6]

While it is not always the ideal to begin one's marriage in poverty, Gonzalo's life reveals that it is better to marry a poor, virtuous woman who will lead one to Heaven than a wealthy, godless woman who will lead one to Hell. True love has been reduced for many to infatuation at first sight, with little understanding of sacrifice. On the contrary, Gonzalo communicates the meaning of true love, which involves risking our family's expectations and inheritance to find our vocation. Gonzalo revealed to his third son, John, that true sacrificial love involved renouncing everything, including wealth, reputation, and family, should God ask. John, on his way to becoming St. John of the Cross, could make the sacrifice to become a Carmelite friar more easily because his own father made a similar sacrifice, that is, he renounced the wealth of this world to do God's will and take a humble, holy bride.

---

[5] St. Alphonsus de Liguori, *The True Spouse of Jesus Christ* (Brooklyn, NY: Redemptorist Fathers, 1929), 212.

[6] Ibid.

Catalina's sacrificial witness was no less important than Gonzalo's in forming their son. Even though her boys often went hungry, she provided for them as best as she could, making sure they were never lacking spiritually. She taught young John how to love God perseveringly and joyfully amidst great trials while being "content with having nothing."[7]

Alonso and Beatriz Sánchez de Cepeda

In addition to Gonzalo and Catalina de Yepes, it is only fitting to mention the parents of another Spanish saint, who was the spiritual mother and at one point a spiritual directee of St. John of the Cross. Teresa Sánchez de Cepeda Dávila y Ahumada was born in Ávila, Spain, on October 4, 1515, to Alonso Sánchez de Cepeda and Beatriz Dávila y Ahumada, is known today as St. Teresa of Ávila. Alonso had been married twice and had three children with his first wife, and nine children with his second wife, Beatriz, Teresa's mother. Details of the death of Alonso's first wife are unknown. However, Teresa's mother would marry Alonso at the age of fourteen and would die in 1528, at the young age of thirty-three, when Teresa was twelve years old. Teresa's parents played a significant role in developing her virtue, despite, in her own opinion, being "so wicked." In Teresa's own words, "We were three sisters and nine brothers; all of them, by the goodness of God, resembled their parents in virtue, except myself though I was my father's favorite."[8] In her autobiography, Teresa testified to her parent's great love for spiritual reading, Our Lady, and the saints as well as their charity, which "began to awaken good desires in me when I was, I suppose six or seven years old."[9] It is never too early to start raising a saint. Specifically, Teresa declared:

> It was a help to me that I never saw my parents inclined to anything but virtue. They themselves had many virtues. My father was a man of great charity towards the poor, who was good to the sick and also to his servants—so

7   St. John of the Cross, *The Collected Works of St. John of the Cross* (Washington, D.C.: ICS Publications, 1991), 89.

8   St. Teresa of Ávila, *The Life of Teresa of Jesus*, 66.

9   Ibid., 65.

much that he could never be brought to keep slaves, because of his compassion for them. On one occasion, when he had a slave of a brother of his in the house, he was as good to her as his own children. He used to say that it caused him intolerable distress that she was not free. He was strictly truthful: nobody ever heard him swear or speak evil. He was a man of the most rigid chastity.

My mother, too, was a very virtuous woman, who endured a life of great infirmity; she was also particularly chaste. Though extremely beautiful, she was never known to give any reason for supposing that she made the slightest account of her beauty; and, though she died at thirty-three, her dress was already that of a person advanced in years. She was a very tranquil woman, of great intelligence. Throughout her life she endured great trials and her death was most Christian.[10]

Teresa's parents planted the seeds of sacrificial love. Most striking was their great charity toward the poor by recognizing Our Lord's presence in every person, regardless of their skin color or social class. Besides their charity, Alonso and Beatriz exercised the virtues of chastity and modesty to the highest degree. In our age, when a married couple's fidelity toward one another is tested like never before due to immodesty, lust, and pornography, Alonso and Beatriz model the depths of sacrificial love by remaining faithful to their spouse in thought, word, and deed, and helping others strive for purity of heart. Teresa was not shy to call her mother "extremely beautiful," but the difference between Beatriz and women who seek vainly to be noticed by dressing immodestly is that Beatriz recognized the true author and admirer of her beauty was God, and not herself or some random stranger. Rather than having false humility by believing that she was not beautiful, Beatriz accepted her beauty as a gift while at the same time recognizing the true beauty of her soul, which is a temple of the Holy Spirit, something far greater than her physical features.

Besides calling their children to the virtues of charity, chastity, and modesty, Teresa's mother provided a most splendid example

[10]   Ibid., 65–66.

of tranquility. We heard Teresa describe her mother as "a very tranquil woman, of great intelligence." Teresa once wrote a prayer that touches profoundly on the tranquility that Our Lord demands of His followers and that personifies the saints—for they were the most peaceful people who ever lived. She declared:

> Let nothing disturb you. Let nothing frighten you. All things are passing away: God never changes. Patience obtains all things. Whoever has God lacks nothing; God alone suffices.[11]

Although the following prayer is attributed to Teresa, the unheralded authors are her father and mother, whose very lives provided the inspiration behind the words to this most beautiful prayer. After all, the parents of the saints were the first models of tranquility for their children. Whether it was serving the poor or serving their children, the peace of God guided these parents to labor without anxiety.

While Teresa praised her mother for her tranquility, she also lauded her father for being a truthful man, who never swore or spoke evil. Thus, Alonso sacrificed his tongue by preventing it from causing scandal to others, particularly his family, but, instead, his mouth became only an instrument to glorify God. Children will either imitate their parents' praise or imitate their blasphemy of God.

Teresa's parents possessed many virtues. However, one area in particular became a double-edged sword, which was the pursuit of wisdom. Most notably, Teresa's father was an avid reader who was particular in his selections. He was "fond of reading good books and had some in Spanish so that his children might read them too,"[12] according to his daughter. Further, Teresa's parents made these edifying spiritual books, such as the lives of the saints, readily available for their children. As Teresa related:

> When I read of the martyrdoms suffered by saintly women for God's sake, I used to think they had purchased

---

[11] St. Teresa of Ávila, "Prayer of Saint Teresa of Avila," EWTN.com, ewtn.com/catholicism/devotions/prayer-of-saint-teresa-of-avila-364.

[12] St. Teresa of Ávila, *The Life of Teresa of Jesus*, 65.

the fruition of God very cheaply; and I had a keen desire
to die as they had done, not out of any love for God of
which I was conscious, but in order to attain as quickly
as possible the fruition of the greatest blessings which, as
I read, were laid up in Heaven. I used to discuss with this
brother of mine how we could become martyrs.[13]

Teresa and her brother were clearly inspired to holiness from
their parents' books on the lives of the saints. Good books, especially
spiritual works, can lead many souls not only to a deep conversion,
but to the path of sainthood. And, sadly, some books can have the
opposite effect by instilling vice as seen in the example below.
According to Teresa:

My mother, as I have said, was very good herself, but
when I came to the age of reason, I copied her goodness
very little, in fact hardly at all, and evil things did me a
great deal of harm. She was fond of books of chivalry;
and this pastime had not the ill effects on her that it had
on me, because she never allowed them to interfere with
her work. . . . For myself, I began to make a habit of it,
and this little fault, which I saw in my mother began
to cool my good desires and lead me to other kinds of
wrongdoing. . . . So excessively was I absorbed in it that
I believe, unless I had a new book, I was never happy. I
began to deck myself out and try to attract others by my
appearance, taking great trouble with my hands and hair,
using perfumes and all the vanities I could get—and there
were a good many of them, for I was very fastidious.[14]

And while we uphold Alonso and Beatriz for their many virtues,
they also missed the mark in a few areas, according to their saintly
daughter. Clearly these chivalrous books had cooled the flames
of young Teresa's love for God, who, instead of glorifying Him,
began to glorify herself. Surprisingly, many Christian mothers take
delight in romance novels because they appear so innocent, yet their
impact, as seen above, can be poisonous, especially if read by one's

---

13   Ibid., 66.
14   Ibid., 68–69.

teenage daughters, by stirring in the hearts of women unrealistic expectations, vanity, and impure thoughts. Besides romance novels, the proliferation and accessibility of pornography continues to distort our children's healthy view of marriage and the proper context of the marital act, requiring parents to be most vigilant.

One of the greatest tragedies for many when they die, other than not becoming a saint, is realizing how easy it would have been, for nothing is lacking on God's end. As mentioned earlier, Teresa said about the martyrs, "They had purchased the fruition of God very cheaply."[15] Every person is called to be not only good stewards of their talents and money, but, above all, their time. The saints became saints because they knew that every moment is to be lived totally for God and never to be wasted. St. Thérèse of Lisieux, the Carmelite spiritual daughter of Teresa of Ávila, once wrote, "We have only the short moments of our life to love Jesus, and the devil knows this well, and so he tries to consume our life in useless work."[16]

Besides not vigilantly safeguarding what books Teresa and her siblings read, along with ensuring they were good stewards of God's time, Teresa's parents failed to protect their children from a pernicious first cousin. According to Teresa, "This person was so frivolous in her conversation that my mother had tried very hard to prevent her from coming to the house, realizing what harm she might do me, but there were so many reasons for her coming that she was powerless."[17] And as a result, Teresa further declared, "I had a sister much older than myself, from whom, though she was very good and chaste, I learned nothing, whereas from a relative whom we often had in the house I learned every kind of evil."[18]

As one of only four female Doctors of the Church, St. Teresa of Ávila is best remembered as one of the greatest mystics, authors on prayer, and reformers of religious life, but the following words, aimed at parents, might be some of her most profound, most forgotten, and least implemented. In fact, Teresa might have ended

15   Ibid., 66.
16   St. Thérèse of Lisieux, *General Correspondence,* Volume I, 568–569.
17   St. Teresa of Ávila, *The Life of Teresa of Jesus,* 69.
18   Ibid.

up in Hell, as the Lord once revealed her place there in a vision, due to her frivolous and lax obedience to her religious vows, which continued for some time in the convent before she repented. These bad habits had been formed in her youth. Teresa declared:

> I am sometimes astonished at the harm which can be caused by bad company; if I had not experienced it I could not believe it. This is especially so when one is young, for it is then that the evil done is greatest. I wish parents would be warned by me and consider this very carefully. The result of my intercourse with this woman was to change me so much that I lost nearly all my soul's natural inclination to virtue, and was greatly influenced by her and by another person who indulged in the same kinds of pastime. From this I have learned what great advantage comes from good companionship; and I am sure that if at that age I had been friendly with good people I should have remained sound in virtue.[19]

Even though Teresa once said, "I do not think I had ever forsaken God by committing any mortal sin, or lost my fear of God, though I was more concerned about my honour,"[20] her parents might have prevented or lessened the spiritual harm inflicted on her by protecting her from her wicked cousin. As seen throughout this book, there are no perfect parents, except for the Blessed Mother and St. Joseph. In light of her own parents' great virtue and flaws, Teresa calls all fathers and mothers to be sacrificial lovers who often prove their love through tough love, yielding only to what is right and true rather than what is popular or what would make them well liked. One can never start too early to form virtue and to play off Teresa's aforementioned quote—the good done is greatest in one's youth.

Anna Velázquez

In the same century, across the Atlantic Ocean in Lima, Peru, around 1579, Anna Velázquez experienced one of the worst imaginable trials for any woman. The man she loved, who was the father of her

---

[19] Ibid., 70.
[20] Ibid.

children, left and never returned. When moments of great suffering arise, opportunities for heroic sacrifice also arise. Anna Velázquez, a freed slave from Panama, of African and possibly Native-American descent, fell in love with Don Juan de Porres, a Spanish nobleman. Their first child, named Martin, was born on December 9, 1579, and their second child, a daughter, Juana, in 1581. After Juana was born, Don Juan abandoned his mistress, Anna, and his young children. Consequently, Anna was forced to sacrifice for her family by taking on various jobs, such as washing other people's clothes, as the family became steeped in poverty. Eventually Anna sent Martin to a primary school for two years, and then to be an apprentice barber. Despite her limited resources, Anna singlehandedly raised one of Peru's greatest saints, St. Martin de Porres. Many single mothers can identify with the sorrow Anna experienced, i.e., to be forsaken by the very man to whom she gave her gift of virginity and become the object of his lust and pleasure. Anna's life confirms what Pope St. John Paul II wrote in his book *Love and Responsibility,* that the "opposite of love is use,"[21] though most people think it is hate.

Despite being used and persecuted for being of African descent, she and her son, Martin, chose to imitate Christ by loving their enemies. Anna's daily sacrificial love, whereby she laid down her life for her children by working menial jobs and enduring the scorn of racism, provided Martin with the most splendid example. Martin could have easily followed his father's poor example as a womanizer, but instead imitated his mother's valiant character. Martin, who became a Dominican lay brother, devoted his life to helping the sick and poor while bearing persecution from some members of his own religious order for being of mixed race. Like Our Lord, Our Lady, and his mother, Martin "came not to be served but to serve" (Mt. 20:28), which is the essence of sacrificial love.

Pope John XXIII, in his homily for the canonization of St. Martin de Porres on May 6, 1962, stated that Martin "loved men because he honestly looked on them as God's children and as his own brothers and sisters. Such was his humility that he loved them even more than himself and considered them to be better and

---

21   Wojtyła, *Love and Responsibility,* 28.

more righteous than he was."[22] Martin chose love over hatred and using others because his mother taught him to see God's image in every person.

Martin and Anna thus embodied the greatest test of love, spelled out by Our Lord, "But I say to you, love your enemies, and pray for those who persecute you" (Mt 5:44), and further, "For if you love those who love you, what reward have you?" (Mt 5:46). They testify that only Christ's love can sustain us when people let us down, even those nearest to us. In the face of Don Juan's departure, Anna, Martin, and Juana would eventually realize that "the LORD who goes before you; he will be with you; he will not fail you or forsake you; do not fear or be dismayed" (Dt 31:8).

Sts. Louis and Zélie Martin

The only way for parents to expect their children to live a life of heroic sacrifice is to model it themselves, as seen by St. Martin de Porres's mother. No less important than a priest laying down his life for his flock, or a soldier laying down his life for his country, is a father and mother laying down their lives for their children, especially in the face of tremendous adversity. In 1873, the year their future saint, Thérèse, was born, Louis and Zélie Martin faced an incredible challenge when their eldest child, thirteen-year-old Marie, came down with typhoid fever and was sent home from her boarding school due to her impending death. Louis responded by staying at his daughter's bedside day and night while his wife tended to her lace-making to financially support the family. Louis was not willing to surrender to his daughter's death just yet, as Zélie wrote in a letter to their second daughter, Pauline, who was at boarding school. Zélie confided, "Her father leaves this morning for Butte de Chaumont on a pilgrimage for Marie. He'll leave fasting and wants to return the same way. He insists on doing penance so that God will grant his prayer. He has to walk six leagues [14.5 miles] on foot."[23]

Due to the intercession of Our Lady, Marie eventually recovered, and the Martin family made a special visit to the local parish church

---

[22]   *The Liturgy of the Hours,* Volume IV, 1541.
[23]   Martin and Martin, *A Call to a Deeper Love,* 122.

in Alençon to give thanks to God. How incredible was Louis's
sacrifice and how bold was his faith! Six years before Louis trekked
several miles to seek a miracle for little Marie, their fifth child
and first newborn son, Joseph Martin, contracted a serious case of
bronchitis, which called for heroic sacrifice. To Zélie's dismay, little
Joseph was placed with a wet nurse as she was unable to breastfeed
him herself. With careful discernment, the Martins selected a peasant
woman named Rose Tallie, who lived in the country, six miles from
Alençon. Though the Martins wanted Rose to nurse in their own
home, she could not due to her own family. As Joseph's condition
was worsened by acute intestinal issues, Zélie would wake up each
morning at 5:00 a.m. and walk six miles one way, just to be able to
hold her suffering son for one hour. Zélie would then walk another
six miles, to be home at 8:00 so her husband could start his work.
She would repeat the same trek at 5:00 p.m. when Louis finished
his workday, and would spend most of the night with her sickly son
before departing for home. Some women run a marathon for the
sake of keeping their bodies toned or for the thrill of reaching the
goal of running 26.2 miles. Zélie's almost daily marathon was none
of the above, but one of complete sacrificial love.

Several years later, while walking home in the bitter cold
one January accompanied by her husband, who would not let her
go alone on this occasion, Zélie came upon a sight that further
confirmed her desire to sacrifice all for God and her family. Zélie
related, "Yesterday, while going with the doctor to see my little
Thérèse who is very sick, I noticed a beautiful château and some
magnificent properties. I said to myself that all of that is nothing.
We'll only be happy when all of us, we and our children, are reunited
in Heaven, and I offered up my child to God."[24]

When children are young, they cannot fully appreciate the
depths of their parents' sacrificial love, particularly their mothers'
self-forgetfulness and daily dying to self. Only years later, when
children become adults and have children themselves, can they fully
understand the depths of such love. A love that was willing to go
into labor, a love that was willing to change countless diapers, a

24   Ibid., 112–113.

love that was willing to spend sleepless nights with a sick child, a love that was willing to prepare meals and transport children to and from a myriad of activities, and a love that was willing to pray for her children more than herself. Céline wrote about such a love in her mini-biography, called *The Mother of the Little Flower*, which she completed on January 2, 1954, five years before her death and what would have been her sister St. Thérèse's eighty-first birthday. Céline fondly recalls her saintly mother's sacrificial love in the following words: "I myself can still remember her distinctly, preparing every morning an excellent breakfast for all in the house; whereas she was satisfied to snatch a little soup for herself which she swallowed hastily, as she was going about. Always the last to retire, around 11 p.m., she often rose at 5:30 a.m."[25]

In essence, Zélie represents all devoted mothers who daily put their husband and children before themselves, who sacrifice sleep and their own comforts to follow Our Lady in being "handmaids of the Lord."

In writing to her sister-in-law, Céline Guérin, on June 24, 1874, when Thérèse was seventeen months old, Zélie described how the little saint forced her to sacrifice even more. Zélie wrote:

> Thérèse is beginning to say everything. She's becoming cuter and cuter, but that's not a little problem, I assure you, because she's continually at my side, and it's difficult for me to work. So to make up for lost time, I work on my lace until ten o'clock at night and wake up at five o'clock in the morning. I still have to get up once or twice for the little one. Oh well, the more trouble I have the better I am![26]

At times, some mothers might feel like their vocation is insignificant, unappreciated, and even frustrating because they can never get anything done due to little children. Perhaps they might even wonder if their time would have been better served in a career, praying for hours in a convent before the Most Blessed Sacrament,

25 Martin, *The Mother of the Little Flower*, 30.
26 Martin and Martin, *A Call to a Deeper Love*, 150.

or serving the poor; but in God's eyes their vocation is foundational, for they are the heart of the family. Most mothers will never be fully repaid in this life by their family for their unseen labors of love, but then again no one can fully repay Christ for His love on the Cross. Though Zélie never became a nun as she once desired, she was an example of what a true vocation looks like to her daughters, i.e., one that leaves self behind and puts God and others first. Those whom Zélie put first, besides her husband, were her daughters: Marie Louise, who became Sr. Marie of the Sacred Heart; Marie Pauline, who became Mother Agnes; Marie Léonie, who became Sr. Françoise-Thérèse; Marie Céline, who became Sr. Geneviève of the Holy Face; and, last but not least, Marie Françoise-Thérèse, who became Sr. Thérèse of the Child Jesus and of the Holy Face. Without a doubt, Zélie was her daughters' first and greatest novice mistress. Thérèse learned what sanctity consisted of from her parents. She declared, "I understood that to become *a saint* one had to suffer much, seek out always the most perfect thing to do, and forget self. I understood, too, there were many degrees of perfection and each soul was free to respond to the advances of Our Lord, to do little or much for Him, in a word, to *choose* among the sacrifices He was asking."[27] Zélie revealed to Thérèse from a young age that there is no sanctity without forgetting oneself and embracing suffering, or better put in the words of Christ, "If any man would come after me, let him deny himself and take up his cross and follow me" (Mt 16:24).

Louis and Zélie were committed to sacrificial love, but this love was not without trouble or testing. Once Louis and Zélie had a small argument. When their seven-year-old daughter, Pauline, overheard their argument, she later approached her mother and said, "Is that what people mean, Mamma, by being unhappy together? Is that why people get 'divorces'?"[28] A surprised Zélie confided to her husband, "We have only too great reason, Louis dear, to watch ourselves very carefully. We have an example which we must set

27   St. Thérèse of Lisieux, *Story of A Soul*, 27.
28   Wust and Wust, *Zelie Martin: Mother of St. Thérèse*, 73.

for our children."[29] Just as parents are called to imitate Christ, in turn do little children learn to imitate Christ through their parent's example. A parent's holy or unholy example can either lead their children to sainthood or mediocrity. Louis and Zélie believed that sacrificial love is the mirror by which they would reflect firsthand to their children how much God loves them and what Christ's true sacrificial love on the Cross looks like. Likewise, parents who show selfishness, the antithesis of sacrificial love, become a mirror of Hell.

Louis and Zélie would not sacrifice their deeply committed beliefs to conform to the culture. Specifically, they ensured their children dressed modestly. Their daughter Céline once recalled, "[Zélie] was very exacting with regard to perfect modesty, and our dresses always reached below the knees."[30] Louis was also on the same page as his wife as Céline stated:

> He would never tolerate, either for himself or for anyone
> in the house, a careless appearance, or any lack of modesty
> in dress. We should not have dared, in his presence, to
> have had short-sleeved dresses, only just to the elbow.
> What would he say of the world today? All vulgar or slang
> words were rigidly forbidden.[31]

In the summertime, Louis would advise his girls not to look up in the windows of the passing houses to prevent seeing someone undressing. Louis and Zélie also made certain their children embraced the gender God made them. According to Céline:

> Sometime after the birth of Thérèse, all the girls played at
> dressing up for her baptism in the garden. The housemaid,
> Louise, got the idea of making me be a godfather and
> dressing me up as a little boy. I was then about four years
> old. The procession was under way when mother arrived
> and put a stop to the play-acting, while scolding Louise
> for the "masculine" exhibition.[32]

---

[29]　Ibid.
[30]　Martin, *The Mother of the Little Flower*, 12.
[31]　Ibid., 48.
[32]　Ibid., 12.

Zélie was countercultural in the nineteenth century and would be considered so today, when sadly many in our society, even some parents, are embracing a gender-fluid ideology. Also, unlike St. Teresa of Ávila's parents, Louis and Zélie closely supervised what books their children read. St. Thérèse recalled in her autobiography:

> I wasn't too good at playing games, but I did love reading very much and would have spent my life at it. I had human *angels*, fortunately for me, to guide me in the choice of books, which, while being entertaining, nourished both my heart and my mind. And I was not to go beyond a certain time in my reading, which was the cause of great sacrifices to me as I had to interrupt my reading very often at the most enticing passage. This attraction for reading lasted until my entrance into Carmel. To state the number of books that passed through my hands would be impossible, but never did God permit me to read a single one of them that was capable of doing me any harm.[33]

Louis and Zélie also guarded their children from vanity by being slow to compliment them on their physical appearances or let others follow suit. Thérèse detailed one time when, at around the age of six, she went to the Atlantic Ocean, which spoke to her "soul of God's grandeur and power"[34] and was less than twenty miles from her home in Lisieux. Thérèse recalled:

> I recall during the walk on the seashore a man and a woman were looking at me as I ran ahead of Papa. They came and asked him if I were his little daughter and said I was a very pretty little girl. Papa said, "Yes," but I noticed the sign he made to them not to pay me any compliments. It was the first time I'd heard it said I was pretty and this pleased me as I didn't think I was.[35]

In addition to making sure their children dressed modestly and understood that their value came from being a child of God and

---

[33] St. Thérèse of Lisieux, *Story of a Soul*, 71–72.
[34] Ibid., 48.
[35] Ibid.

not from their exterior beauty, Louis and Zélie never spoiled their children. In trying to comfort her brother, Isidore, who worried about his daughter Jeanne being "too lively,"[36] Zélie said, "I remember that Pauline was the same way until the age of two. I was very upset about it, and now, she's my best child. I must tell you that I didn't spoil her, and, as little as she was, I didn't let her get away with anything, yet without making a martyr out of her, but she had to obey."[37] At Thérèse's beatification process, her four older sisters gave this testimony: "We were never spoiled. Mother watched very carefully over the souls of her children; even the slightest fault was pointed out to be corrected. It was a kind and loving education, but always vigilant and careful."[38]

Louis and Zélie trained their children to be sacrificial versus being selfish and spoiled. Specifically, the Martins had a coin box for their children to put money in for the poor. The Martin children received money based on their behavior and good grades. They also set aside money for the Society for the Propagation of the Faith, which helped the missions. While the family was living in Alençon before Zélie passed away, some of the lower-class residents would visit their home for food and clothing. According to Céline, "Mother often shed tears when she heard their tales of distress."[39] Céline noted a few stories, which testify to their sacrificial love:

> One day while traveling, she [Zelie] reproved another lady in the railway carriage who showed displeasure at the arrival of a poor woman with her two babies. When they reached Alençon mother helped the women with her children and parcels to get her home. Father, who had been waiting at the station, also helped; and it was midnight before they reached their own home.[40]

On another occasion, for her daughter Léonie's First Communion, "mother selected a poor girl in her class, had her

---

[36] Martin and Martin, *A Call to a Deeper Love,* 49.
[37] Ibid.
[38] Martin, *The Mother of the Little Flower,* 29.
[39] Ibid.
[40] Ibid.

dressed in white also for her First Communion, and invited her to the place of honour at the festive dinner for the occasion."[41] Céline also witnessed her mother ask Thérèse to give alms to a poor old man as they walked in the fields following High Mass. The Martins then invited the man to their home for dinner, where they gave him shoes. Louis even helped him gain admittance to the Little Sisters of the Poor home in the future, where he could spend his final days on earth in dignity.

Before charity could be extended to their less fortunate brothers and sisters outside of their home, Louis and Zélie made sure that charity first reigned in their home. One occasion in particular stands out and shows how a saintly mother rears a saintly daughter. Before little Thérèse became St. Thérèse, she was the overly sensitive baby of the family. Once Thérèse was prevented from getting into a room. As a result, she blocked the door as she lay on the ground. Zélie responded by telling her to get up. When the young Thérèse decided to block the door the next day, Thérèse was told, "You hurt baby Jesus very much when you do that."[42] Thérèse desired to overcome her weaknesses from any early age, as Zélie had impressed upon her daughters that pleasing Jesus was the motivation behind every good action and avoiding every evil action. When Thérèse became impossible, Zélie would say, "I had to reason with Baby."[43] Above all, Zélie mixed firmness with gentleness. In the words of Céline, "Though mother corrected us for the least sign of defects, she also liked to see us cheerful and full of life."[44]

Louis and Zélie also sacrificed in order to send their two oldest daughters, Marie and Pauline, to a boarding school run by the Visitation nuns in Le Mans, where Zélie's older sister was a nun and a teacher. This boarding school was roughly thirty-five miles from the Martins' home in Alençon. Allegedly, it was Louis's decision to send his daughters away for schooling, not only because he trusted the girls' aunt, Sr. Mary Dorothy, to oversee their daughters' spiritual

41 Ibid.
42 Wust and Wust, *Zelie Martin,* 276.
43 Ibid.
44 Martin, *The Mother of the Little Flower,* 23.

welfare, but also because "his intention in this was to lessen the work of his wife, whose health had not ceased to make him anxious."[45] This was no easy sacrifice, especially for Zélie. She penned, "You can't imagine what it costs me to send them away, but we have to learn to make sacrifices for their happiness."[46]

Without the influence and financial assistance of Zélie's sister, the Martins would never have been able to send their daughters to this prestigious boarding school, as most students were from the upper class. Many parents today sacrifice for their children to attend Catholic schools by working two jobs, and still more rely on generous financial aid. Even though her daughters were away, Zélie remained active in their formation and wrote frequently to spur them on in virtue. Zélie penned the following, "My dear Pauline, continue to be a good girl, very gentle, and good towards everybody. You will be rewarded, even here below: 'Blessed are the meek, for they will inherit the earth.'"[47] While Zélie eventually became the breadwinner of the family due to the profitability of her lace-making business, she refused to allow her occupation to rule over her vocation. Instead, "she even willingly played with us, at the risk of having her own day's work prolonged to midnight or after,"[48] according to Céline. Zélie thus reveals that sacrificial love challenges us to always place our occupation at the service of our vocation.

In addition to sacrificing for their children, Sts. Louis and Zélie also sacrificed for their parents as they carried out the words of St. Paul, who declared, "And he died for all; that those who live might live no longer for themselves but for him who for their sake died and was raised" (2 Co 5:15). One of the greatest examples of sacrificial love occurred when Louis and Zélie cared for Zélie's seventy-year-old widowed father when they deemed that it was unsafe to allow him to live alone. Zélie dressed her father twice a day and attended to his needs while amazingly juggling the raising of four young children during the two blessed years that her father lived with them before

---

[45]   Piat, *The Story of a Family*, 84.

[46]   Martin and Martin, *A Call to a Deeper Love*, 64.

[47]   Ibid., 272.

[48]   Martin, *The Mother of the Little Flower*, 23.

passing away on September 3, 1868. Zélie described this opportunity for heroic sacrifice to her brother months before their father died:

> Don't worry, I'm constantly at his side; in other words, I never leave him. I'm the one who dresses his wound twice a day. I give him all that I think is best for him, but he has no appetite, and when it's necessary to make him take something, it's truly torture for him and for me. He can neither move himself nor sit up in his bed. My husband has to come help us, and if this continues, we'll need two men to lift him. We feel so deeply sorry for my poor dear father; he endures all with a great deal of patience.[49]

Louis and Zélie reflected a love that counts no cost, as in tending to their elderly father and father-in-law. True sacrificial love proves itself most through sheer persistence in the face of overwhelming adversity, as seen most visibly in the way of the Cross. One of the greatest tests for a father or mother is instilling virtue in an ornery child. For every Thérèse in the world, there is a Léonie, i.e., Thérèse's older sister who was a handful, to say the least. Zélie had hoped that sending Léonie to a boarding school taught by nuns would help reform her character. Sadly, Léonie persisted in her defiant behavior. Specifically, Léonie was expelled from school three times. According to her mother, "as soon as she found herself in their company [her classmates], she couldn't control herself and displayed a lack of discipline without equal."[50]

Zélie's sister, Sr. Mary Dorothy, who kept a close eye on Léonie while at the boarding school, once described Zélie's reaction to picking up Léonie after her dismissal. She wrote:

> I saw Zélie, she was quite resigned. She indeed thinks that when our children are not like the others, it's the parents' problem. But in the meantime, she doesn't know what to do so she's going to keep her at home. Her pain is great because she had so much confidence that the

---

49 Martin and Martin, *A Call to a Deeper Love*, 38.
50 Ibid., 148.

gentleness and kindness of the Visitation Monastery would change her daughter.[51]

What a reminder to parents that it is their primary duty to properly discipline and form their children rather than expect the school system, nuns and priests, government, and courts alone to instill character. Zélie's following words offer a most beautiful example of hope for any parent dealing with a difficult child:

> Finally, I believe that only a miracle could change her nature. It's true, I don't deserve a miracle, and yet I hope against all hope. The more I see her being difficult, the more I convince myself that God will not permit her to remain that way. I'll pray so much that He'll let Himself be swayed. At the age of eighteen months she was cured of an illness that could have killed her. Why would God have saved her from death and not plan to show her mercy?[52]

Ironically, Léonie sought to enter the convent three times, but either left or was dismissed. It was on the fourth attempt that she obtained entrance at the Visitation Order at thirty-six years old, where she persevered until her death. At the young age of eleven, the "difficult child" Léonie once told her mother that she would become a nun at the Visitation monastery alongside her aunt. Zélie declared, "God willing, this will be so, but it's too beautiful, and I don't dare hope for it."[53]

After being expelled from school, Zélie decided to homeschool Léonie and never gave up on her despite having some reservations. After all, Léonie craved attention partly because she felt that she was not as pretty, smart, or loved as her sisters. Zélie once declared:

> I'm not dissatisfied with my Léonie. If we could manage to triumph over her stubbornness and make her more cooperative, we could make her a good girl, devoted and not afraid of difficulty. She has a will of iron, and she

---

[51] Martin and Martin, *A Call to a Deeper Love*, 148.
[52] Ibid.
[53] Ibid., 141.

wants something, she overcomes every obstacle to get
what she wants.[54]

Zélie also found praying with Léonie to be a struggle. For
instance, Zélie wrote:

> But she's not at all devout. She prays to God only when she
> can't do otherwise. This afternoon I made her come by my
> side and read some prayers. But soon she'd had enough and
> said to me, "Mamma, tell me the life of Our Lord Jesus
> Christ." I wasn't sure I wanted to tell the story because it
> tires me out a lot, and I always have a sore throat. Finally, I
> made the effort, and I told her the life of Our Lord. When
> I arrived at the Passion, she was overcome with tears. It
> made me happy to see her have these feelings.[55]

Regardless, Zélie never lost hope in Léonie, as seen in the
following statement: "I find myself hoping that perhaps God has
merciful plans for this child. If it only took the sacrifice of my life for
her to become a saint, I would give it willingly."[56] Little did Zélie
realize at the time, but those words are coming to fulfillment as
Léonie's cause for beatification and canonization have been opened.

Despite tremendous emotional and physical suffering from
raising Léonie as well as battling cancer, Zélie maintained her sense
of humor, for joy kept her and her family's spirits alive despite her
current struggles. While visiting her older sister and her best friend for
the last time as the forty-seven-year-old Visitation nun was dying of
tuberculosis, Zélie had some important requests for Sr. Mary Dorothy
to take with her to Heaven once God welcomed her into His courts:

> The moment you're in Heaven, go and find the Blessed
> Mother and tell her, "My good Mother, you played a joke
> on my sister by giving her poor Leonie. She's not a child
> like the one she asked you for, and you must fix it."
> Then, go and find Blessed Margaret Mary and tell
> her, "Why did you miraculously cure her? It would have

54 Ibid., 188.
55 Ibid.
56 Ibid., 274.

been much better to let her die, and you are by conscience to repair this misfortune."[57]

In response to these words, Sr. Mary Dorothy "scolded" Zélie. Yet Zélie wrote, "I didn't have any bad intentions, and God knows this very well. It doesn't matter, perhaps I did something wrong, and for my punishment, I'm afraid of not having my request granted."[58] Many people might be scandalized by Zélie's words; however, Zélie did not want to see her daughter Léonie end up in Hell, and thus she questioned St. Margaret Mary's miraculous intervention, which physically cured Léonie as a young girl, but not spiritually. Our Lady and St. Margaret Mary must have heard Sr. Mary Dorothy's requests after she died, because Zélie wrote to Pauline:

> I'd tried everything in my power to draw her (Léonie) to me. It had all failed until today, and that was the greatest sorrow I'd ever had in my life.
>
> Since your aunt died I've begged her to return this poor child's heart to me, and Sunday morning my prayer was answered. Now I have her heart as completely as possible: she doesn't want to leave me for a moment, she hugs me to the point of suffocating me, does everything I tell her without arguing, and works by my side all day long.[59]

Like St. Monica, Zélie is a model for all mothers faced with a difficult son or daughter because she never gave up and stormed Heaven with her prayers and tears. Zélie would join her sister in Heaven only six months later, at the young age of forty-five. Zélie was only two years younger than her sister. But Léonie's noncompliant character was not her fault. Shockingly, it was later discovered that one of the Martins' maidservants, Louise Marais, had secretly manipulated Léonie through physical and emotional abuse. Only after Marie had the courage to notify her mother of Louise's malicious behavior did Zélie take action. Zélie wrote:

---

57   Ibid., 270.
58   Ibid.
59   Ibid., 294.

The maid completely lost her authority, and it's certain
that she'll never again have any influence over Léonic by
the way in which things happened. She found it a severe
blow, and she cried and moaned when I told her to leave
immediately and that I wanted her out of my sight.
I'm going to wait some time before I make her
leave because she begged me so much to stay, but she's
forbidden to direct a word to Léonie. Now, I treat this
child with so much gentleness that I hope to succeed,
little by little, in correcting her faults.[60]

While being held as the epitome of a holy wife and mother,
Zélie was clearly naïve to Léonie's abuse, as was her husband, Louis.
Zélie regretted her oversight and wrote, "Before, it was impossible
for me to take her anywhere without causing a scene. She never
played with her sisters, which surprised me very much. How blind I
was! I didn't notice that she was spellbound by the maid, and I could
have no influence over her."[61] Even the holiest parents can make
mistakes, as seen throughout this book.

Zélie quickly repented and moved on with God's grace. Louis
and Zélie's failure to protect their daughter in this instance reveals
the necessity for parents to be vigilant over their children's lives,
along with being approachable, so that their children are comfortable
sharing anything with them. To Louis and Zélie's credit, they
safeguarded not only their children's purity, but also protected them
from unholy companions. According to Céline, "Mamma carefully
watched over us, and kept away from us even the shadow of evil."[62]
Specifically, Céline related:

> One day, a girl older than any of us came to share in
> our games. Mother noticed her undue familiarities
> and her mysterious whisperings. She called me, and in
> the presence of the other girl, warned me against such
> secretive and out of place manners. To remove all danger
> or suspicion she sent the girl home. Let me add this

[60] Ibid.
[61] Ibid., 300.
[62] Martin, *The Mother of the Little Flower*, 12.

detail: this girl profited by the lesson, and later entered a
religious community.[63]

Louis and Zélie thus avoided the pitfall of St. Teresa of Ávila's
parents, who had failed to protect their daughter from unholy
companions, and, as Teresa declared, "Much harm may result from
bad company."[64] However, if two literally saintly parents such as
Louis and Zélie can be blind to such an evil as abuse, then how much
more must we watch our children, not as overly controlling and
paranoid parents, but rather as a father and mother, who are radically
in touch with every facet of their children's lives—their friends, their
schools, etc. It did not help that Louis and Zélie ran a company full
time, which included overseeing employees on top of taking care
of their children. In terms of their maid Louise's manipulation and
control, which characterizes some parenting styles, Zélie was clear:
"Brutality never converted anyone, it only makes slaves of people,
and that's what happened to this poor child."[65] Sadly, Zélie knew
this firsthand from her own mother's parenting style.

Zélie also sacrificed greatly for her family via her lace-making
business, which proved highly profitable and enabled her husband
to sell his watchmaking business to assist his wife. Zélie worked for
the sole purpose of securing a dowry for her daughters' futures, and
it was "not the desire to amass a great fortune that drives me."[66]
Ironically, none of her daughters would get married. Fortunately,
Zélie did work from home. Still, she felt conflicted by finding a
balance between her tedious work, being a mother, and growing
in spiritual perfection. At times, Zélie felt like a slave to her work,
especially when there were many orders. She would have loved to
take care of her children full time, as she relayed to her sister-in-
law: "But it's such sweet work to take care of little children! If I only
had that to do, it seems to me I'd be the happiest of women. But
it's quite necessary that their father and I work to earn money for

---

[63]   Ibid.
[64]   St. Teresa of Ávila, *The Life of Teresa of Jesus: The Autobiography of Teresa of
       Avila*, 69.
[65]   Martin and Martin, *A Call to a Deeper Love*, 298.
[66]   Ibid., 214.

their dowries. Otherwise, when they're grown, they won't be very happy with us."[67] Zélie further wrote, "If I were alone and had to endure all over again what I've suffered these last twenty-four years, I would prefer to die of hunger, because just the thought of it makes me tremble! I often tell myself that if I'd done half of all this to win Heaven, I could be a canonized saint!"[68]

During her most trying days, Zélie sometimes experienced moments of desolation, when she longed to escape from the crosses and sacrifices of married life for religious life. As Zélie wrote:

> I often think of my holy sister, of her calm and tranquil life. She works, to be sure, not to earn a perishable wealth; she only stores up treasures for Heaven, toward which all her longings go. And me, I see myself here, bent toward the earth, going to trouble to accumulate gold that I can't take with me and that I have no desire to take. What would I do with it up above!
>
> Sometimes, I find myself regretting that I haven't done as she did, but quickly I tell myself, "I wouldn't have my four little girls, my charming little Joseph. . . ." No. It's better that I struggle where I am and that they are here. As long as I reach Heaven with my dear Louis, and see them all there far better placed than I, I will be happy enough like this. I don't ask for anything more.[69]

Zélie checked this temptation by realizing that the greatest struggles and occasions for sacrifice and sanctity were right in front of her eyes and not in some distant convent. Zélie became a saint precisely because she consistently put her children and husband's happiness before her desire for comfort.

One of the most profound examples of sacrificial love came after Zélie passed away. Having to raise five daughters from the ages of four to seventeen while still in his early fifties, Louis faced one of the greatest decisions: whether to place his children in a boarding school as prompted by his spiritual director, or move his family sixty miles away

[67] Ibid.
[68] Ibid.
[69] Ibid., 25.

from their hometown of Alençon to be near his brother-in-law, Isidore Guérin, Zélie's younger brother, and his wife and three children in Lisieux. Rather than make a rash decision, Louis sought the advice of his older daughters, who would be leaving behind their friends. Louis asked them, "For it is solely on your account I am making this sacrifice, and I do not wish to impose a sacrifice on you."[70] The Martins decided to move to Lisieux. Years afterward, Louis explained to Céline the real reason why he left Alençon despite many friends urging him to stay. Specifically, Louis moved his family to Lisieux "to take us away from influences that he considered too worldly among some of his friends, and from the liberal ideas of others."[71] Céline responded, "How grateful we should be to him for a decision so wise and so disinterested!"[72] Only a father who truly loves his children is willing to risk the familiarity of his homeland and friends and move somewhere unfamiliar to protect their immortal souls.

More than keeping his children from the occasion of sin, Louis led his children to a love affair with God. Céline related, "At home our education had piety as its chief lever. There was a complete liturgy of household life: evening prayers all together, Month of May Devotions, Sunday Offices, spiritual reading before the Feasts, etc. Our father aided as much as he could the development of the spiritual life."[73] Though Louis raised his five children in a very strict manner, he also avoided running his household like a military institution or an austere monastery. On the contrary, Louis gave his daughters the freedom to make decisions around the house. According to Céline, "If we had forgotten something, or made some mistake, he seemed to take no notice of it, in order not to make us nervous or timid, according to the recommendations of St. Paul."[74] Louis desired to be a purer reflection of the Heavenly Father by allowing his daughters to grow in confidence rather than have them believe the lie that they must be perfect in order for God to love them.

---

[70] Martin, *The Father of the Little Flower*, 42.
[71] Ibid., 43.
[72] Ibid.
[73] Ibid., 47.
[74] Ibid., 50.

Hence, Lisieux became the ideal setting for the Martin daughters to grow in virtue, away from the secular influences of Alençon. It was only a matter of time before Louis would offer his first of many sacrifices following the death of his beloved wife. As a widower at the age of fifty-four, Louis singlehandedly raised his five daughters. Seeing his first two daughters leave for the convent brought tremendous joy, but also pain. As mentioned earlier, many biographers of the saints can easily gloss over the dark moments of these individuals' lives. While we love to idealize the saints as superheroes, the reality is that they were human, and the more they loved God, the more they loved their families, and, hence, the greater the pain when a loved one was separated either through death or the duties of their vocation. Having said goodbye to his second oldest daughter, Pauline, who became a Carmelite nun in Lisieux a few years earlier, Louis faced the heartbreak of parting ways from another daughter. This time, Louis's eldest daughter, Marie, who was adamantly opposed to religious life most of her life, would follow in Pauline's footsteps. In fact, Zélie once said about Marie, "Here is Marie who dreams of going to live in a beautiful house on the rue de la Demi-Lune across from the Monastery of the Poor Clares. Yesterday she talked about this all evening and you would have thought it was Heaven!"[75]

Upon hearing the news of her entrance into Carmel, Louis sighed, according to Marie, and spoke these words, "Ah! Ah! but without you . . ."[76] As he hugged Marie, Louis further stated, "I thought that you would never leave me!"[77] After all, this was Louis's beloved firstborn child. According to Céline, "In the depths of his soul he was proud of her vocation."[78]

In addition to Marie and Pauline, Léonie and Thérèse also entered religious life as their parents' sacrificial love paved the way for them to freely and courageously follow God's will. Thérèse vividly recalled the tension of revealing her religious calling to her father

75 Martin and Martin, *A Call to a Deeper Love*, 210.
76 Martin, *The Father of the Little Flower*, 61.
77 Ibid.
78 Ibid.

for the first time. It is a moment only few in this life will experience, which often comes with either acceptance or disappointment from one's parents. Thérèse recalled:

> I didn't know what steps to take to announce it to Papa. How should I speak to him about parting from his Queen, he who'd just sacrificed his three eldest? Ah! what interior struggles I went through before feeling courageous enough to speak! However, I had to decide. . . .
>
> Without saying a word, I sat down by his side, my eyes already wet with tears. He gazed at me tenderly, and taking my head he placed it on his heart, saying: "What's the matter, my little Queen? Tell me. . . ."
>
> Through my tears, I confided my desire to enter Carmel and soon his tears mingled with mine. He didn't say one word to turn me from my vocation, simply contenting himself with the statement that I was still very young to make such a serious decision. I defended myself so well that, with Papa's simple and direct character, he was soon convinced my desire was God's will, and in his deep faith he cried out that God was giving him a great honor in asking his children from him; we continued our walk for a long time and, encouraged by the kindness with which my incomparable Father received my confidences, my heart poured out itself to him.
>
> Papa seemed to be rejoicing with that joy that comes from a sacrifice already made. He spoke just like a saint, and I'd love to recall his words and write them down, but all I preserved of them is a memory too sacred to be expressed.[79]

By supporting Thérèse's desire to enter Carmel, Louis reveals his deep love for her and his obedience to God.

When his seventh child and last daughter, Céline, informed Louis that she too wanted to enter religious life after he passed away, Louis was initially taken aback. Louis intended to support his nineteen-year-old-daughter's art career by sending her to Paris if she acquiesced. Louis responded by saying, "Come, Céline, let us

---

[79] St. Thérèse of Lisieux, *Story of a Soul*, 107–108.

go together before the Blessed Sacrament to thank the Lord for all the graces He has granted to our family, and for the honour He has done me in choosing spouses in my home."[80] Louis further declared, "You can all leave. I will be happy to give you to God before I die. In my old age, a bare cell will be enough for me."[81] Louis's words convey a heart of sacrifice, detachment, and simplicity. Most of all, Louis not only supported his daughters' vocation, but also advocated for them. For example, Louis along with Céline accompanied and encouraged fifteen-year-old Thérèse when she sought early entrance into Carmel as they visited the bishop and, later, Pope Leo XIII. When standing before the Holy Father himself, Louis could easily have been embarrassed, allowing such a young child to beg for something that many believed she was too young for. However, Louis was more intent about his daughter doing God's will than the fear of human respect or above all not having his "little Queen," as he liked to call her, by his side. Louis wrote the day after his baby girl entered Carmel to a friend, "Thérèse, my little Queen, entered Carmel yesterday! God alone can exact such a sacrifice; but He helps me so mightily, that in the midst of my tears my heart overflows with joy."[82]

Despite living in the same town as his Carmelite daughters, Louis would only see them periodically. Yet Thérèse's letters kept his spirits high. Thérèse once wrote beautifully to her father:

> I think of all you used to say to us frequently: "Vanity of vanities, all is vanity, vanity of life which passes, etc. . . ." The more I live the more I find this is true, that all is vanity on this earth. When I think of you, dear little Father, I naturally think of God, for it seems to me that it is impossible to see anyone more holy than you on the earth.[83]

---

[80] Martin, *The Father of the Little Flower*, 75.
[81] Piat, *Celine*, 35.
[82] Martin, *The Father of the Little Flower*, 150.
[83] St. Thérèse of Lisieux, *General Correspondence*, Volume I, 432.

While the cloistered walls separated Thérèse and many of the saints from their parents, their love for each other and longing to be reunited in Heaven only increased.

Our Lord made it very clear to His Apostles that their sacrifices would not go unrewarded: "And every one who has left houses or brothers or sisters or father or mother or children or lands, for my name's sake, will receive a hundredfold, and inherit eternal life" (Mt 19:29). Thérèse offers a unique insight on this Gospel passage when she wrote to her married first cousin, Jeanne Guérin, in 1895, a year after Louis passed away, "I know that usually these words are applied to religious souls, however, I feel in the depths of my heart that they were spoken for the generous parents who make the sacrifice of children dearer to them than they are to themselves."[84] And while Thérèse and her four sisters made a great sacrifice by renouncing marriage and children, we must not forget her saintly parents, who made a similar sacrifice in offering their daughters to God.

Stanislaus and Marianna Kowalska

Unlike St. Louis Martin, who allowed his children to freely leave for the convent, one saint, born nearly thirty-two years after Thérèse, failed to receive her parents' blessings to enter religious life. Her parents were not willing to let go of their favorite child. Some sacrifices are just too difficult. The events took place around the year 1823, though the seeds were planted well before, when this saint at the young age of seven heard "God's voice in [her] soul; that is, an invitation to a more perfect life."[85] At the age of eighteen, Helen Kowalska, who later became Sr. Faustina, asked her parents' permission to enter religious life. In Faustina's words:

> The eighteenth year of my life. An earnest appeal to my parents for permission to enter the convent. My parents' flat refusal. After this refusal, I turned myself over to the vain things of life, paying no attention to the call of grace, although my soul found no satisfaction in any of these things. The incessant call of grace caused

---

[84] St. Thérèse of Lisieux, *General Correspondence*, Volume II, 916.
[85] St. Faustina, *Diary: Divine Mercy in My Soul*, 6.

me much anguish; I tried, however, to stifle it with amusements. Interiorly, I shunned God, turning with all my heart to my creatures. However, God's grace won out in my soul.[86]

While attending a dance shortly after, Our Lord appeared to her "racked with pain, stripped of His clothing, all covered with wounds, who spoke these words to me: **How long shall I put up with you and how long will you keep putting Me off?**"[87] Taking only one dress, Helen left home immediately without saying goodbye to her parents, instructing her sister to say goodbye on her behalf. The late Sr. Sophia Michalenko, CMGT, in her book *The Life of Faustina Kowalska*, described the battle between sacrifice and selfishness present in the heart of even some of the holiest parents.

> Helen first broke the news to her mother. "Mother, I must enter the convent." Both parents refused to pay any attention to her pleas. Her father gave the excuse, "I have no money for a dowry [the money and wardrobe expected of a person entering religious life] and I still have many unpaid bills." "Daddy, I don't need any money," she replied. "Jesus himself will lead me to a convent." But the parents, overly attached to this favorite daughter, remained firm in their refusal to allow her to enter the convent.[88]

Later, it was noted that Helen eventually left for Warsaw to enter the convent after working as a housemaid for some time. She left with only the clothes on her back like Our Lord said: "Take nothing for your journey" (Lk 9:3). Her uncle took her to the train station. Once inside the train, Helen shed many tears. "Mother will say I ran away from home when she finds out about this, she sighed. It made her sad, for she knew that her action would hurt her parents, but she felt more deeply the need to be obedient to Him whom she had come to love so much ever since the time she was a small child of seven."[89]

---

[86] Ibid.
[87] Ibid., 7.
[88] Michelenko, *The Life of Faustina Kowalska*, 20–21.
[89] Ibid., 24.

Faustina's parents were still unable to surrender their daughter to God and tried one last time to dissuade her from religious life by sending their eldest daughter, Genevieve, in their stead to convince her to return home. All things considered, they at least had the decency not to kidnap her like St. Thomas Aquinas's parents did with him. "After spending the night in Warsaw, Genevieve returned home to Głogowiec. It was a sad moment for her parents when they saw her returning home without Helen."[90]

Other research indicates that the parish priest at the time encouraged Faustina's parents to sell their family cow, which would have provided the dowry and postulant's wardrobe necessary for her to enter religious life. In fact, many orders at the time refused to accept women from the lowest social class as well as those without a dowry or formal education. Faustina's father said that it would be impossible to sell the cow because it was needed to pull the plow and, hence, support their family. On top of this, the family needed Faustina's income to help with her five younger siblings. Allegedly, after Faustina's death, one of the nuns from her convent asked her parents why they didn't want her to join the convent. After all, the Kowalskas had eight living children at the time, six of whom were daughters. Sr Wilczek asked Faustina's mother why "was she so stingy with the Lord God? With so many daughters, why did she not want to give that sole one to a convent?"[91] According to Faustina's mother, Marianna, it was "because she was the best child, the dearest . . . and so obedient and hardworking. The most loving."[92] Additionally, Faustina's parents were hoping that she would stick around to take care of them in their old age. Even though parents should not have favorites, Faustina, like Thérèse, was her father's favorite. Faustina was the only child who knew where her father's shotgun was in emergencies—not even the eldest daughter or sons knew. According to Faustina's brother, Stanislaus Jr., "We didn't envy her [Faustina] for having won our father's heart, because we

---

[90] Ibid., 27.
[91] Czaczkowska, *Faustina*, 69.
[92] Ibid.

knew that was only fair."[93] Faustina used to say to her siblings, "Be obedient, too, and Father will love you just as much."[94] At the same time, Faustina's joyful disposition and hard work ethic made her very pleasing to her parents. Faustina eventually entered the Congregation of the Sisters of Our Lady of Mercy on August 1, 1925, just twenty-four days shy of her twentieth birthday. Surprisingly, Faustina was turned down by a few orders prior to joining the Congregation, for "she had neither a dowry nor an education to offer. From a material point of view, she had nothing to contribute to a congregation"[95] and was nearly rejected by her own order. The Congregation accepted Faustina under the condition that she wait a year to earn enough money to pay for her wardrobe. Thanks be to God, her superiors looked beyond her physical appearance and recognized something deeper in her, particularly her smile and simplicity. On April 30, 1926, less than one year after entering the convent, Helen became a novice, taking the name Faustina. Sadly, no one from Faustina's family came to the investiture, though invitations had been sent out. There is speculation that Faustina's parents had not yet come to grips with her decision to become a nun. On April 30, 1928, two years later, Faustina professed her first vows. This time Stanislaus and Marianna attended, and they would see their daughter for the first time in four years. As they were walking in the garden, Stanislaus asked his daughter, "My child, don't you feel bored here?"[96] According to family tradition, Faustina responded that boredom was far from the case while living "under the same roof as the Lord Jesus."[97] This time there was no trying to persuade Faustina to come home, though in the back of their minds, I am sure they would have welcomed her with open arms had she left the convent. Instead, Stanislaus remarked, "We have to leave her here. This is the will of God."[98]

---

[93]   Ibid., 38.
[94]   Ibid.
[95]   Ibid., 84.
[96]   Ibid., 151.
[97]   Ibid.
[98]   Ibid.

While Faustina's parents resisted God's will in terms of Faustina's vocation, God's grace filled up what was lacking as they became models in other areas, such as solitude and simplicity. Eventually, Faustina's parents came to embrace their daughter's vocation, as evidenced by attending her first vows and even offering their blessing during her home visit. After Faustina's one and only visit home in 1935, which would be the last time Faustina's parents would see their daughter alive, many emotions filled Faustina as she departed from her family. She would die three years later, but no one dared imagine this would be their last meeting. Faustina recalled, "My father, my mother, and my godmother blessed me with tears in their eyes, wished me the greatest faithfulness to God's graces, and begged me never to forget how many graces God had granted me in calling me to the religious life."[99] Faustina recalled her emotions: "I did not shed a single tear; I tried to be brave and comforted them as best I could, reminding them of heaven where there would be no more parting."[100] Eventually, Faustina's toughness yielded to tears upon entering the car, as she described, "I let my heart have its way, and I, too, cried like a baby for joy that God was granting our family so many graces, and I became steeped in a prayer of thanksgiving."[101] Imagine only seeing your daughter twice in seven years. Such was the sacrifice of Stanislaus and Marianna.

It is also appropriate to describe Faustina's parent's personalities, which helped form their future saint. According to their son Miecislaus, "He [Stanislaus] was severe, unyielding and demanding of everyone at home."[102] Stanislaus Jr. recalls a "spanking that his father gave him for tearing slender birch branches from the neighbor's tree."[103] On the other hand, "[Marianna] was resourceful and hardworking, strong-willed, devoted to her family"[104] and a gentler personality than her husband. Marianna sacrificed daily by serving her husband and children to her best ability. For instance,

---

[99] St. Faustina, *Diary: Divine Mercy in My Soul*, 180.

[100] Ibid.

[101] Ibid., 180.

[102] Czaczkowska, *Faustina*, 36.

[103] Ibid.

[104] Ibid.

Marianna would daily bring her husband a hot meal while he labored on their property. The Kowalska children were also expected to assist around the property by taking the cows out to the pasture, helping with smaller children, and tending to the fields. A sacrificial lifestyle was not an expectation for the Kowalska household, but a necessity, which was visibly communicated by Stanislaus and Marianna's love for each other and their children. Despite their shortcomings in preventing their daughter's vocation, Stanislaus and Marianna ingrained virtue in their children, as seen in the following story. On one occasion, Faustina and her sister Josephine returned home late from a dance accompanied by a gentleman, whom Stanislaus did not seem too fond of. Stanislaus reprimanded Faustina for the first time in her life when he declared to her and her sister, "Is this how I raised you, so you would bring shame and disgrace onto my house?"[105] From this moment, Faustina told her sister that she would "never bring shame on her Father again, but would try hard so as to give him a good reputation and solace, and not disgrace."[106] And that she did by becoming one of the greatest saints.

Julius and Maria Kolbe

In honor of St. Maximilian Kolbe's heroic martyrdom, the Church has appropriately selected the following Gospel to be read on his August 14 feast day: "Greater love has no man than this, that a man lay down his life for his friends" (Jn 15:13). Prior to Maximilian offering his life in the place of the married husband and father, Franciszek Gajowniczek, his parents manifested this Gospel passage on a daily basis. Both Julius and Maria were Third Order Franciscans and worked as weavers. Julius would later open a religious bookstore. Julius eventually joined the Polish legions at the start of World War I to fight for Polish independence from Russia. Sadly, his unit was captured, and he was killed when his saintly son was only twenty-two years old. Julius represents the millions of heroic men and

---

[105] Ibid., 44.
[106] Ibid.

women who have and will continue to lay down their lives for their country for the sake of religious and political freedom.

Like her husband, Maria lived a life of heroic sacrifice. When not attending to her three sons or weaving, Maria acted as a nurse and midwife, which she did gratuitously for many poor tenants of the surrounding area. One firsthand account is worth mentioning. Bronsislava Klys Krakowska recalls one day when Maria helped save her mother's life. After ten hours of unconsciousness after the birth of Bronsislava's younger sibling, her mother, the doctor told Bronsislava, could not be saved. All intervention had been exhausted, and the mother's and baby's lives were hanging by a thread until Maria stepped into the house. Maria remained at the mother's bedside from early evening until well into the night, pleading for God to spare this woman and her child. When medicine could not intervene, it became apparent that "with God all things are possible" (Mt 19:26), as Christ so beautifully reminds His followers. God heard Maria's prayers and the lady awoke.

From a young age, Maximilian learned from his parents that a secret to sanctity is forgetting oneself. Maria's entire life was one of service, even after she resided at the convent. Maria became a mother to many of the postulants, some of whom decided to stay at the convent because of her nurturing heart. On one occasion, Sr. Mary Praxeda was feeling "lost and abandoned"[107] as a young postulant, miles away from her family, until she was assigned to work with Maria cutting communion wafers. Sr. Mary Praxeda recalled the heart of this saintly mother:

> As I walked toward the work area, with a very slow pace, I thought my heart would break, but I tried to smile. Mrs. Kolbe sensed my apprehension and fears. "Child," she emphasized, "God singled you out from among many others." We were alone, she held me close and my "saved-up" tears dried on her special white apron. I listened to her heart beat and she held me, and I listened to her words

---

[107] Zdrojewski, *To Weave a Garment*, 69.

of encouragement to pray, to stay, to serve God because it was His will.[108]

On another occasion, a postulant named Victoria was going to be dismissed from the convent due to a skin infection that needed daily treatment. Maria accompanied her to the doctors and finally encouraged her to beseech the Mother of God, while assuring her of her own prayers. Victoria would become Sr. Mary Sulpicia and credits the intercession of Our Lady and Maria's prayers, which helped clear up her infection within days. Maria sacrificed her time and prayers to help others realize their vocation, especially the young sisters who came to her convent. Maria's sacrificial love was shown most clearly during World War II, as she extended a helping hand, prayers, and a warm bowl of soup to her brothers and sisters in Christ who appeared at the convent door. It must be noted that Fr. Ignacy Podsadcy, Superior General of the Society of Christ, attested to Maria saving his life several times by secretly hiding him behind their convent walls and forewarning him when the Nazis came looking for him. Sadly, one third of Polish priests were murdered during the war. Julius and Maria's sacrificial love clearly paved the way for their son, Maximilian, to freely offer his life for a married man. He learned from his parents that following Christ involves a willingness to risk everything for the love of God—even one's life.

Grazio and Maria Forgione

St. Maximilian Kolbe witnessed his parents' sacrificial love for God, family, and country, which in turn set the bar for his heroic sacrifice. This was also the case in the life of St. Padre Pio, who was blessed by God with two virtuous parents. Born six years before his Franciscan brother, Maximilian Kolbe, Padre Pio may never have been ordained a priest had his father not made a risky but noble sacrifice. With only three years of public education and facing economic hardship, a young Francesco Forgione needed more schooling to be admitted into the Capuchin Order and fulfill his vocation as a religious priest. To help his son's dreams come true, Padre Pio's

108 Ibid., 69–70.

father, Grazio, emigrated to the United States from approximately 1899 to 1903 to earn money so that his son could receive a private tutor. This was not his first trip across the ocean. The previous year he had sailed from Naples to Brazil, but this endeavor failed miserably due to a misrepresentation of employment, which forced Grazio to pay for his way back to Italy. Nearly one third of the men of Pietrelcina were employed overseas. During Grazio's first stint in the United States, he worked in Mahoningtown, Pennsylvania. While in America, he was a laborer on the Myers Farm and worked his way up to foreman. Each week, Grazio would send his family a check along with a dictated letter, as he could neither read nor write. Interestingly, Padre Pio was the only one in the family who knew how to write. Despite the distance, Grazio still exerted his fatherly influence through these letters. He even convinced his wife to have Pio switch schools from one that was run by an ex-priest and lacked sound formation. Grazio emigrated to the United States a second time from approximately 1908 to 1910. One Ellis Island record showed that he arrived in America on April 12, 1910, via the ship *Berlin* from Naples. He was employed on a farm in Queens and in Jamaica, Long Island, where he worked with a pick and shovel on the Erie Railroad. His oldest son, Michele, joined him in New York.

Due to his father's sacrificial love, Francesco Forgione entered the Capuchin Order at the age of fifteen and never looked back, taking the name Pio in honor of Pope St. Pius V, his hometown's patron. While the name Grazio Forgione remains unnoticed and forgotten, his son Padre Pio is one of the Catholic Church's most revered saints and modern-day mystics. Though not canonized, Grazio Forgione could be considered the unofficial patron saint of the Serra Club, those who help promote and financially support priestly and religious vocations. More than anything, Padre Pio's father reveals that no sacrifice is too great to help your son or daughter fulfill their vocation. Grazio's sacrificial nature, which caused him to be temporarily separated from his family and endure several long trips by ship across the Atlantic Ocean, was clearly passed on to his son, Padre Pio, who likewise sacrificed for souls. Even later in life, Padre Pio would never forget his father's heroism.

He would say, "My father crossed the ocean twice so that I could become a monk."[109] Because of World War I, Grazio was unable to attend his son's ordination, which certainly was a great sorrow, but at the same time a great joy . . . for his sacrifice had borne fruit.

Because of Grazio's hard work, he not only paid for Pio's education and helped him reach his vocation, but also enabled his family to purchase two additional buildings and some livestock. At the same time, we must not forget the sacrifice of Padre Pio's mother, Maria, who raised the children by herself while being deprived of her husband while he was away. Marriage is clearly a joint effort in which both spouses sacrifice for the good of their family.

Alberto and Maria Beretta

As Grazio and Maria Forgione paved the way for their son Padre Pio, so too did Alberto and Maria Beretta set forth a legacy of sacrificial love for their daughter St. Gianna Beretta Molla, who was born in 1922, thirty-five years after the holy Capuchin confessor. The Berettas' sacrificial love flowed from the Holy Eucharist. Giuseppe Beretta, the older brother of Gianna, described their father and his authentic love, which permeated the family:

> It was supper time, and everything was ready. After a short prayer, we sat down happily at that long table. How beautiful it is for so many children to be around their parents! He liked to hear a little from everyone about how school had gone, and when some peccadillo surfaced, he frowned to make us understand without saying anything that it should not happen again.[110]

After a long day at work, which began with 5:00 a.m. Mass, Alberto realized his real vocation began when he returned home. Based on his son's account, Alberto was radically present to his wife and children's lives, which would be very countercultural today. For instance, studies have found that parents spend more time

109 Rega, *Padre Pio and America*, 10.
110 Molla and Guerriero, *Saint Gianna Molla*, 25.

watching television and cleaning around the house than talking with their children.

Besides taking the time to hear about his children's day, Alberto disciplined his children by showing disapproval for any less than virtuous actions. Alberto reveals that a father's main role is to help his children get to Heaven by helping them grow in virtue through daily conversion. As the profound words from Proverbs states, "My son, do not despise the LORD's discipline or be weary of his reproof, for the LORD reproves him whom he loves, as a father the son in whom he delights" (3:11–12). Just as God calls each person to greatness, so too did Alberto and Maria call their children to live heroically. In this school of sacrificial love, Gianna would later be inspired to offer her own life rather than abort her child.

Ruggero and Maria Teresa Badano

Another Italian couple raised a future saint in the twentieth century. From an early age, Ruggero and Maria Teresa instilled in Bl. Chiara the virtue of charity: love of God and love of neighbor. Specifically, Maria Teresa asked her daughter if she wanted to help less fortunate children by donating some of her toys.[111] Initially, Chiara refused. After some time by herself, Chiara had a change of heart. In fact, Chiara decided to give away some of her best toys because in her own words, "I can't give broken toys to children who don't have any."[112] Since Chiara was their only child, and Ruggero and Maria Teresa were older, the last thing they wanted was to raise a spoiled daughter.[113] Although they were strict with Chiara, Ruggero and Maria Teresa never demanded "blind obedience,"[114] but gave their daughter the freedom to "express her point of view,"[115] as long as the truth was told.

---

[111] See Michele Zanzucchi, *Chiara Luce: A Life Lived to the Full* (London: New City, 2017), 15.

[112] Ibid.

[113] See Ibid., 16.

[114] Ibid., 17.

[115] Ibid., 14.

Maria Teresa learned a most valuable lesson during her three-month bed rest due to phlebitis, a vein inflammation. After she quit her job, Maria Teresa's eyes were opened to the reality that a mother's greatest role is to be present to her children. Maria Teresa declared, "I had always worked in the biscuit factory and was afraid of being bored by housework. But I soon realized how important it is to be with your own child, not so much talking, but 'being' a mother, in other words, loving. This was the only legacy that I could leave her: to teach her to love."[116]

Ruggero and Maria Teresa set a clear example for Chiara that life is more about giving than receiving and more about dying to self than living for self. Maria Teresa once taught her daughter that she had two fathers—"one who she could see and one [her father in heaven who loved her unconditionally] that she couldn't see."[117] Ruggero and Maria Teresa would often pray with their daughter, and it was through prayer that Chiara fell in love with God and desired to spread His love with various friends. She joined the Focolare Movement, an international Catholic group that promotes unity and universal brotherhood/sisterhood. Although surrounded by a culture of darkness, Chiara was a light for the world.

At the same time, Ruggero and Maria Teresa did not keep Chiara so sheltered that she lived immune from the culture's influences. According to author Michele Zanzucchi, Chiara was a normal girl:

> She wanted to be a flight attendant when she grew up. She loved sport, and took every opportunity to do some kind of physical activity. Besides going for long walks in the mountains with her father, collecting mushrooms, Chiara loved tennis and swimming. Maria Teresa recalls her plunging into the huge waves at the seaside time after time.[118]

---

[116] Ibid., 14.

[117] Christine Sterlini, "Meeting the Parents of Blessed Chiara Luce Badano," Diocese of Westminster (August 18, 2014), dowym.com/voices/meeting-parents-blessed-chiara.

[118] Zanzucchi, *Chiara Luce: A life lived to the full,* 26.

It is clear that Ruggero and Maria Teresa raised their daughter in the ordinary, but taught her the extraordinary love of God and neighbor. Sacrificial love was their greatest legacy.

Nikola and Dranafile Bojaxhiu

Another twentieth-century saint learned sacrificial love from her parents. Our Lord's words, "Truly, I say to you, as you did it to one of the least of these my brethren, you did it to me" (Mt 25:40), have fallen on many deaf ears for over two thousand years, but not to Chiara or this saint. Before the newly canonized Mother Teresa sacrificed for those dying in the gutters of Calcutta by cleaning off their wounds and preparing them for death, she learned Christ's sacrificial love firsthand from her parents' example. According to Kathyrn Spink, who knew St. Teresa of Calcutta personally:

> At least once a week Drana would visit an old woman who had been abandoned by her family, to take her food and clean her house. She washed and fed and cared for File, an alcoholic woman covered with sores, as if she were a small child. The six children of a poor widow became part of Drana's own family when their mother died. Agnes would sometimes accompany her mother on her errands of mercy, for Drana was eager that the lessons of love in action and the importance of leading a Christian life, albeit without deliberately attracting attention to one's own virtue, should be communicated to their own children.[119]

Dranafile taught her daughter the most important lesson, which was "when you do good, do it quietly, as if you were throwing a stone into the sea."[120] Her lesson on humility clearly shaped Mother Teresa for the rest of her life and, at the same time, parallels Christ's words, which are proclaimed on Ash Wednesday: "But when you give alms, do not let your left hand know what your right hand is doing" (Mt 6:3). A motto that Teresa of Calcutta lived by, which

---

[119] Kathryn Spink, *Mother Teresa: An Authorized Biography* (New York: Harper One, 2011), 7.

[120] Ibid.

was on the wall of one of her children's homes, were the following words: "If you do good, people will accuse you of selfish, ulterior motives, DO GOOD ANWAY." [121] And further, "The good you do will be forgotten tomorrow, DO GOOD ANYWAY." [122] Though these words were not attributed to Mother Teresa, they are saturated with her fragrance.

Like his wife, Mother Teresa's father, Nikola, made sure their doors always remained open to the less fortunate. When an elderly woman came to dine frequently at their house, Nikola reminded his children to "welcome her warmly, with love." [123] He also told his future saintly daughter to "never eat a single mouthful unless you are sharing it with others." [124] Once when Mother Teresa's older brother Lazar seemed skeptical of his parent's generosity, Dranafile put him in his place, "Some of them are our relations, but all of them are our people." [125]

Sacrificial love does not count the cost—it simply gives, expecting nothing in return, silent, unseen, and hidden from man's eyes and only visible to God Himself, like a stone thrown in the sea. Some saints like Mother Teresa went so far as to desire that God Himself did not even see their good works, for He alone was their greatest reward. Mother Teresa lived by the lessons of sacrificial love taught by her parents and desired to spread Christ's fragrance by both word and deed. On February 3, 1994, at a National Prayer Breakfast in Washington, D.C., in front of the president, Bill Clinton, and First Lady, Hilary Clinton, Mother Teresa courageously proclaimed that "the greatest destroyer of peace today is abortion." [126] To overcome this war on the child and our society, Mother Teresa revealed that sacrificial love is the answer. Specifically, Mother Teresa declared,

---

[121] St. Teresa of Calcutta, *A Simple Path* (New York: Random House, 1995), 185.

[122] Ibid.

[123] Spink, *Mother Teresa: An Authorized Biography*, 6.

[124] Ibid.

[125] Ibid.

[126] St. Teresa of Calcutta, "An address at the National Prayer Breakfast Feb. 3, 1994," Catholic.org, Washington D.C. (February 3, 1994), catholic. org/clife/teresa/address.php.

"How do we persuade a woman not to have an abortion? As always, we must persuade her with love, and we remind ourselves that love means to be willing to give until it hurts."[127] Mother Teresa went on to say, "Any country that accepts abortion is not teaching its people to love, but to use any violence to get what they want. This is why the greatest destroyer of love and peace is abortion."[128]

The essence of Mother Teresa's life, which she inherited from her mother, were the words "Love means to be willing to give until it hurts,"[129] which she so longed to pass on to every soul she encountered in her eighty-seven years of life. In other words, there is no true love without true sacrifice. By meditating daily on Christ's Passion and Death—a Death in which Christ freely gave every drop of His Precious Blood for sinners—Mother Teresa and her parents knew that self-donation was the only path of a true follower of Christ.

After her father's tragic death from an alleged poisoning incident when she was only eight years old, Agnes Bojaxhui and her two older siblings, Agar and Lazar, were raised by their saintly mother. To help offset their financial losses, Dranafile started her own small sewing and embroidering business. She ensured that her children would have an education, along with attending spiritual talks through the Sodality of the Blessed Virgin Mary, where letters of Jesuit missionaries were often read. While at these conferences, Mother Teresa heard of the missions for the first time, which began to stir a desire in her heart at the young age of twelve. Mother Teresa wrote:

> At the beginning, between twelve and eighteen I didn't want to become a nun. We were a very happy family. But when I was eighteen, I decided to leave my home and become a nun, and since then, this forty years, I've never doubted even for a second that I've done the right thing; it was the will of God. It was His choice.[130]

---

[127] Ibid.

[128] Ibid.

[129] Ibid.

[130] St. Teresa of Calcutta, *Mother Teresa: Come Be My Light: The Private Wrings of the "Saint of Calcutta,"* 14.

Yet it was Dranafile's departing words to Agnes as she left for the convent at the age of eighteen that would guide the future saint. Dranafile told her daughter, "Put your hand in His [Jesus'] hand, and walk alone with Him. Walk ahead, because if you look back you will go back."[131] And Mother Teresa did just that as she journeyed with Christ in the darkness of the night without spiritual consolation for most of her life. Perhaps the memories of her holy parents, like the stars beaming above, provided some consolation during her dark night of the soul.

At the age of seventy-one, a journalist once asked Mother Teresa whether she felt any regret over not having any children. Mother Teresa responded, "Naturally, naturally, of course. That is the sacrifice we make. That is the gift we give to God."[132] Mother Teresa was able to give herself away in love to God because her parents first sacrificed for her. Every vocation requires sacrifice to not only survive, but most of all to thrive.

St. Joseph and Our Lady

Of all the saints, blesseds, servants of God, and venerables listed in this book, the two greatest models of sacrificial love are Sts. Joseph and Mary, who are not exemplars for anything great they achieved, but simply because God "exalted those of low degree" (Lk 1:52), and they responded heroically and unreservedly. Their goal in life was not that they be remembered; on the contrary, it was that their Son be remembered forever. Our Lady offered her will and very body to become God's holy dwelling place on earth. At every moment, she thought only of God and always put Joseph and her Son before herself. Only in Heaven will we be able to appreciate the sacrificial heart of Mary as she stood by Jesus until the very end. Because Our Lady overshadowed her husband, just as the saints overshadowed their devout parents, it is only fitting that Joseph's sacrificial nature be explored in more depth.

As Patron of the Universal Church, St. Joseph provides the unheralded, hidden sacrificial love that was the icon for the holy parents of the saints and should be for all earthly fathers. Besides

---

[131] Ibid., 13.
[132] Spink, *Mother Teresa: An Authorized Biography*, 10.

being the Patron of the Church, who protects Holy Mother Church as he protected Our Lady and Jesus, Joseph is also called "Her [Mary's] most chaste spouse." The latter is the only title ascribed to him in the Divine Praises—a prayer said immediately after Eucharistic Benediction—introduced in 1797 by Jesuit priest Luigi Felici to provide reparation for blasphemes and profane language.

Joseph is a martyr of love by today's standards. In our sex-saturated culture, Joseph's sacrifice would make him the greatest martyr of all. Even though Joseph never offered his life literally by shedding his blood for the Faith, he offered something equally pleasing to the Lord. Above all, he offered his will, which included the gift of his sexuality. Imagine being married to the most beautiful, most gentle, and most loving woman inside and out to ever grace the earth with her presence and never consummate your vows. This was Joseph's martyrdom, but not in a negative sense, as he if suffered emotionally and biologically from living a celibate marriage. In reality, Joseph joyfully offered his will to God when he gave his *fiat*. Thus, Joseph became the New Abraham—the spiritual father of the Church, and not just a father to many nations, but to all men and women who belong to God's family. By God's grace, Joseph did not grapple with lust the way that many men do. He exercised the virtue of chastity to a higher degree than all men because of his special calling to be the spouse of Mary and foster-father to Jesus. Perhaps someday there will be a statue or title of Joseph that reads, "St. Joseph, Martyr of Chastity."

While the parents of the saints and their saintly children sought to imitate St. Joseph and Our Lady as models for sacrificial love, the greatest model for sacrificial love is God Himself. In his January 28, 1979, homily in Mexico—less than four months into his pontificate—Pope St. John Paul II beautifully proclaimed, "God in His deepest mystery is not a solitude, but a family, since He has in Himself Fatherhood, Sonship, and the essence of the family, which is love."[133] At its core, sacrificial love is Trinitarian love, for it seeks to imitate the Father's love for the Son and the Son's love for the

---

[133] Pope St. John Paul II, Homily, Puebla de Los Angeles, Mexico (January 28, 1979).

164

Father and the Spirit, Who proceeds from both the Father and the Son. Sacrificial love begins and ends with the Holy Trinity, and Our Lord's Passion, Death, and Resurrection is the most visible and greatest proof of their love. Our Lord's *kenosis*, Greek for "total self-emptying," became the measuring stick by which the parents of the saints and their children would measure their love. Because Our Lord held nothing back from His bride, the Church, He invites all husbands and wives to love their spouses and children more than themselves, as seen in the following words by St. Zélie Martin, which she penned eleven years into her marriage. Occasionally, her husband, St. Louis Martin, ventured on small business trips, leaving behind Zélie and their children. While away, Zélie would write to him. She once wrote, "I kiss you with all my heart. I'm so happy today at the thought of seeing you again that I can't work. Your wife who loves you more than her life."[134]

The virtue of sacrificial love permeated the hearts of the parents of the saints, making them the most authentic preachers in the world because their words matched their deeds. No sacrifice was too little for these parents and none was too great. Every parent presented in this chapter manifested sacrificial love in his or her own unique way. For some parents, it involved organizing clandestine Masses at the risk of death if caught, feeding the poor, and sheltering the homeless, while for others it meant tending to their sickly children. Each parent had a different spot on Calvary, the mountain of lovers. The love of these parents was not based on convenience, but a free commitment of the will. And, like the image of the vine and the branches taught by Our Lord, these parents sought to abide in Him so that His sap—His most precious Body and Blood—could flow not only on to them, but above all on to their budding, saintly children (see Jn 15:1). Our loving Lord, the Divine Gardener, must occasionally prune the branches in order that we might "bear more fruit" (Jn 15:2). Above all, it is through suffering that Our Lord conforms us to His very likeness. This can be seen when we gaze upon a crucifix, for there is no true love without suffering. The hallmark of suffering will be explored in the next chapter.

---

[134] Martin and Martin, *A Call to a Deeper Love*, 52.

HALLMARK FOUR

Suffering

I have a holy pride: I love my father with all my heart, and I believe
he has a very high place in heaven, because he managed to bear in
such dignified, marvelous Christian way all the humiliation that came
with finding himself out on the street.[1]—St. Josemaría Escrivá

The parents of the saints and their saintly children suffered greatly,
yet joyfully, because they knew that those who seek to resemble
Our Lord the most in His resurrected state must first seek to
resemble Him in His crucified state. Although suffering is the result
of Original Sin, our Crucified Bridegroom desires His bride, the
Church, to resemble Him, not out of punishment, but out of love,
and it is His kiss that allows His bride to taste His love. Perhaps more
than any other hallmark, we can identify with the suffering detailed
in this chapter the most because we have all experienced the "kiss
of Jesus,"[2] as St. Teresa of Calcutta referred to suffering. St. Faustina
went one step further when she declared, "Suffering is the greatest
treasure on earth; it purifies the soul. In suffering we learn who is
our true friend."[3] Few people are able to see suffering as a good, yet
the saints have certainly reached this conclusion.

Our Lord declared, "Enter by the narrow gate; for the gate is
wide and the way is easy, that leads to destruction, and those who
enter by it are many. For the gate is narrow, and the way is hard,

---

[1] de Prada, *The Founder of Opus Dei, Volume I,* 56-57. Cited by Álvaro del
Portillo in *Sum.* 50.

[2] St. Teresa of Calcutta, *Come Be My Light,* 281.

[3] St. Faustina, *Diary: Divine Mercy in My Soul,* 153.

that leads to life, and those who find it are few" (Mt 7:13–14). The
parents of the saints and their children took the road less traveled:
suffering, which is the narrow gate or path that leads to life, for true
happiness can only be found in Heaven. Suffering merely for the
sake of suffering was not the goal of the parents in this chapter, or
of any saint; rather, they sought to patiently embrace suffering with
resignation and joy.

   While Our Lord blazed and finished the trail that ends at
Golgotha, He gave each of us the ability to share in His redemptive
mission, i.e., to save souls by carrying our crosses and helping those
around us carry theirs. At the end of the journey through this valley
of tears and eventual ascent to Mount Calvary, Our Lord and Our
Lady will be waiting for us. Suffering was the path of the parents of
the saints, as will be seen in the following stories, and it is the path
we too must journey if we desire to reach Heaven.

Francis and Margaret Bosco

Two years after Francis Bosco's third son, John, was born on
August 16, 1816, he gave his wife, Margaret, two final requests.
Francis said to Margaret, "Be resigned to God's holy will," [4] and
"Take care of our boys, but of little John in a special manner."[5]
After losing her husband at the young age of twenty-nine, Margaret
Bosco experienced the trial of single-handedly raising three boys.
Ironically, at twenty-four years of age, she had married the widower
Francis Bosco, whose first wife had died young. Margaret initially
refused Francis's proposal, as he had a little son and cared for his
elderly mother, but Margaret's father and friends encouraged her
to accept him. One of St. John Bosco's earliest memories was of
when, at the age of two, his mother said to him, "You have no father
now,"[6] which remained etched in his mind for the rest of his life.
John Bosco was deprived of an earthly father to reflect the Heavenly

---

[4]   Neil Boyton, SJ, *The Blessed Friend of the Youth: Saint John Bosco* (New
      York: Macmillan Company, 1942), 11.
[5]   Ibid.
[6]   Ibid.

Father's love, while his mother was deprived of a spouse to mirror Christ's love.

Despite her tremendous loss and ensuing suffering, Margaret strove to carry out her husband's dying wishes by resigning herself to God's will, which meant being the spiritual head and heart of the family. Although she could never replace her husband, she showed the world how to raise a holy son, for Margaret was unafraid of instilling discipline in John and his siblings because she loved them and wanted them to become the men their father would have wanted them to be. Margaret trained her sons, specifically John, to become saints. As John Bosco was leaving for the seminary in his cassock, Margaret laid her hands on his shoulders and said:

> To see you dressed in this manner fills my heart with joy. But remember that it is not the dress that gives honor to the state, but the practice of virtue. If at any time, you come to doubt your vocation, I beseech you, lay it aside at once. I would rather have a poor peasant for my son than a negligent priest. When you came into the world I consecrated you to our Lady; when you began to study I bade you honor her and have recourse to her in all your afflictions; now I beg you to take her for your Queen.[7]

Margaret did not raise her son to be lukewarm; rather, she raised her son to be a saint after the heart of Mary.

Margaret experienced one last suffering at the age of fifty-eight, when John Bosco invited her to live with him and thirty orphaned boys and serve as their housekeeper and cook. Margaret agreed because she knew it pleased the Lord. Unfortunately, John Bosco had no source of income and lived solely on donations, so Margaret used her own wedding dress to sew priestly vestments for her son, and even sold her wedding ring and jewelry to pay the rent. While initially the suffering of being detached from her most sentimental earthly possessions was very painful, Margaret eventually declared, "When I looked at those things which I was holding in my hands for the last time, at first I felt a little upset . . . but, afterward, I felt

---

[7] Hugo Hoever, *Lives of the Saints Illustrated,* Part 1 (Totowa, NJ: Catholic Book Publishing, 1999), 54–55.

so happy that if I had a hundred trousseaux I'd have given them all up for the same purpose without the least regard."[8] The suffering of being deprived of earthly possessions, like Our Lord, brought peace to Margaret. A reflection by the author Wendy Leifeld sheds light on the suffering of this holy mother:

> Mamma Margarita's life is not one that most of us would choose. It is easy to look at motherhood with a job mentality: "When the kids are grown I'll finally be free to take up my own life again." Mamma Margarita proves that motherhood is not a job, it's a vocation—a holy calling that continues until our children die. God may even give us children besides our own to love.[9]

Margaret never thought she would marry a widower and help raise his son or care for her mother-in-law. Nor did she ever wish to be a widow herself raising three children alone, or the mother to over thirty boys. She looked forward to spending her retirement tending to her small garden in peace and quiet. Yet God had other plans for this holy mother, who fully embraced the suffering that came her way, and who paved the way for her son to become a saint. When John Bosco was trying to decide between the diocesan priesthood or the religious life, and worried about being able to help his mother, she told him, "I want nothing from you, I expect nothing from you. I was born poor, I live poor, and I wish to die poor. But remember this: if, by some misfortune, you become a rich priest I will never darken your doorstep."[10] Margaret's suffering bore fruit, for without this holy mother's joyful acceptance of the Cross it is likely that the Salesian Order, which John Bosco founded, may never have become a reality, for it was founded on his mother's love of poverty.

Margaret died on November 25, 1856, at the age of sixty-eight. At her funeral, many of her spiritual children paid their respects to Margaret, who was the only mother and grandmother figure to many of the orphaned boys she cared for. While John Bosco

8   Leifeld, *Mothers of the Saints*, 164.
9   Ibid., 167.
10   Ibid., 162.

was canonized forty-six years after his death in 1934, it is only in our present time, nearly a hundred years after her death, that his mother's life drew attention from the Congregation for the Causes of the Saints. However, John Bosco knew his mother was the true unheralded saint of the family well before the Church officially recognized her heroic virtue in 2006.

Luca and Anna Maria Danei

Roughly seventy-eight miles from Turin, Italy, where St. John Bosco lived, another future saint learned the value of suffering from his devout parents, but paradoxically also suffered from them, particularly his father. Born in the seventeenth century, 121 years before St. John Bosco, in the town of Ovada, Italy, the heroic life of Paul Danei is undeniable. In fact, Paul Danei, who became St. Paul of the Cross, is one of only a handful of saints who bear the title "the Cross" after their name. Like Margaret Bosco and, of course, Our Lord, St. Paul of the Cross, who founded the Passionists Order, "learned obedience through what he suffered" (Heb 5:8).

As the second child in his family, Paul learned that suffering is never meant to crush, but to heal the soul and unite us to our Crucified Lover. Paul's mother, Anna Maria, had lost six girls in infancy, but did not blame God. Paul's father, Luca, was also not immune to suffering. He had lost his first wife of five years, Maria Caterina, who was childless when she died, making him a widower at thirty. Though he strived to live a holy life, Luca was, unfortunately, incarcerated on a few occasions. Once, he was imprisoned on charges of fraud and another time on allegations of smuggling, related to his work as a tobacconist. Another time, he was falsely accused of a crime in which he claimed no involvement. Because of Luca's inability to conduct his affairs prudently, this once well-off family became financially unstable and had to move frequently, resulting in tremendous suffering for himself and his family. Yet the pillar of the family was Anna Maria, whose fidelity to God, her husband, and her children in the midst of great suffering never wavered. Rather than shrink from her vows during the time of her husband's imprisonment, Anna Maria realized that suffering drew her closer to Christ and her spouse, and provided an opportunity for heroic virtue. While some women would have walked away from their incarcerated husband, Anna Maria patiently bore this trial because she knew that God always brings good out of evil.

Although referred to as "goodhearted and devout,"[11] Luca was his own worst enemy, and his poor choices put his family in harm's way. Once, when Paul was trying to smuggle his father's tobacco over the mountains, he was nearly shot. But, while Luca lacked sound judgment in his business affairs, he did show great prudence in dealing with his future saintly son. On one occasion, Luca found Paul and his little brother John Baptiste scourging themselves with leather throngs, a prevalent penitential practice in those days. Luca immediately took the instrument away from his sons and said, "So you want to kill yourselves?"[12] Luca would also be considered very stern by modern parenting standards, as his children were forbidden to engage in various enjoyments he considered frivolous, such as playing cards or hunting. However, despite his weaknesses, Luca remained faithful to his wife and children, never abandoning them or his strong Catholic Faith. In fact, both of Paul's parents were faithful members of the Confraternity of the Annunciation, and, while on his deathbed after a fall caused by a neighbor, Luca encouraged his children to "forgive and forget"[13] as he united his own sufferings to Christ's.

The Danei household was truly a school of love and suffering, and Paul was gradually being conformed to his Crucified Spouse long before his conversion at the age of twenty, which was primarily due to his mother Anna Maria's profound witness and teaching as well as his father's staunch faith. As a young child, while Paul was getting his hair combed, something which he despised and which often made him cry, his mother would show him a crucifix and repeat, "Look, my child, how Jesus suffered."[14] Anna Maria also

---

[11]   Paul Francis Spencer, CP, *As a Seal Upon Your Heart: The Life of St. Paul of the Cross, Founder of the Passionists* (Maynooth: St. Paul's, 1994), 21.

[12]   Charles Alméras, *St. Paul of the Cross: Founder of the Passionists* (Garden City, NY: Hanover House, 1960), 26.

[13]   Ibid.

[14]   Ibid., 27.

loved to share stories of the saints with her children. Specifically, Paul said, "She would tell me about the lives of the saints and the austere, penitential life of the anchorites in the desert; from then on I had a great desire to serve God and this I have always remembered."[15] Furthermore, Anna Maria would often tell her children, "May God make saints of all of you!"[16] And it is because of Anna Maria's example that Paul once said, "Would to God that I had the virtue of my mother!"[17] While the three words "offer it up" appear to have disappeared from our present-day vocabulary of comfort, Luca and Anna Maria remind parents that our sufferings can become less when viewed in light of Calvary. Because Jesus suffered to a degree that no human being can ever compare, our sufferings become efficacious and powerful when united to His.

Understanding the value of uniting our suffering to Christ's, Anna Maria, when undergoing intense sufferings brought about by illness, did not turn to alcohol, medication, or secular psychologists to numb her pain, but rather gazed upon the Cross and taught her own children to do so as well. And so it was Anna Maria who pointed her son Paul to the crucifix, which became his most precious inheritance. He, in turn, founded the Passionists, a religious order centered on the Passion of Christ.

Ruggero and Maria Teresa Badano

Less than three hundred years after the birth of St. Paul of the Cross, and only twenty miles from his birthplace, another holy Italian girl was born in 1971, in the small town of Sasello, Italy. Clearly, Italy is the land of saints! Bl. Chiara Badano's father experienced great suffering prior to his daughter's birth. Ruggero and Maria Teresa had been married almost eleven years before God blessed them with a child. This was a major source of suffering. "All my friends had plenty of children, and we had none. I really felt that we were missing out,"[18] declared Ruggero.

---

[15] Spencer, *As a Seal Upon Your Heart,* 20.
[16] Alméras, *St. Paul of the Cross,* 26.
[17] Ibid.
[18] Zanzucchi, *Chiara Luce: A life lived to the full,* 13.

Many couples have experienced the cross of infertility like Ruggero and Maria Teresa. This suffering can lead to great disappointment because it appears as if God's will and our wills are not aligned. But, in the case of Ruggero and Maria Teresa, suffering led to the only response possible—surrender. Specifically, Maria Teresa declared, "I considered everything that happened to me to be the will of God. He loved me, and so this inability to have children was love too."[19]

On October 29, 1971, after years of imploring Our Lady for a miracle, the couple finally welcomed their beautiful daughter, Chiara, into this world. Eighteen years later, on October 7, 1990, the Feast of Our Lady of the Rosary, Chiara, after several months of intense suffering caused by bone cancer, left this world for Eternity. So many years of suffering and prayer by Ruggero and Maria Teresa had ended with even more heartache. The worst possible nightmare for any parent, burying one of your children, in this case, their only child, came to fruition. At that moment, Maria Teresa became closer to Our Lady than at any moment in her life, for God allowed her to enter into the Sorrowful Heart of His Mother, whose only Son, Jesus, suffered and died before her eyes.

But, before Chiara went to Heaven, God permitted a final trial, so that she might receive an even greater crown of glory. As Chiara's parents and aunt Mimma tended to her during her last months on bed rest, the devil unleashed his fury. A startled Chiara told her mother, "Mum, the devil came in here."[20] According to the author Michele Zanzucchi, "Maria Teresa tried to calm her, telling her not to be too surprised by such a visit, 'because the devil wants to take the most beautiful souls for himself. Jesus is with you.'"[21] Upon hearing this, Chiara became more peaceful.[22]

As Chiara was nearing her final moments, Maria Teresa continued to be a rock for her daughter. Chiara seemed somewhat unsure when she would die and so asked her mother if it was really

[19] Ibid.
[20] Ibid., 45.
[21] Ibid.
[22] See Ibid.

happening. Maria Teresa responded, "You only leave in God's time. But rest assured, your suitcase is ready, full of acts of love?"[23]

Chiara asked her mother, "Do you think I will meet Grandma there?"[24]

Maria Teresa replied, "You will see Mary first, who will welcome you with open arms."[25]

In a playful manner, Chiara responded, "Be quiet. Don't spoil the surprise."[26] Thus, Ruggero and Maria Teresa embraced their role as spiritual protectors of their daughter from her birth until her death, especially during her sufferings.

Following the example of her parents, who had a great love for the sacraments and Our Lady, Chiara made her final Confession, received Holy Communion, and had her relatives pray with her as she approached the precipice of Eternity. Her last words to her mother were "Ciao! Be happy, because I am."[27] Ruggero wanted to know if his daughter's words were also meant for him, and Chiara "squeezed his hand."[28] Chiara's final request to her parents before dying was to be buried in a wedding dress, as she wanted to be Christ's bride.

Maria Teresa recalls the trial of faith that occurred after her daughter's death, and how this event could have shaken her and her husband's faith. In an interview, she recalls "feeling that this could be a breaking point. She turned to her husband and the two of them grasped hands, knelt down at Chiara's bedside and recited the Creed slowly together."[29] In their moment of unfathomable sorrow, Ruggero and Maria Teresa could have cursed God's holy will. This temptation and trial is prevalent in all mankind. Everyone loves God when things go right, but, when things go wrong, God is often the

---

[23] Ibid., 52.

[24] Ibid.

[25] Ibid.

[26] Ibid.

[27] Ibid., 53.

[28] Ibid.

[29] Christine Sterlini, "Meeting the Parents of Blessed Chiara Luce Badano," Diocese of Westminster (August 18, 2018), dowym.com/voices/meeting-parents-blessed-chiara/.

first one to be blamed. Ruggero and Maria Teresa's recitation of the Creed during their darkest hour provides an incredible witness to all parents who have lost a child—that turning to God at all times, but most especially during the most difficult moments of our lives, when we suffer depression, failure, temptations, sickness, and death, is the only answer to life's miseries, for Christ has conquered sin and death and His grace is sufficient (see 2 Cor 12:9). The Badano's faith in Christ's Resurrection led them to believe that they would one day be reunited with their daughter, Chiara, in Heaven and that their separation was only temporary. In fact, this separation made Ruggero and Maria Teresa long for Heaven with an even greater zeal and not fear death, for their daughter would be waiting for them on the other side.

Nikola and Dranafile Bojaxhiu

In 1919, an eight-year-old girl named Agnes Gonxha Bojaxhiu, who would become St. Teresa of Calcutta, along with her siblings and her mother, Dranafile, experienced their darkest moment. Dranafile' s husband, Nikola, an Albanian activist and nationalist, returned home one night from a political dinner and became gravely ill. After being rushed to the hospital, the doctors declared that it was too late. The forty-five-year-old Nikola had been poisoned. Prior to his death, Nikola had co-owned a construction company and had been the family provider, which enabled Teresa's family to own two homes and live a comfortable life. Although they were very well off, Nikola and Dranafile had instilled in their children a tremendous love for the poor by taking food, medicine, and clothes to them. Now the tables had turned. In addition to losing her husband, Nikola's business partner stole all their assets, leaving only their houses untouched. With God's grace, Dranafile replaced her husband's political zeal with her religious zeal and patience in suffering, which became like a first novitiate for the young Teresa.

Although no one can ever replace a departed spouse or parent, it is their legacy of virtue that never dies if we possess the grace and courage to continue their mission and allow the Holy Spirit to work through us. Clearly, Nikola's zeal spilled over to his daughter, who was ardently pro-life and unafraid to remind political leaders that the "greatest destroyer of peace today is abortion." Dranafile revealed to Teresa that suffering produces the fruits of patience and joy by allowing virtue to triumph over bitterness and regret. In a letter to Fr. Franjo Jambrekovic, her confessor as a young sister, Teresa lauded her mother's joy in the face of suffering: "Mamma is writing regularly—truly she is giving me the strength to suffer joyfully. My departure was indeed the beginning of her supernatural life. When she goes to Jesus, surely He will receive her with great joy."[30] Mother Teresa also described a fellow sister, "She works beautifully for Jesus—the most important is that she knows how to suffer and at the same time how to laugh. That is the most important—to suffer and to laugh."[31] Only in the heart of a holy mother and a saintly daughter can two apparent opposites, "to suffer and to laugh," become one reality. Because God permits suffering for a greater good that we might not understand until we reach Heaven, the parents of the saints and their children could laugh at their trials, for they were just that, temporary. They recognized that a smile in the midst of sorrow is a greater offering to Our Lord than a smile when everything goes well.

Karol and Emilia Wojtyła

St. Teresa of Calcutta's mother, Dranafile, was not the only parent of a saint to lose a spouse. Karol Wojtyła Sr., the father of Pope St. John Paul II, lost his wife, Emilia, who died at the young age of forty-five on April 13, 1929, from kidney failure and congenital heart disease. Although John Paul II spoke little about his mother throughout his pontificate, which, according to his aides, may have been because he had few memories of her, he did keep his parents' wedding picture on a small table at both his Vatican apartment and his summer residence at Castel Gandolfo. Emilia loved to embroider and used her skill to supplement her husband's salary as a lieutenant in the Polish Army. Her death was a deep loss to both her husband and the future pope. Even though Emilia's impact may have been

---

30 St. Teresa of Calcutta, *Come Be My Light*, 21.
31 Ibid., 24.

less than her husband's on John Paul II, he felt her influence. While at the Jagiellonian University in Kraków, young Karol found an outlet in poetry and commemorated his deceased mother with this beautiful poem:

> Oh, how many years have gone by,
> Without you—how many years?
> Over Your white grave
> O mother, my extinct beloved,
> For a son's full love,
> A prayer: Eternal Rest.[32]

In addition to losing his beloved wife, Karol Sr. was dealt another blow three years later when he lost his twenty-six-year-old son, Edmund, a doctor, who contracted scarlet fever from a patient. The scene of his father saying the words "Thy will be done"[33] over his brother's coffin left a deep impression on the future pope.[34] Pope John Paul II wrote, "The violence of the blows which had struck him had opened up immense spiritual depths in him; his grief found its outlet in prayer."[35] As will be discussed later, Karol Sr. would often pray on his knees in the middle of the night, like a contemplative monk in a monastery. Suffering drew Karol Sr. closer to Christ and to his future saintly son. The Wojtyłas pushed their beds together each night and then attended 7:00 a.m. Mass the following morning, where Karol Jr. would serve.[36] In the evenings, they read the Bible together. Following Karol Jr.'s high school graduation, they moved from their apartment in Wadowice to an even smaller apartment in Kraków, where they lived with Karol Sr.'s deceased wife's two sisters, so young Karol could walk to the university. Yet the greatest lessons

---

[32] Robert Sullivan, *Pope John Paul II: A Tribute of Life* (New York: Time, 1999), 9.

[33] Slawomir Oder and Saverio Gaeta, *Why He Is a Saint* (New York: Rizzoli, 2010), 12.

[34] See Evert, *Saint John Paul the Great*, 5.

[35] Andre Frossard, *"Be Not Afraid!"* (New York: St. Martin's Press, 1982), 14.

[36] See Evert, *Saint John Paul the Great*, 5.

John Paul II learned from his father, who retired with the rank of captain, were best described by the papal biographer George Weigel:

> To some, the captain may have seemed a man who bore the tragedies life had thrust upon him with stoic resignation. The moral lesson the son learned from the father was not Stoic, however, but Christian—the lesson of suffering transformed by faith. His father's life was austere, the son would later recall, but austerity for the elder Karol Wojtyła was not simply a matter of the frugality required by living on a small pension. It was born of convictions about Christian asceticism, and from the unshakable certainty that the true measure of man was not his wealth, but his character.[37]

More than asceticism, which Pope John Paul II learned from his father—he often slept on the floor of his Vatican bedroom—he also learned simplicity. He wrote in his March 6, 1979, Last Will and Testament, "I leave no possessions of which it will be necessary to dispose."[38] And more than deep prayer, which John Paul II learned by spending hours before the Most Blessed Sacrament, he learned the "lesson of suffering transformed by faith" by witnessing his father daily carrying his cross. It was through this suffering that both Karol Sr. and John Paul II learned to develop empathy for the world, especially their Jewish friends, who were persecuted and killed. This empathy was manifested daily for the flock that was given to him when John Paul II became a priest, and then later as a bishop and pope. When we ask, "Where is Christ in my suffering?" Christ answers, "I am right there with you, for I suffered in every way like you when I lost My earthly father, My friends abandoned Me, and I died the most horrendous death known to man." Karol Sr.'s unwavering trust in God amidst his sufferings instilled a similar courage in his son. When faced with his own trials, John Paul II was thus able to remain steadfast in his sufferings. Karol Sr. showed his son that suffering is not to be avoided in this life, but to be embraced.

---

[37] George Weigel, *Witness to Hope* (New York: Harper Collins, 1999), 42.

[38] Pope St. John Paul II, *Silence Transformed into Life: The Testament of His Final Year*, 126.

In the words of St. Louis de Montfort, who John Paul II loved, "The most faithful servants of the Blessed Virgin, being also her greatest favorites, receive from her the greatest graces and favors of Heaven, which are crosses."[39]

José and Dolores Escrivá

St. Louis de Montfort's prophetic words came to fruition not only in the Wojtyła household, but also in the Escrivá's home. Like Karol and Emilia Wojtyła, who lost two children, José and Dolores Escrivá experienced a similar tragedy, losing three daughters under the age of ten over a three-year span. Rosario died on July 11, 1910, at nine months old. Lolita died on July 10, 1912, at five, and Chon died on October 6, 1913, at eight. Like the three nails that pierced Christ's hands and feet, causing unimaginable pain, so too did the deaths of José and Dolores's precious daughters cause intense suffering.

A year after Chon's death, José, co-owner of Juncosa & Escrivá textile business and the attached coffee shop, declared bankruptcy. The agriculture economy had suffered a major recession prior to World War I, and, in addition, his former partner failed to uphold his noncompete agreement and allegedly pilfered money from José. Consequently, José decided to liquidate all of his assets in order to pay their creditors, despite having no legal obligation to do so, as his family home and other assets were legally protected. In doing this, José sought to act virtuously, which consequently jeopardized his family's upper-middle-class lifestyle. According to his son, St. Josemaría, José "could nevertheless have remained in a very comfortable situation for those times, had he not been a Christian and a gentleman."[40] The Escrivás felt the financial sting immediately as they had to release their cook, maid, and nanny, and, shortly thereafter, José sought employment in the town of Logroño, some one hundred and thirty miles away. As a result, José would be separated from his wife and children for a few months until the

---

[39]   St. Louis de Montfort, *True Devotion to Mary*, 97.
[40]   de Prada, *Founder of Opus Dei*, Volume I, 55. Cited by Martin Sambeat in *General Archive of the Prelature*, 3. Also cited in *Meditation* of February 14, 1964.

school year finished, when they would move from their house to a small apartment. The once reputable business owner now had to work as a salesman in a clothing and textile store on a reduced salary. Tragically, José and Dolores would have to leave behind all their close friends and the parish where they had exchanged vows and where their children were baptized, as well as the cemetery where their three daughters were buried.

The Escrivás were not the only ones who experienced a devastating blow from this unfortunate economic situation. Sadly, José had to terminate his employees' contracts, many of whom held him in great esteem for his just wages and concern for them as people, and particularly for the salvation of their souls. For example, José encouraged his employees to attend the Lenten conferences each year by paying for their retreats and adjusting their schedules, so all could attend if they desired. José offers a great witness to business owners that employees are more than just a means to an end, but have dignity and, above all, immortal souls. José wanted to create a Christian culture at his business. Therefore, it was a trial for him to break the news to his employees that they no longer had a job, many of whom would now be forced to scramble to provide for their own families and perhaps work for even lower wages or for a less virtuous employer, all because of the sin of one corrupt man.

But José's greatest suffering came not from being stripped of nearly all of his material possessions, including their beloved house, like Christ on the Cross, but being scorned and rejected by his family members and neighbors. In the moments when they needed their relatives' aid both financially and emotionally, they were offered hostility rather than charity. Even Dolores's brother, Fr. Carlos Albas, said of his brother-in-law, "Pepe is a fool. He could have retained a good financial position, and instead he's reduced himself to misery."[41] Josemaría, reflecting on his father's suffering, viewed him as "the personification of Job. He lost three daughters, one after the other in consecutive years, and then lost his fortune."[42]

---

[41] Ibid., 56. Told by Monsignor Escrivá de Balaguer and his sister Carmen to Álvaro del Portillo: *Roman Process of beatification,* 79.

[42] Ibid., 54. Cited in *Meditation,* February 14, 1964.

Despite all these trials, José and his wife surrendered to the will
of God by seeking to bear this cross secretly and heroically. They
sought to console Our Lord rather than receive the consolation and
pity of man, as evidenced by José's words to his family:

> We must look at everything with a sense of responsibility.
> On the one hand, we must not live beyond our means.
> But on the other hand, we must live this poverty with
> dignity, even though it is a humiliation. We must live
> it without others noticing it and without telling them
> about it.[43]

In the crucible of their sufferings, which resulted in greater
poverty, José and Dolores clearly taught their future saint about
resignation to suffering, though it took time and God's graces, as
Josemaría said that he had "rebelled against that situation. I felt
humiliated. I ask pardon."[44]

On March 28, 1971, almost four years before his death, Josemaría
wrote a letter to the mayor of Barbastro, where he grew up, speaking
of his parents' profound influence on his future vocation:

> I remember specifically some things about my father that
> fill me with pride and have not faded from my memory
> at all even though I was only thirteen when we moved
> away: stories of a generous and hidden charity, an upright
> faith without ostentation, abundant strength at the time
> of trial, a strong union with my mother and his children.
> It was thus that Our Lord prepared my soul—by way of
> those examples so imbued with Christian dignity and
> hidden heroism always accompanied by a smile—so that
> later, by God's grace, I could become a poor instrument
> for the carrying out of a work of Divine Providence that
> would not separate me from my beloved city.[45]

Josemaría tried to make sense of his family's suffering as do most
people in this life. The following quote captures a saint's struggle

43   Ibid., 55. Cited by Álvaro del Portillo, *Sum.* 49.
44   Ibid., 57. Cited in *Meditation*, February 14, 1964.
45   Ibid., 62–63. Cited in *C. 4826,* March 28, 1971.

to answer the question most Christians ask: Why do bad things happen to good people and those who do evil or have no want for God seem to have everything go right? Josemaría offered the following insights:

> Even back when I was a child, I thought so often about the fact that there are many good souls who have to suffer so much in this world—sorrows of every type: reversals of fortune, family calamities, the trampling of their legitimate pride. At the same time, I could see other people who did not seem to be good (though I'm not saying they weren't, because we don't have a right to judge anyone), for whom everything was going just great. But then, one fine day, it occurred to me that even the very evil do some good things, although they don't do them for supernatural motives, and I realized that God in some way has to reward them on earth, since he won't be able to reward them in eternity. Then I thought of the old saying, "They also feed the ox that will go to the slaughterhouse."[46]

Later in life, St. Josemaría understood more fully the power and beauty of suffering, largely in part to his parents' example. He once wrote, "Cross, toil, tribulation: such will be your lot as long as you live. That was the way Christ followed, and the disciple is not above their Master."[47] In the world's eyes, José was a failure—he lost his business, his fortune, and died in his fifties, while his business partner, who cheated him, became rich. In God's eyes, José would receive the only reward that mattered: eternal life. José and his wife, Dolores, may never have been revered in the eyes of the world, but that did not truly matter. What mattered most was that their children were left an example of virtue. In the words of Josemaría, "My parents, my quietly heroic parents are my great pride."[48] This testifies to their legacy.

---

[46] Ibid., 72. Cited by Álvaro del Portillo in *Sum.* 67.

[47] St. Josemaría Escrivá, *The Way, Furrow, The Forge,* 175.

[48] de Prada, *The Founder of Opus Dei,* Volume I, 73. *Cited in C 4919,* October 14, 1971.

In addition to losing his business and three daughters, Our Lord permitted additional sufferings to befall the Escrivá family to further detach them from worldly things. Due to his new position as a salesclerk, José began to suffer physically. One of Josemaría's seminary brothers, Francisco Moreno, commented on meeting José, "It made me suffer more than a little to see this man who, though still relatively young, was aging prematurely."[49] He recalled, "His feet were so swollen that he had to take off his shoes as soon as he got home."[50] Eventually José's body could not take the stress and pain of this life.

On November 27, 1924, less than four months before Josemaría would be ordained a priest, his father died. After praying at their statue of Our Lady of the Miraculous Medal, whom he loved dearly, José collapsed. He died two hours later after the parish priest administered the Last Rites. In God's providence, José died on the feast day of Our Lady of the Miraculous Medal.

Following José's death, there was even more suffering and humiliation to come for the Escrivá family, as they did not have enough money to pay for his funeral. Thanks be to God, Josemaría's priest friend, Fr. Daniel Alfara, a military chaplain, loaned the family enough to provide their father with a proper burial. In effect, José resembled Our Lord, who had "nowhere to lay his head" (Lk 9:58) both in life and in death. It must be noted that before closing the coffin, Josemaría removed the cross that lay in his father's hands. José had inherited it from his mother and carried it everywhere with him. And, like his father, Josemaría treasured this little crucifix and kept it with him at all times. At the time of his father's death, Josemaría assumed the role of his family's financial provider, especially for his mother and young brother Santiago, who was only five years old.

Despite losing his father, Josemaría remained resolute in his desire to become a priest despite his new financial obligations to his family. Many mothers might be tempted to ask their son to give up God's calling to the priesthood for the sake of their material well-being. Dolores, however, carried her cross by allowing her son to

---

49   Ibid., 131. Cited in *General Archive of the Prelature*, 10.
50   Ibid.

follow his vocation even at the expense of her continued poverty, for she had surrendered to the will of God. In doing so, Dolores resembled Margarita Sarto, the mother of Pope St. Pius X, who desired her son to continue his seminary studies despite the loss of her husband; both women trusted that God provides, even more so in our most dire moments.

As Fr. Josemaría Escrivá celebrated his first Mass on March 30, 1925, in the Holy Chapel of Our Lady of the Pillar in Saragossa, indescribable joy exuded from his face, according to witnesses. Josemaría had found God's will for his life in the priesthood of Jesus Christ. But he also experienced great suffering over his father's absence, and he offered his first Mass for the repose of his soul. José was not only Josemaría's father, but also his best friend and the inspiration behind his vocation. Sons naturally seek the gaze and approval of their human fathers. What a trial then for Josemaría not to have his father at his first Mass, though he was spiritually present in the Eucharist, as wherever Christ is present so is all of humanity: the souls in Heaven, the souls in Purgatory, the souls on earth, and all the souls in the future who are in the mind of God.

Dolores, even more so than her priestly son, still suffered grief from her husband's recent death. She knew that witnessing her son's ordination and first Mass would have been two of the most joyous moments of her husband's life, for he was the unheralded vocation director of Josemaría, though he never pressured him to be a priest. According to witnesses at Fr. Josemaría's first Mass, Dolores was "dissolved in a sea of tears and at times seemed close to fainting."[51]

The greatest sermon José ever preached on suffering was done silently—providing his son with the clearest answer to his questions on suffering. He left his children with a blueprint for holiness. Specifically, Josemaría said about his father, "I saw him suffer with cheerfulness, without showing the suffering."[52]

José sought more than anything to resemble Our Lord, as both died poor and were mocked by many. Above all, he remained confident and at peace that he was doing the Father's will and

---

[51] Ibid., 171. Cited by José López Sierra in *General Archive of the Prelature*, 1.

[52] Ibid., 163–164. Cited in *Meditation*, February 14, 1964.

preparing the world for his son's vocation, just as Christ prepared the way for the Advocate, the Holy Spirit, to come. In the face of so much suffering, Josemaría's father chose hope over despair, courage over temerity, and love over revenge. In doing so, José blazed the trail for his children and future saintly son, Josemaría, to preach to the world the power of redemptive suffering.

Sts. Louis and Zélie Martin

Like José and Dolores Escrivá, who lost several children in infancy and lived around the same time period, Sts. Louis and Zélie Martin were no strangers to suffering and death. Holding her lifeless child in her arms, Zélie told her brother: "My dear little Joseph died this morning at 7 o'clock. I was alone with him. He had a night of cruel suffering, and tearfully I asked for his deliverance. My heart was relieved when I saw him utter his last sigh."[53] It was not until a few years after Joseph's tragic death that peace and joy permeated their household once again. Zélie wrote a few years later: "Above all, it was on the death of my first child that I felt more deeply the happiness of having a child in Heaven, for God showed me in a noticeable way that He accepted my sacrifice. Through the intercession of my little angel, I received a very extraordinary grace."[54]

What was that extraordinary grace that Zélie obtained through her departed son? When Louis and Zélie's three-year-old daughter Hélène experienced severe earache (*otitis*), which seemed incurable, Zélie said:

> One day, while returning from taking her to the doctor, who didn't have anything good to say, and seeing the helplessness of everyone, the inspiration came to me to turn to my little Joseph, who had died five weeks earlier. So I took the child and asked her to say a prayer to her little brother. The next morning her ear was completely cured. The discharge had stopped all of a sudden, and

---

[53] Martin and Martin, *A Call to a Deeper Love,* 40–41.
[54] Ibid., 91.

the little one never again felt any pain. I've also received
several other graces, but less notable than this one.[55]

In the midst of losing their son Joseph, the Martins had a new
intercessor in Heaven. Further, the loss of her son allowed Zélie to
have empathy for other mothers who had lost a child. Zélie wrote
to her sister-in-law, Céline, on October 17, 1871, a day after Céline
lost her third child, Paul, who was delivered stillborn:

> The tragedy you've just suffered saddens me deeply. You
> are truly being tested. This is one of your first sorrows,
> my poor sister! May God grant you resignation to His
> holy will. Your dear little baby is at His side. He sees you,
> he loves you, and you will see him again one day. That is
> a great consolation I've felt and still feel.[56]

Some incorrectly imagine that these devout couples and their
holy offspring were so detached from this life that they rarely grieved
over their departed loved ones. Being two months pregnant with
Céline and having just lost two sons in consecutive years, one of
whom died only weeks before her own father, Zélie reached her
breaking point while visiting her father's and sons' graves,

> Yesterday, I went to the cemetery. To see me, one would
> have said: "Here is the most indifferent person in the
> world." I was kneeling at the foot of his grave, and I
> couldn't pray. A few steps away I knelt by that of my two
> little angels, the same apparent indifference. . . . I walked
> along a path I had taken five weeks ago with my little
> baby and my father. I couldn't tell you all I was feeling. I
> didn't pay attention to anything happening around me. I
> looked at the places where my father had sat, and I stood
> there, almost without thinking. Never in my life had
> I felt such heartache. When I arrived home, I couldn't
> eat. It seemed as if I would now be indifferent to any
> misfortunate that happened to me. If you knew, my dear
> sister, how much I loved my father! He was always with

---

[55] Ibid.
[56] Ibid., 90.

me, I never left him; and he would help me as much as he could.[57]

From February 14, 1867, with the death of their first son, Joseph, to October 8, 1870, with the death of their eighth child, Mélanie-Thérèse, the Martins mourned the deaths of four children. They had lost their five-year-old daughter, Hélène, only ten months before Mélanie-Thérèse's death. Hélène's death filled Zélie with regret and sorrow because she didn't think Hélène's sickness was serious and, thus, felt guilty. Zélie wrote:

> While I was holding her, her little head fell onto my shoulder, her eyes closed; then five minutes later she didn't exist anymore. . . . That made an impression on me I'll never forget. I didn't expect such a sudden end, nor did my husband. When he came home and saw his poor little daughter dead, he began to sob, crying, "My little Hélène! My little Hélène!" Then together we offered her to God. . . . Before the burial, I spent the night next to the poor darling. She was even more beautiful dead than alive. I was the one who dressed her and put her in the coffin. I thought I was going to die, but I didn't want anyone else to touch her. The church was full of people at her funeral. Her grave is next to grandpa. I'm very sad; write me if you can, to console me.[58]

A month after Hélène's death, Zélie's sorrow turned to depression. She wrote to her sister-in-law on March 27, 1870:

> I have no more energy. I have no stamina for work, and I don't have the heart for it. Sometimes I imagine that I'll go away as gently as my little Hélène. I assure you that I barely care for my own life. Ever since I lost this child, I feel a burning desire to see her again. However, those that remain need me, and, because of them, I ask God to leave me on this earth a few more years.[59]

[57] Ibid., 43.
[58] Ibid., 60–61.
[59] Ibid., 63.

Even the parents of the saints, and Zélie, a saint herself, experienced the agony and emotional trauma of losing loved ones. Following the tragic death of her seven-week-old daughter Mélanie-Thérèse, Zélie wrote to her sister-in-law, whose daughter Marie-Louise was born six days after:

> God has gone to the wrong house because I, who lost my last little girl, would be so happy to have another child. But no, I won't have any more! Now it's useless to wish for it. I'll never get over the death of my little Thérèse [Melanie]. Quite often it keeps me awake at night.[60]

Marie-Mélanie-Thérèse was born two and a half years before her saintly sister Marie-Françoise-Thérèse, who was named after her. Although she lived entirely for her children and would do anything for them, at the age of thirty-five, she was no longer able to breastfeed. This was a great source of humiliation and suffering for Zélie, who now relied on a wet nurse for her children. Unfortunately, the Martins had to use a stranger. To their shock, they discovered their two-month-old Mélanie-Thérèse was suffering from malnutrition and had been neglected and left alone for long periods of time. After her child died in her arms, Zélie wrote, "Tell me that we didn't have misfortune! Finally, it's over, there's nothing else we can do. The best thing to do is to resign myself. My child is happy and that consoles me."[61] Mélanie-Thérèse's cause of death was negligence and starvation at the hands of the Martin's wet nurse, who was an alcoholic. Zélie avoided walking on the street where Mélanie-Thérèse was nursed because of the painful memories it brought back. The fact that the child's death could have been easily prevented only added to her suffering.

After such tragedies, one would think the Martin's friends would be sympathetic to their suffering. Yet a friend at Mélanie-Thérèse's wake said to Zélie, "God surely sees that you could never cope with

---

60   Ibid., 84.
61   Ibid., 73.

raising so many children, and He took four of them to Paradise."[62]
A shocked Zélie replied:

> That's not how I understand it. In the end, God is the
> Master, and He doesn't have to ask for my permission.
> On the other hand, until now, I've very well endured all
> the hard work of motherhood, entrusting myself to His
> Providence. Besides, what do you want? We're not on
> this earth for our enjoyment. Those who expect to enjoy
> life are very wrong and remarkably disappointed in their
> expectations. We see this every day and, sometimes, in a
> very striking way.[63]

Zélie concluded her letter to her sister-in-law by sharing an
account of the recent death of their neighbor, an eleven-year-old
boy, and the impending death of his twelve-year-old sister. Their
parents are "very rich people, who have just bought a beautiful
house in order to retire from business. What's the point, now that
their lives are broken?"[64] Zélie was sharing a great truth: suffering
redirects our desires from the things of this life to the things of
Heaven, should we cooperate.

After a fire destroyed her brother Isidore's wholesale drug
business, Zélie wrote to his wife, "It's true that each person has a
cross to bear, but there are some for whom it is heavier than others.
My dear sister, you've already begun to see that life is not a bed
of roses. God wills this to detach us from the world and raise our
thoughts toward Heaven."[65] Zélie knew firsthand that suffering is
a vehicle by which God reminds us: "For here we have no lasting
city, but we seek the city which is to come" (Heb 13:14). Through
the hallmark of suffering and our own mortality, Our Lord points
us to His Resurrection, to the everlasting city, the world without
end. At the same time, suffering disposes us to a greater intimacy
with Our Lord and our neighbor, for without suffering we can
never appreciate how much God suffered for us nor learn to be

---

[62] Ibid., 82.
[63] Ibid.
[64] Ibid., 82–83.
[65] Ibid., 112.

compassionate to our neighbor. We cannot doubt Zélie felt sorrow for her neighbor's loss.

At the same time, Zélie never sought out suffering. She once wrote, "[Zélie's sister] thinks I desire great suffering because I told her, if I had the choice, that I would prefer to die from a slow illness. But great suffering, no. I don't have enough virtue to desire that; I dread it!"[66]

In addition to burying several children, Zélie experienced a gradual but intense deterioration of health, which caused great concern in her family. In December 1876, as her pain increased, she decided to consult a doctor. The doctor informed Zélie that she had cancer. Céline wrote:

> In the year 1865 she noticed a swelling in her breast. This was the result of an accident years before, in her youth, when she struck herself against the corner of a table. It was a source of great anxiety to father. Our uncle, M. Guérin, was consulted. No immediate treatment was prescribed. For eleven years nothing serious was feared, but then pain developed, revealing the presence of a cancerous tumor. This spread and after causing her terrible suffering, finally, led to her death [67]

Zélie described the dreaded moment she informed her family of her diagnosis:

> I couldn't help myself from telling my family everything. I regret it now because there was a grief-filled scene . . . everyone was crying, poor Leonie was sobbing. . . .
> And yet, I'm quite far from deluding myself, and I have trouble falling asleep at night when I think about the future. However, I'm resigning myself as best as I can, but I was far from expecting such a test.[68]

Louis was devastated. Zélie wrote to her sister-in-law, "My husband is inconsolable. He's given up the pleasure of fishing and

66 Ibid, 253–254.
67 Martin, *The Mother of the Little Flower*, 89.
68 Martin and Martin, *A Call to a Deeper Love*, 262–263.

put his lines up in the attic. . . . It's as if he's shattered."[69] On the advice of her brother, Zélie journeyed immediately to Lisieux on December 23, which would be her last birthday, to meet with two doctors and to see her brother and his family. Zélie would spend her last Christmas away from Louis and their children.

Writing to her beloved husband on December 24, 1876, Zélie penned these words shortly before attending Midnight Mass with her brother:

> So, let's put it into the hands of God because He knows much better than we do what we need. "It is He who causes the wound and He who binds it." I'll go to Lourdes on the first pilgrimage, and I hope the Blessed Mother will cure me, if it's necessary. In the meantime, let's stop worrying. I'm rejoicing very much at the thought of seeing you all again. How long the time seems! How I would like to come home today! I'm only happy when I'm with you, my dear Louis.[70]

In Zélie's case, surrender or despair were her only two options; she took the former. Throughout her suffering, Zélie and Louis's love only intensified as they came to appreciate every moment they had together. Though Zélie resigned herself to her cancer, she recognized the struggle to be holy even more so as her death approached. Zélie wrote on December 31, 1876 to her sister-in-law:

> As for me, I'm trying to convert myself, but I may not get through it. It's quite true that we die as we lived. We can't go against the current when we want. I assure you, I realize it well, and sometimes I become discouraged by it. And yet they say it only takes a moment to make a reprobate a saint, but I think that's only a very little saint! Oh well, there must be all kinds.[71]

Zélie possessed the sense of urgency that epitomized the saints, for they knew that with every beat of their heart, with every breath,

---

69   Ibid., 263.
70   Ibid., 266.
71   Ibid., 267.

and with every step they took, they were drawing nearer to their deaths and Our Lord's return.

Zélie's faith received its greatest test as her days on earth became numbered. Simple tasks like getting dressed or kneeling at Church became increasingly difficult. As her pain worsened, Zélie wasn't able to attend Mass at all, which greatly saddened her.

One month before her death on August 28, 1877, Zélie wrote to her brother, "Yesterday I called out for you in a loud voice, believing that you alone could relieve my pain. For twenty-four hours I suffered more than I'd ever suffered in my entire life, so those hours were spent moaning and crying out. I begged all the saints in Heaven, one after the other, but no one answered me!"[72] Marie recalled the incident as well, but also noted her mother's heroic self-forgetfulness in the face of suffering.

> Yesterday evening, she was suffering so much that she kept saying out loud: "Ah! my God, You see that I have no longer any strength to suffer. Have pity on me! Since I must remain here on this bed of pain, without anyone being able to give me relief, I beg you not to abandon me." Sometimes she weeps, and keeps looking at us one after the other. . . .
>
> In a word, our poor dear mother forgets herself to such a point that she is happy only when she sees us going off for a walk. In order to please and humor her, Papa took my sisters for a boat excursion. But what pleasure can we find, when we know our mother is so ill.[73]

Zélie's sacrificial nature did not allow her sufferings to become an occasion for self-pity. Instead, she kept her eyes on Our Lord, Who loved mankind more than Himself when he offered His life on Good Friday. Like Our Lord, she sought to make others happy even in the throes of death.

It was only one month earlier, on June 21, that Zélie made a pilgrimage to Lourdes with her three oldest daughters, Marie, Pauline, and Léonie. She did not receive a cure. She wrote, "I wish

---

72 Ibid.
73 Martin, *The Mother of the Little Flower*, 104.

I could have sent you a joyful telegram, but unfortunately, I'm not cured. On the contrary, the trip made my illness worse."[71] Her pilgrimage was a disaster, to say the least. In her own words, "When I arrived at the Grotto, my heart was so tight I couldn't even pray. During Mass, I was very close to the altar, but I was so exhausted I didn't understand a thing."[75]

Despite her dire circumstances, Zélie kept hoping for the best. She wrote, "I'm still expecting a miracle from the goodness and omnipotence of God through the intercession of the Holy Mother. Not that I'm asking Him to take away my illness completely, but only to let me live a few years to have time to raise my children, and, especially, poor Léonie, who needs me so much and who I feel so sorry for."[76]

On July 15, 1877, when it became clear that Our Lady was not going to cure her, Zélie wrote to her sister-in-law some of her most poignant words on suffering and surrender.

> You tell me not to lose confidence, and I'm certainly not losing confidence. I know very well that the Blessed Mother can cure me, but I can't help fearing that she doesn't want to, and I'll tell you honestly that a miracle seems very doubtful to me now. I've taken that stand and am trying to act as if I have to die. It's absolutely necessary that I not lose the little time I have left to live, these are days of salvation that will never come again, and so I must make the most of them.[77]

Further, Zélie penned so beautifully, "I'll have double the benefits. I'll suffer less by resigning myself, and I'll do part of my Purgatory on earth. So please, ask for resignation and patience for me, I need it very much. You know that I have hardly any patience."[78]

---

74 Martin and Martin, *A Call to a Deeper Love*, 324.
75 Ibid., 326.
76 Ibid., 331.
77 Ibid., 339.
78 Ibid.

She wrote her final letter to her beloved brother on August 16, 1877, twelve days before her death, which concluded with these words, "I can't write any longer, my strength is at an end. . . . What can you do? If the Blessed Mother doesn't cure me it's because my time is at an end, and God wants me to rest elsewhere other than on earth."[79]

Marie wrote to her aunt Céline three days before her mother's death, "I have sad news to tell you. Mamma is very much worse. Her illness is making frightful progress from day to day. The nights are terrible for her. She is obliged to rise every quarter of an hour, as her suffering prevents her from remaining in bed. . . . On Monday and Tuesday we did not know what to do. Her sufferings were atrocious. We could not relieve her in any way, and no remedy seems to quiet her."[80] In that same letter, Marie said, "Last night she had a hemorrhage; which has increased her weakness. Papa spent the whole night beside her; he was so distressed."[81] The following day Marie wrote to her uncle Isidore imploring his presence.

As Zélie received the Last Rites, her countenance changed. According to Louise, their former maid, Zélie's "serenity in the face of death was amazing!"[82] Forty-six years later, still moved by Zélie's last moments, Louise wrote to Louis and Zélie's living Carmelite daughters:

> During her illness, one day she received at her office a call from the parish priest of Montsort, who was her confessor, while I was present. She spoke to him of her death with so much resignation that the priest said "Madame, I have met many valiant women, but never one like you." The good pastor was less calm than Madame.[83]

Standing at the foot of Zélie's cross in her final moments was her husband, her brother Isidore, and her older daughters. Zélie died at 12:30 a.m. on August 28, 1877. Thérèse, who was four years

---

[79] Ibid., 346.
[80] Ibid., 370.
[81] Ibid.
[82] Wust and Wust, *Mother of St. Thérèse*, 310.
[83] Martin, *The Mother of the Little Flower*, 90.

old at the time, was not present when her mother died; she was already asleep as it was past midnight. Zélie's funeral Mass took place the next day on Wednesday, August 29, at 9:00 a.m. in the Church of Notre-Dame d'Alençon—the same church where only nineteen years earlier she married Louis. Zélie's burial followed at the Cemetery of Notre-Dame. In October 1894, after Louis's death, her body was exhumed and moved, along with her four children, to the family vault in Lisieux at the request of Zélie's brother.

Zélie's oldest daughter, Marie, recalled gazing upon her mother's dead body:

> During the course of the day I often went close to the body of my dear mother. I never tired of looking at her. She seemed to be but twenty years old. I thought that she was beautiful. I felt a supernatural impression as I stood beside her. It struck me, which was quite true, that she was not dead, but more alive than ever.[84]

Thérèse added, "Our father's *very affectionate heart* seemed to be enriched now with a truly maternal love!"[85]

In the midst of our sorrows, we ask: What is the point of so much suffering? Are we not on this earth to be happy? Zélie answered that question best, and she passed it on to her children in these words: "Happiness can't be found here below, and it's a bad sign when all goes well. In His wisdom, God wanted it this way to make us remember that the world is not our true home."[86]

Zélie died at the age of forty-five; Louis would live to be seventy. And both of them suffered long illnesses before death. Louis suddenly became paralyzed on May 1, 1887, when he was sixty-four, and would have two other strokes that year. Did Louis ask for such suffering? Thérèse recounted what her father said to her and his two other Carmelite daughters upon visiting them at Carmel:

> "Children, I returned from Alençon where I received in Notre Dame church such great graces, such consolations

84 Ibid., 111.
85 St. Thérèse of Lisieux, *Story of a Soul*, 35.
86 Martin and Martin, *A Call to a Deeper Love*, 8.

that I made this prayer: My God, it is too much! yes, I
am too happy, it isn't possible to go to heaven this way.
I want to suffer something for you! I offer myself..." the
word victim died on his lips; he didn't dare pronounce it
before us, but we had understood.[87]

Louis began to show early stages of cerebral arteriosclerosis,
which brought with it forgetfulness, anxiety, and hallucinations
related to dementia. But he told his daughters, "Children, do not
be afraid for me, for I am a friend of the good God."[88] As Louis's
health declined, and he even once disappeared for three days, Louis's
brother-in-law suggested that he be admitted to the Bon Sauveur
Mental Home, which was staffed by a few religious sisters. Louis
eventually agreed. Thérèse described how painful this was for her
and her sisters.

> I didn't know that on February 12, a month after my
> reception of the Habit, our dear Father would drink the
> *most bitter and most humiliating* of all chalices. Ah! that
> day, I didn't say I was able to suffer more! Words cannot
> express our anguish, and I'm not going to attempt to
> describe it. One day, in heaven, we shall love talking
> to another about our *glorious* trials; don't we already feel
> happy for having suffered them? Yes, Papa's three years
> of martyrdom appear to me as the most lovable, the
> most fruitful of my life; I wouldn't exchange them for
> all the ecstasies and revelations of the saints. My heart
> overflows with gratitude when I think of this inestimable
> *treasure* that must cause a holy jealousy to the angels of the
> heavenly court.[89]

How many children can say this of a parent's suffering? Only one
who is a masochist, or someone who knows the power of redemptive
suffering! Thérèse and her sisters were the latter and declared, "We
were no longer walking in the way of perfection, we were flying,

[87] St. Thérèse of Lisieux, *Story of a Soul*, 154.
[88] Martin, *The Father of Little Flower*, 88.
[89] St. Thérèse of Lisieux, *Story of a Soul*, 156–157.

all five of us,"[90] thanks to their father's sufferings. Thérèse was so inspired that she herself desired to suffer as well. She wrote, "My desire for suffering was answered, and yet my attraction for it did not diminish. My soul soon shared in the sufferings of my heart. Spiritual aridity was my daily bread and, deprived of all consolation, I was still the happiest of creatures since all my desires had been satisfied."[91] Louis himself said, "I was always accustomed to command, and here I must obey, it is hard! But I know why God has sent me this trial. I never had any humiliation in my life; I needed one."[92]

In the midst of his suffering, Louis tried to forget himself. Such is the heart of a saint. Those who personally knew Louis said he never complained, but possessed a grateful heart. Even when his daughters told him they were praying a novena to St. Joseph for his cure and to return to his beloved home, Louis replied, "No, you must not ask that, but only the Will of God."[93] Louis's words echo those of Zélie, who, on her way to Lourdes, resigned herself to God's will. The doctors and the sisters who cared for Louis had never met a patient like him. One sister, whose eyes were filled with tears upon seeing Louis's joyful resignation, said, "We're caring for a saint."[94]

Louis, whose legs were fully paralyzed, returned to Lisieux in May 1892. He moved into a small rented home facing his brother-in-law's house. Louis asked to pay his Carmelite daughters one last visit. His daughter Céline, who tended to him for his final two years, described the visit:

> On May 12, our father was taken to Carmel. It was his last visit as it was feared that too much emotion would harm him. When at the moment of his leaving the Carmelites were saying good-bye to him, he raised his eyes, pointed with his finger to Heaven, and remained thus quite a while, being unable to express his thoughts except by the words, uttered in a voice full of tears: *"In Heaven!"*[95]

---

[90]   Ibid., 157.
[91]   Ibid.
[92]   Martin, *The Father of the Little Flower*, 92–93.
[93]   Ibid., 95.
[94]   Piat, *Celine*, 38.
[95]   Martin, *The Father of the Little Flower*, 105.

Louis, of course, meant that he would be reunited with his departed wife and children someday. Their aunt Céline recalled that his three Carmelite daughters "were so delighted to see their father; but after the first moments, the tears they had held back did flow."[96] It was the last time they would see him alive. Louis's last words to his daughters were probably his shortest yet most important, for they provided hope to Thérèse and her sisters that suffering does not have the final say. Like Louis, parents must never lose sight of Heaven in the midst of their sufferings.

On July 29, 1894, Louis entered eternal life at the age of seventy as Céline invoked the names of Jesus, Mary, and Joseph. In doing so, she gave her father the most beautiful gift a child can give her parent in his final moments, which is to support him and pray for him at his Calvary. Céline described the peaceful death of her father to her cloistered sisters in Carmel.

> Papa is in Heaven! . . . I received his last breath, I closed his eyes. . . . His handsome face took on immediately an expression of beatitude, of such profound calm! Tranquility was painted on his features. . . . He expired so gently at fifteen minutes after eight. My poor heart was broken at the supreme moment; a flood of tears bathed his bed. But at heart I was joyful because of his happiness, after the terrible martyrdom he endured and which we shared with him. . . . Last night, in a sleep filled with anguish, I suddenly awakened; I saw in the firmament a kind of luminous globe. . . . And this globe went deeply into the immensity of heaven.[97]

She also told her sisters that their father had received the Anointing of the Sick, Absolution, and a plenary indulgence the night of his death.

Louis's legacy is undeniable. Thérèse gave him the greatest glory by becoming a saint, which was only possible because he showed her and his other children how to suffer with serenity. Thus, Louis revealed to his daughters that one should not expect others to

---

96   Ibid.
97   St. Thérèse of Lisieux, *General Correspondence,* Volume II, 875.

walk the path of sainthood unless they themselves have taken the first steps.

Thérèse wrote to Léonie (Sr. Thérèse-Dosithee) about her father less than one month after his death:

> Papa's death does not give me the impression of a death but of a real *life*. I am finding him once more after an absence of six years, I feel him around *me*, looking at me and protecting me . . . . Dear little Sister, are we not more united now that we gaze on the heavens to find there a Father and a Mother who offered us to Jesus? . . . Soon their desires will be accomplished, and all the children God gave them are going to be united to Him forever.[98]

Louis and Zélie taught their daughters to carry their crosses with resignation. As Zélie declared, "We have to carry our cross in one way or another. We say to God, 'I don't want that one.' Often our prayer is answered, but often also to our misfortunate. It's better to patiently accept what happens to us. There's always joy alongside the pain."[99] In fact, Thérèse herself died a very painful death at the young age of twenty-four from tuberculosis. But she was inspired by her parents' example to suffer even more for God. Having seen her saintly parents embrace their crosses serenely and joyfully, Thérèse was able to say to God, "Thy will be done" (Mt 26:42). Céline believed that "Papa will certainly have no purgatory in the other world, but these sorrows are so sharp for us that they can, I think, bring about changes in our souls that will make us saints. I don't believe the saints had harder trials."[100]

Louis's suffering and death certainly contributed to the sanctity of his daughters. Thérèse declared, "Our dear Father must be much loved by Jesus to have to suffer in this way, but don't you find that the misfortune that is striking him is really the complement of his beautiful life?"[101]

---

[98] Ibid., 884.
[99] Martin and Martin *A Call to a Deeper Love*, 88.
[100] St. Thérèse of Lisieux, *General Correspondence,* Volume I, 540.
[101] Ibid., 537.

On July 21, 1891, Thérèse had written to Céline something so profound that it encapsulates the virtue of suffering.

> Dear Celine, the image of this world is passing, the shadows are lengthening, soon we shall be in our native land, soon the joys of our childhood, the Sunday evenings, the intimate chats . . . all this will be restored to us forever and with interest. Jesus will return to us the joys which He has deprived us of for one moment![102]

Due to their parents' example of patient and joyful resignation to suffering, Thérèse, Pope John Paul II, Josemaría Escrivá, and countless other saints were inspired to save souls. In the midst of their trials, the hope of seeing their beloved parents one day at the eternal family reunion with God provided the motivation to keep pressing forward. And while some will contend that sanctity entails giving alms to the poor, going to Mass daily, making a Holy Hour, or perhaps praying the Rosary, Thérèse asserted, "Sanctity does not consist in saying beautiful things, it does not even consist in thinking them, in feeling them! . . . It consists in *suffering* and suffering *everything*."[103]

St. Monica and Patricius

St. Augustine, who lived nearly fifteen centuries before St. Thérèse and her godly parents, once wrote:

> In my youth, miserable wretch that I was, yes, most wretched from the first dawning of adolescence, I had begged You for chastity, and said: "Give me chastity and continence, but, not for a while," for I was afraid that You might hear me too soon and heal me of concupiscence, which I wished rather to satiate than to extinguish.[104]

Just as virtue is taught in one's home, so too is vice. The former takes great discipline and toil while the latter can easily

---

[102] Ibid., 732.
[103] Ibid., 557–558.
[104] St. Augustine, *The Confessions of St. Augustine*, 215.

be transmitted to our children, resulting in great suffering for the
entire family. Even though St. Monica provided a solid witness,
Augustine chose instead to adopt the vices of his father, Patricius.
Augustine wrote about his mother, "She so discreetly endured his
wrongdoing of her bed, that she never had any jealous quarrel with
her husband for that matter. Because she still expected Thy mercy
upon him, that believing in Thee, he might turn chaster."[105] Besides
his infidelity, Monica endured Patricius's anger and cautioned her
maidservants with this advice, "Guard your tongue when your
husband is angry."[106]

Augustine fathered an illegitimate child at the age of seventeen
and lived with the child's mother for fifteen years, during which he
renounced the Faith. Monica's grandson, Adeodatus, which means,
"gift of God," was baptized with his father on April 24, 387, by St.
Ambrose. Adeodatus died a holy death in the year 389, less than
two years later, when he was sixteen. In addition to the suffering
caused by her husband and son, Monica also experienced great
hardship from permanently living with her mother-in-law, which
was largely due to malicious gossip about Monica spread by their
maidservants. Their fractured relationship was eventually repaired
when the truth prevailed. Regardless, Monica suffered more in a
lifetime than most. Yet her sufferings had not been in vain. God
rewarded this heroic women's tears, perseverance, and suffering by
bringing about the conversion of her husband and son, as well as a
harmonious relationship with her mother-in-law.

Augustine's life reminds us that a father's holy or unholy example
can lead his children to great virtue or great vice. Had Patricius
loved Monica freely, faithfully, totally, and fruitfully, Augustine may
never have fathered a child out of wedlock. Even the most devout
parents cannot prevent the misguided free will of their children; yet
parents living a virtuous life and with a rich prayer life have won
half the battle.

Augustine converted to the Faith at the age of thirty-two, and
four years later he was ordained a priest. Even though he lived to

[105] Cruz, *Secular Saints*, 535.
[106] Ibid.

seventy-five, he might have experienced an even greater intimacy with God and helped save many more souls—let alone caused his mother less suffering—had he not spent fifteen years of his life seeking the pleasures of the flesh rather than laboring in the Lord's vineyard. Augustine himself admitted his regret for delaying the Lord's invitation of love, with these most splendid words: "Too late have I loved Thee, O Beauty so ancient, O Beauty so new, too late have I loved Thee! Behold, Thou were within me and I was outside, and it was there that I sought You. Deformed as I was, I ran after those beauteous things that Thou have made."[107]

The late Mother Angelica, a Poor Clare cloistered nun and founder of EWTN Catholic television network, lived a saintly life and died on Easter Sunday 2016. She offered her sisters one of the greatest lessons on the value of suffering.

> We don't understand the awesomeness of living even one more day. . . . I told my sisters the other day, "When I get really bad give me all the medicine I can take, all the tubes you can stuff down me." "Why'd you want that?" "I want to live." "Why?" "Because I will have suffered one more day for the love of God. . . . I will exercise you in virtue. But most of all I will know God better. You cannot measure the value of one new thought about God in your own life."[108]

Many of the saints experienced an acute awareness of suffering from an early age, due to the death of one or both of their parents, some of whom died while still in the prime of their lives, for instance, the fathers of Sts. Jeanne Jugan, John Bosco, John of the Cross, and Maria Goretti; and the mothers of Sts. Katherine Drexel, Thérèse of Lisieux, and Pope John Paul II. Perhaps many of these parents of the saints had an intuitive sense that their time on earth would be but a blink of an eye, and, therefore, they lived with a greater sense of urgency than most.

---

[107] St. Augustine, *The Confessions of St. Augustine*, 297.

[108] Ivana Hrynkiw, "Mother Angelica, Founder of EWTN, Dies on Easter Sunday," al.com, al.com/news/index.ssf/2016/03/mother_angelica_founder_of_ewt.html.

Whether the Lord gave these parents five or forty years with their children, they wanted their children not only to know the love of God, but also to have an example of someone who suffers well. They sought to savor every moment while embracing their crosses, for each moment brought them one step closer to death. After death, there would be no more opportunities to help Our Lord carry His Cross or merit a greater crown in Heaven. That is why the present moment is so rich and why we need to embrace this reality. There is no question that, in the words of Mother Angelica, the "awesomeness of living even one more day" beckoned the parents of the saints and their children not to waste another day, but to use it to love God better and to suffer for Him so as to bring many more souls to Heaven with us. Whether these parents died first, or their children—God forbid—they would be spiritually ready to be meet their Maker, Lover, and Redeemer. Perhaps God took many of these holy parents in the prime of their lives as a way to better prepare their children for their future vocations, that is, lives completely attached to God and detached from this world. Can you imagine the anticipation and joy that Pope John Paul II felt to see the face of God as he lay dying on April 2, 2005, while the entire Catholic world prayed for his peaceful death? Can you imagine the longing in his heart to be reunited with his departed family in Heaven?

There is no question that the parents of the saints and their children suffered tremendously. In fact, they experienced some of the most intense suffering humans can experience. Why? Because Christ wants us to be conformed to Him, and suffering is the "narrow gate" (Mt 7:13) by which we enter into Him so as to be transformed into another Christ. St. Vincent de Paul, a seventeenth-century French priest, offers one of the most clear answers to the question: Why must the innocent suffer? Vincent declared, "God, to procure His glory, sometimes permits that we should be dishonored and persecuted without reason. He wishes thereby to render us conformable to His Son, who was calumniated and treated as a seducer, as an ambitious man, and as one possessed."[109]

---

[109] "Saint Vincent de Paul," CatholicSaints.Info, catholicsaints.info/saint-vincent-de-paul/.

The sufferings in the lives of the saints and their parents give hope to all of us who suffer. Know this, that those who suffer greatly in this life are the closest to Our Lord. For God only gives suffering to His closest friends because He loves them. We need to look no further than the Blessed Mother. No one can conceive a greater suffering than Mary watching her child be violently murdered in front of her own eyes, hanging upon a cross to slowly suffer and die. Many saints say that Our Lord suffered more watching His own mother suffer than from His own torture. Mary could do nothing but simply be with Him and pray for those who killed her Son, which is you and me, and that there would be courageous souls in every generation who would not be afraid to stand at the foot of the Cross alongside her rather than abandon Him when their own sufferings come.

The salient lesson is that the parents of the saints reveal that we cannot become saints without suffering, which perfects us in virtue and detaches us from the things of the world so that we might be conformed to Christ Crucified. A rose grows surrounded by thorns, and so too did these holy parents and their saintly children flourish not despite their crosses, but because of them. St. Zélie once wrote to her brother.

> You know that we're all given to pride, and I often notice those who have made their fortune are, for the most part, unbearably arrogant. I'm not saying that I've reached that point, or you either, but we've been more or less marred by this pride. It's certain then that constant prosperity takes us away from God. Never has He led His chosen ones down that road. They have passed through the crucible of suffering beforehand to be purified.[110]

Suffering is never an end itself, but a means to a deeper union with Christ. In the midst of our sufferings, we might experience the temptation to blame God or ask God, "Why me?" We would do well to remember that Our Lord leads His chosen ones, as Zélie said, "through the crucible of suffering."

---

[110] Martin and Martin, *A Call to a Deeper Love*, 101.

Our crosses frequently open our eyes to what is most important in this life: God, Faith, and family; while stripping us of what is least important: pleasure, power, prestige, and wealth. Hence, suffering led many of these devout parents and their children to adopt a simple lifestyle. For Heaven is our true home, and we are merely pilgrims walking on the path to the Eternal Shrine, where there is no beginning or end. Our Lord once told St. Rose of Lima, "This is the only true stairway [afflictions] to paradise, and without the cross they can find no road to climb to heaven."[111]

---

[111] *The Liturgy of the Hours,* Volume IV, 1342.

HALLMARK FIVE

Simplicity

*Everything that a man owns over and above his personal
needs is excess and should be shared compassionately
with others.*[1]—St. Bridget of Sweden

Married to one of the wealthiest men in the early fourteenth century,
St. Bridget of Sweden is one of the least likely souls to appear in a
chapter written on simplicity. Yet the virtuous parents of the saints
and their holy offspring have proven time and again that they are the
exception to the rule. Their lives contradict the world and serve as a
reminder that God's grace can allow someone who is very wealthy
to be simple. To quote Ven. Fulton Sheen:

> Character is nothing more or less than the reconciling of
> opposite virtues. In other words, a really great character is
> not just a brave person, for if a person was brave without
> being tender, he or she might very easily become cruel.
> Tenderness is what might be called the other wing to
> bravery.[2]

As Sheen further declared, "The possession of one virtue in
an eminent degree no more makes a great person than one wing
makes a bird."[3] By definition, simplicity refers to the freedom from
complexity, the absence of luxury, and sincerity, among other things.
It is also the mean between excess and deficiency. Simplicity is often

---

[1] Holbock, *Married Saints and Blesseds Through the Centuries*, 248.
[2] Fulton Sheen, *From the Angel's Backboard: The Best of Fulton J. Sheen, A
Centennial Celebration* (Liguori, MO: Triumph Books, 1995), 173.
[3] Ibid.

associated with poverty, but one who is poor may not necessarily possess the virtue of simplicity, while one who has wealth may in fact. In many cases, souls who are poor by circumstance and those who embrace poverty willingly for the sake of the Gospel tend to acquire simplicity more easily than those with great wealth and material possessions because the former are more detached from the things of this world. Our Lord even said, "Again I tell you, it is easier for a camel to go through the eye of a needle than for a rich man to enter the kingdom of God" (Mt 19:24). Our Lord does not disdain the rich. What Our Lord disdains is attachment to anything other than Himself, including riches. That is why Our Lord calls everyone to be generous with their money and, above all, their talents. In fact, the Church is filled with saints who were well off, but still embraced a penitential and simplistic lifestyle, such as Bridget of Sweden, King Louis IX, Thomas More, and many more. These saints came to realize how precious simplicity is. St. Vincent de Paul once wrote, "Simplicity ought to be held in great esteem. . . . It is a virtue most worthy of love, because it leads us straight to the kingdom of God."[4]

To understand what simplicity truly is, we must look to the greatest example of simplicity, which is God Himself. "God is truly and absolutely simple,"[5] according to St. Augustine. This was further expounded upon by St. Thomas Aquinas, who wrote, "There is neither composition of quantitative parts in God, since he is not a body; nor composition of form and matter."[6] The foundation for the Church's teaching on simplicity flows from the Gospel of St. John, which declares, "God is spirit" (4:24). In essence, God is not composed of parts or divisible by any physical or metaphysical means. God is simple in terms of His substance, His nature, and His very being. Aside from all the philosophical intricacies of God as stated above, Our Lord chose a simplistic lifestyle from His humble birth, living far below His worthiness more so than any of the saints were capable.

---

[4]   *A Year with The Saints* (Rockford, IL: TAN Books, 1988), 199.
[5]   St. Thomas Aquinas, *Summa Theologica*, Volume One, 19. Originally cited in *De Trin.* iv, 6.7.
[6]   Ibid.

St. Peter Damian, Doctor of the Church, once beautifully wrote, "The Creator of Angels is not said to have been clad in purple, but to have been wrapped in rags. Let worldly pride blush at the resplendent humility of the Savior."[7] During His earthly life, Christ traded the praises of the angels for the reviling of men, and His heavenly throne for a simple dwelling at Nazareth and a wooden cross at Calvary. Our Lord's simplistic lifestyle flowed from who He is. It could be argued that the Holy Eucharist is the greatest manifestation of Our Lord's simplicity. As St. Teresa of Calcutta once wrote, "Christ made Himself Bread of Life. He wanted to give Himself to us in a special way, in a *simple*, tangible way because it is hard for human beings to love a God whom they cannot see."[8] If Our Lord appeared in the Holy Eucharist in His full glory, we would scarcely approach Him. Yet, in His simplicity and poverty under the species of bread and wine, Our Lord longs for us to receive Him, provided we have no stain of mortal sin. And, by receiving Our Lord under the appearance of bread and wine, we receive the grace to become more like Him, thus growing in the virtue of simplicity.

St. Bridget of Sweden

Desiring to imitate the simplicity of God, St. Bridget, a daughter of a knight who was one of the richest landowners in Sweden, understood that she was a steward of the Lord's gifts, which included her time, her talents, and her money. Though not totally free from luxury while her husband lived, Bridget used God's money not for herself, but for others. She lived an authentic vocation as a mother of eight children, one of whom was St. Catherine of Sweden, by putting her family and the less fortunate before herself while painfully ridding herself of vanity. In doing so, Bridget exemplified the virtue of simplicity, which is one of the main reasons the Church reveres her. In fact, the Bull of Canonization promulgated by Pope Boniface IX,

---

[7] St. Alphonsus de Liguori, *The Incarnation Birth and Infancy of Jesus Christ* (Brooklyn, NY: Redemptorist Fathers, 1927), 116.

[8] St. Teresa of Calcutta, *No Greater Love* (Novato, California: New World Library, 1997), 117.

who presided over Bridget's canonization in 1391, sheds light on her heroic simplicity and generosity:

> She opened her hand to the poor and reached out her hands to the needy [cf. Prov 31:20], because for God's sake she untiringly performed the duties of an inexhaustible charity toward the needy, the sick, and the despised. Even while her husband was still alive, she invited twelve poor people to dine at her house each day, waited on them herself and gave them all they needed; every Thursday she washed their feet in memory of the Lord's Last Supper. Using her own income, she restored ruined hospitals in several regions of her native land, she visited the poor and the sick there most diligently as a loving, merciful, and industrious servant. . . . She touched, washed, bandaged, and tended their wounds without horror or loathing. . . . She praised the Lord and became more and more steadfast in faith, firm in hope, and ardent in charity. . . . Being noble-minded, she looked down on the vainglory of empty show and reputation.[9]

While her husband's fame increased throughout Sweden, Bridget, like Our Lady, quietly devoted herself to the simplicity of being a mother and another handmaid of the Lord, while shunning prestige and comfort in order to make others more comfortable. In fact, Our Lady once appeared to Bridget and shared with her the centrality of simplicity and poverty when she declared, "From the beginning I vowed in my own heart that I would never possess anything on earth."[10] Our Lady and the parents of the saints knew that to possess anything less than God was to be truly poor, for the one who possesses God alone is truly rich. How easy it would have been for Bridget to waste her husband's money, or, even worse, to choose not to have children because they wanted to "eat, drink, [and] be merry" (Lk 12:19). Instead, Bridget took Our Lady's message of poverty to heart as well as the words that Our Lord spoke to His disciples when He told them to "invite the poor, the maimed, the

---

9 Holbock, *Married Saints and Blesseds Through the Centuries*, 246.
10 St. Alphonsus de Liguori, The *Glories of Mary*, 576.

lame, the blind, and you will be blessed, because they cannot repay you. You will be repaid at the resurrection of the just" (Lk 14:13–14). To cultivate the virtues of simplicity and generosity in her children, Bridget would often bring them with her while performing works of charity.

Bridget also entrusted her children to wise and virtuous instructors. She desired to instill in her children a simple heart that holds no air of superiority, or inferiority, over others, but only sees Christ present in one's neighbors. More intelligent than her husband, Bridget taught him how to read. However, her simplicity combined with the virtue of humility protected Bridget from a condescending attitude toward both her husband and the vast majority of people who could not read at the time. In the book *My Way of Life*, a short, simplified version of the *Summa Theologica*, the following description of a saint brings to light the great virtue of simplicity.

> The saint head over heels in love with God, finds the most perfect fellowship with every least and greatest thing in the universe, with every least and greatest man and woman. He understands them, he is at one with them, being himself so closely one with the God Who is their source, the model on which they are formed, the goal to which they are so drawn. He is so close to the world and to men because his heart is so close to God.[11]

How fitting is this quote, which in a special way seems to describe Bridget and echoes the foundation of simplicity—God Himself. Bridget's simplicity overflowed to generosity and evangelization. She ensured that her children and maids were instructed in the Faith and, each evening, would read them selections from Sacred Scripture or the lives of the saints. Besides God, her family and Christ in her neighbor were everything to Bridget. Her simplicity was such that there was no hiding anything from God—there was total transparency—and she felt no need to impress others by her

---

[11] Walter Farrell, OP, and Martin Healy, *My Way of Life: Pocket Edition of St. Thomas, the Summa Simplified for Everyone* (New York: Confraternity of the Precious Blood, 1952), 12.

Like most parents who one day must let their children leave home, Philip's parents allowed him, at the age of eighteen, to live with their generous cousin who owned a prosperous business on the outskirts of Rome. By taking this position, Philip would inherit a huge fortune due to his cousin having no heirs. However, after working there for a little while, Philip found himself in a crisis and soon left his cousin to work for the next ten years as a caretaker for two children in Rome, both of whom would become religious later in life, thanks to Philip's influence. Even as a layman, Philip, who would eventually become a priest and founder of the Oratorian Order, would often hold all night prayer vigils in the caves under the Church of San Sebastian.

Francesco and his wife willed the best for their son, even if it meant he would never become rich, add recognition to the family name, or, worse, cause family friction. Philip and his parents never compromised God's will, peace, or joy in exchange for money or human respect, or for the sake of pleasing others, including their relatives.

Bernard and Anne Emmerick

Nearly three centuries after St. Bridget of Sweden and two centuries after St. Phillip Neri, on September 8, 1774, in Flaschen, Germany, Bernard and Anne Emmerick welcomed their daughter Bl. Anne Catherine, one of ten children, into their humble abode. Unlike Bridget of Sweden, who came from money and married into money, Bernard and Anne were very poor farmers. As a result, their children were expected to assist in the work, and their schooling was cut short to provide labor on the farm. Anne Catherine learned to appreciate the importance of manual labor from her youth due to her parent's tireless example as well as her own various chores around the farm and, later, as a seamstress for several years. As she grew older, her desire for prayer intensified as did her call to the religious life. However, there was one obstacle keeping Anne Catherine from entering the convent. Unlike many women today, it had nothing to do with her parents' opposition to her vocation, her desire to have a family, or even her love for the world and natural repugnance toward the more austere life of being nun. In fact, she was already living a simple, poor, and prayerful life like her parents, so surely religious life would not have been that much of an adjustment from her current lifestyle of *ora et labora*, Latin for pray and work, and the motto of the Benedictine Order. The real obstacle to Anne Catherine's vocation was her family's poverty. The custom for many convents at that time was to insist that their candidates provide some monetary offering, while other convents with more wealth could dispense with the dowry. Anne Catherine had applied to several convents, but was turned down by all of them because she could not supply a dowry.

One convent though, the Poor Clares in Münster, accepted Anne Catherine under the condition that she learn to play the organ before joining. Unselfish and simple hearted, Bernard and Anne highly supported this proposition and encouraged their daughter to follow her heart and fulfill God's will instead of imposing their own will on their daughter when they could have profited from her help on the farm. The Emmerick's simplicity of heart was not only detached from the material things of this life, but, even greater, from their own will, knowing that "the LORD preserves the simple" (Ps 116:6).

Seeking to fulfill the condition of her entrance into the convent, Anne Catherine made arrangements to be trained as an organist by Mr. Söntgen. However, she was so touched by the poverty of the Söntgen family that she gave them her earnings and served them instead, which further delayed her vocation. Such was the daughter of simplicity, who was detached from money and even her own will to help others.

After putting her vocation on hold for several years to obtain a dowry, Anne Catherine, at the age of twenty-eight, entered a convent of Augustinian nuns instead of the Poor Clares. Having learned the virtue of simplicity from her parents' example, Anne Catherine was not afraid of the drudgery of menial labor that many of her religious sisters despised. However, due to her poor upbringing, Anne Catherine was sometimes treated as an inferior by sisters from more affluent families and was even mocked for her strict observance of the rule. Anne Catherine bore all this in silence

and submission, learning from the example of Christ's suffering and
that of her own parents, simple and poor farmers, who never desired
the wealth and titles of this world, but simply to remain humble,
working with their hands in the dirt of the fields.

Tragically, Anne Catherine's convent was suppressed by the
King of Westphalia in 1812, forcing Anne Catherine to live as a
laywoman before dying on February 9, 1824. For her beatification
on October 3, 2004, Pope St. John Paul II wrote these inspiring
words about both Anne Catherine and her parents:

> The fact that the daughter of poor peasants who sought
> tenaciously to be close to God became the well-known
> "Mystic of the Land of Münster" was a work of divine
> grace. Her material poverty contrasted with her *rich
> interior life.* We are equally impressed by the new Blessed's
> patience in putting up with physical weakness and
> her *strong character,* as well as her *unshakable faith.*[15]

The Emmericks reveal that true poverty, particularly poverty of
spirit, leads to simplicity. Bernard and Anne taught their children
that poverty and simplicity are the pathways to Christ's heart and
the best remedy against raising spoiled, entitled children. The
Emmericks could not offer their daughter much, I dare say little in
material goods, but they could offer her the precious gift of faith, an
example of hard work, and a great devotion to prayer. In doing so,
Bernard and Anne revealed to Anne Catherine that Christ calls His
brides to be like the Bridegroom and His Mother Mary, who are
poor and simple. The Emmericks were true laborers, "farmers" in
Christ's vineyard. Through their poverty and simplicity, they tilled
the soil and planted the seeds, but it was their children, especially
Anne Catherine, who were their greatest harvest.

While the Church and her members celebrate the harvest, that is
her saints, blesseds, and holy children with various feast days, many
forget that there would be no harvest, no canonized saints, were
it not for holy married couples, who were unafraid to toil silently,

---

[15] Pope St. John Paul II, Homily for the Beatification of Five Servants of
God, October 3, 2004.

heroically, and simply for the glory of God and not the glory of man. In this case, there would have been no Bl. Anne Catherine Emmerick had her parents failed to put their hands to the plow and till their children's hearts with their own example for "the harvest is plentiful, but the laborers are few" (Mt 9:37).

François and Louise Soubirous

On January 7, 1844, twenty years after Bl. Anne Catherine Emmerick's death, François and Louise Soubirous gave birth to their first of nine children, Bernarde-Marie, known today as St. Bernadette. She was only fourteen years when Our Lady appeared to this poor, simple, and humble girl. Perhaps Our Lady saw something in Bernadette that reminded her of herself when the Angel Gabriel appeared to her, surely both were around the same age and both were very simple and humble women. Does not Our Lady throughout history purposely appear to lowly and simple people? Perhaps she knows they will not become prideful after receiving these heavenly messages; instead, the visionaries of Our Lady, like Bernadette, resemble her Magnificat, becoming even more humble for such a gift as seeing Our Lady and being conduits of her message. Or, best put by St. Paul, "God chose what is foolish in the world to shame the wise, God chose what is weak in the world to shame the strong" (1 Cor 1:27).

Although Bernadette was not born simple, it was through her parents' example that she was aided in acquiring this virtue. François and Louise lived a very simple lifestyle, which was clearly influenced by their great poverty. François was a poor miller, who eventually lost his job. Consequently, the Soubirous family, which included four children (five had previously died in infancy), lived in a single room that had previously been a jail. The view from their one-bedroom apartment was not the ocean or some wooded forest, but a dung heap and stable yard. Their neighbors were not even real human beings, but their cousin's livestock. Their tiny stone house was damp and had a foul odor, which only worsened Bernadette's asthma. In fact, the apartment was so small that they could only fit one cupboard, three family beds, and a fireplace. While François and Louise worked various jobs to help support their family, none seemed to advance their current situation. A standard breakfast for the Soubirouses involved sliced maize bread with garlic and sprinkled salt. However, despite their poverty, Bernadette always appeared clean.

Unfortunately, due to their difficult situation, François and Louise sent Bernadette, at the age of thirteen, to live with a foster mother, Marie Lagues, who promised to send her to school and instruct her in the Faith. The latter she did, but not the former, as Bernadette would attend to the sheep and pray her Rosary. Eventually, Bernadette would return to her family as she wanted to make her First Holy Communion and her unique dialect made it difficult to understand Madame Lagues's French.

Despite their difficult financial circumstances, François and Louise's faith, and especially Bernadette's, kept them joyful and loving. While most families do not choose to be poor, God calls all families to slowly detach themselves from the things of this life because Heaven is our true native land. Regardless, poverty and simplicity only have value if they lead a family and their children to God and a life of continual conversion and joy. More than anything, Bernadette's simplicity and humility must have come from her parents, who practiced both of these virtues. Years later, when writing to her younger brother and godson, Pierre, from the convent, Bernadette offered some advice on whether he should become a priest, if it be God's will, or follow some trade. She made it clear that she did not want Pierre to become a priest for the prestige, which would have afforded him a better financial life than their father. If that were his motives, she told him, "I would rather you become a rag picker."[16]

Our Lady loves the simple of heart in a special way for they best resemble her and her Son; and, even after Our Lady appeared to their daughter, François and Louise remained simple and humble. In fact, they offered Bernadette to the convent without a dowry at a time when most convents only accepted girls with a dowry unless they were convinced the aspiring nun had a true vocation. Deep

---

[16]   Ball, *Modern Saints,* Book One, 76.

in their hearts, or perhaps even written on the walls of their one-bedroom apartment, paralleling the Holy Family's humble abode in Nazareth, were the words of Our Lady to Bernadette, "I do not promise you happiness in this world, but in the next."[17]

When asked about her apparitions in the convent by other sisters, Sr. Bernadette at the time would calmly ask the sister what she did with a broom when she was finished and replied, "You put it behind the door, and that is what the Virgin has done with me. While I was useful, she used me, and now she has put me behind the door."[18] And, while François and Louise's life changed forever when Our Lady appeared to their simple daughter, their virtue never changed because they remained grounded in humility and simplicity. Perhaps the townspeople and their relatives would call them the parents of a visionary. Yet, like their daughter, they felt blessed to be God's little broom. They were not inflated with pride that their daughter was a famous visionary, but recognized that everything is a gift from God.

Unlike many families who blame God for unemployment or financial debt, or many children who complain that they do not have enough, we need to look at the example of the Soubirous family, who always remained faithful to God and Our Lady during their difficult financial times. Simplicity brought contentment to the Soubirous family despite being poor and living in a one-bedroom apartment, and simplicity beckons us to be at peace with whatever God decides to give or take away: richness or poverty, sickness or health. And, while poverty is not necessarily simplicity, the Soubirouses reveal that being content with what we have, albeit riches or poverty, and holding nothing back from God, including our own children, is the secret of true peace amidst the sufferings of this life.

Isaac and Clothilde Bessette

In addition to François and Louise Soubirous, another French couple would lead their children to a life of simplicity while embracing poverty at around the same time period in French Canada, thirty miles from Montreal, in the farming village of Mont-Saint-

---

17   Ibid., 73.
18   Ibid., 76.

Gregoire. Like François and Louise Soubirous, Isaac and Clothilde Bessette have been long forgotten, yet their eighth out of twelfth children, Alfred, is one of Canada's most cherished saints. Alfred, who took the religious name of Br. André when he joined the Congregation of the Holy Cross, remained rooted in his parents' simplicity, which is one of the main reasons that he was canonized on October 17, 2010, by Pope Benedict XVI. Just as Jesus learned the value of hard work and simplicity from St. Joseph, the same could be said of André with his father Isaac. Like Joseph, Isaac was employed as a carpenter and a woodcutter. The family was forced to move several times as Isaac sought to better provide for his growing family. Unfortunately, tragedy visited the Bessette family when Isaac died in a freak lumbering accident, leaving his six-year-old future saint without a father and his wife to provide for ten children by herself—two had died before André was born. Six years later, tragedy again struck the Bessette household again when Clothilde became sick with tuberculosis and died on November 10, 1857. As a result, André became an orphan at the young age of twelve. Despite his mother's unexpected death, André was fortunate to have had some critical years of formation with his devout mother. One of Br. André's religious brothers and friends, Fr. Henri-Paul Bergeron, CSC, described André's saintly mother:

> Virtuous, meek, hardworking, the mother of little Alfred proved herself an ideal Christian parent. At the knee of this illiterate woman of the people, he learned to lisp the names of Jesus, Mary, and Joseph along with those of Papa and Mamma, and thus came to associate in his childish mind the love of his dear ones on earth with the love of the Heaven Family.[19]

Though Br. André had few memories of his father, his mother clearly made a strong impression on the saint. He once wrote:

> Because I was sickly, my mother always showed me a deeper affection than she showed the others. She used

---

[19] Henri-Paul Bergeron, CSC, *Brother André: The Wonder Man of Mount Royal* (Montréal: Saint Joseph's Oratory, 2007), 11.

> to kiss me repeatedly and often gave me little dainties.
> During the family evening prayer, I used to kneel beside
> her and follow the Rosary on her beads. My mother was
> always smiling—such a lovely smile! Even since her death
> she often smiles at me. Sometimes I see her looking at me
> and loving me though she utters not a word. I seldom pray
> for my mother, but I often pray to her.[20]

André would be raised by his aunt (his mother's sister) and uncle who kept him on the narrow path, while his other siblings were spread out among other relatives. By the time of his mother's death, André could hardly read or even pen his own name. In terms of education, André once said the following words, which hearkens back to his illiterate parents and their great simplicity, "It is not necessary to have been well educated, to have spent many years in college, to love the good God. It is sufficient to want to do so generously."[21] In effect, André received from his parents the greatest inheritance that money can never buy, which is a deep faith and love for God. Some parents may never be able to afford the best education for their children, or even the latest iPhone, but they can give their children the best gift: an example of simplicity and an unshakable faith in God.

As Br. André experienced health issues from his birth and throughout his life, there were rumors that he might be dismissed by his order. A tear-filled Br. André once approached the Bishop of Montreal, who was visiting their college, and begged him to intervene so that he could stay in the order. Br. André told the bishop that his only desire was to serve God in the most menial duties. The bishop reassured him, telling him to not be afraid.

Br. André never wrote volumes of theological treatises or preached heart-moving sermons at Mass as he was a simple religious brother who served as a humble porter (door keeper) for forty years. However, his simplicity resembled that of his parents and his favorite saint, St. Joseph, who sought to live a quiet, hidden prayer life. Fr. Henri-Paul once wrote in André's biography that "destinies are

---

20 Ibid., 11–12.
21 Ibid., 337.

almost as a rule shaped at the knees of a mother."[22] When Clothilde prayed her Rosary with her little son next to her, did she ever dream that her son would become a saint? Yet it was this mother's simplicity, profound faith, and joy that helped shape her son's destiny to become a great saint.

Anyone who has seen a picture of Br. André, especially in his later years, notices a little twinkle in his eyes and many years of wrinkles surrounding them, perhaps from smiling like his mother, who loved to smile. There is no doubt that Br. André seemed to smile with his eyes. And it was not a fake smile to cover his pain, which he too experienced, but both his mother and he realized that a smile conveys the inward simplicity of a person who believes the fundamental truth that all is well, and all will be well no matter the crosses, or, in the words of Bl. Columba Marmion, "Joy is the echo of God's life in us!"[23] Like his mother, Br. André did not wallow in his miseries, but instead reflected Christ's face.

Simplicity and humility flowed from André's parents to him and his siblings. Like his father and mother who lived obscure lives—one as a carpenter, and the other as a housewife and mother who changed diapers, cleaned, and cooked—Br. André knew that simplicity was the heartbeat of God. At the same time, Br. André always gave God and St. Joseph the glory and remained aware of his smallness before God when he said the words, "It is with the smallest brushes that the artist paints the most exquisitely beautiful pictures."[24]

Simplicity safeguarded the Bessettes from pride and vanity as they preferred the menial jobs and praise of God to splendid works and self-seeking human praise. If the God of the Universe is willing to wash the feet of His Twelve Apostles and calls each of us to follow Him, why then should we, His true friends, think we are exempt from such humble service? Simplicity is not just an attitude, but an act of the will that recognizes that degrees and lofty positions in society or the Church do not make a saint; instead, a humble

[22] Ibid., 11.
[23] Anne Ball, *The Saints' Guide to Joy that Never Fades* (Atlanta: Charis Books, 2001), 11.
[24] Bergeron, *Brother André*, 96.

and simple heart, which is unafraid of the messiness of life, is the blueprint for holiness.

Sts. Louis and Zélie Martin

At the age of sixty-two, around the year 1885, the widower St. Louis Martin toured Central Europe with his parish priest, Abbé Marie. He traveled to the Bavarian Alps, Athens, and to St. Peter's Basilica in Rome, which he called "the most beautiful thing in the world."[25] While at St. Peter's, Louis wrote to his daughter Marie, "I place you all in the grace of God and pray for you every day in St. Peter's. The thought of your mother also follows me constantly. I'll see you soon . . . soon . . . soon!"[26] In spite of his great love for traveling and seeing the beauty of this world, Louis clung to the virtue of simplicity. Specifically, Louis wrote to his daughters in Milan while en route to home on October 6, 1885:

> Everything I see is splendid, but it's always an earthly beauty, and our heart is satisfied with nothing as long as we're not seeing the infinite beauty that is God. Soon we'll have the intimate happiness of family, and it's this beauty that brings us closer to Him. I kiss all five of you with all my heart. Your father who loves you.[27]

Before her passing, Zélie echoed similar words to her daughter Pauline, "In short, my Pauline, one cannot be happy in this world. When one has a fortune, one wishes for honors. I see this in all the people who become rich."[28] Zélie preferred to associate herself with other simple-minded people rather than the wealthy and desired for her daughters to follow suit. Zélie wrote:

> I know Marie has nothing to fear in this gathering of young ladies, but I don't like seeing her with such people because it arouses unhealthy envy. I have no desire to associate with these people. I would be rather humiliated

---

[25]   Martin and Martin, *A Call to A Deeper Love*, 363.
[26]   Ibid., 364.
[27]   Ibid., 365.
[28]   Ibid., 250.

by them. I think that it's from pride on my part, but what can you do, I would have to spend too much to please them, and I would risk wasting my time and my money.[29]

Despite her initial reservations, Zélie later agreed to allow Marie to attend the gathering of upscale ladies because she wanted her daughter to improve her social skills even to her sister's dismay. Zélie declared:

> Then, her aunt didn't like Marie telling Pauline that she was going to Madame X's house every two weeks. Although there's no harm in this; there are a dozen young ladies there, all well brought up, who have a good time among themselves. So, do I have to shut her up in a cloister? We can't live like wolves in the world! I would take all "the holy girl" (Sr. Mary Dorothy) tells us with a grain of salt. First, I'm not sorry that Marie finds a little entertainment, it makes her less unsociable, and she's already too much so.[30]

Although Zélie tried to protect her daughters from an "unhealthy envy" by keeping them away from their wealthy peers, Zélie also realized her daughters were not in the cloister yet. She recognized her daughters needed recreation as long as sin was not involved. Zélie's quote also sheds light on the sin of vanity, whereby we seek the approval of others by placing our security in what they think of us, including our family and friends. And, as a result, we can make decisions based on being accepted by them even if it compromises our values and we fear disappointing them. In this case, Zélie followed her own heart rather than seeking her sister's approval for she saw no harm in allowing her daughter to have some fun.

From an early age, St. Thérèse and her sisters learned from their parents that the material things of this life can never satisfy—a nice house, fancy clothes, good looks, or recognition—but the simple things in life do—the love that permeates from a family in love with God and one another. Simple hearts treasure the gift of each moment

---

[29] Ibid., 251.
[30] Ibid., 254.

we are alive and the gift of delighting in God in everything and everyone. Practically speaking, Zélie purchased what her children needed and not what they wanted, even if their children's peers had the latest and greatest items. For example, Zélie wrote to her sister-in-law the day before Christmas:

> Since you wanted to give New Year's gifts to Marie and Pauline, you couldn't have chosen better gifts to make them happy. So many times, they've told me they would like a travel bag and that all their companions have one except for them. I let them say it, but because I only buy things that are necessary, and, as they could do without them, I didn't consider it appropriate to satisfy them. But now I see their happiness.[31]

Zélie's simplistic heart prevented her from spoiling her children and or from buying things that were superfluous, though, on special occasions, such as Christmas, she would allow her relatives to pamper her children. Although written for monks, the Rule of St. Benedict offers practical advice to help parents foster a simplistic lifestyle—advice that Zélie seemed to embrace. Specifically, "Whenever new clothing is received, the old should be returned at once and stored in a wardrobe for the poor."[32]

Though extremely generous with their time and financial resources, Louis and Zélie lived frugally by only purchasing what was necessary. Yet, when it came to helping their children grow in holiness, Louis and Zélie were not afraid to spend their money once they were on the same page. One instance is worth mentioning. After having a profound retreat experience the year before at the Visitation Monastery, Marie, the Martin's oldest daughter, desired to attend again. This time, however, Louis insisted his daughter stay home. Like Our Blessed Mother who pleads before Jesus for her children, Zélie reassured Marie that she would be going with these words, "Let me take care of it. I always manage to get what I want without fighting. It's still a month away, that's enough time to persuade your

---

[31] Ibid., 162.
[32] St. Benedict, *The Rule of St. Benedict*, 76.

father ten times."[33] Zélie said the reason behind Louis's refusal was
that "he, who likes neither absences nor expenditures, declared to
me again yesterday, 'I don't want her to go, and she certainly won't
go; the trips to Le Mans and Lisieux are never ending.'"[34] Zélie's
persistence paid off as Louis eventually allowed Marie to attend the
retreat. Specifically, Zélie declared:

> And I found that I had a good reason to want Marie
> to go on the retreat. It's true that's it an expense, but
> money is nothing when it's about the sanctification and
> perfection of a soul, and last year Marie returned to me
> completely transformed. The fruits still last, yet it's time
> for her to renew her reserve. Besides, deep down, your
> father feels the same way, and that's why he gave in so
> kindheartedly.[35]

While many husbands and wives resort to arguing, the silent
treatment, or even threats to get their way, Zélie persistently, yet
lovingly, utilized sound reasons to convince Louis to change his
mind concerning Marie's retreat. Most notably, Zélie believed the
supernatural end, which was "the sanctification and perfection of
a soul," ought to justify the means, which was spending money
along with Marie's absence. And, while the Martins were thrifty
with their money, they were never stingy with God or things that
involved the holiness of souls, such as attending a conference, retreat,
or owning solid religious books or art.

In addition to encouraging their children to attend a retreat,
even if there was some financial sacrifice, Louis and Zélie's deep
faith and detachment from this world led their children to realize
that they were more citizens of Heaven than earth. Specifically, Sr.
Geneviève declared, "My father and mother had a deep faith. In
listening to them speak of Eternity, we were disposed, although
quite young at the time, to look on all things of this world as pure
vanity."[36] Yet the Martins by no means viewed the world as evil.

---

[33]   Martin and Martin, *A Call to a Deeper Love*, 309.
[34]   Ibid.
[35]   Ibid., 309–310.
[36]   Martin, *The Mother of the Little Flower*, 37.

They clearly enjoyed the simple things in life. Thérèse captured this so beautifully when she wrote:

> What shall I say of the winter evenings at home, especially the Sunday evenings? Ah! how I loved, after the *game of checkers* was over to sit with Celine on Papa's knees. He used to sing, in his beautiful voice, airs that filled the soul with profound thoughts, or else, rocking us gently, he recited poems that taught the eternal truths.[37]

Louis also loved to imitate birds, dialects, and military bugle calls. On top of this, Louis was practical by making toys for his daughters. For example, he was known to make tiny carriages from melon skins for his daughters. Thérèse's childhood was a far cry from her mother's supremely unhappy childhood. On a side note, Louis was also a great fisherman who once caught a nearly twenty-four-inch-long carp. Being the generous soul that he was, Louis saved his best catches for the sisters in Carmelite convent in Lisieux, which his four daughters would join one day. In her autobiography, *Story of a Soul*, Thérèse recounted one of these memorable fishing outings with her father:

> Speaking of clouds, I remember one day when the beautiful blue sky became suddenly overcast and soon the thunder began to roll and the lightning to flash through the dark clouds. I saw it strike a short distance away, and, far from being frightened, I was thrilled with delight because God seemed to be so close! Papa, however, was not as delighted as his little Queen. It wasn't because the storm frightened him but because the grass and the tall daises (taller than I) were beginning to sparkle with precious stones. We had to cross several fields before coming to a road, and Papa, fearing the diamonds would soak his little girl, picked her up and carried her on his back in spite of his bundle of lines.[38]

---

[37] St. Thérèse of Lisieux, *Story of a Soul*, 43.
[38] Ibid., 37–38.

Just as Louis and his daughter Thérèse could treasure the simplicity of God present in the Holy Eucharist on a supernatural level, so too both could treasure the simplicity of God all around them on a natural level. Though cliché, simple people tend to delight in the simple things in life for they recognize God's goodness imbues the entire supernatural and natural realm. Through fishing, Louis experienced God's presence and witnessed to the heights of simplicity by means of the tranquil, flowing water, the thrill of a big catch, and, above all, the companionship of his children. On the other hand, while many children, and even adults, are terrified by storms, the Little Flower, Thérèse, was fearless and found God's presence even in the lightning bolt for she was a true saint of simplicity. No one would second guess Louis's instincts to protect his daughter from the storm, but, sadly, some adults lose their childlike simplicity due to the monotony of life or waiting for the next big event, such as a holiday or trip. However, God is found in the ordinary events of our lives, and those saints like Louis, Zélie, and Thérèse discovered Him in a cup of coffee, an enchanting song, a tasty meal, a hot shower, a winter snowfall, a warm fire on an autumn night, a summer breeze, the sight and sound of ocean waves, a dazzling sunset, fishing, lightning, and even sewing, as Zélie wrote when she said, "To tell you the truth, I only enjoy myself when I'm seated at my window assembling my Alençon lace."[39]

Zélie's simplicity also manifested itself in being utterly transparent before God. The saints were the most real people— honest with God and themselves. For instance, Zélie once wrote:

> We're in full-time penance. Fortunately, it will be over soon. I'm suffering so much from the fasting and abstinence! Yet it's not a very severe mortification, but I'm so tired of how my stomach feels, and especially so cowardly, that I wouldn't want to do it all if I listened to my nature. For a week, we've had two missionaries who give three sermons a day. In my opinion, one doesn't preach any better than the other. We're going to hear

---

[39] Martin and Martin, *A Call to A Deeper Love*, 102.

them anyway out of a sense of duty, and, for me at least, it's an extra penance.[40]

How refreshing to know that even the saints struggled with the Church's prescribed Lenten fasts, which were more severe at that time. The fast days called for no food until noon and only a light meal at night. Moreover, unlike her husband, who never spoke any ill of the clergy or their sermons, Zélie was not as reserved with her tongue. Clearly, God's faithful are never wanting in opportunities to offer something to God albeit fasting or listening to poor preaching. However, Zélie did have a soft spot for the Capuchin Order. She once wrote, "We're going to have a Capuchin friar begin instructions this evening. I'm finishing my letter to go hear him. Whether he preaches well or badly, I'll like him because he's a Capuchin. Just seeing them converts me."[41]

When Zélie's cancer made her homebound, she said the following:

> I also, would like to be a saint, but I don't know where to begin. There's so much to do that I limit myself to the desire. I often say during the day, "My God, how I would like to become a saint!" Then, I don't do the work! Though it's high time I started because I could very well do what two people did this week; they died, and their deaths affected me noticeably.[42]

Zélie's words offer a beautiful contrast to the many sugarcoated biographies of the saints, which frequently pass over their weaknesses, like complaining, in favor of their more heroic virtues, such as their courage and purity. Far from being "cookie cutters," the parents of the saints were the simplest people because they were fully aware of God's gifts, but also fully aware of their own imperfections. In a letter written on October 1, 1871, Zélie, a mother of four children under the age of eleven, once told God, "You know well that I don't

---

[40] Ibid., 174.
[41] Ibid., 219–220.
[42] Ibid., 216.

have time to be sick."[43] Zélie felt as if God said to her, "Since you don't have time to be sick, perhaps you'll have time to suffer a lot of pain?"[44] Zélie further wrote, "And I haven't been spared, I assure you!"[45] Zélie reveals that simple souls speak to God from the heart about everything in their lives, especially their joys, but also their sorrows and sufferings.

Zélie once declared, "Under what illusion do the majority of men live! Do they possess money? Forthwith, they want honors. And when they obtain these, they are still discontented, for the heart that seeks anything but God is never satisfied."[46] Céline once asked Louis why he went to the 6:00 a.m. Mass. Louis responded, "Because it is the Mass of the poor and the working people."[47] When traveling, Louis preferred to travel third class for the same reason and also to practice some mortification. Specifically, Céline relates about her parents:

> I do not remember even once having heard him complain if anything disagreeable turned up. It must be said that we also admired the same self-denial in our mother, who was just as forgetful of self. How often I have seen her carefully preparing the family breakfast with the greatest care, while contenting herself with a bowl of broth, taken standing up and alone by herself, while serving the others.[48]

St. John of the Cross, whom St. Thérèse loved to read, once wrote, "Anyone who complains, or grumbles is not perfect, nor even a good Christian."[49] Simple hearts, as seen in the lives of Louis and Zélie, were totally content with God's providence and provisions.

---

43   Ibid., 88.
44   Ibid.
45   Ibid.
46   Piat, *The Story of a Family*, 141-142.
47   Martin, *The Father of the Little Flower*, 29.
48   Ibid., 29.
49   St. John of the Cross, *The Collected Works of St. John of the Cross* (Washington, D.C.: ICS Publications, 1991), 97.

Unfortunately, many of us complain frequently because we lack a simple heart and desire that things go our way and go perfectly.

While simplicity is a most splendid virtue to acquire with God's help, it is even more beautiful if we can instill this virtue in our children. There is no doubt that Louis and Zélie's simplistic and childlike faith, especially in the Holy Eucharist, was passed on to their children as seen in the following example. As a little girl, Céline inquired about Our Lord's Real Presence in the Holy Eucharist, which led to a most beautiful, simplistic response from her little sister Thérèse. Zélie recounted, "Céline said to her the other day, 'How is it that God can be in a tiny host?' Thérèse answered, 'It's not surprising, since God is all powerful.' 'And what does all-powerful mean?' 'It means He can do whatever He wants!'"[50] Thérèse's words were imbued with a childlike simplicity, which contradicts the hardness of heart and intellectual pride that filled the Scribes and Pharisees and sadly lives on in every generation. While even the most brilliant theologians cannot fully explain the Holy Eucharist, nor can we wrap our minds around this mystery for it is God Himself, only simple souls are truly capable of either explaining or understanding this great mystery with God's grace. With a childlike faith, these simple souls were freed from the mental constraints of trying to figure out everything about God.

Alberto and Maria Beretta

Alberto and Maria Beretta, the parents of St. Gianna, were financially comfortable, but always sought ways to help those less fortunate. More than their wealth, this couple prized the glory of home life. One of the main reasons that Alberto in particular cherished his wife and children was due to the fact that he himself never knew what it was like to experience such love. At the age of four, Alberto became an orphan and resided at Milan's San Carlo Diocesan School. As a result of these unfortunate circumstances, Alberto desired earnestly one day to have his own family where his children could experience the closeness and love that he lacked growing up. God answered that prayer. In fact, Alberto's children would often greet him every

---

[50] Martin and Martin, *A Call to a Deeper Love*, 310.

evening at the railway station after a long day at the Cantoni cotton mill. One of the greatest fruits of these devout parents' simplicity, regardless of their wealth or poverty, was the love and joy that permeated their family.

Alberto's simplicity was noted both in his demeanor and personality. Specifically, his son Giuseppe described him as "a man of few words, but those few were the fruit of reflection and wisdom. His faith and piety were as great as Mamma's. He was a gentleman you could trust with your eyes closed."[51] After dinner, Alberto loved to smoke a cigar and listen to his daughter Amalia play Chopin, Bach, and Beethoven on the piano followed by the family Rosary. Alberto resembled St. Joseph, who has no recorded words in the Gospel. Moreover, Alberto was clearly a simple man, who, like Joseph, took the greatest thrill in spending time with his family. Just as Joseph gazed upon the Divine Child with wonder and awe, so too did Alberto look upon his children with the greatest tenderness and amazement because his children were made by God and deified at their Baptism, i.e., that is infused with the indwelling Trinity. Simple hearts like Alberto and Maria recognized that the home life is where God's presence can be found . . . in their precious children, a tasty cigar, music, a home cooked meal, and the family Rosary—here, the Berettas had everything they needed; God's love in the simple things.

Bernard and Ellen Casey

All virtues strive for the mean, which for simplicity includes neither living above nor below one's means. One of the risks of taking simplicity to the extreme is that we miss out on enjoying God's goodness present everywhere because we can fall into the erroneous belief that all material things are an impediment to holiness. After all, we are not just spiritual beings, but physical beings, who need material things to live: clothes, food, shelter, books, recreation, etc. These material things are gifts from God, which only furthered these parents' gratitude toward God's benevolence. Bernard and Ellen Casey knew that simplicity meant living life to the fullest

---

[51] Molla and Guerriero, *Saint Gianna Molla*, 24.

and using the material world as a means to further encounter and glorify Our Lord, Who "came that they might have life, and have it abundantly (Jn 10:10).

Residing on their eighty-plus-acre farm and then later on a 345-acre farm near Prescott, Wisconsin, by the Mississippi River around the end of the nineteenth century, Bernard and Ellen, Third Order Franciscans, raised their sixteen children with joy and simplicity. Immigrants from Ireland, they probably never imagined that their sixth child, Bernard Francis, who would later take the religious name Solanus, would become the second American-born man beatified and may eventually become the first American, male canonized saint.

Describing his upbringing in the lush state of Wisconsin, Bl. Solanus wrote, "No doubt what heightened the appreciation of those days was our innocence—and how the hawks were wont— as we would play on the grass stopping to watch them—to circle around and around in their upward flight. They seemed to me as they circled to the clouds to invite us to strive with them to get to heaven."[52] The Caseys lived like Catholic Amish, that is, they had no television, automobile, or electricity, though not by choice as these modern technologies had not been invented at the time. The Caseys had moved from Philadelphia, Pennsylvania, to live closer to their relatives while also seeking a more simplistic lifestyle in the rural setting. The green, rolling hills of Wisconsin and giant bluffs near the Mississippi River would have certainly reminded Bernard and Ellen of their native Ireland. In fact, the land where Solanus was born was situated on a bluff overlooking the Mississippi and St. Croix Rivers, offering a most splendid view. Though the midwestern rivers offered a different beauty from the famous Irish Cliffs of Moher with its breathtaking views of the Atlantic Ocean, the Caseys simplicity allowed them to marvel at the awesome Providence of God, Who loves to spoil His children from time to time with familiarity and beauty. The Casey farm with its open land, scenic river views, and various trees offered a most appropriate

---

[52] Leo Wollenweber, OFM, CAP, *Meet Solanus Casey: Spiritual Counselor and Wonder Worker* (Cincinnati, OH: Servant Books, 2002), 17.

background for the cultivation of virtues, recreation, and, above all, prayer. And, like the creatures in nature, the Casey family sought with all their might to soar to Heaven.

At the heart of Bernard and Ellen's life was prayer, which was a daily fixture in the Casey household. According to Br. Leo Wollenweber, OFM Cap., who lived with Solanus at St. Bonaventure Monastery in Detroit, Michigan:

> Solanus often described the way their father would get them together in the evening by calling out, "Prayer, boys, prayer!" Even Solanus Casey himself described his life in the 12' x 30' log cabin as a "mansion." Well, he said, "You'll be wondering how it might be called a mansion. Well, every decent mansion has a chapel of some dimensions. Ours was at times all chapel, and at times something of a church."[53]

The family had fixed hours for prayer each night beginning at 7 p.m. Yet the home was far from a Carthusian monastery, that is, one of the most austere religious orders where silence is the norm. Br. Leo further relates:

> Barney (Solanus' nickname) grew up in a wholesome American family, rich in love and a solid Catholic faith. All the children had a love for sports and the outdoors. Hunting, fishing, swimming, and winter skiing and skating provided healthy exercise alongside their daily farm chores. With ten boys in their family, they had their own baseball team, the "Casey Nine."[54]

The Caseys also enjoyed singing Irish and American songs along with having lively discussions. Barn dances were frequent, and Solanus learned to play the fiddle. Sometimes tempers flared in this close-knit Irish family, and, on one occasion, Solanus threw a fork at one of his sisters. His father threatened him with lashings if he repeated that behavior. As a Capuchin, Solanus recalled how his parents had instilled the virtue of self-control. Outside of school,

[53] Ibid., 18.
[54] Ibid.

prayer, and games, the Casey children were expected to assist around the farm. Yet, when the crops failed and the economy was struggling, young Solanus lived with his uncle and aunt Murphy near his other uncle, Fr. Maurice Murphy, who was a priest in Stillwater, Minnesota. There, he helped to support his family by working as a prison guard. Because Solanus missed school in his youth to help his family, he had only average and passing marks in seminary, which resulted in him being ordained a simplex priest, which meant he could not hear confessions or preach doctrinal sermons, both of which Solanus resigned himself to joyfully.

Celebrating his first Mass on July 31, 1904, at St. Joseph's Parish in Appleton, Wisconsin, which happened to be the closest Capuchin parish to his parents some 200 miles away, Fr. Solanus described the joy of seeing his mother. It had been eight years since he had last seen her. According to Br. Leo, "His father wept for joy that God had blessed his family with a priest."[55] However, Fr. Solanus would not be the only priest in the family. His older brother Maurice, whom Solanus had always looked up to, and who had previously left seminary due to a nervous condition, was now inspired by his little brother's ordination and decided to re-enter another seminary. Later, another brother, Fr. Edward, became a priest. On the occasion of his parents Golden Wedding Anniversary (fifty years of marriage) on October 6, 1913, a Solemn High Mass of thanksgiving was celebrated with all fourteen of the living Casey children, along with the spouses of those who were married and numerous grandchildren, at Immaculate Conception Church in Seattle, Washington, where the Caseys had relocated. Fr. Solanus preached his one and only sermon as a priest on his parents' great love and faith, which they passed on to him and his siblings. What a glorious sight for Bernard and Ellen to see three of their sons on the altar as priests, in addition to having other holy children who were lawyers and businessmen. Any couple would praise God to have one son as a priest, and the Caseys had three.

Long before Solanus became a priest, he proposed to a neighbor girl, Rebecca Tobin, whose mother rejected the offer and sent her

---

[55] Ibid., 39.

away to boarding school because she was too young. It was likely his parent's rich conjugal love that first inspired Solanus to pursue marriage, but later Divine Providence led him to the Capuchin Order and then to the priesthood. Solanus's parents never preached about religious life, but simply revealed authentic love, which is the foundation of every vocation. And it was because of Bernard and Ellen's love that Solanus was free to listen and respond in love to God's call for his life by neither running away from marriage or the priesthood. Fr. Solanus would often speak about his parent's virtues to encourage those married couples to whom he offered spiritual direction. Specifically, Fr. Solanus wrote, "We were fortunate children to whom the good God gave such sturdy, honest, virtuous parents."[56] The simplicity of the Casey household and the rural setting conducive for prayer clearly paved the way for Solanus to follow in the footsteps of St. Francis as a Capuchin. Like so many of the saints and blesseds, his home was his first monastery!

Newton and Delia Sheen

Simplicity flowed down the Mississippi River and moved to central Illinois, some 431 miles southeast of Bl. Solanus Casey's homestead, where the young Ven. Fulton Sheen was growing up in El Paso, Illinois. Specifically, Fulton Sheen was born twenty-five years after Solanus Casey on May 8, 1895. Though not canonized at the present time, Fulton's cause for canonization is currently progressing. Long before this holy American bishop, prolific writer, and famed television personality grew in holiness, Fulton first learned the importance of simplicity, sacrifice, and humility from the example of his parents, Newton and Delia. Fulton's father had a third-grade education due to his duties on the family farm, while his mother had an eighth-grade education. It is only fitting in his autobiography, *Treasure in Clay,* that Sheen wrote:

> Clay has to be molded, and that is done primarily in the family, which is more sacred than the state. The determining mold of my early life was the decision of

---

[56] Fink, "The Doorkeeper," *The Anthonian*, 6 (1987), 19.

my parents that each of their children should be well
educated. The resolve was born not out of their own
education, but their lack of it.[57]

Owning a hardware store, which tragically burned down,
Newton and Delia moved their four sons, Fulton being the oldest,
to a farm. Eventually, they returned to the City of Peoria to ensure
their children had an education. Peter John Sheen, who would be
named "Fulton" after his mother's maiden name, once lamented to
his mother that his father never praised him for his holy pictures and
medals, which he earned at school. Delia responded, "He does not
wish to spoil you, but he is telling all the neighbors."[58] Sheen further
described the virtue of his parents by saying:

> The molding of clay was done by great sacrifices on
> the part of my father and mother, who would deny
> themselves every personal comfort and luxury in order
> that their sons might be well clothed and well cared for.
> Our family life was simple and the atmosphere of our
> home Christian. Grace was said before and after each
> meal; when we had visitors none of us were permitted to
> sit at the table without wearing a coat and tie; the Rosary
> was said every evening; the priests of the cathedral visited
> the home once every week; and visits of the old country
> cousins were very frequent.[59]

On one occasion, the young Fulton stole a ten-cent geranium
plant from a grocery store, which he intended present to his
mother. When Fulton gave the plant to his mother, she asked, "Did
you buy it?"

"No, Mother," he replied.

"Did you steal it?" she then asked.

"Yes, Mother,"[60] Fulton answered. Delia made her son use
his own earned money and pay the storeowner fifty cents for

---

[57] Fulton Sheen, *Treasure in Clay, The Autobiography of Fulton J. Sheen* (New York: Image Books, 2008), 9.

[58] Ibid., 14.

[59] Ibid., 18.

[60] Ibid., 20.

restitution even though the plant cost less. Fulton learned that his act of "dishonesty thus punished by restitution taught me for life that honesty is the best policy."[61] On another occasion, Fulton related that while playing baseball at the age of ten his mother asked him to go to the grocery store to purchase something very important for dinner. Sheen responded:

> "Why can't I finish the game? There only are two more innings to play." Her answer was: "You are out there for exercise. What difference does it make whether you are running the bases or running to the grocery store?" Years later when I fell into the wisdom of Thomas Aquinas I received the answer to her question. This learned philosopher asks. "What is the difference between work and play?" and he answers: "Work has a purpose, play has none, but there must be time for purposeless things, even foolishness." But when I learned that distinction it was too late for a clever answer to my mother. By this time, she would hardly ever call me from a book.[62]

In addition to cultivating honesty, the Sheens, who loved to work in the kitchen and on the farm, fostered in their children a strong work ethic. Fulton related that this "habit of work was one I never got over, and thank God I never did."[63] Fulton was known to have plowed and shucked corn, fed cows, etc. While he spent his youth working on the farm, Fulton, who discerned a priestly vocation from an early age, believed that his hands were made for chalices and not callouses. Above all, Newton and Delia revealed that simplicity breeds honesty, humility, and hard work because we all stand naked before God Who sees everything—our thoughts and our motives—and knows our deepest sins, fears, and joys. While Newton and Delia seemed to prize work and study over play, their emphasis on ensuring their children had an education bore great fruit. One son became a lawyer, another a doctor, and the youngest entered industry, while Fulton became a priest and later a bishop.

[61] Ibid.
[62] Ibid., 21–22.
[63] Ibid., 21.

While Fulton learned the importance of work, he often argued with his dad that farming was not a good life and that you could become rich only if you found oil. However, Fulton, ordained on September 20, 1919, learned the greatest lessons from his parents' simplicity and sacrifice. Specifically, Fulton believed that priests are meant to be victims and to live simply. The Sheens's simplicity was such that they wanted their children to live virtuously and pursue the vocation God had called them to without imposing their will and or expectations on their children. Like many of these devout parents, Newton and Delia prayed that their son would become a priest without openly communicating that desire. According to Fulton, "Never once did my mother or father say a word to me about becoming a priest, nor did I speak to them about it until the day I went to the seminary. Their only response then was: 'We always prayed that you might become a priest; if it is your vocation, be a good one.'"[64] Fulton once wrote:

> On the last day, God will ask priests: "Where are your children? How many vocations have you fostered?" Though it is not given to any of us to implant the vocation, it is nonetheless within our power to widen the capacity for receptivity. We fertilize the soil by good example and encouragement.[65]

Finally, Fulton added, "The best vocation leaders should be the priests themselves. We may not mount pulpits to urge parents to bear children, unless we priests bear spiritual children."[66] Fulton stated that "being an altar boy at the cathedral fed the fires of vocation, as did the inspiration of the priests who visited our home almost once every week."[67] In the same sense, a father and mother cannot expect their son or daughter to become detached from the world, avoid the near occasion of sin, and live simply if they themselves do not provide the example as seen in the lives of Newton and Delia. Though Fulton did not explicitly credit his vocation to his parents, it

64   Ibid., 32.
65   Ibid., 39.
66   Ibid., 38–39.
67   Ibid., 32.

is clear that without their prayers and virtuous example, there would have been no Bishop Fulton Sheen. In fact, Fulton himself declared:

> There are many more vocations to the priesthood than those which result in Ordination, as there are more seeds planted than those which bear fruit. St. Thomas Aquinas holds that God always gives the Church a sufficient number of vocations, "provided the unworthy ones are dismissed and the worthy ones are well trained."[68]

Finally, the Sheens modeled the words of Pope Benedict XVI, who in an interview once said:

> I think there is today in general terms of seeing children as a right, as a possession. Parents not only want to represent themselves in their child, but to achieve whatever they failed to do in their own lives in order to make a second attempt at their lives and thereby validate themselves. In these circumstances, the children necessarily rebel against the parents. This is a rebellion in defense of being oneself, of having a right to one's own life. Every person comes, of himself, out of the freedom of God and stands in that freedom as of his own right. The upbringing by his parents must be a matter of leading the child to what is his own, and not of laying a claim on their own behalf, for that is the true heart of authoritarian programming.[69]

Parents are never meant to live vicariously through their children. One historical example is enough to prove the point that pushing your children to be what you want them to be is a recipe for disaster. This family also proves the point that simplicity for the sake of simplicity without love is a contradiction, for simplicity ought to lead families to union with God, Who is love, and allow His love to saturate us.

On November 10, 1483, in Eisleben Germany, Hans and Margaret Luther welcomed their son Martin, named after St.

---

[68] Ibid., 38.

[69] Joseph Cardinal Ratzinger, *God and the World: A Conversation with Peter Seewald* (San Francisco: Ignatius Press, 2002), 136–137.

Martin of Tours, into their home. Martin's father was a miner and so
longed for his son to become a lawyer to better their family's social
position, so much so that he was heartbroken when Martin joined
the Augustinian monastery. Tragically, Hans and Margaret, noted
for their "extreme simplicity and inflexible severity,"[70] beat their
son on a few occasions to the point of shedding blood. Concerning
his mother, Martin recounted that upon the occasion of stealing a
nut, "My mother . . . beat me until the blood flowed, and it was
this harshness and severity of the life I led with them that forced me
subsequently to run away to a monastery and become a monk."[71]
Martin admitted to joining religious life out of fear of his salvation.

Every parent is called by God the Father to reflect His face of
mercy, love, and justice. Yet some parents tragically reflect only
a tyrannical, diabolical love as seen by Martin's parents. Hans
and Margaret's love was conditional rather than unconditional.
Consequently, Martin projected his parents' tyrannical love, which
he could see, onto God the Father Whom He could not see. His
parents wounded him deeply and caused neurosis in him, especially
scrupulosity, as he felt he had to earn God's love. In fact, Martin
recounts that he was so terrified of God that he almost collapsed
while celebrating his first Mass. His later rejection of this false
understanding of God's love led to the heretical belief that man
is saved by faith alone and other skewed biblical interpretations.
Consequently, the Catholic Church will never have a St. Martin
Luther, partly due to his parents, who taught him to fear God more
than to love Him and to follow their dreams rather than listen to
his own heart.

John and Agnes More

Only five years before Martin Luther's birth, St. Thomas More was
born on February 6, 1478, to John and Agnes More in London,
England. Peering into Thomas More's life, there is no question
that his father's simplicity and love helped lay the foundation for
this future saint. Many fathers desire their children, especially their

---

[70] "Martin Luther," New Advent.org, newadvent.org/cathen/09438b.htm.
[71] Ibid.

sons, to follow their footsteps in their respective professions or to follow some noble career as seen in the life of Hans Luther. Although John More was a lawyer and a judge and sent his son to some of London's finest institutions, such as St. Anthony's on Threadneedle Street and Oxford, he never coerced his son to become a lawyer; rather, he ensured that Thomas received the best education possible and allowed him the freedom to follow his heart, but not without guidance. John did steer Thomas in the pursuit of law, but not for the same reasons as Hans Luther did, who only wanted to improve his family's social position. Like many parents, John had an intuitive sense about his son's talents. Regardless, Thomas, like many children, felt the need to please his father and so began his pursuit of becoming a lawyer. According to historian and author, James Monti:

> While Oxford may have nurtured the young More's aspirations to seek "the things that are above" (Col 3.1), John More had very different ambitions for his son. Hence it seems likely that Thomas' transfer around 1494 from the halls of the university to a London institution that trained students destined for a career in law, the "New Inn", was prompted by the young man's desire to comply with his father's wishes.[72]

Thomas lost his mother unexpectedly at the age of twenty-one, which led him to further discern his calling in life. Between the ages of twenty-three to twenty-seven, Thomas "gave serious consideration to the idea of entering the priesthood and religious life."[73] While beginning his law career, Thomas lived and worked near the Carthusian monks where he would regularly join the monks in prayer when his schedule allowed. In today's terms, Thomas would be considered an "aspirant" of a religious order, i.e., that is someone who is seriously discerning a vocation with an order prior to joining. While Thomas never joined the Carthusian Order, their austere and strictly contemplative life clearly inspired his spirituality as a married layman as seen in the following account:

---

[72] James Monti, *The King's Good Servant but God's First: The Life and Writings of St. Thomas More* (San Francisco: Ignatius Press, 1997), 25.

[73] Ibid., 32.

(Thomas) rose at two o'clock in the morning, devoting the first five hours of his day to prayer and study. He attended Mass daily and often served the priest at the altar. After the children had risen from bed, he would gather them together to recite the seven "Penitential Psalms" (Psalms 6, 32, 38, 51, 102, 130, 143) followed by the Litany of the Saints. At meals, More would have one of his children read aloud a passage from Scriptures and after it, an appropriate commentary or spiritual book (usually the Scripture commentaries of the popular medieval exegete Nicholas of Lyra), during which there was not a word of conversation.[74]

Prayer was the most important thing in Thomas's life, and certainly his father, John More, provided Thomas with his first witness of prayer. In addition to helping kindle his son's prayer life, John sought to bestow his love and blessing upon Thomas. The following story offers a glimpse into John and Thomas's simplicity, while at the same time revealing the tremendous love between this father and son, which, after God's love, became the foundation for Thomas's future relationships with his wife and children. According to Monti:

The filial love More bore toward his father was as genuine as his love for his children. Thomas' mother died when he was in his early twenties, but John More lived well into More's adult life, dying only five years before his illustrious son. In life and in death the younger More manifested his unchanging devotion. Thus while serving as Lord Chancellor it was his habit, on passing through Westminster Hall where John More sat as judge in the Court of the King's Bench, to pause and kneel down before his father to ask his blessing. This custom of his was all the more notable, for according to the anonymous author of the "Ro: Ba:" biography, at the time "men after their marriages thought themselves not bound to these duties of younger folks." Thomas was most attentive to his father's spiritual and bodily needs in his last illness,

---

[74] Ibid., 57–58.

and when the older More passed away, his son, "with tears taking him about the neck, most lovingly kissed and embraced him, commending him into the merciful hands of almighty God" and causing "many good prayers to be said for his soul's ease."[75]

St. Ambrose of Milan, Doctor of the Church, who was more of a father to St. Augustine than his own father, reaffirms this importance of a father's blessing in the following words directed at parents. Specifically, Ambrose declared, "You may not be rich; you may be unable to bequeath any great possession to your children; but one thing you can give them [is] the heritage of your blessing. And it is better to be blessed than to be rich."[76] While John More was financially well off and provided Thomas and his siblings with everything they could need in terms of material goods, it was his blessing that Thomas sought daily even well into adulthood. According to one biographer, Peter Ackroyd, "Every morning and evening, when he was a child, he (Thomas) would also have knelt down in reverence before his father."[77]

One of the greatest tragedies in life is that we often lose our childlike simplicity by outgrowing our parents' blessing and affection even when we become adults. By daily seeking his father's blessing as an adult, married man, and his father still freely bestowing it upon him, which was unconventional at the time since it was for "younger folk," Thomas and John More reveal what it means to possess a simple heart. For only simple souls can truly appreciate something so ordinary, yet so meaningful albeit bestowing or receiving a blessing. Without his father's love and blessing, Thomas would have felt poor despite being rich in worldly things: a prestigious law career, house, fine food, etc.

[75] Ibid., 78.

[76] Mellis Muck and Anna Keating, *The Catholic Catalogue: A Field Guide to the Daily Acts That Make Up a Catholic Life* (New York: Image Books, 2016), 316.

[77] Peter Ackroyd, *The Life of Thomas More* (New York: Anchor Books, 1998), 65.

When Thomas became a father himself, he seemed to embrace his father's simplicity and tenderness. For instance, Thomas "never beat his own children except, on occasions, with peacock feathers."[78] Further, "his eldest daughter, Margaret, said that she had seen her father angry only twice—they must have been striking occasions to be so firmly retained in her memory."[79]

Few people shed tears unintentionally or over trivial matters. We tend to shed tears over someone or something that has inestimable worth. Upon seeing his father die, Thomas embraced him and shed a plethora of tears, which made visible the Fourth Commandment, namely: "Honor your father and your mother, that your days may be long in the land which the LORD your God gives you" (Ex 20:12). Thomas's love and gratitude for his father, who was at times described as sweet and other times as strict, was most apparent. Does not every parent long to be appreciated during their final moments on earth as they are surrounded by their loved ones and, above all, missed after they die? While Our Lord instituted the Holy Eucharist so that we would never forget Him, every parent wants to be missed by their family when their time on earth comes to an end, not in some depressed way, but because their lives were sacred and utterly unique—there will never be someone like them again. By embracing his father with tears, Thomas showed just how great was his impact on him, which helped provide the paternal guidance and love that formed him into a man who would rather die for his faith than compromise the truth.

As Thomas was devoted to his father, John, both in life and even after his death by praying for him, so too were Thomas's children toward their saintly father, particularly his daughter Margaret, even well after her father's martyrdom on July 6, 1535. According to Monti:

> As was customary with beheaded traitors, More's head was parboiled and impaled on Tower Bridge as an intimidation and threat to the King's subjects. It would have eventually been hurled into the river had not

[78] Ibid., 66.
[79] Ibid., 145.

Margaret bribed the executioner to let her take it. She
kept it with her for the rest of her life, and when she died,
only nine years later, she was buried with her father's head
in her arms as she desired.[80]

St. Louis Martin

Over three hundred years after the death of St. Thomas More,
another saint was profoundly moved by her father's blessing.
Although St. Louis Martin was already mentioned earlier in this
chapter, along with his bride, St. Zélie, it seems only fitting, in
light of Thomas More, to highlight the most important blessing
that Louis gave to his daughter Thérèse moments before entering
Carmel on April 9, 1888. So profound was this blessing that Thérèse
described it in her autobiography, *Story of a Soul*. Thérèse related:

> After embracing all the members of the family, I knelt
> down before my matchless Father for his blessing, and to
> give it to me he placed *himself on his knees* and blessed me,
> tears flowing down his cheeks. It was a spectacle to make
> the angels smile, this spectacle of an old man presenting
> his child, still in the springtime of life, to the Lord! A
> few moments later, the doors of the holy ark closed upon
> me, and there I was received by the *dear Sisters* who
> embraced me.[81]

Thérèse would later recall how, when she received her veil, "the
day was veiled in tears. Papa was not there to bless His Queen."[82]
Through his tears, and above all his blessing, Louis communicated
to Thérèse and her sisters that they were loved and treasured by
him, but above all by their Heavenly Father, Whom Louis sought
to reveal.

---

[80] Monti, *The King's Good Servant but God's First*, 451.
[81] St. Thérèse of Lisieux, *Story of a Soul*, 147–148.
[82] Ibid., 167.

Grazio and Maria Forgione

Grazio and Maria Forgione raised their children near the end of the twentieth century in the little town of Pietrelcina, in southern Italy. Pietrelcina, which consisted of 4,000 people, was a simple town of farmers and peasants, similar to Nazareth where Jesus grew up. Their son Francesco Forgione, who later was given the religious name Pio, was born in a one-room house on the street named *Vico Storto Valle,* or Crooked Valley Lane. The family also owned a second building that had a kitchen, dining area, and bedroom. Author Frank Rega puts it best about this family, relating that they were:

> Hard-working country folk, the salt of the earth, and well-liked by their neighbors. As farmers, they tilled a small plot of land consisting of a few acres that was about a thirty-minute walk from the town, in an area called the Pianna Romana (the Roman plane). They used an old stone farmhouse to store their goods, and to sleep in overnight during the busy periods.[83]

Despite the fact that Grazio emigrated temporarily to the United States for better wages on two occasions, this was not done to become wealthy, but so that his family could survive and, above all, so that his son Francesco, "Padre Pio," could attend seminary. It goes without saying that a simplistic lifestyle demands sacrifice from all family members.

Both Grazio and Maria, along with Padre Pio's grandparents, could neither read nor write, though they memorized Holy Scripture and shared these Bible stories with their children. Passing on a love for the Word of God was the greatest bedtime story the parents of the saints imbedded in their children's minds. Hence, it was on his mother's lap that Francesco "Pio" learned about Jesus' teachings on the "birds of the air" (Mt 6:26) and the "lilies of the field" (Mt 6:28), where Our Lord teaches us about total trust in Divine Providence. This became the catalyst for Padre Pio's recommended spiritual advice, "Pray, hope and don't worry."[84] In light of Padre Pio's story,

---

[83] Rega, *Padre Pio and America*, 3.
[84] Ibid., 267.

parents can sometimes feel inadequate in their pursuit to raise holy children, especially when it comes to their knowledge of the Faith. Some might contend that if only they had a theology degree, or did not receive such poor catechesis when they were younger, then they would be better able to pass on the Faith to their children, or even homeschool them. They question: Who am I to share these Divine Mysteries? The parents of the saints, especially Padre Pio's parents, remind us that a great love for God, especially the Holy Eucharist and Sacred Scripture, is the most important qualification to be teachers of our children, and not whether we have read St. Thomas Aquinas's *Summa Theologica*. Above all, it is best to live simplicity than preach it, as seen in the following story, which testifies to Maria Forgione's simplicity and humility.

> The winter of 1928–1929 was biting cold. Guiseppa (Maria), who was about 70 at the time, had arrived on the mountain with only light clothing. She was frail and in poor health, and plagued with a constant cough. It seemed to many that she had actually come to San Giovanni Rotondo to die close to her son. Mary and her friends offered her a heavy fur coat and woolen dress to wear during her trek up the steep hillside, often in the snow and frigid wind, to attend her son's daily Mass. But she politely declined, saying she did not want to appear to be a "great lady." She preferred to wear her simple peasant garb, especially when talking to her son.[85]

It is no wonder that Padre Pio's yearning for the things of God and a life of simplicity began at a young age due his parent's occupation as farmers and their down-to-earth personalities. While her son was regarded as a saint long before he was canonized and, thus, had more followers than most do on Twitter, Maria never let her son's holiness go to her head. Instead, Maria knew who the real great lady was—Our Lady. On a side note, one would think that Padre Pio was first drawn to religious life by the friars' impressive monastery, the opportunity for ample prayer, or the thought of saving many souls. Instead, Padre Pio, around the age of ten, was inspired by a certain Capuchin brother's dark beard. Over the years, Padre Pio would say, "I had gotten the idea of Br. Camillo's beard into my head and no one could take away my desire to be a bearded friar."[86] Simplicity is thus not only a virtue, but it is part of who God is, and the more we live simply, the more we draw others to God Himself. Clearly, Grazio and Maria's simplistic lifestyle, along with Br. Camillo's beard, were like little seeds that God sowed in Pio's heart, which helped draw him more and more to the consecrated life.

Luigi and Assunta Goretti

In addition to St. Padre Pio's parents, the parents of St. Maria Goretti embraced the virtue of simplicity both materially and spiritually in late twentieth-century Italy, some 125 miles from Padre Pio. In their profound simplicity, the Gorettis resembled the twelfth-century married saint and farmer, St. Isidore the Laborer, and his bride, María de la Cabeza, whose cause for canonization is currently progressing with the Congregation for the Causes of Saints. While Luigi was not so fortunate as Isidore, who, according to pious legend, had his land plowed by the angels so he could attend Holy Mass, both couples counted their blessings despite being very poor. In fact, Maria's mother Assunta, a former orphan, never knew how to read or write. After Maria's father Luigi completed his military duties, they established roots on their little plot of land where he would farm to support the family, which would soon grow to six children. Author Ann Ball said it best when she declared about the Goretti parents, "Rather than feel bitter about their poverty and way of life, this valiant couple accepted all as God's Will, and greeted the birth of each of their children as a gift from God."[87] Like Isidore and his wife, María, the Gorettis experienced the tragedy of losing their first-born son. However, the Gorettis were very detached. As Ball pointed out:

---

[86] Augustine McGregor, OCSO, *Padre Pio: His Early Years* (San Giovanni Rotondo: 1981), 83.

[87] Ball, *Modern Saints,* Book One, 164.

The family had few possessions, and a small image of Our
Lady was considered their greatest treasure. The children
had no toys, so an apple or rock often took the place of the
ball another child played with. Maria never had a single
doll. Because of their poverty, the children never attended
school. But in spite of this type of life, the entire family
was happy, until the food shortage became so critical that
something had to be done.[88]

While the Gorettis were happy in their humble abode, their
only hope to provide for their children, as seen in a previous chapter,
was to move to a different part of Italy to become tenant farmers.
Luigi once declared, "We must not think of ourselves; but they
[the children] are gifts from the Good God and we must show
our gratitude by taking care of them."[89] The point is that while
simplicity presupposes a detachment from the things of this life, it
does not mean that one ought to resign oneself to a life of material
destitution, especially when little mouths need to be fed. Above
all, a father and mother have a sacred obligation to provide for their
children, not only materially, but also spiritually. And, at the same
time, simplicity kept Luigi and Assunta from being both greedy and
bitter over that which they did not possess, and instead filled them
with gratitude for all of God's blessings, especially their children.
Even when moving from their native land in search of a better life for
their children, the Gorettis were by no means seeking great financial
prosperity; rather, Luigi and Assunta desired that their children's
basic needs of food, shelter, and clothing were met. Ironically, even
parts of Maria's First Communion accessories, like shoes and a veil,
were donated to her because of the family's poverty. St. Alphonsus
de Liguori seems to personify the simple faith of the Goretti family
when he declared, "He who desires only God is rich and happy: he
is in want of nothing, and may laugh at the whole world."[90] By daily
mediating on the mysteries of the Rosary, particularly the mysteries
of the Nativity and Crucifixion, Luigi and Assunta came to "imitate

---

88   Ibid.
89   Ibid.
90   St. Alphonsus de Liguori, *The True Spouse of Jesus Christ*, 726.

what they contain and obtain what they promise," including Our Lord's most splendid example of simplicity.

José and Dolores Escrivá

Like the Gorettis, José and Dolores Escrivá also experienced Our Lord's poverty when they too were forced into financial destitution by a most unfortunate circumstance, as discussed earlier. Despite their poverty, however, the Escrivás sought to embrace a simple and frugal lifestyle. In terms of material goods, the Escrivás economized even before their financial collapse. Specifically, Andrés Vázquez de Prada wrote in his book *The Founder of Opus Dei*, "If a child broke a vase or some valuable object, it would be immediately glued back together or sent out for repair."[91]

When José's business went bankrupt, simplicity became even more pronounced in their home. He would daily impose a ration of six cigarettes on himself and Dolores was known as saying, "Don't extend your arm further than your sleeve will go."[92] Later in life, St. Josemaría learned to appreciate the poverty of his parents, though as a youth he never fully embraced it as he once wrote, "My father's business did not go at all well. And I thank God for that, because in that way I learned what poverty is. If not, I wouldn't have known."[93] Josemaría' s mother also set a most holy example of simplicity by treasuring every moment and using every breath to glorify God rather than waste her time on frivolous things. Specifically, Josemaría described his mother by saying, "I don't ever remember seeing her with nothing to do. She was always busy, whether knitting, sewing or mending some piece of clothing, reading . . . I never remember seeing her idle. She was a good Christian mother of a family, and knew how to use her time well."[94]

On a spiritual level, José grew in simplicity, along with the grace to persevere in suffering, from the font of the Holy Eucharist, from

---

[91] de Prada, *The Founder of Opus Dei*, 43.
[92] Ibid., 73. Originally cited in *General Archive of the Prelature*, 267.
[93] *Coverdale, Uncommon Faith*, 23. Originally cited by Manuel Garrido in *El Beato Josemaria Escriva y Barbastro*, 56.
[94] "A Christian Family," OpusDei.org, opusdei.org/en-us/.

which he partook nearly every day. Moreover, José and Dolores
were known to teach their children short and simple prayers, which
Josemaría would say every morning and evening for the rest of his
life. One in particular was the Guardian Angel Prayer:

> O Guardian Angel, to you I pray,
> Desert me not, by night or day.
> If you were to leave me, where would I be?
> O Guardian Angel, pray for me.[95]

In addition to his parents, Josemaría's grandmothers taught him
some prayers like the following, which reflects their simplicity and
the often-forgotten role of grandparents to be spiritual warriors for
their families:

> Yours am I, I was born for Thee.
> What is it, O Jesus, you want of me?[96]

Josemaría was certainly impacted by the prayers his parents
so beautifully taught him that he once wrote, "Don't forget your
childhood prayers, learned perhaps from your mother's lips. Say
them each day with simplicity, as you did then."[97]

In addition to a life of simple prayer, José revealed to his son
the importance of spending time with those we love. José loved to
take walks through town accompanied by one of his children. On
their walks together, José and Josemaría discussed various topics.
José listened attentively and imparted wisdom should Josemaría seek
advice. Josemaría liked the fact that whenever he asked his father
a question, "He always took him seriously."[98] José and Josemaría
were best of friends because the father made himself available and
"invited him [Josemaría] to open his heart."[99] Outside of his prayer,

95   de Prada, *The Founder of Opus Dei*, 29. Originally cited by Joaquin
     Alonso in *Roman Process of Beatification*, 1651.
96   Ibid.
97   St. Josemaría Escrivá, *The Way, Furrow, The Forge,* 137.
98   de Prada, *The Founder of Opus Dei*, 32. Originally cited by Álvaro de
     Portillo in *Sum.* 27 and Javier Echevarria in *Sum.* 1794.
99   Ibid., 32.

nothing seemed more important to José than being with his wife and children.

This openness between parents and children as seen in the life of the Escrivás serves as a stepping stone for a child's relationship with God where they can experience the sheer delight of being loved and realize that prayer is a conversation with God. José became more than just a biological father, but a spiritual father and somewhat quasi-spiritual director. In his book *The Way*, Josemaría extolled the necessity of spiritual direction, which his father helped provide some impetus for this belief:

> Your own spirit is a bad adviser, a poor pilot to steer your soul through the squalls and storms and across the reefs of the interior life. That's why it is the will of God that the command of the ship be entrusted to a master who, with his light and knowledge, can guide us to a safe port.[100]

José's total availability certainly helped Josemaría navigate himself through his crucial adolescent years. While parents are never substitutes for spiritual direction, their wisdom and, above all, their listening ears when their children are young can provide a medium for them to discover their vocation in freedom without pressure or self-interest. A spiritual director, a trusted confessor, and a listening parent can help guide a soul from duplicity to simplicity where disordered attachments are slowly removed. It must also be noted that José and Dolores never opened Josemaría' s mail or spied on him, which gave their son the freedom to become self-controlled. José and Dolores expected the best from their children and corrected them when appropriate. At the same time, José offers a great example for all parents to really get to know their children rather than simply provide for them. After all, children do not choose their parents; instead, God chose these children for their parents.

In addition to José and Josemaría's heart-to-heart talks, the Escrivá family took walks every Sunday along the banks of the Ebro River as their family recreation. The Royo family would

---

[100] St. Josemaría Escrivá, *The Way, Furrow, The Forge*, 14.

often accompany them. Both families would conclude their walk
with a snack or some games. Before the advent of television and
the Internet, more families like the Escrivás took advantage of the
Lord's Day for rest and outside recreation. The Escrivá's simplicity
delighted in God's magnificent nature, such as the beautiful sun or a
gorgeous river, which, like an outdoor cathedral, lifted their bodies
and souls as their Sunday liturgy spilled over to their entire day.

One walk with his father would be different from the others. In
the spring of 1918, a sixteen-year-old Josemaría told his father about
his wishes to enter the seminary. This news caught José by surprise
as he had counted on his eldest son to carry on the family name
and resurrect the family's business. Filled with tears, which was the
only time Josemaría had witnessed his father cry, José told his son,
"Priests have to be saints. It is very hard not to have a house of your
own, not to have a home, not have a love on this earth. Think about
it a little more, but I will not oppose your decision."[101]

The young Josemaría remained resolute in his vocation and
would enter the seminary, but asked God to bless his family with
another son to take his place—something which God did in his
younger brother Santiago. Perhaps it was his father's words, "Priests
have to be saints" that really struck Josemaría because he knew all
along what we are learning now—that his father was a true saint
and that without holy parents there will be fewer or no saints at
all. Josemaría would spend his life trying to spread the message
that his father had only half expressed. When he founded Opus
Dei, he stressed that not only do "priests have to be saints," but
married people (and all people) as well. Josemaría once beautifully
wrote, "You have the obligation to sanctify yourself. Yes, even you.
Who thinks this is the exclusive concern of priests and religious?
To everyone, without exception, Our Lord said: 'Be perfect, as my
heavenly Father is perfect.'"[102]

Parents like José Escrivá were not naïve to the awesome
responsibility and sacrifices that comes with the priesthood and

---

[101] Coverdale, *Uncommon Faith*, 27. Originally cited by Jose Luis Illanes,
       Dos de Octubre de 1928: Alcance y Signifcicado de una Fecha, 66.
[102] St. Josemaría Escrivá, *The Way, Furrow, The Forge*, 69.

the ramifications for those who do not live it heroically, for they understood the gravity of their own vocations. That is why José wanted his son to really pray about his vocation. He did not want his son to be a mediocre priest, but a saintly one. Thankfully, in his own father, Josemaría saw a glimpse of what the priesthood ought to be because his father was the priest of his family: one who lives simply and poorly so that others can live comfortably; one who sacrifices everything for his beloved; one who suffers cheerfully and courageously even when misfortune and persecution come and forgives others; and one who makes prayer the most important priority in his life. And, hence, there is a reason Josemaría could speak the following words about his father, "I don't recall ever seeing him frown. He was always serene, I recall, with a smile on his face. He died worn out, at only fifty-seven years of age. I owe him my vocation."[103] The latter words are the most edifying words any father could ever hear from their son, "I owe him my vocation." And, therefore, God calls every earthly or spiritual father and mother to cultivate the vocations He entrusts to us rather than suppressing them. Reflecting on the role of his parents in his vocation, Josemaría said, "I was given a Christian upbringing. I received more formation in the faith there than at school, even though at the age of three I was taken to a school run by nuns, and then, at the age of seven, to one run by a religious order of priests."[104]

Stanislaus and Marianna Kowalska

In the early twentieth century, two Polish couples strove to live a very simplistic lifestyle, albeit in a different way, only 206 miles away from each other in the cities of Głogowiec and Wadowice, Poland—a roughly four-hour car ride today. It could be argued that their two children, Sts. Faustina and Pope John Paul II—both missionaries of Divine Mercy—are the two greatest Polish saints of the twentieth century. Faustina's parents, Stanislaus and Marianna,

---

[103] Coverdale, *Uncommon Faith*, 24. Originally cited by Manuel Garrido, *El Beato Josemaria Escriva y Barbastro*, 57.

[104] de Prada, *The Founder of Opus Dei,* 34. Originally cited in *Meditation*, February 14, 1964 and by Francisco Botella in *Sum.* 5609.

embraced simplicity while living on their twelve-acre land, five of
which was used as a pasture. According to author Ewa Czaczkowska:

> The soil was barren and could support mainly rye
> and potatoes. The house was in great despair, so the
> Kowalskis decided to build a new one. They could afford
> only the cheapest building material-marl, quarried in
> nearby Rozniatow. The light yellow stone was hewn
> into rectangular, somewhat uneven blocks and then
> bound with clay mortar that crumbled quiet easily. The
> building was covered with a thatched roof. Stanislaus
> Kowalksi completed all of the carpentry work himself.
> It was not a large home and boasted a layout typical for
> peasant farmhouses of the day: two rooms separated by
> a large hall. On the right was a kitchen with a stove,
> where Stanislaus moved his carpentry in winter, and on
> the left, a large room. In the rear of the house was a door
> leading to the backyard. Little remains of the original
> furnishings of the Kowalksi home from the time when
> Helen lived there; just her father's carpentry bench and
> three paintings depicting the Sacred Heart of Jesus, the
> Holy Family, and St. Agatha.[105]

Further, several children slept in the same bed and the girls
shared one dress. In fact, the latter was the main reason why Faustina
and her sisters missed Sunday Mass on some occasions. To miss
Sunday Mass was so painful for Faustina, who used to follow the
readings at home, despite her mother sometimes getting angry
with her for not assisting in the kitchen. Faustina would respond,
"Mommy, don't be cross, because the Lord Jesus would have been
more cross if I didn't do that."[106] Faustina's one dress was already a
preparation for her future life as a religious sister, many of whom
have only one or two religious habits. So important was the religious
habit to Faustina that when, as a nun, some of her religious sisters
tried to convince her to wear work clothes when cooking in the

[105] Czaczkowska, *Faustina*, 34–35.
[106] Ibid., 43.

kitchen instead of her habit, Faustina would say, "The Lord's bride should always wear the habit."[107]

The seven acres of poor land used for crops, combined with Stanislaus's occasional carpentry jobs, along with working as a carpenter at a local brewery, barely allowed the Kowalska family to make ends meet. After laboring during the day as a carpenter, Stanislaus would often work on his land well into the night. However, despite his best efforts, Stanislaus still could not afford to pay for his children's education, provide ample clothes for them, or provide a necessary dowry for his daughters. This likely caused him intense suffering and some humiliation, for every father aims to provide for his family, not only spiritually, but materially. Stanislaus did everything in his power to provide for his wife and ten children, but even that was not enough. As a result, Stanislaus and Marianna's daughters were expected to work as maids when they were old enough. So impoverished was this family that their eight-year-old daughter Natalia left home to work as a nanny for distant relatives. Faustina matriculated for nearly three years from 1917 to 1920 before her wages were needed by the family. Surprisingly, at the age of twelve, Faustina knew how to read, which was rare in their village. In fact, her father Stanislaus was one of only two people in his village who could read, and the family subscribed to magazines and religious books. Adding to their difficulties, when the Kowalskas had their horse stolen during the First World War, they could not afford another one, and instead had to use their cow to pull the plow.

Though it would seem easier to embrace simplicity either by renouncing external possessions, as did many saints when called to religious life, or by circumstance, as did several of the parents presented in this chapter, it is a far greater feat to possess simplicity of heart, which, according to Our Lord, makes one the greatest in the Kingdom of God. While Marianna was known for her gentler demeanor compared to her husband, she struggled at times to possess the simplicity of heart that so captured her saintly daughter. From a young age, Helen (Faustina) had dreams of the Blessed Mother and various visions of God. One time, during the night, the thirteen-

---

[107] Ibid., 153.

year-old Faustina was awakened by a light. Marianna recalled telling her daughter, "Where's it at, then? Are you stupid? You're just seeing things and talking nonsense."[108] Upon which Helen would sit up and pray, which caused Marianna to tell her, "You'll lose your mind from not sleeping and waking up so suddenly. Go to sleep!"[109]

Helen would say to her mother, "But no, Mommy, it's probably an angel that's waking me so that I don't sleep, so that I would pray."[110]

Not surprisingly, Helen would be tired during the day and asked to take a nap, which her mother was not always amenable to because she knew Helen traded sleep for prayer. Faustina must have experienced some frustration because her parents, the people she loved and trusted most, were indifferent to her spiritual encounters.

A parent has an obligation to guide their children to the truth, but it is not unusual for certain souls, especially the saints, to have had mystical experiences even in their youth. For example, as little boys, Padre Pio conversed with his guardian angel, and Maximilian Kolbe saw Our Lady. Perhaps God reveals certain things to little children because they are so innocent, simple, and without pride. Even Our Lord suggested this, "I thank you, Father, Lord of heaven and earth, that you have hidden these things from the wise and understanding and revealed them to infants" (Mt 11:25). While these mystical experiences of seeing our guardian angels or Our Lady are not the norm, nor should they be sought, for "blessed are those who have not seen and yet believe" (Jn 20: 29), parents who possess a simple heart must remember the words of the Lord: "Let the children come to me, and do not hinder them; for to such belongs the kingdom of heaven" (Mt 19:14), i.e., their children are above all God's children.

Each night, the Kowalska family recited their prayers together while Faustina and her siblings knelt beside their parents, and, throughout the day, Faustina invited her siblings to pray. She was in charge of their family altar in the main room, which consisted of a small cross and two clay statues of Jesus and Mary. These religious

---

[108] Ibid., 40.
[109] Ibid.
[110] Ibid.

items were purchased at the Jasna Góra Shrine, where the famous image of Our Lady of Częstochowa is venerated. Faustina's advanced piety from her youth provides an important reminder for parents to encourage their children to meet Our Lord in the sacraments along with Eucharistic Adoration and, most importantly, for parents to pray for a simple heart for themselves and their children. Parents ought to never dismiss their children's mystical experiences without striving to further understand and deepen them in light of the Gospel.

Besides her family's simplistic lifestyle and prayer life, which helped prepare Faustina for religious life, Faustina received schooling in the classroom of the Cross well before she donned her habit. The many crosses and sacrifices that Faustina met in religious life, such as sleeping in a small cell, working difficult and mundane jobs, and bearing hurtful comments from a few, cruel religious sisters were not foreign to her. Faustina had experienced all of the latter sufferings in a similar manner at home, including misunderstandings from her parents and humiliations from her own siblings and classmates.

On one occasion, Faustina's classmates would not sit next to her at school because of her "shabby attire,"[111] which resulted in tears. According to Faustina's mother, "the children (Faustina's siblings) would hit and bully her because she was in daddy and mommy's graces."[112] While in the convent, some sisters would even mock her by calling her a "princess," to which Faustina candidly responded, "Indeed, I am a princess, because the royal Blood of Christ flows in my veins."[113] Once, a religious sister told Sr. Faustina, "Sister, you can get it out of your head that the Lord Jesus might be communing in such an intimate way with someone who is miserable and imperfect! The Lord Jesus only communes with holy souls— remember that!"[114] If only this sister knew that this is the precise reason Our Lord communicates with someone like Faustina— because God draws near to the humble and simple of heart, those who recognize their misery before a God that has "not come to

---

[111] Ibid.

[112] Ibid., 38.

[113] Ibid., 238.

[114] Ibid., 108.

call the righteous, but sinners to repentance" (Lk 5:32). This is the message of Divine Mercy.

In a mysterious way, the simplicity and poverty of Faustina's parents not only prepared their daughter, who had only three years of elementary education, for religious life but, more importantly, prepared her heart for union with God. In fact, Faustina was once instructed by the infant Jesus in a vision that "true greatness of the soul is in loving God and in humility."[115] Our Lord could have spoken these words of simplicity to Faustina from the Cross, or in His splendid glory, but He chose to appear as a child to reiterate to Faustina and the world that "whoever humbles himself like this child, he is the greatest in the kingdom of heaven" (Mt 18:4). Above all, whoever becomes like the infant Jesus, Who, in His great simplicity, great humility, great poverty, and total dependence on His Father in Heaven and Joseph and Mary while He lived on earth, is on the right path to Heaven. At the same time, Faustina's parents realized that poverty as a manifestation of simplicity was a means to an end—the end being a heart that belongs completely to God.

The Crucified Bridegroom calls forth not just religious to be conformed to Him in their poverty and simplicity, but also families. The Kowalska family was clearly pleasing in the eyes of God because they relied solely on God's providence and let their simplistic lifestyle be an outlet to partake of the Holy Family's simplicity in Nazareth with joy and surrender. Faustina would continue her parent's simplicity in the convent as she would be admitted to the second choir of sisters rather than the first. The first choir of sisters was reserved for the more educated sisters from a higher class, while the second class was for the poorer nuns without a dowry. First class sisters had longer veils and wider sleeves and were given gold rings after their perpetual vows compared to the second choir sisters who had shorter veils, narrower sleeves, and silver rings. Fortunately, this practice was abolished after World War II. Nevertheless, Faustina's religious vows were clearly a continuation of her simplicity and poverty from her home life.

[115] St. Faustina, *Diary: Divine Mercy in My Soul*, 189.

One final story concerning the Kowalska family is worth mentioning as it testifies more so to their poverty than their simplicity. Faustina's funeral took place on October 7, the Feast of Our Lady of the Rosary, two days after her death on October 5, 1938. Ironically, no one from Faustina's family attended her Requiem Mass. Faustina, being sensitive to their poverty, did not want any of her relatives to be notified of her death due to the high travel expenses. While news of her death did not reach her parents and most of her siblings immediately, Faustina appeared to her younger sister, Natalia, in her room. Natalia recalled:

> She was as white as a communion wafer, so thin, with folded hands. And she said to me, "I have come to say goodbye to you, because I'm leaving. Remain with God. Do not cry, you mustn't cry!" She kissed me on the cheek, and I couldn't say a word. I just pressed my face into the pillow. When she left, I started to cry. . . . Then, the door opened again, and my sister stood there, so white, and said: "I have asked you not to cry and you are crying. There's no need to cry, and I beg you: do not cry!"[116]

Natalia traveled the following day with her husband to visit her parents and siblings as they mourned the loss of their thirty-three-year-old daughter and sister, who had died from tuberculosis. While this chapter focuses on the simplicity of Stanislaus and Marianna, and that of their daughter Faustina, those who read Faustina's diary with a cursory glance can easily miss the faith and simplicity that epitomized the Kowalskas, but which was overshadowed by their daughter's vast mystical experiences, including visions, dreams, and messages given by Our Lord (and some by His Mother). Despite all the mystical experiences, however, many forget that Faustina went through the dark night of the soul for six months as a novice. She offered these terrible sufferings for the salvation of souls both the dead and the living, including her siblings. It was not the visions that made her a saint; rather, it was her simplicity and faith, which she inherited from her parents, that led to her canonization. And

---

[116] Czaczkowska, *Faustina*, 354.

that is why at the heart of Faustina's life and spirituality was the virtue of simplicity. One of her spiritual directors, now Bl. Fr. Michael Sopocko, testified to this amazing virtue, "Naturalness and simplicity characterized her relations both with the sisters in the convent, and also with persons outside the community."[117]

Behind the gentleness, simplicity, and the smile of Faustina lies Stanislaus and Marianna Kowalska, parents of great simplicity and faith, who were also not without their flaws. And, despite initially opposing their daughter's vocation, somehow, God used their detachment, their sheer poverty, and their simplicity of faith to be the training grounds for one of the Church's greatest twentieth-century saints. Though Stanislaus and Marianna's land produced a scant harvest, and they themselves were infertile for nine years, God blessed them with ten children. With God's grace, this couple helped scatter the seeds of virtue, especially simplicity and faith, to their children. And, just as the Kowalska parents were deemed average Catholics by their pastor,[118] so too was their saintly daughter deemed an ordinary sister by many of her sisters in the convent. Faustina's simplicity and humility were such that she preferred to pass unnoticed in this life like her own parents. Only after her death, would her religious sisters, family, and the entire world see just how far from ordinary she was, for, while being a woman of great simplicity, her obedience to fulfilling and spreading Our Lord's message of Divine Mercy was extraordinary.

Three Polish words, *Jezu, Ufam Tobie,* seemed implanted in Stanislaus and Marianna's hearts well before Our Lord privately revealed these most powerful words to their daughter in 1931. Most notably, Our Lord asked Faustina:

> Paint an image according to the pattern you see, with the signature: Jesus I trust in You. I desire that this image be venerated first in your chapel, and then throughout the world.
>
> I promise that the soul that will venerate this image will not perish. I also promise victory over [its] enemies

---

[117] Ibid., 303.
[118] See Ibid., 37.

already here on earth, especially at the hour of death. I
Myself will defend as it as My own glory.[119]

The words, *Jezu, Ufam Tobie*, translated into English as "Jesus, I
trust in You," were lived out by Stanislaus and Marianna Kowalska,
not in an image, as commanded by the Lord to Faustina, but truly
in a life of simplicity and trust as they imperfectly relied on God
to provide for their family of ten children despite their poor land
and low wages. Stanislaus and Marianna struggled at times to trust
God with their finances, their fertility, their land, their health, and
their children, especially when their daughter Faustina went to the
convent; yet somehow their simplicity was a safeguard against the
words from the Psalmists, "Put not your trust in princes, in a son of
man, in whom there is no help" (146:3), or "if riches increase, set not
your heart on them" (62:10). Most of all, Stanislaus and Marianna's
simplistic lifestyle as seen in this chapter inspired their daughter
Faustina and her siblings to recognize that one should not put their
trust in some "prince," i.e., some political leader, or even our health,
land, or wealth, for security, for that too shall pass away someday;
rather, our entire trust ought to be rooted in Our Lord, especially
His words, "Jesus, I trust in You," for His mercy and love endure
forever. Over time, Stanislaus and Marianna, in their simplicity of
heart, came to realize that, despite their material deprivations, they
lacked nothing as they possessed God, Who is everything.

Karol and Emilia Wojtyła

Besides Stanislaus and Marianna Kowalska, Karol Wojtyła Sr. and his
wife, Emilia, embraced a simplistic way of life in the early twentieth
century. Unlike the Kowalskas, the Wojtyłas were wealthier, had
fewer children, and resided in a more urban area. Still, both couples
embraced the Lord's call to "not lay up for yourselves treasures on
earth, where moth and rust consume and where thieves break in and
steal, but lay up for yourselves treasures in heaven, where neither
moth nor rust consumes and where thieves do not break in and
steal. For where your treasure is, there will your heart be also" (Mt

---

[119] St. Faustina, *Diary: Divine Mercy in My Soul,* 47.

6:19–21). In his biography, *Witness to Hope*, Weigel related that the "Wojtyła apartment was modest, but certainly middle class, housed in a solid brick structure covered by stucco."[120] Further, Weigel described their apartment as having "several rooms and a kitchen. The extant furniture, china, cutlery, and decorations suggest solidity, piety, and a simple, but hardly impoverished standard of living."[121] Their apartment was far from some well-kept museum where parents' energies are directed toward keeping a pristine home versus letting their children discover the joy of play. It was not uncommon for Karol Sr. and Karol Jr. to play indoor soccer where the future pope would excel as a goalie.

Giovanni and Marianna Roncalli

One story worth mentioning recapitulates this entire chapter of simplicity from the eyes of a saint in reference to his father. According to Pope St. John XXIII, "Angelo Giuseppe Roncalli," who lived and served as pope during the lives of many of the saints mentioned in this book, such as John Paul II, Josemaría Escrivá, Fulton Sheen, Solanus Casey, and Mother Teresa, "My father is a peasant who spends his days hoeing and digging, among other things, and I, far from being better than my father, am worth much less, for my father at least is simple and good, while in me, there is nothing but malice."[122] On one occasion, when the pope was a young boy, his father lifted him up on his shoulders to watch a religious procession. This was a foreshadowing of him being carried into St. Peter's Basilica on the *sedia gestatoria*, the portable papal throne on which popes were carried prior to the Second Vatican Council. He reminisced about this event when he wrote, "Once again I am being carried, carried aloft by my sons. More than seventy years ago I was carried on the shoulders of my father at Ponte San Pietro. . . . The secret of everything is to let oneself be carried by God, and so

---

[120] Weigel, *Witness to Hope*, 28.

[121] Ibid.

[122] Pope St. John XXIII, *Journal of a Soul* (New York: McGraw-Hill, 1964), 91–92.

to carry Him [to others]."[123] The simplicity of Pope John XXIII's father, Giovanni Roncalli, paved the way for his son to be the pope of the common people. Though not mentioned explicitly, Marianna Roncalli would have likely tucked her thirteen children in bed each night, especially after the little ones fell asleep in her arms. There truly is no safer place in this world than in our father and mother's arms—a glimmer of God the Father and Our Lady's love for us.

It must be noted that where simplicity reigns there also happiness reigns. It is no wonder that the saints were some of the most joyful, most down to earth, and funniest people that ever lived. Fulton Sheen, John Paul II, Phillip Neri, Solanus Casey, and Thérèse, to name a few, all learned from their parents that our possessions or the approval of others will not bring happiness. Instead, a loving family atmosphere where prayer, play, household responsibilities, quality time, and virtue are prized above everything helps bring Heaven a little closer to earth. The parents of the saints were interested in forming the whole person and not making their children into spiritual robots or even replicas of themselves. They wanted to mold them into the sons and daughters that God the Father wanted them to be. Author, Mary Ann Budnick, sums up one of the greatest lessons we can learn from these simple and devout parents:

> Living our Catholic faith is more than rigidly performing actions, reciting specific prayers or defending the teachings of the Church. It must first of all be a conversion of heart. This conversion gives birth to holiness whose fruit is happiness. One cannot raise happy, holy children unless one is happy and holy oneself.[124]

That is why the parents of the saints prayed for simplicity and adopted a simplistic lifestyle as a safeguard against pride, envy, avarice, and sadness. Simplicity is indeed a virtue and, like an aqueduct, it allows grace to flow more freely from the hearts of Jesus and Mary. Without simplicity, there can be no true conversion

---

[123] Hebblethwaite, *John XIII: Pope of the Century* (New York: Bloomsbury Academic, 2005), 7.

[124] Mary Ann Budnick, *Raise Happy Children . . . Teach Them Virtues!* (Springfield, IL: R.B. Media, Inc., 2002), 9.

of heart. Just as God's very being is simple, so too ought simplicity to be at the heart of who we are, for it surely was at the heart of these parents and their children's identity. As alluded to earlier, simplicity is connected with humility. Upon meeting someone who lacks simplicity and humility, we can look past the façade to see who they truly are—a person with duplicity. However, upon meeting a saint or a holy parent of a saint, we may encounter something that we have never encountered before in another human being, something that escapes us, which is none other than God's presence fully radiating through this soul. God's presence pervades simple and humble souls like a glass prism or stained glass window, reflecting so many splendid virtues. We are moved by this person because we feel as if we are in the presence of God just like those who saw Moses after he came down from Mount Sinai (see Ex 34:29). A seasoned Carmelite sister, Sr. Febronie, once told St. Thérèse, "Your soul is extremely *simple*, but when you will be perfect, you will be even *more simple*; the closer one approaches to God, the simpler one becomes."[125] The simpler we become, the more we disappear, and the more God appears in us. Though his parents were not mentioned in this chapter, St. Giuseppe Moscati offers one of the greatest quotes on simplicity. As a prestigious doctor, Giuseppe could have easily been arrogant, pretentious, and rich. Instead, he used his own home to treat his poor patients for free as well as priests and religious. The following quote says all there needs to be said on simplicity:

> Love truth; show yourself as you are, without pretense, without fears and cares. And if the truth means your persecution, accept it; if it means your torment, bear it. And if for the truth's sake, you should sacrifice yourself and your life, be strong in your sacrifice.[126]

The background for simplicity, which set the bar for so many saints and their parents, was and is Bethlehem—the first residence of the King of Kings. Our Lord did not choose to be born at the

---

St. Thérèse of Lisieux, *Story of a Soul*, 151.

126 "Lives of the Saints—St. Joseph Moscati" (2006), piercedhearts.org/theology_heart/life_saints/st_joseph_moscati.html.Piercedhearts.org.

Ritz Carlton, but in a stable. His mode of transportation was not a Mercedes Benz, but a donkey. The parents of the saints learned simplicity not by reading *People* magazine or aspiring after degrees for the sake of appearing learned in the eyes of men, but by immersing themselves in the life of the greatest Man of simplicity, Jesus Christ. At the heart of simplicity is the belief that these parents were content with who God made them to be, what God gave them, and also what He took away. Ultimately, simplicity was a means to an end, for its purpose was to lead these devout parents and their children to union with God. For, in simplicity, we not only live an authentic life without pretenses, but slowly detach ourselves from the things of this world in order to be attached to things of Heaven. These parents also reveal that the ordinary things in life do in fact lead us to God like incense rising up to Heaven, such as a home-cooked meal with strangers and family members, happily completing daily tasks for the praise of God and not the praise of man, living joyfully in our poverty, fishing with our family, delighting in a lightning storm, savoring a delicious cigar, playing games with our children, receiving a blessing from our parents, and, above all, partaking of the Holy Eucharist. Only those with a simple heart can find delight in spending time alone with God for they know that He is the One most worthy of their time. For what we do now will continue on in Eternity, which leads us to our next chapter on solitude.

HALLMARK SIX

Solitude

*When I saw how my father prayed, I was very much ashamed
that, after so many years in the convent, I was not able to
pray with such sincerity and fervor. And so I never cease
thanking God for such parents.*[1]—St. Faustina

At some point in our lives, we are all novices when it comes to
learning a skill. And, like any skill, prayer takes effort, repetition,
perseverance, and, above all, God's grace. Even before these
conditions occur, however, we first need someone to show us how,
just as a child needs a father or mother to teach them how to ride
a bicycle for the first time. Even Jesus learned how to pray from
the example of his foster father, St. Joseph, and His mother, Mary,
"(who) kept all these things in her heart" (Lk 2:51). Some Scripture
scholars have posited that the burning bush, which manifested the
presence of God in the midst of the Israelites, prefigured Mary's
Immaculate Heart, which burned because of the presence of the Son
of God in the midst of the Holy Family.

From His birth in a hidden, quiet cave in Bethlehem, roughly
six miles from the clamor of Jerusalem, Our Lord showed us how
precious solitude is and how precious silence is—oh silent night,
which changed the world forever. After Bethlehem, we encounter
Our Lord's first taste of solitude during the Holy Family's visit to
Jerusalem during the Feast of the Passover. St. Luke's Gospel says
that Joseph and Mary were "astonished" (2:48) when they found
their twelve-year-old Son in the Temple after He had disappeared

---

[1]   St. Faustina, *Diary: Divine Mercy in My Soul*, 178.

for three days. While Scripture relates that Jesus was "sitting among the teachers, listening to them and asking them questions" (Lk 2:46) during this point in His pilgrimage to His Father's house, we are left to our imaginations as to how He spent the rest of His time. Though purely speculation, it would seem very plausible that Our Lord, Who unceasingly communicates with His Father from all eternity, would have readily conversed with Him in the solitude of the Temple, which was the Father's House and His dwelling place on earth. Perhaps more than anything, the young Jesus wanted to remain a little more time in the home of His Heavenly Father rather than return to the earthly home of His parents, Joseph and Mary. While, in the perspective of Joseph and Mary, Our Lord may have been lost for three days, He was not lost in the perspective of His Heavenly Father, for he who discovers solitude is truly found by his Father in Heaven.

Little is known about Jesus' childhood, but Joseph and Mary may have occasionally checked on their Son in the middle of the night only to find Him talking with His Heavenly Father in solitude and silence. No doubt this experience of witnessing a glimpse of the inner life of the Trinity here on earth—one of the most beautiful sights any human eye could behold this side of the pearly gates!—would have filled them with awe and humility. Many of the saints were greatly inspired by their parents' reverence in prayer. How much more then would St. Joseph, Our Lady, and even the Apostles be moved to tears at the sight of witnessing Our Lord, the true Divine Master of prayer, commune with His Heavenly Father in solitude?

Inspired by Our Lord's life of prayer and the desire to pray like Him, one of His disciples asked Him directly, "Lord, teach us to pray, as John taught his disciples" (Lk 11:1). It was then that Our Lord revealed the "Our Father" prayer. This disciple knew that if you want to become the best, you have to learn from the best. Yet Our Lord did not stop there. He showed us all throughout His entire life how to live not only by what He said, but, most importantly, by what He did and, above all, by how He prayed. Scripture paints the best picture of Our Lord's prayer life: "And after He had taken leave of them, He went up on the mountain to pray" (Mk 6:46). Or, in St. Luke's Gospel, just before St. Peter's declaration that Jesus is the Christ, "Now it happened that as he was praying alone the disciples were with him; and he asked them, 'Who do the people say that I am?'" (9:18–19). Or, just prior to calling His Apostles, "In these days he went out to the hills to pray; and all night he continued in prayer to God" (Lk 6:12). Or, before Our Lord walked on the sea, St. Matthew tells us, "And after he dismissed the crowds, he went up into the hills by himself to pray" (14:23). In essence, Jesus' human nature needed contact with His Father, while His Divine nature was always in contact with the Father.

It must be noted that the words "praying alone" are often translated as "solitude." In fact, the word solitude comes from the Latin word *solitudinem*, meaning loneliness, or the state of being alone.[2] It may also be used to indicate a lonely place, such as the desert or the wilderness. In referring to the original meaning of solitude found in Genesis, Pope St. John Paul II articulated that "man is 'alone': this is to say that through his own humanity, through what he is, he is at the same time set into a unique, exclusive, and unrepeatable relationship with God himself."[3] We are the only creatures God has made in His image and likeness (see Gn 1:26). God, therefore, Who desired us for Himself, has set us apart from the rest of living beings by our self-consciousness and self-determination.[4] Solitude beckons us back to the author of our being, Who is God Himself.

Of all the Scripture accounts that capture Our Lord praying, Jesus' agony in the garden is the most courageous, memorable, and painful example of solitude recorded in human history. As St. Luke declared:

> And he came out, and went, as was his custom, to the
> Mount of Olives; and the disciples followed him. And
> when he came to the place he said to them, "Pray that you

---

[2] "Solitude," Online Etymology Dictionary, etymonline.com/index. php?term=solitude.

[3] Pope St. John Paul II, *Man and Woman He Created Them*, 151.

[4] See Ibid.

may not enter into temptation." And he withdrew from
them about a stone's throw, and knelt down and prayed.
Father, if you are willing, remove this chalice from me;
nevertheless, not my will, but yours be done.[5]

Notice that Jesus leaves His Apostles temporarily to be alone with
His Father. After the angel strengthened Him to be able to suffer
even more for us, St. Luke further declares, "And being in an agony
he prayed more earnestly; and his sweat became like great drops of
blood falling down upon the ground" (22:44). Our Lord's blood
descended to the ground like heavy raindrops. Through His bitter
agony in the garden, Our Lord shows us that prayer is harder than
any battle we will ever encounter for we face the greatest enemy of
the world, Satan, who stops at nothing to keep us from our mission
of hearing the Good Shepherd's voice and boldly following His
will. Yet prayer is also sweeter than any earthly delight because it is
only in prayer that we experience the unmerited, infinite mercy and
love of God Who thirsts for our love. Without prayer, particularly
solitude, Our Lord would not have been able to discern the Father's
will and then pray for the courage to accomplish it. If Jesus needed
solitude to fulfill His mission, then we certainly need solitude to
fulfill ours.

As the greatest teacher and example of prayer, Our Lord showed
His Apostles that if we are to love someone, namely, the Father,
"Abba" (Mk 14:36), we must set aside quiet time daily to be alone
with Him. And, therefore, the Apostles sought to not just preach
Christ to their followers, but above all to imitate Our Lord's life of
prayer, particularly His great love for solitude. And, going one step
further, the Apostles desired to enkindle in their flock the absolute
necessity of solitude. Can you imagine listening to Sts. Peter, Jude,
or John the Evangelist preach on Our Lord's agony in the garden,
which they certainly witnessed as they were only a "stone's throw"
(Lk 22:41) away? Solitude is truly an apostolic prayer, which has
been handed down by Our Lord to His Apostles, who handed it on
to their followers, who in turn shared it with the Desert Fathers and
other religious founders like St. Benedict, and, finally, to parents

[5]   Lk 22:39–42.

who in turn passed it on to their saintly children. And, while new forms of prayer have come and gone, the Catholic Church will never deviate from the necessity of solitary prayer, not as a replacement for the Holy Sacrifice of the Mass or the Liturgy of the Hours, but as a perfect complement. From generation to generation, solitude is the "one thing" (Lk 10:42) that will endure forever, and it is the "one thing" that the following parents of the saints wanted to hand on to their children aside from their great love for the sacraments. These devout parents were not passing on some new technique or some sensational musical experience, but were literally imitating how God Himself prayed and how we all ought to pray. Solitude leads us to union with the Father for it was how Our Lord Himself prayed, which in turn became, as seen in the following accounts, the preferred prayer encounter of the parents of the saints and their children outside of the Holy Sacrifice of the Mass.

Stanislaus and Marianna Kowalska

In February of 1935, a nun, obscure at the time, named Sr. Maria Faustina Kowalska of the Most Blessed Sacrament was being summoned to visit her severely ill mother, Marianna, who was battling acute liver pain. Thirteen years had passed since Faustina had last been home, and it had been seven years since she saw her parents when they attended her first vows in 1928. Only two years before visiting her ill mother, the twenty-seven-year-old Faustina had made her perpetual vows on May 1, 1933, in Kraków, where, just a few miles away, lived a thirteen-year-old boy named Karol Wojtyła. At her final vows, Sr. Faustina made three requests, the first being:

> The triumph of the Church, particularly in Russia and in Spain; for blessings on the Holy Father, Pius XI, and on all the clergy: for the grace of conversion for impenitent sinners. And I ask You for a special blessing and for light, O Jesus, for the priests before whom I will make my confessions throughout my lifetime.[6]

---

[6]　St. Faustina, *Diary: Divine Mercy in My Soul,* 119.

Her second request included blessings on her congregation, her superiors, her homeland, and her "dearest parents." Her third request was a plea for souls in need of prayer: the dying and the Holy Souls in Purgatory.

Faustina longed to see her mother, whose life was hanging in the balance. The fact that she included her "dearest parents" in her offering of final vows reveals that Faustina's religious formation from a young age was truly blessed. After receiving permission from her Mother Superior, Faustina arrived the next morning at her home. Although the context for the family gathering was sad due to her mother's supposed impending death, Faustina recalled with great joy how beautiful their meeting was. Faustina wrote, "We knelt down to thank God for the grace of being able to be together once again in this life."[7] Marianna fondly recalled their encounter, "She came to my room, praised God, and knelt down beside me, by the bed, and said at once, 'Mommy, you will get up yet.'"[8] Miraculously, the next day, Marianna joined her family for Sunday Mass and declared her good health ever since. Faustina's mother would recover and live another thirty years before going to her eternal reward in 1965, while her father died in 1946, eight years after Faustina's death.

Two years after having made her final vows, Faustina, inspired so much by the prayer life of her father, Stanislaus, highlighted this in her own diary: "When I saw how my father prayed, I was very much ashamed that, after so many years in the convent, I was not able to pray with such sincerity and fervor. And so I never cease thanking God for such parents."[9] How, in fact, did Faustina's father pray? In her book *Faustina, The Mystic and her Message*, Czaczkowska declared:

> Stanislaus was devout and very hard-working. He would wake up at dawn to sing the *Little Office of the Blessed Virgin Mary*, the hymn "When the Morning Dawn Rises," and during Lent, the *Lenten Lamentations*. Helen's father's chosen form of devotion was often trying for the whole family, since the house was cramped and several

7   Ibid., 178.
8   Czaczkowska, *Faustina*, 46.
9   St. Faustina, *Diary: Divine Mercy in My Soul*, 178.

children slept in one bed. He would get up first, when the family was still asleep and—without taking into consideration the children or our exhausted mother, worn out by taking care of the children day and night—would sing his *Hours* loudly and fervently, desiring foremost to honor the Virgin Mary. Mother, barely alive, would ask him not to, or even get angry at him for waking her. Nothing helped.[10]

Stanislaus believed his first duty each day was to give glory to God and honor Our Lady, even at the expense of his wife and children's sleep. Like her father, Faustina, too, found herself lost in solitude before the gaze of the famous icon of Our Lady of Częstochowa, also known as the Black Madonna, where she once prayed from 5 a.m. until 11 a.m., or, in her own words, "I prayed without interruption until eleven, and it seemed to me that I had just come."[11] Though both Faustina and her father loved Our Lady dearly, they clearly had different methods of prayer when praying in solitude. Stanislaus prayed more vocally and utilized devotional books. On the other hand, Faustina's desire for solitude, which she inherited from her father's example, took on a different shape, that is, mystical prayer instead of devotional prayer. One of Faustina's religious sisters, Sr. Justine Golofit, described Faustina's prayer life as such:

> She prayed, and she loved to pray. She was always recollected when she was praying and immersed in her prayer. She prayed kneeling, but with her back straight. Her prayer was mental prayer. While praying, she rarely used devotional books or the Holy Scriptures.[12]

Despite the fact that Faustina did not rely on prayer books, she imitated her father by singing religious hymns, such as "When Morning Dawn Rises," to start her day and various songs to Our Lady and Our Lord throughout the day. Yet, unlike her father's

[10] Ibid., 36.
[11] St. Faustina, *Diary: Divine Mercy in My Soul,* 127.
[12] Czaczkowska, *Faustina,* 235.

spouse, Faustina's spouse, Our Lord, seemed more receptive to such morning hymns!

Although Sr. Faustina would pass away only three years and eight months after her home visit at the age of thirty-three—like her Divine Lover at His Death, which was truly providential—she was reenergized by her father's prayer life. Most people would think that the opposite would be the case, that is, Faustina's prayer life would have inspired her parents, but a holy father and mother are like fine wine in that their prayer life and love for one another, for their children, and, most of all, for God becomes sweeter with age.

As a young girl, Faustina had listened to the stories of hermits and monks from her father's lap, which helped plant the seeds of a religious vocation. Stanislaus also read missionary magazines, biblical stories, and the lives of the saints, which helped ignite the flames of heroic virtue in his children. Describing her home visit in her diary, the tides were now turned as "they [Faustina's family] listened with great interest to my account of the lives of the saints. It seemed to me that our house was truly the house of God, as each evening we talked about nothing but God."[13] Yet the solitude and love for prayer that her father had modeled and instilled in Faustina became somewhat trying surrounded by twenty-five-plus relatives and friends. At times, Faustina felt like a fish out of water from her convent, where solitude permeated, saying, "When, tired from these talks and yearning for solitude and silence, I quietly slipped out into the garden in the evening so I could converse with God alone, even in this I was unsuccessful; immediately my brothers and sisters came and took me into the house."[14] Faustina recalled asking her brothers to sing for her and to play the violin and the mandolin. During this time, Faustina stated, "I was able to devote myself to interior prayer without shunning their company."[15] While holding the Infant Jesus in a vision, Our Lady once instructed Faustina how best to pray with these words:

---

13 St. Faustina, *Diary: Divine Mercy in My Soul,* 179.
14 Ibid.
15 Ibid.

My daughter, strive after silence and humility, so that
Jesus, who dwells in your heart continuously, may be
able to rest. Adore Him in your heart; do not go out
from your inmost being. My daughter, I shall obtain for
you the grace of an interior life which will be such that,
without ever leaving that interior life, you will be able
to carry out all of your external duties with even greater
care. Dwell with Him continuously in your own heart.
He will be your strength.[16]

Though the saints reveal that we can converse with God at
any time and any place because of the indwelling Trinity, solitude
seems more easily found in an adoration chapel, the cloister, a
nature walk, a small prayer corner in our home, or even a garden,
as Faustina sought solitude there before her family discovered her.
These environments are more conducive for hearing God's voice
because they tend to be away from the exterior noise, including the
conversation of men, allowing us to be alone with Him Who seeks
to be alone with us. We must never forget that Jesus, the greatest
lover of solitude, preferred prayer spots were in the mountains or the
desert, away from the crowds and even His own Apostles.

The Kowalska's property, with its vast acreage away from the
din of the city, provided a peaceful setting favorable for deep prayer.
It is no wonder that many contemplative religious orders built their
monasteries and convents on the top of mountains, in the woods, or
in the countryside, where the beauty and solitude of nature leads one
to God, for the purpose of solitude is to hear the voice of God even
if it is a voiceless word. It is no surprise that many laypeople flock to
these religious houses for retreats, for it is here that they can escape
the hustle and bustle of the world and encounter God, Who dwells
not only in the Tabernacle, but also throughout the property in the
rustling of the leaves and the star-studded sky. It is by no accident
that many of the saints were raised in the countryside, away from
the city and its secular influences, because their holy parents desired
a simple, contemplative atmosphere where they could ascend to God
through prayer, work, and family love. Above all, these parents

---

[16] Ibid., 312–313.

276

wanted their children to hear God's will, which can only be found in silence and solitude.

Like the Fatima seers who were all born less than five years after her, Faustina attended to livestock, most notably the family's cows. She also enjoyed reading books. The rural setting gave her a taste of solitude, of which she longed to drink more heavily, later, in religious life. One story, which sheds light on how God draws us to Himself through nature, is significant in Faustina's life. A year after her first vows in 1929, while visiting a lake in Kierz, Our Lord revealed something that only those who appreciate solitude can grasp. Specifically, Faustina wrote:

> One afternoon . . . on the shore of the lake; I stood therefore a long time, contemplating my surroundings. Suddenly I saw the Lord Jesus near me, and He graciously said to me. **All this I created for you My spouse; and know that all this beauty is nothing compared to what I have prepared for you in Eternity.**[17]

And solitude, like all the hallmarks present in this book, points us to Eternity, to the place that "no eye has seen, nor ear heard, nor the heart of man conceived, what God has prepared for those who love him" (1 Cor 2:9). And, at the same time, Our Lord reminds us through His messenger Faustina that there is no sight on this earth—not even the most spectacular sunset, harvest moon, or crystal-clear ocean water, or even seeing our children for the first time—that can compare to what awaits us in Heaven, which is God Himself. In the meantime, Stanislaus, Marianna, and Faustina reveal to us that while we are citizens of Heaven, we must not forget that everything God created is good, particularly nature, which can be a means to lift our hearts and minds back to Him in praise and thanksgiving.

Sts. Louis and Zélie Martin

St. Faustina was not the only saint whose own prayer life was greatly influenced by watching her father pray. In her autobiography, St. Thérèse described the lasting impression her father's prayer life

---

[17] Ibid., 88.

made on her. She wrote, "Then we all went upstairs to say our night prayers together and the little Queen was alone near her King, having only to look at him to see how the saints pray."[18] Louis was likely Thérèse's first and most important example of prayer as her mother died while she was just four years old. Long before his marriage at the age of thirty-five, Louis was an ardent lover of prayer and solitude. On April 24, 1857, a year prior to meeting Zélie, Louis purchased a small property, which he dubbed the "the Pavilion," in a secluded part of town away from his work and his parent's home. At the Pavilion, which was more like an austere, monastic cell, Louis possessed a haven for him to store not only his fishing items, but, more importantly, it became a place of prayer with a simple crucifix on the inside and his thirty-six-inch statue of Our Lady surrounded by his garden on the outside grounds. Written on the walls of his room were Louis's favorite mottos: "God sees me," and "Eternity is drawing near."[19]

Throughout his life, Louis made retreats at the Trappist Monastery of Soligny when his duties permitted. Specifically, Zélie wrote, "[Louis] has to leave on the twentieth for *L'Abbaye de la Trappe* near Mortagne together with several gentlemen, and they will stay there three days."[20] A worldly person might think making a retreat is time poorly spent. Even a deeply religious wife might hesitantly allow her husband to leave the family for a three-day retreat once a year because she needs him at home. Louis and Zélie knew they were called to love God before their spouse and children, and, therefore, solitude was not an afterthought, but the very life of their vocation. These devout parents came to believe that without solitude we can neither lead our families to Heaven nor become saints ourselves because only in the silence is Our Lord's voice heard.

In addition to supporting their spouse's desire to be holy by allowing them to take time away from their daily duties for a retreat, Louis and Zélie also fostered this desire in their children. In a letter to her sister-in-law, Zélie recalled how her oldest daughter, Marie,

---

[18] St. Thérèse of Lisieux, *Story of a Soul*, 43.
[19] Martin, *The Father of the Little Flower*, 3.
[20] Martin and Martin, *A Call to a Deeper Love*, 182.

who was sixteen years old at the time, had a deepening conversion due to a five-day retreat directed by a holy Jesuit priest named Fr. Cartier. Specifically, Zélie wrote:

> Marie is completely changed since her retreat. It seems the Jesuit priest who gave it is a saint. There were mysterious things said between them. I asked her for information, but there was no way of finding out anything. . . . What I learned was from Pauline. Moreover, it was very little information. I told her aunt about it, who begged me not to publicize it, since Marie prefers to hide everything from me. I wouldn't want you to mention what I'm telling you for anything in the world, neither in letters (she reads them) nor in any other way. In short, I think she's going to be a nun, although she does everything possible to convince me otherwise.[21]

Ironically, this was the same girl who always dreamt of living in a "beautiful house,"[22] according to her mother. Zélie further stated, "Though so unworldly, [Marie] is never happy where she is. She aspires to something better; she would need very large and well-furnished rooms."[23] After Marie's retreat, it appears as if she heard God's voice, particularly concerning her vocation, and, at the same time, perhaps received a grace to detach herself from the desire to live comfortably. Our world has lost its appreciation for silence and solitude in favor of background noise and activity, which only drowns out the voice of God. Parents like Louis and Zélie remind the world of the importance of solitude. If a parents' most fundamental duty is to get their children to Heaven, then the second most important duty is to help their son or daughter discover their vocation through prayer, and what better way than by encouraging their children to make a retreat.

Besides encouraging their children to make a retreat, parents must provide a home life that is conducive to prayer. The Rule of St. Benedict offers great wisdom for cultivating solitude and silence.

---

[21] Ibid., 236.
[22] Ibid., 210.
[23] Ibid., 210.

Specifically, in Chapter 42, "Silence After Compline," it declares, "Monks should diligently cultivate silence at all times, but especially at night." Though a home is not a monastery, parents must provide the environment where God's voice can permeate the hearts of their family and allow them to make time for spiritual reading. And, while solitude and silence are different, they flourish together.

Whether it was in their home, on a retreat, at Church, or in nature, Louis and Zélie wanted their children to discover God's presence everywhere for solitude knows no boundaries. Specifically, Louis and Zélie often took their children for a picnic in the countryside or to the ocean. Thérèse wrote about these fond memories:

> Ah! how quickly those sunny years passed by, those years of my childhood, but what a sweet imprint they have left on my soul! I recall the days Papa used to bring us to the *pavilion*; the smallest details are impressed in my heart. I recall especially the Sunday walks when Mama used to accompany us. I still feel the profound and *poetic* impressions that were born in my soul at the sight of the fields enameled with *cornflowers* and all types of wildflowers. Already I was in love with the *wide-open spaces*. Space and the gigantic fir trees, the branches sweeping down to the ground, left in my heart an impression similar to the one I experienced still today at the sight of nature.[24]

The Martin family clearly loved the outdoors. In fact, throughout their marriage, Zélie supported Louis's favorite recreation, which was fishing, and, although he loved taking his children with him, on occasion, he would go by himself. Zélie wrote to her sister-in-law on June 24, 1874 that "[Louis] left this morning to go fishing and won't return until eight o'clock this evening."[25] Louis probably needed some carefree time away from his female dominated house, which consisted of six women, including his wife Zélie and their children, who, at the time, ranged from Marie at fourteen to Thérèse

[24] St. Thérèse of Lisieux, *Story of a Soul*, 29–30.
[25] Martin and Martin, *A Call to a Deeper Love*, 149.

at seventeen months. Besides refreshing his soul, fishing allowed Louis to be with God in solitude. Louis and Zélie reveal how essential it is for spouses to allow each other to do things they enjoy, which should make them come alive and draw them nearer to God. Louis's love for fishing reiterates the sentiments of St. Bernard, who once said that "he learned more among the trees of the forest than from books and masters."[26] St. Alphonsus de Liguori also pointed out that "the saints, in order to live in solitude and far from tumult, have so ardently loved the caves, the mountains, and the woods."[27]

According to his daughter Céline, who tended to Louis until his passing, her father's delight for solitude never waned:

> I will always remember his beautiful face when, in the evening, as night fell in the deep woods, we stopped to hear a nightingale: he listened . . . with what expression in his gaze! It was like an ecstasy, some inexpressible part of heaven was reflected in his features. Then after a good moment of silence, we were still listening, and I saw tears streaming down his dear cheeks. Oh! what a fine day![28]

Thérèse and Céline inherited their great love for nature from their father, for only a person of solitude can allow everything around him or her, albeit wheat fields, flowers, or nightingales, to transport them to Heaven, for God created everything to reflect His beauty, truth, and goodness. Specifically, in her autobiography, *Story of a Soul*, Thérèse described how her outings with her father led to deeper communion with God. She related:

> They were beautiful days for me, those days when my "dear King" took me fishing with him. I was very fond of the countryside, flowers, birds, etc. Sometimes I would try to fish with my little line, but I preferred to go *alone* and sit down on the grass bedecked with flowers, and then my thoughts became very profound indeed! Without knowing what it was to meditate, my soul was absorbed in real prayer. I listened to distant sounds, the murmuring

---

26   St. Alphonsus de Liguori, *The True Spouse of Jesus Christ*, 481.
27   Ibid.
28   Piat, *Celine*, 58.

of the wind, etc. At times, the indistinct notes of some military music reached me where I was, filling my heart with a sweet melancholy. Earth then seemed to be a place of exile and I could dream only of heaven.[29]

As the saying goes, "Give a man a fish and he'll eat for a day. Teach a man to fish and he'll eat for the rest of his life." The same is true with solitude. Teach your children to love solitude, and they will hear the voice of God for the rest of their lives. That is why the saints were the greatest admirers of God's beauty. They recognized the Divine fingerprint in all things from a flower to a sunset. In fact, Our Lord once revealed to a twentieth-century mystic, "My sunsets are also My love. So few of My children look at them and praise Me . . . and yet My love is there."[30]

Like her husband, Louis, Zélie's desire for solitude never faded, but only increased through the years, even some seventeen years after being married. She once wrote to her daughter Pauline on January 16, 1876:

> As for me, I imagine that if I were in a magnificent chateau, surrounded by everything one could wish for on earth, the emptiness would be bigger than if I were alone, in a little attic room, forgetting the world and being forgotten. So I do nothing but dream of the cloister and solitude. With the ideas I have, I really don't know how this wasn't my vocation or how I didn't remain a spinster, or retreat into a convent. Now I'd like to be very old, so I can withdraw in solitude when all my children are grown. But I feel that all these are only empty ideas, so I hardly pay attention to them. It's better to use the present time well than to think so much about the future.[31]

After an exhausting day of work and being surrounded by her workers, not to mention her children, Zélie longed for a little solitude. She once wrote, "I had intended to spend a nice evening with my Pauline and also to read. It disturbs me a little to receive

---

[29] St. Thérèse of Lisieux, *Story of a Soul*, 37.
[30] Gabrielle Bossis, *He and I* (Boston: Pauline Books, 2013), 7.
[31] Martin and Martin, *A Call to a Deeper Love*, 211.

Madame Tessier. I have no need of company because I quite enjoy myself all alone."[32] In her moments of solitude, Zélie often read spiritual biographies, such as Sts. Frances de Chantal and Frances of Rome. Zélie identified closely with these saints, who were also mothers like herself, and who joined religious life after their husbands died. Zélie recalled, "As for me, I'd begun my reading about the torments of the damned seen by Saint Frances of Rome; it makes me tremble. I don't like this kind of reading material, but it can be very beneficial. I talked to your father about it all morning, and he wanted to take the book to his Pavilion."[33] How beautiful that Louis and Zélie discussed with one other their spiritual reading, but also literally shared their books! Few married couples experience the intimacy and love Louis and Zélie experienced, a love that God wills for every marriage, because few tap into their sacramental graces through prayer along with discussing with their spouses the deeper, spiritual things. After the Fall, harmony was severed between man and woman, husband and wife. Yet, through Our Lord's Passion, Death, and Resurrection, and the graces received through Sacrament of Holy Matrimony, an indissoluble bond is created between a husband and wife, and they are granted the grace to love each other supernaturally and to help each other attain true holiness in their lives. And therefore, contrary to many, solitude actually leads us closer to our spouses and loved ones because, the closer we come to God, the more we become like Him, and the more we love like Him.

After Zélie's death, Louis's pining for solitude grew as he preferred to walk home silently after Mass while accompanied by his five daughters. Louis would tell his daughters, "I like to continue my conversation with Our Lord."[34] After moving to Lisieux to be near his brother-in-law and sister-in-law, who would help him raise his five daughters, Louis's home, "Les Buissonnets," had a room referred to as the Belvedere, Italian for "beautiful view." In his Belvedere, which was an upstairs room with a view of the entire city

---

[32] Ibid., 216.
[33] Ibid., 218.
[34] Martin, *The Father of the Little Flower*, 5.

of Lisieux, Louis spent hours praying and reading spiritual classics, such as the Gospels, *The Imitation of Christ*, *Clock of the Passion*, entire volumes of *The Liturgical Year* by Dom Geuranger, and works of St. Alphonsus de Liguori. He also enjoyed *The History of France*, *The History of the Church*, and *The Reformer of La Trappe* among other books. Louis delighted in poetry, especially Lamartine and Victor Hugo. According to Céline, he was known to repeat the poem of Lamartine: "Man! Time is nothing for an immortal being. Unfortunate he who tried to store it up. Foolish he who weeps for it. Time is your sailing-ship and not your home."[35]

After Louis retired, he dedicated his energies even more fully to raising saints and developing a rich prayer life, which included spiritual and intellectual formation. Louis's passion for spiritual reading was passed on to his children, especially Thérèse, who would often quote *The Imitation of Christ* in her letters to her sisters. More than anything, Louis and Zélie used their solitude not only to enrich their spiritual lives, but, equally important, their children's as well—a practice that reflects one of the mottos of the Dominican Order: "To contemplate and to share with others the fruit of one's contemplation." Specifically, Pauline Martin, the second oldest daughter, who later became Mother Agnes of Jesus in the Carmelites and superior for her little sister, Thérèse, wrote, "My mother and father possessed a profound faith. When we heard them talking together of eternity, and reading aloud certain passages from *The Imitation of Christ*, we were led, young as we were, to look upon the things of this world as pure vanity."[36]

Louis and Zélie encountered Our Lord through spiritual reading. At the same time, they communicated the fruits of their prayer and the lessons from these spiritual writers to their children. Solitude for the sake of solitude is pointless if it does not transform us and those around us into great lovers of God and neighbor.

---

[35] Ibid., 8.
[36] Wust and Wust, *Zelie Martin*, 73.

Karol Wojtyła Sr.

Besides Sts. Faustina and Thérèse, another saint described his encounters of witnessing his father pray, this time in the solitude of the night. Seeing his father pray had such a profound impression on this saint that he wrote about it on the occasion of the fiftieth anniversary of his priestly ordination:

> After my mother's death, his life became one of constant prayer. Sometimes I would wake up during the night and find my father on his knees, just as I would always see him kneeling in the parish church. We never spoke about a vocation to the priesthood, but *his example was in a way my first seminary*, a kind of domestic seminary.[37]

Clearly, the prayer life of Pope St. John Paul II's father helped inspire the vocation of this future pope. Following the death of his mother, the young Karol and his father, Karol Sr., would frequently read the Sacred Scriptures and pray the Rosary together. Whether it was praying before the Most Blessed Sacrament or hiking in the Italian Alps, John Paul II, like his father, would sometimes be immersed in prayer for hours. On one occasion, John Paul II's secretary, Cardinal Dziwisz, described John Paul II's desire to be alone as they hiked the snow-covered Alps, "I had the very clear sensation that I was observing someone endowed with a spiritual power that was no longer human; someone who no longer belonged to his world, but was living those minutes in complete communion with God, with the saints, and with all the souls of heaven."[38] Both Karol Sr. and his son, John Paul II, reveal that solitude is a prerequisite for sanctity, and through solitude God is transfigured before us daily in prayer, and we become lost in the Eternal Love. Though John Paul II had at one time wanted to be a Carmelite friar, probably because of his great love for solitude that he inherited from his father, along with his great interest in the writings of the

---

[37] Pope St. John Paul II, *Gift and Mystery* (New York: Image Books, 1996), 20.
[38] Lino Zani and Marilu Simonescho, *The Secret Life of the John Paul II* (Charlotte, NC: Saint Benedict's Press, 2012), 57.

Carmelite friar St. John of the Cross, God had better plans. Above all, Karol Sr. and his saintly son lived by the words written by John of the Cross: "The knowledge of God is received in divine silence."[39]

There is no greater or more memorable impression that Karol Sr. could have made on his son than the one above, for a father is most powerful and most vulnerable on his knees. Most powerful because a father communicates to his son who the real Father of the house is. At the same time, he reveals the source of his strength and, at the same time, how weak and little he is—totally dependent on God's mercy just as a child is dependent on his or her parents for everything. One of the most beautiful sights is when a father and mother teach their children bedtime prayers. Little did Karol Sr. know that as he kneeled next to his little son "Lolek," as he called him, he was praying next to a future pope and saint. Though Karol Sr. would die from a heart attack on February 18, 1941 at the age of sixty-one, leaving his twenty-year-old son alone in this life, he would be a constant intercessor from Heaven. Imagine the joy Karol Sr. might have experienced when he died, if God had told him, "Well done good and faithful servant, a child of yours will one day become pope, but more importantly one of the Church's greatest modern-day saints."

At a glance, Karol Sr. did nothing spectacular to raise a saint. Yet his greatest lesson was not something he said, but what he did, for just as John Paul II, through his love for the Holy Eucharist, opened the floodgates of hope and peace for millions of Catholics oppressed by Communism, so too did Karol Sr. lift the veil of Heaven for his son by his contemplative presence. Many fathers might feel unworthy of the task of raising saints and, therefore, sadly abdicate their role as the spiritual head of their families by allowing their wives to lead. Perhaps Karol Sr. at one point doubted whether he himself was competent to raise his young son by himself for women often tend to be more devout than men. Yet the truth of the matter is that Karol Sr. came to embrace the words of St. Paul, "My grace is sufficient for you, for my power is made perfect in weakness" (2 Cor 12:9). Karol Sr. preached the greatest lesson to his son not by quoting

---

[39] St. John of the Cross, *The Collected Works of St. John of the Cross*, 88.

the catechism, but by making prayer, particularly solitude, his most treasured time on earth, while at the same time not neglecting both communal prayer at Mass and praying the Rosary with his son.

Sante and Agnes Possenti

One of the greatest examples of solitude could be seen in the lives of Sante and Agnes Possenti in Assisi, Italy, during the nineteenth century. Living seven centuries after St. Francis of Assisi and one century before the Wojtyłas, Sante and Agnes's prayer life was at the heart of everything they did, which laid the foundation for their son, St. Gabriel of Our Lady of Sorrows, who lived a most holy life as a Passionist religious brother before dying at the age of twenty-three from tuberculosis. Agnes created a special prayer room with a replica sculpture of the Pietà where she devoted many hours to contemplating this great mystery of Christ's Death and His Mother's sorrow. She also journaled her thoughts and used these for her daily meditations. It is no coincidence that her son Gabriel took the title of Our Lady of Sorrows, which was likely instilled in him by seeing his mother's great devotion. Besides Gabriel, his other twelve siblings were profoundly impacted by their parents' love for prayer. Gabriel's brother, Michael, described their father as "very pious,"[40] but not a fanatic. Every morning, Sante, the governor of Assisi, would set aside an hour for meditation in his room, not taking any guests. Following his meditation, Sante would attend Mass with one of his children before beginning his work. Each evening, the family joined together to pray the Rosary. Sante would also pay a visit to the Pietà statue before going to bed.

It is no surprise that his son, Gabriel, once declared, "My Heaven is the suffering of my dear Mother,"[41] referring to the Blessed Mother's pain over witnessing the brutal Crucifixion of her Son. Gabriel's religious brothers were edified by his devotion to prayer. Specifically, his Passionist brother Bernardo Silvestrelli declared, "It was beautiful watching him pray. I am not exaggerating when I say

---

[40]   Gabriele Cingolani, CP, *Saint Gabriel Possenti, Passionist: "A Young Man in Love"* (Staten Island, NY: Alba House, 1997), 7.

[41]   Ibid., 107.

that he would bring tears to people's eyes, and move their hearts to devotion. I saw people who were not so devout come to see him, and they were visibly moved and had tears in their eyes."[42]

Like Gabriel, parents ought to never doubt that authentic piety is contagious, especially when it comes to their children. In what would be his last letter before dying, Gabriel, around Christmas, wrote the following unforgettable words to his brother Michael, who, at the age of forty, was a doctor and widower caring for six children from the ages of nine to one month: "Do you want to love? Love Mary. People on this earth cannot make you happy. The drama of this world passes quickly. Farewell dear brother. Do as I have recommended, it is a matter of eternal happiness."[43] Such words can only be born of someone who is radically in touch with God through solitude. By virtue of his parent's example and insights acquired in solitude, Gabriel came to realize that only Our Lord and His Blessed Mother could truly make him happy amidst the fleeting things of life.

Alberto and Maria Beretta

Compared to those in religious life or priesthood, a married couple has less opportunities for solitude due to the demands of work, rearing children, maintaining a clean and orderly home, etc. Those in religious life and the priesthood set their day around their prayer lives, particularly Holy Mass and meditation. However, unlike a nun, a mother is not fortunate enough to be able to slip away for two hours to pray in a chapel, especially at the expense of her duties. In fact, many of those in married life struggle to focus on just one thing, which is being alone with God for a short period of time. St. Paul highlighted this struggle when he declared, "The married man is anxious about worldly affairs, how to please his wife, and his interests are divided" (1 Cor 7:33–34). Far from making excuses, the parents of the saints were convinced that solitude was essential to their holiness and sanity as much as oxygen is to life, and, therefore, prayer was not an afterthought. Though most homes, especially

---

[42]   Ibid., 96.
[43]   Ibid., 144.

those with large families, oftentimes resemble a circus more than a monastery, many of the parents of the saints sought not only to quiet their hearts and receive God's grace to guide their family, but most of all to fall head over heels in love with God and, in turn, to fall more deeply in love with their spouses and children. They knew that only in solitude can we hear the Holy Spirit's whisper of love. Yet how can one find solitude with so many distractions and responsibilities? In the life of St. Gianna's mother, Maria Beretta, she found her solitude through spiritual reading. According to her son, "After mamma straightened up the house and made our beds, she sat in the armchair beside a big basket overflowing with laundry to mend and socks to darn. She never complained, she always smiled, she never seemed tired. With all her work, she found time to meditate on a little book called *The Gift of Self*, written by a French author."[44]

Like her parents, Gianna valued the importance of solitude. According to her husband, Pietro, "From the time we were married, Gianna would spend a few minutes of recollection and meditation in the chapel of Ponte Nuvoro. Silence was very important for her too."[45] The following quote about Gianna could also be applied to her parents and every couple in every generation who allows the graces from their prayer lives to spill over to their family and neighbor:

> Gianna is a saint because she reminds us that life is beautiful, that God is happy when we climb a mountain to contemplate a snow-covered valley, when we help our brother, when we play with our children. Then there is the heavy load of pain and suffering. But we must not allow them to prevail.[46]

Like her parents, Gianna was passionately in love with God. Above all, Gianna understood that God was the source of anything good she did for her family, patients, and neighbors: "Only if we are

[44] Molla and Guerriero, *Saint Gianna Molla*, 24.
[45] Ibid., 68–69.
[46] Ibid., 15.

rich in grace ourselves, can we spread it around us, for we cannot give what we do not have."[47]

It must be noted that the Berettas lived near a Capuchin friary in Milan's Piazza Risorgimento where both Alberto and Maria were Third Order Franciscans. What a grace to be able to walk to the friary for daily Mass, Confession, spiritual direction, and some quiet time in solitude before the Most Blessed Sacrament. It is no small wonder that two of Alberto and Maria's children became priests and one became a sister.

Angelo and Maria Angelerio

In the four Gospel accounts, Our Lord is recorded as asking his accusers, Apostles, bystanders, and, most of all, you and me over one hundred questions. However, probably the greatest question Our Lord ever posed was asked not only once, but three times: "Simon, son of John, do you love me?" (Jn: 21:15). Our Lord asked St. Peter this question when He appeared to His disciples after His Resurrection. Our Lord poses this very same question to each of us every day of our lives, but especially at the hour of death. For instance, every time Satan tempts us to some pleasure, Our Lord asks us: "Do you love Me more than this fleeting pleasure?" This question surely penetrated the heart of Peter and undid his threefold denial of the Lord. Like Our Lord, parents can and should ask their children many questions. Have you been courageous today? Have you done anything that may have upset Jesus, and what can you do differently next time? Have you completed your chores and finished your homework? While the question to Peter demanded only a yes or no response, Our Lord was not afraid to use open-ended questions. In fact, on several occasions, Jesus did just that: "Why are you afraid, O men of little faith?" (Mt 8:26). "But who do you say that I am?" (Mk 8:29). "Why do you sleep?" (Lk 22:46).

Throughout the centuries, parents have and continue to ask their children open-ended questions like: What do you want to do with your life? This question is asked by many parents, but falls short of a deeper question, which many parents of the saints asked:

---

[47]   Ibid., 148.

What is it that God wants you to do with your life? Some parents might even ask their children these beautiful questions: Have you considered the priesthood or religious life? Or, if a son is considering marriage: Have you considered pursuing such and such girl from church who appears very virtuous? Or, to a daughter: What do you think about this man? Surely questions about their particular or secondary vocation are some of the greatest questions parents can and should ask. Unfortunately, many parents tend to focus solely on their children's occupation: Have you considered being a nurse since you are so good at helping other people or being an architect since you are skilled at math and drawing? And, while the aforementioned questions are necessary and praiseworthy, they do not get to the heart of the matter. There is, however, one question that one mother of a saint asked all of her children that might be the greatest question any parent can ask, and a question that helped lead her son to become one of the greatest lovers of solitude in the Church's history.

Around 1210, some seven centuries before the Beretta family, Angelo and Maria Angelerio from Abruzzi, Italy gave birth to their eleventh of twelve children, whom they named Pietro. From a young age, Pietro gravitated toward silence and solitude. Who can blame him for wanting a little peace and quiet from his large family? Perhaps Pietro's mother challenged him to holiness when she asked him and his siblings the following question after their father's unexpectant death, namely, "Which one of you is going to become a saint?" Pietro would answer emphatically, "Me, Mamma! I'll become a saint!"[48] Notice Maria did not ask, "Which one of you will become a priest to bring honor to our family?" "Which one of you will be married to increase our family's name?" or "Which one of you will become a doctor to ensure my financial stability when I am old?" She simply, but profoundly, asked, "Which one of you is going to become a saint?" In effect, Maria's question lit a fire in Pietro's heart, who, at the age of twenty, became a hermit where he prayed, worked, and read the Bible as he embraced the Benedictine Rule in various remote wilderness settings, such as Mt. Majella. At

---

[48] "St. Celestine," Catholic.org, catholic.org/saints/saint_id=172.

the same time, Maria's question allowed her children to reflect on their first vocation or primary vocation, which, for every baptized person, is nothing less than becoming a saint. Holiness is our primary vocation, while our secondary or particular vocation—marriage, Holy Orders (priesthood, diaconate), religious life (religious priest, brother, or sister), or a generous single life—is the vehicle by which we are called to fulfill our primary vocation to holiness.

While most people will never remember the name Pietro Angelerio or his mother for that matter, many will remember his papal name, Pope St. Celestine V, the 192nd successor of St. Peter. Unfortunately, Pope St. Celestine V is more remembered for resigning as pontiff than for what he set out to do, which was to reform the clergy. Celestine's resignation as pope would be a first in Church history, but not the last. Pope Celestine V did not want to be pope in the first place and so, five months and eight days into his office, he resigned, citing, among other reasons, humility and his desire to return to his former state of life—namely his deep longing for solitude found in the monastic life. Following his resignation, Pope Celestine V was kept hidden in a tower in the castle of Furmone, perhaps under house arrest, by his successor Boniface VIII. There he spent the last nine months of his life in prayer, fasting, and solitude—something which he probably enjoyed more than being pope. With God's grace, Celestine fulfilled his mother's question when Pope Clement V canonized him only seventeen years after his death in 1313. The Church does not canonize someone just because he was a pope. In fact, there have only been eighty popes who have been canonized or recognized as saints out of 266 popes since St. Peter, which is roughly thirty percent. And, while Pope Celestine V's papacy was far from spectacular, he nevertheless was a man of prayer and a saint of solitude, who showed that there can be no saint who does not prize solitude. However, his life testifies to an even greater lesson for parents. Just as God was pleased with this servant's faithfulness and prayer, even though his papacy seemed like a failure, so too parents must teach their children this same reality. St. Teresa of Calcutta once declared to a senator, "We're not always called to be successful, but we're always called to be faithful."[49] Even if our children never make the varsity team, are never accepted into an Ivy league college, never become pope, or never obtain a reputable profession, that really does not matter in God's eyes. What matters most is that we and our children become holy by making prayer the most important reality in our lives and do everything for God's glory and honor, leaving the outcome to Him alone. Even in our prayer lives, we are called to be faithful and not successful. Saints like Celestine and Faustina remind us to leave our agendas behind as well as our need to get something out of our prayer. Or, as best put by St. John of the Cross, "Preserve a loving attentiveness to God with no desire to feel or understand any particular thing concerning him."[50]

While Maria likely never climbed Mt. Majella or its 9,000-foot summit where the young Celestine loved to pray, she found her solitude closer to the ground, perhaps in a small prayer corner of her home after her twelve children went to sleep. Whether we are called to be a hermit, a pope, or a mother of many, solitude beckons us to spend time alone with God so that we might answer like St. Peter, "Lord, you know everything; you know that I love you" (Jn 21:17) with each moment of our lives.

Joseph and Anna de Liguori

On October 5, 1696, near Naples, Italy, exactly 400 years after the death of Pope St. Celestine V, Holy Mother Church welcomed one of her greatest saints. In his ninety years on earth, the bishop, St. Alphonsus de Liguori, wrote over one hundred works on spirituality and theology. Because of his holiness and breadth of teachings, Alphonsus, who is sometimes referred to as the Doctor of Prayer, was declared a Doctor of the Church and a patron of moral theologians. Our Lord said, "You will know them by their fruits" (Mt 7:20). What was the tree that enabled Alphonsus to produce so much fruit? After all, fruit cannot grow by itself; it needs nutrients, which come from the soil. In examining Alphonsus's upbringing, it seems clear that prayer, particularly solitude, was the tree, which allowed the

---

49   St. Teresa of Calcutta, *A Simple Path*, 153.
50   St. John of the Cross, The *Collected Works of St. John of the Cross*, 92.

grace of God to produce so many virtues in him. With God's grace, Alphonsus kept his purity intact throughout his entire life, though not without temptations.

One of the most impressive features of Alphonsus's life was his prolific writings on top of founding the Redemptorist Order and serving as a bishop. We often think that the more responsibilities we have, the less time we have for prayer. On the contrary, the opposite was the case for Alphonsus, who realized that solitude is the vessel, especially before the Most Blessed Sacrament, whereby we come to experience God's infinite love as well as other Divine truths. And, through solitude, Alphonsus sought to impart the fruits of his prayer life to His flock and to every generation interested in advancing in the spiritual life.

As the eldest of seven children, Alphonsus was raised by two fervent Catholics, Joseph and Anna de Liguori. Joseph was a naval officer of the Royal Galleys and his mother, who came from noble blood, was Spanish. Yet his parents belonged to the poorer side of the family. Despite this, they had complete trust in God and a commitment to life, and so welcomed seven children despite their modest income.

Reflecting their great love for the saints, they gave their son the baptismal name Alphonsus Mary Anthony John Cosmas Damian Michael Gaspard de Liguori. Anyone who has ever read any of his rich spiritual works, especially on the Holy Eucharist, or the Passion of Christ and Our Lady, will discover a man in love with God, His Church, and the saints—a love that he inherited from his parents. In fact, the writings of St. Alphonsus are saturated with countless quotes from his saintly brothers and sisters to a degree that is unmatched by most spiritual authors.

Just as a bishop or priest has the responsibility of leading his people into a deeper intimacy with the Holy Trinity, Joseph had a similar mission in his family. While navigating the waters as a captain to provide for his family, Joseph understood that his most important calling from God was to steer his family to Heaven by providing a sound example of virtue and prayer. Therefore, he wanted to share with his son Alphonsus the "one thing," as Our

Lord told Martha, "One thing is needful. Mary has chosen the good portion, which shall not be taken away from her" (Lk 10:42).

Joseph and Anna fulfilled their primary duties as parents by not just telling their children about Jesus, which is necessary, but by providing a concrete witness to the value of prayer. Specifically, as a young child, Alphonsus frequently accompanied his father on spiritual retreats at a local monastery. God has blessed most of us with five amazing senses via smell, touch, taste, sight, and hearing, yet what distinguished the de Liguoris from most people is that their five senses were used for the glory of God, especially the sense of hearing, which was used profoundly. St. Benedict, one of the spiritual masters on prayer, wrote in his Rule, "Let us listen with the ears of our hearts," and there is a spiritual adage that testifies to the importance of listening, which states that God gave us two ears and one mouth for a reason, meaning we should listen twice as much as we speak. The Old Testament is clear about silence: God's voice is heard in "a still small voice" (1 Kgs 19:12).

As the world fills our lives with more distractions and noise, the de Liguoris knew the secret to hearing God's will and "the still small voice" was being alone with Him and removing as much exterior and interior noise as possible. This lies at the heart of solitude. Because of Joseph's great love for solitude, which he transmitted to his son, Alphonsus came to realize that his love for God on earth would be the basis for his relationship with God for all eternity. Alphonsus once declared, "He who would love God exceedingly in heaven must first love him very much on earth. According to the degree of love which we bear towards God when we finish the journey of life, will be the degree of love with which we shall continue to love God for all eternity."[51] The famous words from the movie *Gladiator* says it all, "What we do in life, echoes for all eternity."[52] There are no minimalistic saints in Heaven; rather, Heaven is filled with saints who maximized their time on earth. Our union with God in Heaven will take off where it left off on earth. Those who had

---

[51] St. Alphonsus de Liguori, *The Incarnation Birth and Infancy of Jesus Christ*, 124.
[52] *Gladiator*, DVD.

the greatest union with God on earth, i.e., those who prized the sacraments and solitude above everything will enjoy the greatest union in Heaven, while those who put little effort into their prayer lives will have a lesser union, but still pleasing nevertheless.

The Church encourages everyone to make an annual retreat, just as Joseph and Alphonsus did at their local monastery. However, some saints sought solitude so much that they literally built their "domestic church," most notably their house, away from the city. Although not a parent of a saint, St. Thomas More's quote below offers some wisdom for married couples when choosing to purchase a home. As realtors say, location is everything. In fact, some saints' homes seemed to foster greater spiritual growth by virtue of their proximity to a Catholic Church or perpetual adoration chapel like Gianna Molla, Josemaría Escrivá, and Thérèse, while others grew in their spiritual lives due to their proximity to the countryside like Bernadette, Faustina, Francesco, Jacinta, Maximilian Kolbe, Padre Pio, Pius X, Solanus Casey, Thomas More, and countless others.

The countryside with its clear, starlit skies, radiant sunsets that permeate the horizon, and vivid wildflowers served as a secondary educator to the parents of the saints as they pointed their children to the Divine Presence in nature. Furthermore, many of these devout parents discovered that the countryside offered a quiet, slower-paced, simplistic lifestyle conducive for solitude and silence not to mention the protection of traditional values compared to that of the city. For instance, St. Benedict fled from the debased fifth-century culture of Rome to the hillside to form a community of men set on prayer, work, and perseverance in virtue. While St. Thomas More lived the first forty years of his life in the city, it was roughly around the year 1525 that the More's moved to what was then the countryside of Chelsea. There, away from the city, Thomas and his family's prayer life seemed to soar due to the privacy of the country along with the construction of a chapel on their estate. More testifies to the advantages of the countryside as a divine meeting place:

> In the city, what can incite a man to a good life, and does not rather, by a thousand devices call back him who is struggling to climb the hard tracks of virtue? One sees

nothing but false affection and flattery on the one hand; hatred, quarrelling, and the wranglings of the law courts on the other. Wherever you look you see nothing but caterers, fishmongers, butchers, cooks, confectioners, poultrymen, all occupied in serving the body, the world, and the devil! Even the houses block out a great part of the light, so that one cannot freely see the heavens; it is not the arc of the horizon that bounds the view, but the roofs of the houses. I cannot blame you if you are not tired of the country, where you see simple people, ignorant of the wiles of the town, and wherever you turn your eyes, the beautiful face of the country refreshes you, the soft air exhilarates you, and the sight of the sky delights you.[53]

And, while not every family can own a home in the country, many of these saintly families, like the Martins, made it a practice to take long walks in the countryside as they wanted their children, like St. Francis of Assisi, to experience the presence of God in nature. These saintly families desired to "freely see the heavens," which the countryside so beautifully affords.

In addition to ensuring their children's spiritual needs by refreshing their bodies and souls through a retreat, Joseph and Anna ensured their children had a well-rounded education. For instance, they made Alphonsus practice his harpsichord daily for a few hours in addition to his schooling. Alphonsus went on to receive his doctorate in civil and canon law from the University of Naples at the age of sixteen. This eventually led him to a successful career as a lawyer. However, after losing a vital case at the age of twenty-seven, Alphonsus renounced his career to follow the Lord, which at first was met with great resistance by his father. Perhaps Joseph took delight in having a successful son and was disappointed when his son renounced everything, which meant his pride and family's honor were at stake. All those years of education gone to waste must have been a thought that crossed Joseph's mind when he first learned that Alphonsus renounced his prestigious law career. Further, Alphonsus wanted to join the Oratory of St. Phillip Neri, which would result

---

[53] Monti, *The King's Good Servant but God's First*, 45.

in him leaving home and seeing his family less depending on his assignment.

Like the father of St. Francis of Assisi some 500 years earlier, Joseph could have reacted as Pietro di Bernadone did by using threats and beatings to persuade Alphonsus to return to his former job. However, these harsh tactics employed by Pietro, a wealthy Italian merchant, only drove his son, Francis, away from him, eventually leading Francis to renounce his own father. On the contrary, Joseph conceded two months later that Alphonsus could study for the priesthood under the condition that his studies occur at home and he serve as a secular missionary rather than join the Oratory. Such was the closeness of the tight-knit Catholic family that they did not want their son to leave them even in his adult years.

Joseph never raised Alphonsus to be remembered for his success, wealth, or intellect, but that his Catholic Faith would permeate society through his vocation as a lawyer and married man. Joseph's heart was in the right place, but he lacked the wisdom of God as written in the words of the Psalmist, "Teach us to number our days that we may get a heart of wisdom" (90:12). Something changed in those two months. Perhaps Joseph received an insight from God while making a retreat, which allowed him to fully support Alphonsus's new calling. Through solitude and surrender, Joseph was conformed to God's will rather than trying to inform God of his will. Like every imperfect, earthly father who believes they know what is best for their children, Joseph had his flaws because only the Heavenly Father knows what is truly best. However, in spite of their own weaknesses, the de Ligouris laid the fertile soil for a future saint by passing on their love for solitude, the Eucharist, Our Lady, and the saints to their seven children.

Joseph and Anna also created a home environment where the virtue of purity was instilled in their children. For instance, Alphonsus would remove his glasses when going to the theatre to avoid seeing anything scandalous. Through their rich sacramental and personal prayer lives, Joseph, Anna, and their children came to experience God's love, which allowed them to grow in modesty and chastity as they respected their own sexuality as well as that of their neighbors. In fact, Joseph, on a few occasions, sought to arrange a marriage for Alphonsus to the best available bride—a very holy and virtuous woman. Alphonsus declined his father's attempts. Though little is known about Joseph and Anna compared to their saintly son, a spirit of affection and respect seemed to pervade their home. As a result, the seven Liguori children did not need to look for love in all the wrong places as often happens in homes where affection is lacking. The de Liguori household was built on the love of God, which they drank of daily in solitude.

Outside of the Holy Sacrifice of the Mass and spending time with their families, the greatest moments of the parents of the saints were spent intimately conversing with the Blessed Trinity. In fact, several of them, such as Sts. Louis and Zélie Martin, had, at one point in their lives, set foot in a convent or monastery to seriously discern God's will. Other parents of the saints even started their own orders, for example, St. Bridget, who sought to contemplate Our Lord's unfathomable love, particularly His Passion. While discerning their vocation in the convent or monastery, the desire of these devout parents for union with God only intensified, and the lessons they acquired from the holy religious men and women they encountered there would shape their vocation and that of their children. For example, Louis and Zélie grew to appreciate labor, silence, solitude, spiritual reading, and the Divine Office that forms the rhythm of religious life, which they sought to incorporate into their own family life. While many in the world view strictly contemplative orders, who devote their entire lives to prayer and work, as wasteful, these devout parents and their children believed the opposite to be true. In fact, many of these pious parents and their saintly children believed that God's presence could be found more in a convent or monastery than anywhere else in this world because God's spoken language is silence. There is no place in this world save a convent or monastery, especially a cloistered one, that esteems silence so much that it is mandated by their rule. Hence, there is a reason Louis would make retreats at various monasteries even after being married—he longed to be alone with God Who longs to be alone with us. He longed to hear the voice of the Father more clearly outside of his pressing responsibilities. The same is true for Zélie who dreamt of the cloister even after being married for many years because she desired to be alone with Our Lord. Perhaps this is a reason many of the parents of the saints sought the monastic life in the first place, or later joined, like Maria Kolbe, while others supported their children's vocations, such as the parents of Sts. Alphonsus de Liguori, Pope Celestine V, Thérèse, Padre Pio, and many more. Above all, the Martins and all of the parents mentioned in this chapter wanted to make their home a house of prayer.

Many of us would have loved to witness Our Lord praying while He lived on earth. In truth, we can witness Our Lord praying simply by gazing at the Most Blessed Sacrament where He prays day and night to the Father. And while many of us, especially the saints, have been blessed with pious parents to show us how to pray, we often feel like we are still novices. Our Lord never desired that we keep our training wheels forever. That is why He gave us the Holy Spirit, the master of the interior life, to guide and inspire our prayer life, particularly our times of solitude. As St. Paul's letter to the Romans so beautifully declares, "Likewise the Spirit helps us in our weakness; for we do not know how to pray as we ought, but the Spirit himself intercedes for us with sighs too deep for words. And he who searches the hearts of men knows what is the mind of the Spirit, because the Spirit intercedes for the saints according to the will of God" (8:26–27). In this exchange of love, we lose track of time with God Who knows no time as we slowly move from trying to control God with our prayers and instead rely on the Holy Spirit "with sighs too deep for words." For the purpose of prayer is never about us informing God of our plans, but allowing God to instruct us in His ways and, above all, allowing God to love us. Or, as St. Teresa of Calcutta so succinctly wrote about prayer, "The essential thing is not what we say but what God says to us and through us."

At the heart, solitude is the desire to be alone with God just as Jesus sought to be alone with His Father. Since we were created for nothing less than to spend all eternity contemplating, loving, and praising the Blessed Trinity, solitude is a foretaste of the Beatific Vision while on earth. That is why without solitude, we cannot become saints or raise saints. Like simplicity, which expresses itself in many ways, solitude, though essentially referring to being alone with God, manifests itself in a variety of encounters with God. Some parents of the saints found solitude in the early hours of the morning, others in the darkness of the night, others while making a retreat, others before the Most Blessed Sacrament, others through spiritual reading, others in the depths of their heart where the Holy Trinity dwells, others before a religious statue in their home, and still others on a fishing excursion. In fact, many saints like Teresa of Ávila utilized and recommended her spiritual children to use Scripture or some spiritual book to better enter into conversation with God.

Furthermore, the prayer life of these parents was not some technique to be mastered, but, above all, a relationship with God. The end goal of solitude is union with God and not consolations, locutions, and visions—all of which should not be sought, according to St. John of the Cross. Nothing is "achieved" in prayer and, therefore, for the worldly mind, solitude may seem like a waste of time. On the other hand, many of us know that solitude is essential, but still relegate it, or sadly neglect it altogether, behind other tasks, such as maintaining a clean house or shuttling our children to the next event. St. Alphonsus pointed out one of the main reasons why we avoid solitude: "Worldlings shun solitude, and with good reason; for in solitude they feel more acutely the remorse of conscience, and therefore they go in search of the conversations and tumults of the world, that the noise of these occupations may stifle the stings of remorse."[54] Perhaps this is one of the reasons the late twentieth-century Benedictine abbot Benedict Baur wrote, "The fundamental evil that afflicts our times and from which we all suffer is that the interior life of men, even of Christians has grown weak."[55] Satan loves nothing better than for us to be distracted by this world and its passing things rather than focus our interior lives on the world which never passes away. His strategy is very subtle—flood the world with constant noise so that God's voice can no longer be heard in silence and solitude. When we no longer hear God's voice, we remain in the darkness of our sins rather than allow God's light to shine through us and heal us because the truth hurts.

54 St. Alphonsus de Liguori, *The True Spouse of Jesus Christ*, 483.
55 Benedict Baur, *Frequent Confession: Its Place in the Spiritual Life* (New York: Scepter, 1999), 129.

The parents of the saints understood the sign of the times and the evil that surrounded their families more so than any other married couples. That is why solitude was not an option, but a priority. And, while many of us waste time on trivial things and shun solitude altogether, the holy parents of the saints desired to never waste this precious time. These devout parents and their children believed wholeheartedly that prayer was the best usage of their time. Like many of the saints listed before, such as Alphonsus, Faustina, Gabriel, Gianna, John Paul II, and Thérèse, John Bosco came to appreciate solitude from the example of his mother, Margaret, who, though illiterate, would take little John outside to contemplate the universe of God, particularly the stars of sky, by pointing out that God was the author of such splendid works. Little did she know that her son's name would be written in the stars as Our Lord prophesized, "Rejoice that your names are written in Heaven" (Lk 10:20). Margaret and the parents of the saints in this chapter reveal a timeless truth: parents are not only the primary educators of their children; they are above all their children's primary witnesses of prayer.

Many of the saints have their names written in Heaven precisely because of their parents' profound prayer lives, which set the pace for them to be docile to the Holy Spirit's inspirations. The angel of the Lord once told Abraham that God would "multiply [his] descendants as the stars of heaven and as the sand which is on the seashore" (Gn 22:17), which in a mysterious way was referring to those parents in future generations who would courageously raise up saints, who in turn would bring countless souls to Heaven. What a lineage of spiritual children the parents of the saints have! Above all, because these parents sought God daily in solitude, they were able to radically embrace God's will for their lives, including how many children He wanted for them as well as the plans He had for those children, which leads us to our next chapter on the sacredness of life. Hence, solitude prepares our hearts and the hearts of our children to be men and women who live the Gospel of Life heroically in a culture of death.

HALLMARK SEVEN

Sacredness of Life

*All life is beautiful, and to live well is so important,
for life is of God.*[1]—Maria Kolbe

The Creator of the universe, the invisible hand guiding all of creation and mankind, Who made over 100 billion galaxies, Who covered the Earth with over 332 million cubic miles of water, ninety-seven percent of which makes up the oceans, Whose highest mountain peak towers over 29,000 feet, and Who created myriads of species of animals ranging from single-celled creatures to the blue whale, was not finished with His work of creation, for none of these could love Him as the human heart can. And so God sought someone with whom to share His goodness and love outside of His very self, that is, outside of the very love shared between the Father, the Son, and the Holy Spirit. Human life is the crown of His creation for man is the "only creature on earth that God has willed for its own sake."[2]

Despite God's amazing works—spectacular sunsets, the sun to warm us, a breeze to cool us, and beautiful mountains to gaze upon—none of these come close to the masterpiece that is one human soul. One human being made in God's image and likeness, who alone is capable of knowing and loving his Creator, and who is animated by an immortal soul to become a temple of the Holy Spirit, is God's greatest masterpiece. We only need to marvel at the miracle of how each human life is formed to recognize the utter greatness of God as two cells come together to form a human being, who,

---

[1]   Zdrojewski, *To Weave a Garment*, 21.
[2]   *CCC*, 356.

infused with an immortal soul, will grow with all of its subsequent complex cell signaling and stages of development. No one besides God can so perfectly knit together a human life. We are wondrously made by God (see Ps 139:14). The Church, who never ceases to proclaim that each soul is created immediately by God, tells us: "It is not 'produced' by the parents—and also that it is immortal: it does not perish when it separates from the body at death, and it will be reunited with the body at the final Resurrection."[3]

As the author of our lives, God did not stop there. He would not let His glory, or the veil of Heaven, keep us from Himself, so He became one of us. Our Lord once told a mystic, "I know all about your emotions as I know every wave of the sea. Even before you speak I hear you, since I live in you."[4] And yet we have a Father, Who, though He knows everything about us because He created us, still waits to hear everything about our lives as if He knew nothing, for the Divine Lover seeks union with His greatest creation. God willed us into existence and longs for us to be with Him for all eternity, even after we caused Him to sweat drops of blood in the garden, scourged Him for our impurity, crowned Him with thorns for our pride, and nailed Him to the Cross. Such is God's love for souls that even when we give up on Him, and even when we give up on ourselves, He continues to pour out His love and grace on us in the Eucharist and in Confession. Our Lord once revealed to St. Gertrude the Great that each time we look at the Cross, we ought to be convicted of the following words:

> Behold how, for your love, I have been fastened to this cross—naked, despised, torn, and wounded in My Body, and in all My members; and still My Heart has such tender charity for you, that were it necessary for your salvation, and were there no other means of saving you, I would even at this moment suffer for you alone all that I have suffered for the whole world.[5]

---

[3] Ibid., 366.
[4] Bossis, *He and I*, 113.
[5] St. Gertrude the Great, *The Life and Revelations of St. Gertrude the Great* (Rockford, IL: TAN Books, 2002), 211.

Our lives are so sacred to God that He would have died for each one of us alone, for we are unique and unrepeatable. For century upon century, mankind has attempted to destroy God's most precious gift, human life, through horrendous acts contrary to the dignity of life, such as abortion, abuse, contraception, euthanasia, genocide, human sacrifice, human trafficking, pornography, war, etc. Shockingly, many individuals have forgotten that "all life is beautiful" and "all life is sacred" and that God is the author of life Who decides when a person's life begins and ends—a decision that does not belong to the government, a religion, or a race of people, incursions of which have been seen throughout history. Maria Kolbe's statement, "All life is beautiful, and to live well is so important, for life is of God,"[6] reveals the heart of a mother who valued the sacredness of life, which is desperately needed today. This wisdom was so ingrained in her son St. Maximilian that he was willing to take the place of a married man at Auschwitz who was about to be executed. Maximilian, who became a martyr, realized that this man's life was of God and that his wife and children had need of their father. Unfortunately, this wisdom has become ignored by many souls today, especially by many pregnant mothers who would rather abort their babies than care for and love them, by those who pressure them to make this decision, and by the organizations and governments who promote the culture of death. For example, in the United Kingdom, over the last nine years, twenty-six babies were aborted for cleft lips or palates—a physical defect that can be easily corrected by surgery. These are only the reported figures, and surely there are many more unreported cases. Equally shocking is the reality that nine out of ten babies diagnosed with Down syndrome are snuffed out of the womb worldwide. The devout parents of the saints presented in this chapter were truly the heralds of the Gospel of Life.

Count and Countess of Altshausen

The child born on July 18, 1013, in Altshausen, Germany, might have been just another statistic in the vast number of babies aborted

---

[6] Zdrojewski, *To Weave a Garment,* 21.

each year because of a disability had he been conceived today; yet his parents understood that a child is the greatest gift from God, regardless of his physical appearance or mental aptitude. His name was Hermanus Augiensis, and he was born with a cleft palate, cerebral palsy, and spina bifida, though more recent research believes it may have been a myotrophic lateral sclerosis or spinal muscular atrophy. Though we do not know the name of his parents, his father was a count. While it is only natural to want a healthy child, giving birth to a deformed son would have been especially shocking for a member of the nobility. One could imagine the disgrace that Herman's parents felt for having a child with special needs when, in fact, a child with special needs is a gift from God to teach us to be innocent, pure, and simple like children. Yet Herman's parents heroically did not abandon their son. However, when Herman reached the age of seven, his parents recognized they could no longer provide the necessary support to address their son's mobility and speech impediments. As a result, they handed their precious son over to the Benedictine Abbey of Reichenua, located on an island on Lake Constance. Herman's parents were not alone in offering their son to the Abbey. Throughout the middle ages, many parents offered their sons or daughters at a young age to the various monasteries as they were the first universities in Europe. Herman eventually became a Benedictine brother and flourished to say the least. He became a renowned astronomer, historian, mathematician, musical composer, and poet. Further, Herman constructed musical and astronomical instruments and became literate in several languages, including Arabic, Greek, and Latin. Going blind in his later years, Herman wrote two of the Church's most famous Marian hymns, *Alma Redemptoris Mater (Loving Mother of our Savior)* and *Salve Regina (Hail Holy Queen)*. Herman was beatified in 1863, and the Church reveres him as Bl. Herman the Cripple, celebrating his feast day on September 25, the day of his entrance into Heaven at the age of forty when his blind eyes were opened to the sight of the most beautiful woman in the world, Our Lady, who turned her eyes of mercy upon him. As the last lines of the *Salve Regina* read, "Pray for us, O Holy Mother of God that we may be worthy of the promises of Christ."

Thanks be to God that Bl. Herman's parents found their son worthy of life, even if it meant they could not raise him themselves. This is a tremendous witness to young fathers and mothers that adoption is a loving and heroic option. Herman's parents also provide an example to fathers and mothers of a son or daughter with special needs who are constantly pressured from doctors and relatives to abort their child. Herman's life was a miracle, and so is every child. Every person has the potential to become a saint regardless of their disability. All it takes is a father, mother, adopted parents, or even Benedictine monks to cherish, nourish, and challenge this soul to become who God made him or her to be.

Tescelin and Aleth Sorrel

In twelfth-century France, Tescelin and Aleth Sorrel strove to leave their mark on the world, not through their nobility and wealth, but by transforming the culture through their seven precious gems—their children. Aleth offered each of her six boys and one daughter to God at their birth. As a member of the noble class, Aleth could have easily employed a wet nurse for her children, as was the custom of the day, but Aleth insisted on nursing them herself. She also insisted on visiting the sick and poor. While Tescelin and Aleth's lives were unassuming and their legacy most likely forgotten, their third child, born in 1090, lived a life that is worthy of remembering nearly one-thousand years later. Aleth was not the first pregnant woman who had a strange dream about one of her children. Aleth once dreamt during her pregnancy that instead of carrying a child, she had a red and white barking dog in her womb. Upset by this dream, Aleth asked a holy monk for advice. The monk told Aleth, "Don't worry, it is all right. The child within you will be a watchdog for the Church. He will bark mightily against the enemies of the faith. He will be a great preacher and shall heal many of their sins."[7] Aleth took this as a sign to raise her son even more carefully than her other children. Every August twentieth, the day of his entrance into eternal life, the Church celebrates the feast day of St. Bernard of Clairvaux, who founded over 300 monasteries. There was power

---

[7] Leifeld, *Mothers of the Saints,* 95.

in Aleth's consecration as all of her sons ended up following Bernard
to become monks in the Cistercian Order, which follows the Rule
of St. Benedict. Tescelin and Aleth lives mirrored the words in the
Catechism (no. 2367):

> Married couples should regard it as their proper mission
> to transmit human life and to educate their children;
> they should realize that they are thereby *cooperating with*
> the love of *God the Creator* and are, in a certain sense, its
> interpreters. They will fulfill this duty with a sense of
> human and Christian responsibility.

Just as the Cross was Jesus' revelation of the Father's love, so, too,
the love of a father and mother reflects the love of Christ: "When
you see our love, you should no longer see us, but Christ's love for
the Church." By consecrating their children to God, Tescelin and
Aleth wanted to give their children to God from their very birth,
which was not meant to replace Baptism, but to express a personal
commitment from the parents to God. Specifically, the Sorrels knew
that their children belonged to God. It was God Who had loved
their children first and had created them, and it was God Whom
they would stand before at the end of their lives. Tescelin and Aleth
wanted to make sure they formed the entire person when raising
their children, including a particular focus on their intellectual
and spiritual formation while teaching them the corporal works of
mercy. Even after her death, Aleth never left her children's side. As
Bernard was encouraging his brothers to join the Cistercian Order,
his younger brother, Andrew, who was seeking human glory as a
knight, saw his mother standing next to Bernard. Andrew's vision
of Aleth caused him to change his plans and immediately join the
Cistercians. In addition to Andrew, Bernard's four other brothers
and twenty-five friends joined the Abbey of Citeaux. Even Bernard's
own father joined the abbey after his wife passed away, and Bernard's
younger sister, Humbeline, became a Benedictine abbess. Initially,
Humbeline was married like her parents, but was so moved by her
saintly brother that her husband granted her permission to enter the
convent. Abbess Humbeline died in her brother Bernard's arms and
became the second canonized saint in her family. Holiness is often

contagious in families. In most cases, it is the parents that lead the way, but, in this family, it was both the parents and their saintly son Bernard who helped inspire the rest of their family, including their daughter, to become saints.

Bl. Joan and Félix Guzmán

In the neighboring country of Spain, lived another devout couple named Félix and Juana (Joan) Guzmán. God blessed the Guzmáns with four children, which is large by today's standards, yet small compared to other families in this chapter. Yet, out of those four children, there were three vocations to the priesthood. The first child, Anthony, became a canon regular at Santiago and divested his possessions that he might serve in a hospital tending to the ailing and poor. The second, Friar Mannes, would later join his younger brother's community and served as a Dominican superior in Paris and Madrid. He would be declared blessed in 1834. The next child, a daughter whose name is not known, married, and their youngest son would found the Order of Preachers.

Despite the fact that Joan and Félix were in their mid-thirties with two grown sons, they still desired more children and prayed that God might bless them with another son. Specifically, Joan frequented the abbey church of Silos where the eleventh-century Benedictine abbot, St. Dominic of Silos, once lived. He is alleged to have appeared to Joan in a dream and assured her that her prayer would be granted, and that the child would be a shining light. Because of this, St. Dominic of Silos became the patron of expectant mothers, and, until 1931, his crozier was used to bless the queens of Spain and was placed by their beds when in labor.

In thanksgiving for his intercession, Joan named her son Domingo after St. Dominic (Domingo) of Silos. Her fiat to God gave the world one of her greatest saints, known as St. Dominic, founder of the Dominican Order, born in Caleruega, Spain, in the year 1170. Interestingly, Dominic is one of the few saints whose feast day occurs on the day of his birth (August 8) and not the day of his death (August 6). This is most likely due to Feast of the Transfiguration, which falls on August 6. However, perhaps the

Church also wants to communicate a subtler point, which is to show the sacredness of our entrance into this world.

Before Dominic was born, Joan had a second dream. In this dream, Joan seemed to hear that she was bearing a black and white dog, and the dog broke forth from her womb with a flaming torch in its mouth, carrying light into the world. These two symbols would be cherished by the Dominicans, and Dominic has since been represented with a star shining on his forehead. The black and white dog carrying a flaming torch in its mouth is also used by the Dominicans, whose habits are black and white, as one of the symbols of their order. Punning on the Latin phrase *Domini canes*, they have been proud to call themselves the "hounds of God." Although little is written about Joan, except through the legacy of her children, she became a "blessed" in 1828 when King Ferdinand VII of Spain asked the Holy See to confirm this ancient veneration of the mother of St. Dominic. Pope Leo XII approved and granted her the title "blessed."

By remaining open to children regardless of age, Bl. Joan heroically witnesses to all mothers, especially when the idea of going to another little Calvary, "labor," seems daunting. And, by being unafraid to sacrifice her body and her very life for her children, Joan reveals that we become most like God when we give ourselves away. Joan's holy example paved the way for the vocations of her children, especially Dominic, who became a tireless preacher of the Faith. At the same time, Joan's confidence in the saints' intercession ought to inspire all parents to seek help from their heavenly family, especially when seeking to conceive. While Joan and Félix may have wanted a large family, God gave them, and gives each of us, what we need. On our end, we must be generous and grateful to God.

The Church does not confer the title of saint or blessed on just anyone. You cannot buy this title, though the process of canonization does require significant finances and takes years due to the extensive gathering of information about these saintly souls. This is one reason why many saintly parents are not canonized. Unlike a saint from a religious order, which can devote years and resources to promoting a person's cause for canonization, children of holy parents normally have limited resources and limited time.

When the Church canonizes someone as a saint, she is officially recognizing that this person lived a life of heroic sanctity in cooperation with God's grace and is now in Heaven. Or, in the words of St. Paul, "Do you not know that in a race all the runners compete, but only one receives the prize? So run that you may obtain it" (1 Cor 9:24). Bl. Joan competed, not just once, but every day of her life. There was no sprint to sanctity for Joan, but a marathon of waking up in the middle of the night when her babies were crying, preparing meals for her family, getting up early for daily Mass, disciplining her children when necessary, and preparing them for their vocation. Make no mistake, there is a special place in Heaven for mothers who sacrifice in this life and raise their children to be holy, even if they never are raised to the altar by being officially recognized as blesseds or saints. God sees everything and will reward everything done for His glory in Heaven. Every parent wants to be appreciated and loved by not only their spouse, but also their children, which is sadly not always the case. Yet the greatest gift any son or daughter can give to their parents is to become a saint. It would be foolish to say that Dominic's love for Our Lady was something he acquired personally; rather, Dominic's mother passed on her own devotion. In essence, Joan revealed the heart of Mary to Dominic by her own maternal love, which was only a fraction of Our Lady's love for Dominic and each one of us. While the Church remembers St. Dominic's holy life every August 8, eclipsing his mother's feast day only six days prior on August 2, Bl. Joan preferred to be overshadowed by her son both in life and even now after their death, just like Our Lady. And, though Dominic's feast day is celebrated with an optional memorial Mass while Joan's is not, we must never lose sight of the fact that August 8 (Dominic's birthday and now feast day) was the fruit of his mother's fervent prayers, labors of love, and profound witness.

Compagnonus and Amata de Guarutti

In 1245, less than twenty-five years after St. Dominic's death, a childless middle-aged couple named Compagnonus and Amata de Guarutti prayed to God for the miracle of life. Like Bl. Joan, Compagnonus and Amata sought the intercession of a specific saint to help them conceive. With an ardent faith, this holy couple made a pilgrimage to a shrine dedicated to St. Nicholas, the great Bishop of Myra, who the Church associates with Christmas, and who always looked upon the needs of his flock. Specifically, Nicholas tended to the poor and once paid for three women's dowries, which enabled them to get married rather than be sold as prostitutes as their own father had lost all his money and could not support his daughters. Informed of their lot, Nicholas threw some gold in the window of the father's house in the middle of the night and, thus, the legend of Santa Claus (derived from the Dutch name for St. Nicholas, Sinter Klaas) began. Nicholas's love for families and the centrality of marriage made Compagnonus and Amata believe that this saint might have even more influence in Heaven now that he was before the throne of God. In a miraculous twist of fate, Amata soon became pregnant and named her son after "Good Ole St. Nick." Less than twenty years after St. Francis died, their son, Nicholas, was born in the little town of Sant' Angelo, Italy, about sixty-six miles from Assisi.

Compagnonus and Amata's son would become St. Nicholas of Tolentino. Like his namesake, Nicholas developed a great love for the poor, especially the Holy Souls in Purgatory of whom he is now the patron saint. One legend says that Nicholas of Tolentino's prayers helped save the lives of over one hundred children, including several who had drowned, and parents in Bolivia have attributed his intercession for the conception and safe delivery of their children. Perhaps Nicholas wanted to assist, with an even greater zeal than most saints, those parents who experienced the same struggle that his did in conceiving because he knew how fervently his parents prayed for him and how patiently they waited for God's intervention. The saints are clearly touched by our concerns and miseries because they experienced the same struggles. Nicholas also knew that his life was a pure gift and he wanted somehow in God's divine plan to intercede for infertile couples. At the same time, Compagnonus and Amata's faith expresses a profound truth declared by the Catholic Church:

> A child is not something *owed* to one, but is a *gift*. The
> "supreme gift of marriage" is a human person. A child

may not be considered a piece of property, an idea to which an alleged "right to a child" would lead. In this area, only the child possesses genuine rights: the right "to be the fruit of the specific act of the conjugal love of his parents" and "the right to be respected as a person from the moment of his conception."[8]

Only God is the author of life, and many parents, like Compagnonus and Amata, have been blessed by God with a child via the intercession of some particular saint. In turn, these families have named their children after certain saints like Dominic, Nicholas, Gerard, or Gianna, etc. The name our parents bestowed on us, and the name we bestow on our children, is not mere chance. It was often discussed, inspired, and prayed over. The name we bestow on our children grants them not only a heavenly intercessor, if named after a saint or some biblical figure, but also perhaps an indication of their mission in life. For instance, Our Lord changed the name of Simon to Peter (from the Greek word for "rock"), which eventually ushered in his mission to be the leader of the early Church as the first pope, the "rock" on which Christ would build His Church. St. Nicholas of Tolentino followed in the footsteps of his patron, St. Nicholas of Myra, though not as a bishop, but rather as an Augustinian friar who dedicated his life to helping the poor, particularly the Holy Souls in Purgatory, who have a greater need of our prayers and mortification than those on earth because they cannot help themselves.

Nicholas of Tolentino's parents remind us that every life is a miracle. Sadly, many infertile couples may feel as if God has ignored their prayers and even experience anger toward Him, especially when nearly 4,000 babies are aborted daily in the United States. In addition, many married couples, and others in same-sex relationships, have begun to take matters into their own hands through *in vitro* fertilization (IVF), which only adds to the pain of many devout, faith-filled infertile couples, perhaps even tempting them to follow suit. Make no mistake, IVF is gravely immoral because it separates the unitive from the procreative aspect of the conjugal act and oftentimes deprives the child of their fundamental right to be born

---

8   *CCC*, 2378.

of a father and a mother known by them. When all else fails, the Church offers consolation with these beautiful words:

> The Gospel shows that physical sterility is not an absolute evil. Spouses who still suffer from infertility after exhausting legitimate medical procedures should unite themselves with the Lord's Cross, the source of all spiritual fecundity. They can give expression to their generosity by adopting abandoned children or performing demanding services for others.[9]

Parisio and Emilia

In 1287, forty-two years after the birth of St. Nicholas of Tolentino, and more than 200 years after the death of Bl. Herman the Cripple, two wealthy parents, Parisio and Emilia, waited with tremendous joy for the birth of their first child. If this child was a boy, perhaps it would become a national war hero like Parisio, or, if a girl, perhaps she would marry a wealthy prince charming and bless them with numerous grandchildren. These noble parents, whose last name is unknown, desired a healthy son. However, God had other plans for this wealthy noble couple—a plan that sadly they rejected. Had Parisio and Emilia embraced God's plan for their lives, they too may have also been declared "blessed" alongside their daughter.

Born into a family of nobles in the castle of Metola, located southeast of Florence, Italy, their daughter was born blind, deformed with kyphosis, had difficulty walking, and was a dwarf. Upon seeing their daughter, Parisio and Emilia were filled with anger and disappointment over her physical deformities. Their daughter was immediately given over to a maidservant for several years, where she was hidden to avoid any shame that would come to the family. So disgraced were the parents by their daughter that they did not even name her. The maidservant, however, named her Margaret, which means "Pearl."

Because Margaret loved to pray, Parisio and Emilia literally imprisoned her at the age of six in a cell with a window at the

---

[9]   Ibid., 2379.

nearby Church of St. Mary so that she could assist with Mass. Sadly, she was deprived of all contact from the outside world and, worst of all, of her parent's love. Margaret eventually entered the religious life, but was soon forced out when the community became jealous that she was living the rule so faithfully while they were lax. At the age of twenty, Margaret's parents took her to the city of Costello to the tomb of Fra' Giacomo to seek a cure for their daughter as many alleged miracles had taken place. After no cure occurred, even after several hours of prayer, Parisio and Emilia abandoned their daughter. Margaret was now homeless. In the meantime, various families had taken in Margaret, and she eventually became a Third Order Dominican. Throughout her life, Margaret held no bitterness toward her selfish parents, but prayed for them and led a life of heroic prayer while helping others more in need—if there was such a person.

We do not know whether Margaret's parents repented on their deathbeds for their utter cruelty, pride, and vanity. However, if this was indeed the case, such a change would have been due to none other than their daughter's prayers and sufferings united with Our Lord's suffering on the Cross. Though this book focuses overwhelming on the holy parents of the saints, it would be biased if we did not shed light on those parents of the saints and blesseds who failed to embrace the Gospel of Life. The only reason for reading about the scandalous behavior of Margaret's parents, far from infusing pride in ourselves as if we are better parents than most, is to learn from their bad example what we should not do if we are the parents of a child with special needs. Such a child will experience, at some point, cruel stares, frustration, and shame. Sadly, some in society only perpetuate suffering because they think such a child has no right to live as they have no economic value. Because children with special needs have many physical and mental disabilities that will remain forever in this life, they can easily push our patience to the limit. The frustration may seem to never end. We may feel shame because we worry about what people will think of our special needs child, and perhaps even ourselves. In the depths of every parent's heart with a special needs son or daughter is the cry,

"Why Lord couldn't you have made my child normal?" And, "Please Lord, cure my child!" Parents like Parisio and Emilia continue to exist today, but rather than imprison their child, they abort their child before he or she is even born. Ironically, Margaret was born in a castle and lived as a prisoner her whole life. She was imprisoned literally for many years by her parents, but also imprisoned by her own handicaps of being a dwarf and blind. To never see a sunset or the face of another human being, which we take so lightly, must have been a huge cross. Yet Margaret's greatest imprisonment was that she was rejected by the very parents of whose love she was the fruit. Still the greatest prisoner was not Margaret, but her parents, who were imprisoned by selfishness and anger at God. Her parents rejected the greatest gift God had given them—a child—and the greatest good— God Himself—when He did not cure their daughter. When Jesus said there are many mansions in Heaven, you can be assured that Margaret now lives in one of them as the princess in her Heavenly Castle under the gaze of her Heavenly Father and Mother Mary, who love her just the way she is. And, like Our Lord, Margaret died at the age of thirty-three on April 13, 1320. Nearly 300 years later, Margaret was beatified on October 19, 1609 by Pope Paul V. She is the patron saint of the pro-life movement, the disabled, the poor, and the unwanted. Ironically, Parisio and Emilia locked Margaret away for fear that her physical appearance would bring shame upon their noble name. They wanted her to be forgotten, and, yet, it was Bl. Margaret of Costello whose name spread throughout all of Christendom while their lives have been forgotten with the exception of being remembered as wicked parents. A saintly soul's virtue and memory never dies, even after 700 years, and will shine throughout all eternity, while those who spend their short life trying to advance their name or their wealth, rather than God's holy name, will be forgotten soon enough.

Parisio and Emilia's vocation to be saintly parents was not lacking on God's end, for He desires our perfection more than we do. Rather, their failure to embrace their daughter might best be explained by the "domino effect," a term that describes a cumulative effect produced when one event initiates a succession of similar events. Parisio and Emilia were so set on a healthy boy that anything less would be unacceptable. Another real possibility is that they were not receiving the sacramental graces offered through the Holy Eucharist and Confession as well as a rich, personal prayer life. By languidly seeking, or even neglecting, the graces offered by the sacraments as well as other occasions of grace, Parisio and Emilia were unable to surrender to God when this great trial came, which led to their unwillingness to sacrifice, causing themselves and Margaret to suffer because they rejected God's will. Had Parisio and Emilia meditated fervently on Our Lord's Passion like their daughter, they may have responded courageously to Our Lord's words, "Greater love has no man than this, that a man lay down his life for his friends" (Jn 15:13). There is no greater love for parents than to lay down their lives for their spouses and their children like Christ did for His Bride. When God does not become our greatest good in this life, and we are more concerned with our honor than His honor, a domino effect of selfishness and unwanted suffering will transpire. And when we lose touch with God, we lose touch with reality and truth. We are unable to see the blessing of having a special needs child or any suffering that comes our way. We become like Parisio and Emilia, who wanted the glory without the Cross.

Despite all the evil that Margaret endured from her parents and even one religious order that rejected her because they were jealous of her sanctity, Margaret's life offers hope to all people, especially those who have felt the scourge of being abused or unwanted. She also offers hope to those with a disability, teaching us that the only real handicaps in life are the ones we put on ourselves or allow others to put on us. Sadly, many of us project our parent's imperfect love onto God. We succumb to the lie that we must be perfect for God to love us. Margaret reminds us that we have a Father in Heaven Who cherishes us a million times more than our earthly parents, and Who loves us as if we were the only soul on earth. It was said that Margaret prayed the entire 150 Psalms daily from memory, mainly because she was blind. There is likely one Psalm verse that spoke to Margaret's heart more than others: "For my father and my mother have forsaken me, but the LORD will take me up" (Ps 27:10). Only God's unconditional love can turn a physically, deformed woman, rejected by her very own parents, into one of the most beautiful souls in the world and a future saint. Margaret came to understand her Heavenly Father's fathomless love, which enabled her to press forward in love rather than bitterness.

Giacomo and Lapa di Benincasa

Sixty years after Bl. Margaret of Costello's birth in Italy on March 25, 1347, twin daughters, Caterina and Giovanna di Benincasa, were born prematurely. Fortunately, the situation was a far cry from what Parisio and Emilia faced. This time, parents Giacomo and Lapa rejoiced over the birth of their daughters, who were the family's twenty-third and twenty-fourth child. Giacomo and Lapa had tragically lost nearly half of their children from the bubonic plague, so they prayed fervently that God would spare them. Unfortunately, the family lost Giovanna, but Caterina, known in English as Catherine survived and would become one of the Church's greatest saints as a Third Order Dominican, like Margaret of Costello. Perhaps it was the intercession of her twin sister from Heaven that helped lead Catherine to become a saint. Regardless, the di Benincasas knew that all life is precious.

Families that lose a child from a miscarriage, stillbirth, or illness all participate in the sufferings of Christ. No one can replace this precious and unique soul. These parents and their relatives will never be the same for a part of them has died. Eventually the sorrows of death are replaced with the longing to be reunited in Heaven with their loved one. Still, losing a child pierces the heart of any father or mother because the parents had wanted this child—some had even felt the kicks in the womb. Even some who have had abortions may have wanted the child, but were sadly coerced. For a married couple, this child was the fruit of their love. This child was hiding behind their smiles on their wedding day, not yet conceived, but in God's mind, according to the prophet Jeremiah, "Before I formed you in the womb I knew you" (1:5). Rather than lamenting over the children that were lost, Giacomo and Lapa focused their attention on counting their blessings and raising the children they did have.

In today's culture, Giacomo and Lapa would be mocked for having such a large family. In fact, Lapa was around forty years old when she gave birth to Catherine and Giovanna—an age when many women are no longer open to life and use artificial birth control for fear of having a child with a disability. When God blessed Giacomo and Lapa with their twenty-fifth child, they named her Giovanna after her deceased older sister. To support his large family, Giacomo worked tirelessly and industriously as a cloth dyer, often employing his sons' help. While God is not calling all couples to have twenty-plus children, He does call every married couple to welcome life, which was reiterated in Pope Paul VI's papal encyclical *Humanae Vitae*. In other words, "each and every marriage act must remain open to the transmission of life."[10]

Giacomo and Lapa overcame human respect, which often stifles many parents from having a large family because they worry about what their family, friends, and neighbors will think. The di Benincasas were more concerned with God's opinion. Had they decided to focus solely on building up their cloth dyeing business for the sake of being wealthy and happy, the Church would likely have never known St. Catherine of Siena. This holy couple also gave God twenty-four other souls destined to live for all eternity! On a curious note, a couples' odds of raising a saint increase as they have more children as these parents often trust in God more and seek His will over money or their own pleasure.

Despite their tremendous openness to God's will by being truly pro-life, Giacomo and Lapa were not so quick to allow Catherine to embrace celibacy. Instead, they wanted Catherine to marry the widowed husband of her older sister, who had died young. Perhaps it was selfishness on their part, perhaps sympathy for their son-in-law, or perhaps even the fact that they wanted Catherine to experience the joys of married life, including many children. Regardless of the true reason, Giacomo and Lapa eventually supported Catherine's desire to embrace a life of celibacy, just as they surrendered to God's plan in having more children. Catherine's parents reveal that God knows what is best for our families, and we become holy through the crucible of suffering, learning from our mistakes, and trusting in God. Being open to God's will can be unsettling at times because

---

[10] Pope Paul VI, *Humanae Vitae*, 5–6.

we let God lead the dance of our lives—yet when we follow His will, He will never lead us astray nor let us go where His grace won't protect us. The di Benincasas knew that the only thing you can take to Heaven with you is, God willing, yourself and your family. In fact, "Sacred Scripture and the Church's traditional practice see in *large families* a sign of God's blessings and the parents' generosity."[11] The more generous we are with God, the more He will bless us, and blessed are those couples like Giacomo and Lapa, who allow God to be Lord of their marriage bed, Lord of their finances, and Lord of their lives, and Who, in turn, blesses our world and the Church with the gift of saintly children.

John and Agnes More

While Italy had no shortage of saints, England welcomed one of her most illustrious saints on February 6, 1478. John More and Agnes Graunger entered into the Sacrament of Matrimony on April 24, 1474, at the Church of St. Giles in Cripplegate, England. This holy couple accepted children willingly as Agnes bore her first child during their first year of marriage. Within a span of six years, God blessed this couple with six children: Joan, Thomas, Agatha, Elizabeth, John, and Edward. Their second child, Thomas, would follow his father's career in law as well as his parent's holiness of life and their openness to life. In 1499, at the age of twenty-one, Thomas tragically lost his mother, which only furthered his desire to be holy, particularly by discerning a vocation to the religious life. Thomas eventually discerned that his calling was to the married vocation, where he flourished, not despite, but precisely through his unforeseen sufferings. Around 1504, Thomas married Jane Colt, and they were blessed, like his own parents, with a child during their first year of marriage, and together they had four children: Margaret, Elizabeth, Cecily, and John. In 1511, at the age of twenty-three, Jane became sick and died shortly thereafter. The young Thomas had become a widower at around thirty-three years of age. As a single father with four children under the age of six, Thomas felt that he needed a mother for his children. Like his father, who lost his bride

---

[11] *CCC*, 2373.

at a young age, Thomas remarried a month later to Alice Middleton, a widow, who was six to seven years older than him. Alice had several children of her own, though all of them were adults, except for one who lived at home. Thomas would benefit financially from marrying Alice, who had inherited estates in Essex, Yorkshire, and various other places following the death of her husband, who was a merchant.

A contemporary of Thomas More, Robert Whittington, described Thomas as "a man for all seasons,"[12] for he remained true to God, his conscience, and his wife and children despite the changing seasons and trials of life. This phrase later became the title of a play and movie about his life. But before Thomas could become "a man for all seasons," it was his own father's daily blessing that was the one constant in his life after God's love—and this blessing certainly shaped the way he raised his own children. After all, parents are called to be their children's greatest champions, motivators, and shelters, particularly through their storms and shifting emotions of life. In testimony to his unwavering and ever-deepening love for his children, Thomas once wrote to one of his children:

> It is not so strange that I love you with my whole heart, for being a father is not a tie which can be ignored. Nature in her wisdom has attached the parent to the child and bound their minds together with a Herculean knot. Thence comes that tenderness of a loving heart that accustoms me to take you so often into my arms. That is why I regularly fed you cake and gave you ripe apples and fancy pears. That is why I used to dress you in silken garments and why I never could endure to hear you cry. . . . Ah, brutal and unworthy to be called father is he who does not himself weep at the tears of his child. . . . But now my love has grown so much that it seems to me I did not love you at all before.[13]

---

[12] Beatrice White, *The Vulgaria of John Stanbridge and the Vulgaria of Robert Whittington* (London: Early English Text Society, 1932), xxvii.
[13] Monti, *The King's Good Servant,* 63.

Every season in our lives brings tremendous challenges and, therefore, having a father and mother to lean on and catch our tears is one of the greatest graces God can bestow on us and, in turn, the greatest grace we can bestow on our children. When John More died, Thomas shed tears because the person who was his unchanging season among the changing seasons, his rock as every father or mother is called to be, would no longer be there to offer his encouragement and blessing. Moments before being decapitated, having been convicted on false testimony of refusing to recognize Henry VIII as the head of the Church in England and to accept his annulment from his wife Catherine, Thomas declared "that he died the King's good servant but God's first,"[14] which testifies to the man of God that John and Agnes More raised their son to be— someone who loved his wife and children more and more each day, someone who would rather taste death than compromise God's law, and someone who would rather die with God's blessings and his father's blessings than with the world's blessing.

While Thomas More lived several centuries ago, his impact stretches well beyond the fifteenth century to the present day. In fact, Thomas More's children went on to have children, who also went on to have children, many of whom would heroically embrace the deep faith of their direct ancestor. According to some records, Thomas More's posterity included a Jesuit priest, a few Benedictine nuns, and many holy married couples to name a few. The relatives of Thomas More must have taken great pride to know their last name hailed from a saint who chose to die for Christ and His Church rather than compromise his beliefs. Parents must never doubt not only their influence on the lives of their children, but on the lives of their future descendants as well. The retired Archbishop Charles Chaput of Philadelphia described it best when he declared, "The future belongs to people with children, not with things. Things rust and break. But every child is a universe of possibility that reaches into eternity, connecting our memories and our hopes in a sign of

---

[14] Ibid., 449.

God's love across the generations. That's what matters. The soul of a child is *forever*."[15]

Beltrán and Marina Yañez de Oñaz

Only thirteen years after St. Thomas More's birth, Iñigo Yañez de Oñaz Loyola was born in Spain's Basque region on October 23, 1491, in his parents castle. Iñigo was the son of the Spanish nobles Beltrán and Marina Yañez de Oñaz and the youngest of thirteen children. Today, the Church heralds him as St. Ignatius of Loyola. Most people's legacy either ends at the grave or with their children's passing. The Church, however, never ceases to remember its saints for they are the exemplars of what we ought to be and can be with God's grace. At the same time, the world never ceases to remember its Neros, Hitlers, Stalins, and Osama Bin Ladens as what we ought not to be! Nearly 500 years after his death on July 31, 1556, Ignatius of Loyola's legacy endures. As the founder of the Society of Jesus, known as the Jesuits, Ignatius's legacy was already coming to fruition before his death as the Jesuits helped lead the Counter Reformation along with establishing thirty-five schools and boasting 1,000 members. Today, some of America's most prestigious Catholic universities, such as Boston College, Georgetown, Fordham, and, of course, Loyola University, named after Ignatius himself, owe their existence to this saintly soul and his order. Those who belong to the Jesuit order, who teach at her institutions, or who graduated from these institutions, which are founded on Ignatius's motto "*Ad Maiorem Dei Gloriam,*" Latin meaning "For the Greater Glory of God," would do well to remember Beltrán and Marina's openness to life. Had Ignatius's parents used contraception or, God forbid, aborted one of their own children because of financial strain, Ignatius and his institutions may never have come to fruition. Instead, Beltrán and Marina gladly welcomed thirteen children. Sadly, Ignatius's mother died when he was just seven years old, which resulted in him being

---

[15] Archbishop Charles J. Chaput, "What's next: Catholics, America and a world made new," CatholicPhilly.com, catholicphilly.com/2017/07/homilies-speeches/whats-next-catholics-america-and-a-world-made-new/.

raised by María de Garin, the wife of a blacksmith. Ignatius's father later died when he was sixteen.

While Beltrán was very pro-life, he sadly was not very pro-marriage as he had several children by another woman. Beltrán's vices were likely learned from his own father, Ignatius's grandfather, whose immoral actions once resulted in the two top floors of their castle being leveled by the king's order. According to Jesuit scholar Fr. George Traub, Ignatius was "raised in a family culture of Catholic piety but lax morals. He experienced the contradictions between the ideals of the church and crown and the realities of his own family."[16] Not surprisingly, Ignatius followed his father and grandfather's scandalous lifestyle prior to his conversion for he too was a "fancy dresser, an expert dancer, a womanizer, and sensitive to insult."[17] In other words, Ignatius's personal motto before his religious conversion, after a cannonball shattered his leg, seemed to be "for the greater glory of Ignatius." When we don't worship God, we end up worshiping ourselves as can be seen in so many conversion stories like that of Ignatius.

Many Catholic families and Jesuit institutions face the same struggle Ignatius's family did when they lived in a "family culture of Catholic piety but lax morals." No family, institution, or religious order is perfect, but somehow the family books that Ignatius read on Christ's life and the saints while recovering from his battle wounds challenged him to become a spiritual soldier for Christ. These holy books taught Ignatius about the vanity of this fleeting world, and the necessity of living entirely for God's glory. Obedience to Christ and obedience to the pope in regard to the missions, which Ignatius initiated as his order's fourth vow, leads to freedom.

While little is known about Ignatius's parents, except the fact that his father was unfaithful and his mother died young, they were generous to God with their fertility. Further, Ignatius's parents

---

[16] George Traub, SJ, and Debra Mooney, "St. Ignatius of Loyola: Founder of the Jesuits," Xavier University (2015), xavier.edu/mission-identity/heritage-tradition/documents/1IgnatiusLoyola-RevisedText-June20151.pdf.

[17] Ibid.

communicated a valuable lesson that the Gospel of Life is not only about joyfully welcoming life, but, more importantly, teaching your children to be faithful sons and daughters of the Church by protecting and nourishing their souls with the truths of the Faith. This is in keeping with the Sacrament of Baptism when the priest or deacon questions the parents prior to baptizing their child. Specifically, the ordained minister says:

> You have asked to have your child baptized. In doing so you are accepting the responsibility of training him (her) in the practice of the faith. It will be your duty to bring them up to keep God's commandments as Christ taught us, by loving God and our neighbor. Do you clearly understand what you are undertaking?"[18]

Even though Ignatius's parents failed to effectively transmit the Faith to their children, they did own several, readily accessible, orthodox Catholic books. This was a good start.

Two of Ignatius's brothers also chased the dream of chivalry. One went on Christopher Columbus's second voyage, while another died in battle. Perhaps Ignatius tried to recruit his brothers for his order, but the call for personal glory was too much　we will never know. Things might have been different had Ignatius's own mother not died so young. Yet God's grace can work even in the most trying family circumstances. While Ignatius became a saint, it is also sad to think that he was the only one out of his thirteen siblings who was officially canonized.

On May 20, 1521, at the age of twenty-nine, Ignatius received a physical wound at the battle of Pamplona that could have been mortal and nearly cost him his leg. On the surface, Ignatius was merely physically wounded, but, in reality, it was a spiritual wound that God used to tear out his vanity, greed, and lust and replace it with His righteous zeal, poverty, and love. Without his battle injury and religious books, Ignatius may never have become a saint due to

---

18　"Rite for the Baptism of the Child (1970 Roman Missal)," Catholic Liturgical Library, Catholicliturgy.com, catholicliturgy.com/index.cfm/FuseAction/TextContents/Index/4/SubIndex/67/TextIndex/7.

his lax upbringing and his parent's unforeseen deaths. Prior to his conversion, Ignatius was an avid reader of romance and chivalry books, but, recuperating from his battle injury, he encountered the lives of Sts. Francis and Dominic. After reading about these heroic men, Ignatius pondered following in their footsteps. He was challenged to go deeper in his faith through silence, meditation, and spiritual reading. Ignatius concluded that life is not about living for oneself but spreading the Gospel of Life by living for God and others.

In light of Ignatius's life, parents that curse misfortune and suffering when it is heaped upon them or their children ought to remember that the Divine Physician only permits physical or spiritual blows in order to heal us. God calls every soul to daily conversion and waits patiently for His prodigal sons and daughters to return, sometimes sending tragedy as the last resort. Had Beltrán been faithful to his marriage vows, there is no telling what might have been with Ignatius and his siblings. Perhaps Ignatius would have joined religious life earlier and maybe several of his siblings would have accompanied him. Who knows, maybe a thousand more souls might have been saved? We cannot delay the call to sainthood or wait until some terrible event occurs before we follow the Lord. The time is now!

Above all, the sanctity of life is tied to holiness, for all life is sacred. Yes, children must have access to holy books, but parents must read these books and, above all, provide the best witness possible—a living book of virtue for their children to imitate. In the words of St. John Vianney, "Christian fathers and mothers: if you wish to have pious, good children, you must first of yourselves be God-fearing and lead good lives. As the tree, so will the fruit be, says an old proverb, and the Divine Word verifies this."[19]

Vincenzo and Cinzia Bellarmine

After St. Ignatius's conversion, he dedicated his life to God, dying at the age of sixty-four on July 31, 1556. While this chapter highlights the parents of the saints who were biologically fruitful, we cannot

---

[19]   Francis W. Johnston, *The Voice of the Saints* (Rockford, IL: TAN Books, 1986), 102.

forget those who were spirituality fruitful. Only four years after Ignatius's death in 1860, his virtue was already bearing fruit when an eighteen-year-old boy named Robert Bellarmine entered the Society of Jesus. Though we do not know if Ignatius and Robert ever met, many of the saints' lives were intertwined. Several years later, Robert Bellarmine became a spiritual father to another future Jesuit saint, Aloysius Gonzaga. So close was their relationship that Robert Bellarmine asked to be buried by his spiritual son. In the Church of Sant' Ignazio di Loyola in Rome, you can find Robert buried next to his saintly spiritual son.

Before Robert became St. Robert Bellarmine, a renowned theologian, cardinal, and Doctor of the Church, he was born Roberto Francesco Romolo on October 4, 1542, in Montepulciana, Italy (Southern Tuscany) to Vincenzo and Cinzia Bellarmine. His parents gladly accepted ten children, Robert being their third. Despite the fact that Cinzia was the sister of Pope Marcellus II, the Bellarmines were poor nobles, albeit rich in virtue. Vincenzo and Cinzia exemplified the virtues of generosity and simplicity as they taught their children the importance of sharing as well as not being overly attached to material things. Cinzia was noted for her "almsgiving, prayer, meditation, fasting, and mortification of the body."[20] In effect, large families are training grounds for raising saints. A large family forces parents and children to not only sacrifice, as seen throughout this book, but also provides ample occasions to grow in virtue. As displayed in St. Faustina's life, it was not unusual for the siblings of these families to share their clothes, toys, and beds. Also, the older siblings were expected to assist their younger brothers and sisters. At the time, Robert's younger brothers thought they were simply getting his hand-me-down clothes, but later these would be second-class relics. Canonized on June 29, 1930, by Pope Pius XI, St. Robert Bellarmine grew in virtue due to his solid upbringing, especially his devout mother's influence. Like his mother, he remained humble and simple despite the fact that his uncle was the pope. As a cardinal, he gave away most of his money

---

[20] "St. Robert Bellarmine," Catholic.org, catholic.org/saints/saint. php?saint_id=101.

and furnishings to the poor. Specifically, the tapestries from his living quarters were used to clothe the poor. Robert would reply, "The walls won't catch a cold."[21]

Luca and Anna Maria Danei

Less than seventy-five years after St. Robert Bellarmine's death in 1621, Luca and Anna Maria Danei welcomed their seventh child, Paul, who was born on January 3, 1694. Luca and Anna Maria had sixteen children together. Tragically, their first six died during infancy. Their seventh child would become St. Paul of the Cross, founder of the Passionists Order. A large family like the Danei's affords parents so many blessings and celebrations: Baptisms, birthdays, First Communions, Confirmations, graduations, weddings, vocations to the priesthood, and, of course, future grandchildren. Yet those parents who are radically open to life often experience the cross of losing one of their precious children. The blessings of a large family clearly outweigh the sufferings, for our children are destined to live forever with us in Heaven. There is nothing like the gift of raising a saint. Parents like Luca and Anna Maria, who lost a child, or even several children, know more than any other couple just how sacred life is, and how every moment we have with our children is a total gift never to be taken for granted, but to be cherished.

It could be said that Anna Maria was either pregnant or nursing a child throughout most of her married life.[22] Despite her duties as a mother, however, Anna Maria never shirked away from her duty to teach the Faith. She had a great love for the Holy Name of Jesus, which she handed on to her children, especially her future saint. Unlike many of her contemporaries, Anna Maria was educated and was able to teach her children how to read and write. On one occasion, Anna Maria sought to teach Paul prudence by encouraging him to not give away all of his possessions to the poor, including the very clothes on his back, which he so desired. Anna Marie feared

---

[21]   Andre Marie, "Saint Robert Bellarmine," Catholicism.org, Catholicism.org/ad-rem-no-269.html.

[22]   See Spencer, *As a Seal Upon Your Heart,* 19.

Paul would return naked. Yet the greatest lesson Luca and Anna Maria taught their son Paul was never to lose his joy amidst the crosses of his vocation. Suffering, sacrifice, and the sacredness of life all go hand in hand because the more children that parents welcome into this world, the more God will require of them. Paul of the Cross never forgot his parents' joy when suffering came to him as he once said, "Live in the joy and the peace of the divine Majesty. Live lost in divine love. Live for divine love and of divine love. Oh cherished cross! Through thee my most bitter trials are replete with graces![23] And so too, if parents want to inspire their children to live their future vocations to the fullest and generously embrace life, especially their children called to marriage, they must exude joy and peace no matter their sufferings and trials.

Jean-Baptiste and Jeanne Grignion

Nearly fifteen years after St. Paul of the Cross's birth, Jean-Baptiste and Jeanne Grignion gave birth to their first son, Louis-Marie (Louis) on January 31, 1673, in the town of Montfort, France, where Jean-Baptiste worked as a notary. God blessed Jean-Baptiste and Jeanne with another seventeen children after Louis-Marie. Unfortunately, ten of their children died in infancy. Some accounts state that this marriage produced some eleven saints in total. Their first child would become a saint and a great lover of Our Lady, and his books *True Consecration to Mary* and *The Secret of the Rosary* are two of the most widely read books in the Church, even some 300 years later. Louis was surrounded by parents who treasured and welcomed life. They also ensured that Louis would pursue a solid, Catholic education. At the young age of twelve, Louis attended the Jesuit College of St. Thomas Becket in Rennes, and he was fortunate to have an uncle who was a parish priest in Rennes.

Canonized in 1947 by Pope Ven. Pius XII over 200 years after his death, St. Louis-Marie Grignion de Montfort battled anger his entire life, something that he likely inherited from his father. One

---

23   "Sayings of Saint Paul of the Cross" (2009), saintpaulofthecross.com, saintpaulofthecross.com/2009/10/words-quotes-of-st-paul-of-cross. html.

source said that Louis "confessed in later years that his most difficult struggle against passions of the flesh was in subduing his violent temper."[24] Unfortunately, Jean-Baptiste would occasionally lash out at Louis and his other siblings. Perhaps the difficulties of raising a large family combined with their poverty caused Jean-Baptiste tremendous frustration at times. At the same time, it is consoling to know that even the saints and their parents wrestled with their passions throughout their lifetime. God kept them humble, as He does with us, by permitting various temptations and weaknesses. It cannot be overstated that children are greatly influenced by their parents' virtues and vices, likes and dislikes, faith or disbelief, and respect or disrespect for human life. And, just as Louis was influenced by his father's temper, so too was he likely influenced by his parent's great love for Our Lady. And, while we know little about Jean-Baptiste and Jeanne's life, Louis's mother Jeanne surely was an imperfect, yet beautiful, mirror of Our Lady's love. Without his own earthly mother's tenderness, Louis may never have come to understand the Blessed Mother's unfathomable love for him. And, most of all, Jean-Baptiste and Jeanne's willingness to welcome eighteen children testifies to their heroic love for life.

Jean-Baptiste and Anne-Barbara Labre

The Grignions were not the only pious French couple to raise a large family. On March 25, 1748, Jean-Baptiste and Anne-Barbara Labre gave birth to their first of fifteen children, whom they named Benedict Joseph. Jean-Baptiste and Anne-Barbara were blessed by God both spiritually and financially as they belonged to the middle class, which allowed them to offer their children a reputable education. On top of this, Jean-Baptiste's brother, François-Joseph, was a priest, and he took Benedict Joseph under his wing at the age of twelve to train him for six years in Latin and history. At the age of sixteen, Benedict Joseph asked his parents for permission to enter the Trappist Order, which they declined due to his age. Obedient to his parents, Benedict Joseph waited a few years before asking again.

---

24   Slaves of the Immaculate Heart of Mary, "Saint Louis de Montfort," Catholicism.org, catholicism.org/louis-de-montfort.html.

This time his parents agreed as they didn't want to oppose God's will. One biographer of Benedict Joseph said his parents definitely wanted at least one priest in the family. The odds were in their favor.

Above all, every parent wants their children to be happy, while most devout parents want their children to do God's will. And many devout parents desire to have at least one son or daughter become a priest or religious. Yet no parent dreams that their child will one day become a homeless wanderer, especially their oldest child who the younger siblings look up to. Rejected by the Carthusians, Cistercians, and Trappists because of his age and unstable health, Benedict Joseph drifted throughout Europe, especially Rome, where he spent his time meandering through the streets while visiting various churches. Benedict Joseph never asked for alms and always gave away any excess to those poorer than himself. He died at the young age of thirty-five and is revered as the patron saint of the homeless, unmarried men, and those rejected by the religious orders. Perhaps Benedict Joseph acquired the courage to overcome human respect, i.e., to not care what other people thought about him being a hobo because his parents seemed unaffected by what people thought about their family size. In fact, Jean-Baptiste and Anne-Barbara likely experienced pressure from their relatives and friends to have fewer children for the sake of their financial and emotional stability, yet they followed the will of God for their lives.

At the age of twenty-five, Benedict Joseph wrote his last letter to his beloved parents explaining his further determination to enter an Italian monastery as he left all that was dear to him: his parents, his siblings, his native France, and his comfortable living for Rome. The last sentences of his letter read, "Again, I ask your blessing, and your pardon for all the uneasiness I have given you, and I subscribe myself. Your most affectionate son, Benedict Joseph Labre."[25]

The next time Jean-Baptiste and Anne-Barbara would hear about their son would be years later when word spread concerning his death and holy life. Though Benedict Joseph once desired to spend his life hidden in a monastery, the Holy Spirit made it clear

---

[25] Alban Goodier, *Saints for Sinners* (Huntington, IN: Our Sunday Visitor, 2005), 153.

that his cloister was Rome, and especially wherever the Most Blessed Sacrament was present. In fact, Benedict Joseph is known as the patron saint of the Forty Hours Devotion because of his great love for the Holy Eucharist. Benedict Joseph lived a very penitential and eremitic life, avoiding those who sought to proclaim his virtue. On December 8, 1881, he was declared a saint and serves as a model for the single vocation. Specifically, St. Benedict Joseph reveals that life is not about feeling sorry for ourselves when failures arise, or even trying to figure out why the Lord has not called us to something "more." Rather, each person is called to be a servant to all and a great lover of Jesus—the one, true Spouse for all eternity.

In the world's eyes, and perhaps in their friend's eyes, Jean-Baptiste and Anne-Barbara's son was a failure—he never became a priest, got married, or held a respectable job, but instead lived as a vagrant, for "God chose what is low and despised in the world, even things that are not, to bring to nothing things that are, so that no flesh might boast in the presence of God" (1 Cor 1:28–29). Who would have thought that the son of a wealthy shopkeeper would one day become a homeless saint?

Before Benedict Joseph was born, the priest asked Jean-Baptiste and Anne-Barbara the following question, which every Catholic married couple answers at their Nuptial Mass: "Will you accept children lovingly from God and bring them up according to the law of Christ and his Church?" This holy couple responded with an unequivocal "yes," both on their wedding day and each day of their lives. In effect, Jean-Baptiste and Anne-Barbara gave God permission to work His greatest miracle outside of the Holy Eucharist, which is to create a new soul. Without Jean-Baptiste and Anne-Barbara's unfailing and serious commitment to their marriage vows, there would have been no fertile soil for a future saint to be planted. The Labres knew that God takes us at our word, and therefore our vows are sacred, sealed and pronounced not just before mortal men, but before the Blessed Trinity.

The Labre's mission in life was not to control their children's destiny; rather, they exemplified heroic generosity, patience, prayer, and unfailing support for their children's vocations. Such was the beauty of Jean-Baptiste and Anne-Barbara that despite not understanding God's will for their oldest son's life, and perhaps even their son not understanding it at times, they were Benedict Joseph's greatest fans. The sacredness of life is at the heart of the Gospel where parents till the soil and then allow the Holy Spirit to pour forth the rain that raises saintly sons and daughters for God.

Joseph and Marie Jugan

On October 25, 1792, Jeanne Jugan was born to Joseph and Marie Jugan in Brittany, France. Jeanne was the sixth of eight children. Tragically, Marie raised all of her children by herself in a one room, dirt floor cottage after her husband, a fisherman, tragically drowned at sea when Jeanne was only three and half years old. Their future saint, Jeanne Jugan, would later found the Little Sisters of the Poor, a religious order devoted to helping the poor and especially the aged. Before Joseph's unexpected death, this holy couple prized bringing many immortal souls into this world rather than living comfortably with many possessions. Joseph's humble occupation as a fisherman, certainly endeared himself to the Apostles, who shared the same profession. After Joseph's death, Marie boldly assumed the spiritual leadership of her family despite the anti-clerical movement from the French Revolution. Marie would secretly make sure her children attended morning prayers at the local church, Our Lady of the Orchard. Marie was a simple, pious woman like her late husband. In the face of sufferings from the French Revolution, many true, Catholic families like the Grignions, Vianneys, and Jugans arose. Joseph and Marie prepared their children and, above all, their daughter Jeanne for a life that values all people, regardless of age or status. The famed English novelist Charles Dickens once met St. Jeanne Jugan and had the following to say, "There is in this woman something so calm, and so holy, that in seeing her I know myself to be in the presence of a superior being. Her words went straight to my heart, so that my eyes, I know not how, filled with tears."[26]

---

[26] Weigel, "St. Jeanne Jugan, We Need You Now," Catholic Exchange.
com (October 29, 2009), catholicexchange.com/st-jeanne-jugan-we-need-you-now.

Would that all those who encounter us be drawn to God for the more we see God in them, the more they will be drawn to God's goodness and love through us. The saints were God's greatest magnets for their presence alone could draw all peoples to Himself, even the most decorated authors.

Sante and Agnes Possenti

On March 1,1838, in the famous village of Assisi, Italy, Francis Joseph Vincent Pacific Rufinus Possenti was born to Sante and Agnes Possenti, the eleventh of thirteen children. Francis, who would later become St. Gabriel of Our Lady of Sorrows, joined the Passionists Order and died just shy of his twenty-fourth birthday as a young religious seminarian. There were many ups and downs in the Possenti family. For instance, their eldest son, Lawrence, committed suicide rather than be forced to murder someone due to his own Masonic ties. Sante and Agnes also lost their nine-year-old daughter, Adele, and another daughter, Rose, after her birth. Adele's death was a serious blow to Agnes. According to their son Michael, "It was a source of tremendous pain for her and after a few days she too fell ill with meningitis, which in seven days took her to the grave."[27] The forty-one-year-old Agnes went to her eternal reward on February 9, 1842, leaving behind her husband and eleven surviving children, which included their almost four-year-old future saint, Gabriel. As she lay on her deathbed, Agnes embraced each of her children one last time with some departing words of wisdom. The sacredness of life calls each person, particularly parents, to not wait until their deathbed to tell their children they love them— though very important—but each day of their lives. Surely Agnes loved her family more than anything in this life outside of God, so much so that the sorrow over Adele's death contributed to her own death. After Agnes's death, the spirit of joy left the family for quite some time.

Though the Possentis experienced many sorrows, God blessed this family with many graces. Their son Lewis became a Dominican

---

27   Gabriele Cingolani, CP, *Saint Gabriel Possenti, Passionist* (Staten Island, NY: Alba House, 1997), 13.

priest. Teresa and her brother, Michael, a doctor, both had six children. Henry became a diocesan priest. Both Vincent and Mary Louisa remained single. Vincent devoted his life to helping his father, while Mary Louisa helped raise her little siblings after their mother died. Hence, the sacredness of life calls each family member to no longer live for themselves, but to selflessly give of themselves, living for something greater than their own needs and pleasure, which is the salvation of each family member. When Pope Benedict XV canonized St. Gabriel on May 13, 1920, he confirmed that Gabriel was in Heaven and lived a most heroic life of virtue, which at the same time reaffirmed the Possenti family's devotion to God, authentic commitment to life, and sacrificial love for each other. In their nineteen years of marriage, Sante and Agnes provided a most excellent example of fidelity toward each other and an openness to God's will by welcoming life, which certainly left a lasting impact on their children. Above all, they provided the foundation for their children to follow the path God had ordained for them, which involved becoming holy in their respective vocations: priesthood, religious life, married vocation, and the single vocation.

Charles and Brigid Savio

On April 2, 1842, in the village of Riva in northern Italy, Charles and Brigid Savio welcomed their second of eleven children, Dominic, only four years after St. Gabriel Possenti was born. Charles and Brigid were described as "poor but upright citizens,"[28] according to St. John Bosco, who wrote a biography of their saintly son Dominic, who died just shy of his sixteenth birthday. John Bosco, who was Dominic's spiritual father, further declared:

> The good parents' only concern was to give their boy a Christian upbringing. Up till now he had given them much pleasure. Dominic was naturally good, with a heart which was easily given to piety. He learned his morning and night prayers readily and could already say

---

[28] St. John Bosco, *Life of Dominic Savio: Pupil at the Oratory of St. Francis de Sales*, sdb.org/en/Don_Bosco/Writings/Writings/Life_of_Dominic_ Savio__Pupil_at_the_Oratory_of_St_Francis_de.

them by himself when he was only four years old. He was
constantly beside his mother, eager to help her in every
way. If he did go off sometimes, it was only to go into
some corner of the house and try to say some prayer.

Charles was a blacksmith, but, more importantly, like his humble
profession, which heats pieces of wrought iron or steel until they
become soft enough for shaping with hand tools, he and his wife
helped shape his children into saints with God's help along with
John Bosco's guidance. Charles had the wisdom to entrust his son to
a saint in Fr. John Bosco, who further helped Dominic's formation
when he joined the oratory.

Dominic also helped mold his parents into saints. According to
John Bosco, "One day, distracted by something unusual, his parents
sat down to the meal without saying grace. Dominic immediately
said, 'Dad, we have not said our grace yet' and began himself to
make the Sign of the Cross and say the prayer."[29]

Another interesting story occurred on the eve of Dominic's First
Communion, which he was given permission to receive at the age
of seven. Dominic told his mother:

> "Mother, tomorrow I am receiving Jesus in Holy
> Communion for the first time; forgive me for anything
> I have done to displease you in the past: I promise you
> I am going to be a much better boy in every way. I will
> be attentive at school, obedient, docile, respectful to
> whoever tells me what to do." Having said this, he burst
> into tears. His mother, who had only received consolation
> from him, was also emotional and found it difficult to
> hold back her tears, but she consoled him saying: "It's ok
> dear Dominic, everything is forgiven. Ask God to always
> keep you good, and also pray for me and your father."[30]

The sacredness of life also means that every life that is born
will inevitably die. While many live as if they were never going
to die, the Savios prepared each day for death by living a holy life.

---

[29] Ibid.
[30] Ibid.

Sometimes God grants consolations to parents who have lost a young child by giving them little signs to comfort them and to let them know their child is safe in Heaven. For instance, some parents may report seeing their loved one in a dream, hearing their child's favorite song on the radio, or encountering a remarkable sign in nature like rainbows or a dazzling sunset on the child's birthdate or anniversary of their death. At the same time, we must be careful not to tempt God for a sign.

However, the following sign that Charles experienced after Dominic's death is clearly out of the ordinary and should not be the norm for any parent, for faith in the Resurrection is our greatest sign. However, this incredible story is worth mentioning. After Dominic's death, John Bosco said that Charles was lamenting and trying to make sense of his son's death as any parent naturally does. According to Charles, Dominic's death:

> Was a source of deep sorrow for me and was further stirred by the desire to know what had happened to him in the next life. God wanted to give me consolation. About a month after Dominic's death, one night after I had been unable to sleep, I thought I saw the ceiling of the room spring wide open and there, surrounded by a bright light, Dominic appeared, smiling and happy but majestic and striking. I was beside myself at such a sight and cried out, "Dominic, how are you? Where are you? Are you already in heaven?" "Yes, yes father", he answered, "I really am in heaven". "Well", I replied, "if God has been so good as to let you enjoy the happiness of heaven, pray for your brothers and sisters so they may be with you one day". "Yes father", he answered, "I will ask God on their behalf that they may be able to enjoy the immense happiness of heaven with me one day". "And pray for me, for your mother too" I said, "so that we may be saved and be together with you one day in heaven". "Yes, yes, I will pray for that". And having said that he disappeared, and the room returned to darkness as before. His father gives assurance that he is simply witnessing to the truth and

says that neither before or after this, either when awake or asleep, did a similar consolation happen again.[31]

While God gave Charles Savio a great consolation, and perhaps other parents have had a similar experience, those who have not seen their departed children via some supernatural vision or dream should remain just as hopeful, for "the souls of the righteous are in the hand of God, and no torment will ever touch them" (Wis 3:1). And, as Our Lord reminds us, "Blessed are those who have not seen and yet believe" (Jn 20:29). Charles's mystical encounter also testifies to a father's great longing to have his entire family saved and reunited in Heaven with their departed loved ones for all eternity where they will enjoy the immense happiness of seeing God face to face. What greater prayer can pour forth from a father and mother's heart? The sanctity of life bears witness to the desire written in our hearts that every human life created by God returns one day to its Creator!

Sts. Louis and Zélie Martin

On January 2, 1873, Marie-Françoise-St. Thérèse Martin was born, the ninth child of Louis and Zélie Martin, just thirty years after St. Dominic Savio's birth. She would later become St. Thérèse of Lisieux. Zélie was always seen in town with one or two children by her side. After the birth of their seventh child, Céline, born on April 28, 1869, four years passed before Thérèse's birth. During that time, Zélie lost a child, Marie-Mélanie-Thérèse, who died in infancy two years before Thérèse, and for who Thérèse was named. Also, during this period, Zélie expressed grief for not having a little one. She wrote the following words to her sister-in-law, Céline Guérin, on December 15, 1872, a month before St. Thérèse was born: "As for me, I'm crazy about children, I was born to have them, but it will soon be time for that to be over. I'll be forty-one years old the twenty-third of this month, old enough to be a grandmother."[32] Such are the words of a pro-life mother and a reminder to all women

---

31   Ibid.
32   Francis Renda, *A Call to a Deeper Love* (Staten Island, NY: St Paul's, 2011), 103.

that being a mother either biologically or spiritually is inscribed in their very bodies. When Zélie learned that a neighbor was having triplets, she responded, "Oh! Happy mother! If I had only twins! But I shall never know that happiness! I am madly fond of children. It is such sweet work to take care of babies."[33]

During Zélie's time, not every woman felt the same way she did concerning children. Zélie once described a wealthy, childless woman from her hometown, who made it a point to share the following with those she encountered. This unfortunate woman would declare, "My God! Oh, how happy I am! I lack nothing. I have my health, I have wealth, I can buy all that I desire, and I don't have any children to disturb my rest. In short, I don't know anyone as well off as I am."[34] Shortly thereafter, this woman and her husband died tragically when they fell in a ditch while taking a short cut during the night.

Zélie once declared, "I don't want to become attached to anyone except God and my family."[35] She and her husband knew that welcoming and nurturing life was the most noble and most challenging of missions. Had Louis and Zélie given up having children after losing Mélanie-Thérèse, the world would have been deprived one of the greatest saints, St. Thérèse of Lisieux. Like any parents with many children, Louis and Zélie had to overcome human respect along with the gossip and subtle persecution that comes with being open to God's will— the criticism from family members, the stares at Mass, the whispers in the grocery store, etc. While standing beside the casket of her little babies, neighbors and townspeople would cruelly say to her face and behind her back, "It would be much better never to have had them."[36] Zélie reacted to such harsh words by writing to her sister-in-law, "I can't bear that kind of talk. I don't think the sorrows and problems could be weighed against the eternal happiness of my children. So they weren't lost forever. Life is short and full of misery. We'll see them

---

[33] Martin, *The Mother of the Little Flower*, 5–6.
[34] Martin and Martin, *A Call to a Deeper Love*, 7.
[35] Ibid., 99.
[36] Ibid., 90.

in Heaven."[37] When Zélie lost her fourth child, Hélène, who was only five years old, some of Zélie's alleged friends insisted that she should stop having children, especially since her health was poor. Yet, because Louis and Zélie were attached to God and their family, they sought only to please Him.

After Hélène's death, Zélie's sister comforted her with these prophetic words written on February 23, 1870:

> Be certain, then, that the Lord will bless you, and that the measure of your troubles will also be that of the consolations stored up for you. In a word, will you not be fully rewarded, if the good God, so pleased with you, will grant you that Great Saint whom you have so much desired for His glory.[38]

Thanks be to God, Zélie listened to the advice of holy people like her sister and not her neighbors' noxious opinions. Parents committed to the Gospel of Life by welcoming as many children as God wants to give them, like Louis and Zélie, must never expect the world's applause nor should they be surprised by their persecutions. Yet the joy of bringing one more soul to Heaven always outweighs any criticism from family members, friends, and strangers, as seen in the words of Zélie.

Living at the same time as Sts. Louis and Zélie Martin, Michael and Anne Higgins embraced the sacredness of life, that is, until suffering led their family to anger and disobedience. On the surface, this American couple was even more pro-life than the Martins. Over a span of twenty-two years, Michael and Anne had eighteen pregnancies, eleven of whom survived. The Higgins were given the same baptismal graces as the Martins, and both Zélie and Anne died in their forties. However, unlike Louis and Zélie and their daughter Thérèse, Michael and Anne and their daughter, Margaret, will never be canonized. Ironically, Margaret was born only six years after Thérèse on September 14, 1879. Biographers believe Margaret blamed her mother's death on her many miscarriages. At the same

---

[37] Ibid., 90–91.
[38] Martin, *The Mother of the Little Flower*, 81–82.

time, Margaret's father, Michael, a stonemason, who in later years became an activist for women's suffrage and free public education, went from being a practicing Catholic and an artisan of angels, saints, and tombstones to an avowed atheist. Perhaps Michael blamed God for his beloved wife's death. There is no question that both her mother's death and her father's loss of faith ignited Margaret's passion to provide birth control for women. For most, the name Margaret Higgins does not stand out, but her married name surely does—Margaret Sanger.

The death of their beloved wife and mother dealt such a devastating blow to Michael and Margaret that she followed in her father's footsteps by advocating for a world-wide campaign for birth control and eugenics, which eventually evolved into Planned Parenthood, as she opened the first family planning and birth control clinic in the world in Brooklyn, New York. Margaret and her sister were eventually arrested for breaking a New York law, which prohibited the distribution of contraception. Eventually this law was repealed in 1918, and the opposite is now the case. Religious orders, such as the Little Sisters of the Poor, have been sued for not providing health care that covers contraception for its employees. Times have changed. Though the natural law never changes, man's interpretation of the natural law surely has. Sadly, though Anne was very pro-life, a Catholic Church in New York will never be named after Michael and Anne Higgins or their daughter, Margaret Sanger. Anne's death, like the death of Zélie Martin, could have been a time for Michael and Margaret to reclaim their Catholic Faith, but instead sorrow and suffering led them to rebel against God.

Louis Martin experienced the same trial as Michael Higgins when his wife Zélie died young. Yet Louis found the answer to the mystery of suffering and death in the Cross. In the midst of his pain, Louis never forgot the blessings that God had already bestowed on him, the greatest being his children. No doubt, Louis battled at times with frustration, grief, and loneliness from his wife's absence, but, with God's grace and time, he devoted his energies to the most important thing left to do, which was to raise his children to become saints like their godly mother would have wanted. In effect, Louis

Parents of the Saints

remained committed to the sanctity of life by striving to forget himself, to help those God had placed in his path, particularly his five daughters, and to hide himself in the wounds of Christ rather than run away wounded. Such was not the case with Michael Higgins and his daughter, who by all accounts abandoned their Faith. Michael dulled his pain through alcohol and politics rather than prayer. One can only imagine how different the Catholic Church in America might have been had one father, Michael Higgins, kept his faith and fostered a pro-life ideology in his daughter, Margaret Sanger.

Any parent who doubts their impact on their children ought to heed the following words by Dr. Bernard Nathanson, who was forty years old at the time of Margaret Sanger's death, and certainly followed in her footsteps before his conversion. Dr. Nathanson wrote,

> I teach medical students at Cornell and Columbia. The problem of low medical ethics is not in the medical schools, but with the parents. You don't learn respect for life in high school, you don't learn decency in college, nor ethics in medical school. The way parents bring up their children account for their attitudes.[39]

Dr. Nathanson gained a reputation as the former director of NARAL (National Association to Repeal Abortion Laws). However, he did not become pro-abortion overnight; rather, he was heavily influenced by his father, who happened to be a staunch pro-choice, secular Jewish obstetrician and gynecologist. Tragically, before his conversion, he supervised over 60,000 abortions as director of a facility, trained others responsible for 15,000 abortions, and personally performed roughly 5,000 abortions, including the abortion of his own child who was conceived with a girlfriend in the 1960s.[40]

---

[39] Pumphrey, "Dr. Bernard Nathanson's conversion highlighted in Cleveland speech 35 years ago," Cleveland.com (September 13, 2015), cleveland.com/articles/16929039/dr_bernardnathansons_conversi.amp.

[40] Deacon Keith Fournier, "Pro-Life Hero and Prophetic Voice is Dead: Rest in Peace Dr. Bernard 'Bernie' Nathanson" (February 23, 2001), catholic.org/news/saints/story.php?id=40450.

After technology revealed a fetal heartbeat, Dr. Nathanson became one of the twentieth-century's greatest pro-life converts. Once a child of darkness, Dr. Nathanson became a child of light, joining the Catholic Church in 1996 just five years before he died of cancer. Dr. Nathanson's above words testify to the irrefutable impact that parents have on their children, especially when it comes to moral issues. Had Dr. Nathanson's own father been pro-life, thousands of babies might have been saved. The moral of the story as seen in this chapter is that if parents want their children to respect the sanctity of life, then they must first cultivate and defend the sacredness of life at all stages no matter the cost.

Siegfried and Auguste Stein

The sacredness of life is not only for Catholic parents as will be seen by the following couple, whose daughter became one of the greatest converts and martyrs of the twentieth century. On October 12, 1891, Edith Stein, the youngest of eleven children, was born in Breslau, Germany, to Jewish parents, Siegfried and Auguste Stein. She was born on the feast day of Yom Kippur, the holiest day in the Jewish religion, which made Edith "very precious to her mother."[41] Tragically, four of Edith's siblings died in childhood, likely from scarlet fever. Both parents were devout Jews. Surprisingly, Edith's mother went to Catholic school from the age of five to twelve. Unfortunately, her father died of heat stroke at work when Edith was two years old. Her mother valiantly took over their timber business, while ensuring her children received a solid education. One of Auguste's greatest struggles came when Edith was a teenager and decided to "give up praying,"[42] which ultimately led Edith to embrace atheism. Besides fervently praying for Edith's conversion, Auguste humbly reminded her intelligent daughter Who the true

---

[41] "Teresa Benedict of the Cross-Edith Stein (1891–1942), *nun, Discalced Carmelite, martyr*," Vatican.va, vatican.va/news_services/liturgy/saints/ns_lit_doc_19981011_edith_stein_en.html.

[42] Ibid.

author of everything is when she declared, "After all, I can't imagine that I owe everything I've achieved to my own ability."[43]

Edith converted to Catholicism from Judaism in 1922 at the age of thirty. When Edith told her mother the following words, "Mother, I am Catholic,"[44] both mother and daughter cried. Edith's conversion was "the most severe blow for Mother, for she was a truly devout Jewess,"[45] according to Edith's sister Erna. Furthermore, Auguste felt betrayed as she "considered Edith's adoption of another religion an act of deep disloyalty."[46] Still, Auguste's love for her baby daughter went deeper than her religious ties. Tragically, many parents have renounced a child when faced with a similar situation.

Eighteen years younger than St. Thérèse of Lisieux, Edith would eventually follow in her footsteps and become a Carmelite sister on October 14, 1934, at the age of forty-three. Edith had wanted to enter the convent immediately following her conversion, but delayed her vocation due to her spiritual director's advice combined with her sensitivity toward her mother. While visiting the synagogue one last time together, Auguste expressed her concerns about Christianity to Edith, "Why did you get to know [Christ]? I don't want to say anything against him. He may have been a very good person. But why did he make himself God?"[47] Prior to departing, Edith's mother wept as they said their final goodbyes, which would be the last time they saw each other. While on a train to Cologne the next day, Edith said, "I did not feel any passionate joy. What I just experienced was too terrible. But I felt a profound peace—in the safe haven of God's will."[48] While in the convent, Edith wrote her mother every week but received no response except from her sister Rosa. Auguste felt that Edith had abandoned her when she entered religious life. Later in life, Rosa also converted to Catholicism and served at the convent.

[43] Edith Stein, *Life in a Jewish Family: Her Unfinished Autobiographical Account* (Washington, D.C: ICS Publications, 1986), 60.
[44] Teresa Benedict of the Cross Edith Stein (1891–1942), Vatican.va.
[45] Stein, *Life in a Jewish Family*, 17.
[46] Ibid.
[47] Teresa Benedict of the Cross Edith Stein (1891-1942), Vatican.va.
[48] Ibid.

Edith came to embrace the sacredness of life from her parents, who welcomed and treasured eleven children. Even after her conversion to Catholicism, Edith never forgot her Jewish roots. While in the convent of Cologne, Edith, who became St. Teresa Benedicta of the Cross, wrote, "I simply want to report what I experienced as part of Jewish humanity. We who grow up in Judaism have a duty to bear witness . . . to the young generation who are brought up in a racial hatred from early childhood."[49] Unlike the Nazis, Edith and her parents embraced the Gospel message, particularly the words, "Love your neighbor as yourself" (Mt 22:39) well before Edith's conversion and despite not being Christian. The sacredness of life beckons parents to imitate the Stein's example, who taught their children to treat every person as a child of God regardless of their ethnicity or religion.

On September 14, 1936, Edith renewed her vows, which providentially coincided with her mother's death. Edith mysteriously felt her mother next to her. She wrote, "As I was standing in my place in choir waiting to renew my vows my mother was beside me. I felt her presence quite distinctly."[50] The sacredness of life reveals that those who have gone before us are closer to us because they are united with God. Reflecting on her mother's amazing faith, Edith once wrote, "My mother held onto her faith to the last moment. But as her faith and her firm trust in her God . . . were the last thing that was still alive in the throes of her death, I am confident that she will have met a very merciful judge and that she is now my most faithful helper, so that I can reach the goal as well."[51]

Nearly six years later, Edith would lose her own life after being gassed at Auschwitz on August 9, 1942. The sacredness of life is the circle of life where we are born into this life and born again through the waters of Baptism and eventually die to this world, so as to live in Heaven for all eternity.

---

[49] Ibid.

[50] Freda Mary Oben, Ph.D., *Edith Stein: Scholar, Feminist, Saint* (Staten Island, NY: Alba House, 1988), 31.

[51] "Teresa Benedict of the Cross Edith Stein (1891–1942)," Vatican.va.

Innocenzo and Angela Pampuri

They say it takes a village to raise a family, but for some parents this is really the case. On August 2, 1897, in Trivolzio, Italy, Innocenzo and Angela Pampuri welcomed their tenth of eleven children named Erminio. When Erminio was just three years old, his mother died suddenly of tuberculosis, and, seven years later, Erminio's father died tragically in a traffic accident. As a result, Erminio was raised by his maternal grandparents and aunt. As a young boy, Erminio dreamt of becoming a missionary priest, but, due to his frail health and the influence of his uncle Carlo, who was a doctor, he pursued medicine and graduated at the top of his class at Pavia University in 1921. Dr. Erminio treated the poor for free along with organizing retreats for lay people. It was declared about him, "Throughout his practice he visited them (patients) both by day and night, never sparing himself no matter where they lived, even in places difficult to find. Since most of his patients were poor, he gave them medicines, money, food, clothing, and blankets."[52]

Wanting to give himself more fully to the Lord, Dr. Erminio joined the Hospitaller Order of St. John of God in 1927 around the age of thirty. He took the name Br. Riccardo and utilized his medical skills solely for God's glory. Dying a few months shy of his thirty-third birthday from tuberculosis and pneumonia, Br. Riccardo had embraced the sanctity of life when he wrote to his sister, who also became a religious sister, these beautiful words: "Pray that neither self-indulgence nor pride, nor any other evil passion prevent me from seeing in my patients Jesus Who suffers, and from healing and comforting them."[53] Some grandparents, uncles, aunts, and siblings will be called by God to help raise children that are not their own due to unforeseen tragedies, as seen in Br. Riccardo's life, or other reasons, such as an unwed mother who lacks the means to take care of her child. The important lesson is that while parents are the primary educators of their children, God calls all family members to offer a virtuous example. Had Br. Riccardo's grandparents and

---

[52] "Richard Pampuri, O.H. (1897–1930)," Vatican.va.

[53] "Saint Richard Pampuri," CatholicSaints.Info, catholicsaints.info/saint-richard-pampuri/.

relatives been lax in their faith, there is a great likelihood that he and his sister may have never joined religious life and, perhaps, abandoned the Faith of their parents. All vocations are meant to build up the culture of life and can either be a sign of sanctity or scandal. Grandparents and especially single uncles and aunts need to realize that they too beget life, albeit spiritual life, each time they provide a concrete witness. When Pope St. John Paul II canonized Br. Riccardo Pampuri on November 1, 1989, the Feast of All Saints, perhaps he was trying to prove a subtler point—it takes a family of heavenly and earthly saints to raise a saint.

Stanislaus and Marianna Kowalska

On August 25, 1905, Helen Kowalska was born the third of ten children to Stanislaus and Marianna. She would later become St. Maria Faustina, the Apostle of Divine Mercy. Stanislaus and Marianna were twenty-four and seventeen years of age, respectively, when they were married on November 9, 1892, in the Church of St. Nicholas in Dabie, and, for the first nine years of their marriage, they experienced the cross of infertility. In 1902, they gave birth to their first daughter, Josephine. Later, they would have Eve in 1903, Helen "Faustina" in 1905, Natalia in 1908, Stanislaus in 1912, Miecislaus in 1915, Lucy in 1916, and, finally, Wanda in 1920. Unfortunately, two daughters, Casimira and Bronislava, died in infancy. Marianna, who was once thought to be infertile, gave birth to ten children in a span of eighteen years, which echoes the words of the Angel Gabriel to Our Lady during the Annunciation: "And behold your kinswoman Elizabeth in her old age has also conceived a son; and this in the sixth month with her who was called barren. For with God nothing will be impossible" (Lk 1:36–37). Nothing is impossible for married couples like Stanislaus and Marianna, who persistently prayed during those nearly ten difficult years. How providential that God would bless them with ten children, and what a joy!

Even further, Stanislaus, who was born on May 6, 1868, and his wife, Marianna, who was born on March 8, 1875, conceived their last child at around fifty-two years of age and forty-five years of age, respectively—a testament to their continued openness to life. Even though their daughter Faustina never became a biological mother like her own mother; nevertheless, she was a spiritual mother to many and her maternal intercession continues from Heaven where she draws souls to the ocean of God's mercy most present in the Sacraments of Reconciliation and Holy Communion. In her own words, "I feel certain that my mission will not come to an end upon my death, but will begin. O doubting souls, I will draw aside for you the veils of heaven to convince you of God's goodness."[54]

Though Pope St. John Paul II once proclaimed Faustina as "the great apostle of Divine Mercy," many overlook the fact that she was also an apostle for the sacredness of life—a victim soul for the unborn child. On September 16, 1937, almost one-year shy of her death, God wanted to use his spiritual daughter, Sr. Maria Faustina, to offer her bodily suffering to become a spiritual mother to many souls by making reparation for their sins of abortion. While Sr. Faustina never experienced the pain and the joy of delivering a baby as her mother did with her, God, in a mysterious way, invited Faustina on a few occasions to become a victim soul to save babies from abortion, along with calling down God's mercy upon many souls destined for Hell, especially women who had aborted their children without repentance. Specifically, Faustina wrote:

> I was seized with such violent pains that I had to go to bed at once. I was convulsed with pain for three hours. . . . Jesus had me realize that in this way I took part in His Agony in the Garden, and that He Himself allowed these sufferings in order to make reparation to God for the souls murdered in the wombs of wicked mothers. . . .
>
> I understand the nature of these pains, because the Lord himself has made this known to me. . . . If only I could save even one soul from murder by means of these sufferings![55]

Faustina's final words, "If only I could save even one soul from murder by means of these sufferings!" lie at the heart of the sacredness of life. It is no coincidence that one of the greatest sins of

---

[54] St. Faustina, *Diary: Divine Mercy in My Soul*, 134.

[55] Ibid., 460.

the last century, abortion, was atoned for by one of the greatest saints of the last century, St. Faustina. She was a prophetess of the final days whose mission was to convince the world of God's mercy before it is too late. As St. Faustina once beautifully proclaimed, "Satan hates mercy more than anything else. It is his greatest torment."[56] It must also be remembered that not all women who have had abortions are wicked for many were pressured by their parents and boyfriends while others have repented and have sought God's mercy. Even after an abortion or some serious sin, many people still doubt God's forgiveness or can't forgive themselves. Faustina reassures them with these words of hope:

> O soul, whoever you may be in this world,
> Even if your sins were as black as night,
> Do not fear God, weak child that you are
> For great is the power of God's mercy.[57]

In response to this holocaust toward the unborn child, which springs from the culture of death, there is one sure defense, and that is when couples like Stanislaus and Marianna respond generously and heroically to Our Lord's words "Be fruitful and multiply" (Gn 1:28). By embracing life, this couple allowed their children to become warriors for the Gospel of Life by following their example that a human life, cherished and loved by either its biological or adopted parents, is the most vulnerable and most beautiful creation of God. A human soul is the greatest wonder of the world, greater than all of the seven wonders of the world, for nothing compares to it and nothing can replace it. Nothing is more worth fighting for and suffering for than an innocent child, as Sts. Faustina and Gianna showed the world. This was ingrained in them from their parent's openness to life and their love for them and their siblings.

Karol and Emilia Wojtyła

When Pope St. John Paul II canonized St. Faustina on April 30, 2002, he was reported as saying, "This is the happiest day of my

---

[56]   Ibid., 306.

[57]   Ibid., 584.

life."[58] When most parents find out they are pregnant or see their child for the first time, these same sentiments can fill their hearts. A new life reminds us of God's unfailing love and the reality that He won't abandon us even though sometimes we wonder how much evil God can tolerate. For Karol and Emilia Wojtyła, who welcomed their child on May 18, 1920, at their home in Wadowice, Poland, it truly was of the happiest days of their lives because this child was not supposed to be there in the first place. Several months prior, according to author Milena Kindziuk, Emilia's doctors advised her to abort the child. "You have to have an abortion"[59] were the doctor's words to the then thirty-six-year-old Emilia, who was born on March 26, 1884. Prior to Emilia's pregnancy with Karol, her daughter Olga had died shortly after birth. Emilia's health issues, which would claim her life nine years after Karol's birth, were the main reason the doctor advised her to terminate the life of her future saint. Emilia's doctor worried that she was jeopardizing her health by keeping this baby. Emilia and Karol Sr. trusted boldly that God knew what was best for their son and not their doctor. It also comes as no surprise that Emilia chose life for she was the fifth of thirteen children. In God's providence, Karol Wojtyła Jr., who became Pope St. John Paul II, was born on the feast of Pope St. John I, who was a sixth-century pope and martyr. Emilia's decision to keep her child at the expense of her own health and even death was a foreshadowing of another saint, who was born only two years after her son.

Alberto and Maria Beretta

Only two years after Pope St. John Paul II's birth on October 4, 1922, St. Gianna was born at her paternal grandparent's house in Magenta, Italy, near Milan on the Feast of St. Francis. Alberto and

---

[58] "The Divine Mercy," Divinemercy.org, thedivinemercy.org/message/ john-paul-ii#:~:text=The%20feast%20day%20falls%20on%20the%20 Second%20Sunday,in%20Lagiewniki%2C%20a%20suburb%20of%20 Krakow%20in%20Poland.

[59] Steven Ertelt, "Book: Pope John Paul II's Mother Rejected Doctor's Abortion Suggestion" (October 16, 2013), Lifesitenews.com, lifenews. com/2013/10/16/report-pope-john-paul-iis-mother-rejected-doctors- abortion-suggestion.

Maria Beretta named their daughter Giovanna Francesca—likely after St. Francis. In a documentary about her, called *Love is a Choice*, St. Gianna once declared, "I was number ten of thirteen children. My parents had a strong, strong faith. We all felt it. I lost three of my siblings when the Spanish influenza hit us. I would later lose my older sister Amalia when I was fifteen. I don't think I felt a hurt like this before."[60]

In 1942, at the young age of nineteen, Gianna lost both of her beloved parents in a span of four months, events that surely pierced Gianna's heart. In 1949, Gianna received her degree in medicine and surgery, becoming a doctor. In 1952, Gianna obtained her degree as a specialist in pediatrics from the University of Milan. On September 24, 1955, Gianna and Pietro married at the Basilica of San Martino in Magenta. As mentioned earlier, Gianna was not the only child with a prestigious degree. Her brothers and sisters included two engineers, four physicians, a pharmacist, and a concert pianist. The late Cardinal Carlo Martini, SJ, Archbishop of Milan, pointed to the reason behind these upstanding individuals. "But I believe that the determining factor was the parents' way of listening to their children."[61] This hearkens back to the family meal when Alberto took a genuine interest in his children's life by asking about their day. The Beretta children felt appreciated, loved, and respected by their parents, which enabled them to revere the dignity of each soul they encountered.[62]

Alberto, who worked at the Cotoni cotton mill, never sought to direct his children to be what he wanted them to be, or to achieve success in the world's eyes. He was noted for his "responsibility and hard work,"[63] which he and his wife expected of their children. Above all, Alberto and Maria loved their children with God's love, seeing them through His eyes as the crown of His creation as a pure gift rather than something owed to them. Guerriero said it best about couples like Alberto and Maria,

---

[60] *Love is a Choice*, DVD.
[61] Molla and Guerriero, *Saint Gianna Molla*, 30–31.
[62] See Ibid., 31.
[63] Ibid., 25.

In those days there was no talk of family planning
or "responsible parenthood." Parents welcomed
children from the hand of God and trusted him for
their upbringing and education. In this spirit, Alberto
and Maria had thirteen. Three—David, Rosina, and
Pierina—died during the Spanish flu epidemic; two
others, Guiglielmina and Anna Marie died very young.
In order of birth the other eight were: Amalia (nicknamed
Iucci), Francesco, Ferdinando, Enrico, Zita, Giuseppe,
Gianna, and Virginia.[64]

On September 6, 1961, just shy of her thirty-ninth birthday,
Gianna developed a uterine tumor while two months pregnant with
her fourth child. Gianna was advised of the following options: have
an abortion and remove the entire uterus, or remove only the tumor,
which could spare the baby, but might result in further medical
issues and perhaps even death. Gianna elected for the latter as she
wanted to protect her baby even if it would take her life. Just a few
hours after giving birth to her daughter Gianna Emmanuela on April
21, 1962, Gianna took a turn for the worse, due to a fatal infection
at the time called septic peritonitis. Throughout her pain, Gianna
sought Our Lady's intercession. Gianna wanted to live, to be with
her husband and help him raise their children. Being an orphan at
the age of nineteen was hard enough. Not having her parents alive
to witness her becoming a doctor, attend her wedding, and meet her
grandchildren surely weighed heavily on Gianna's heart.

Gianna's husband Pietro recalled her final days of immense
suffering, which coincided with the Easter Triduum. Specifically,
Pietro described the day after little Gianna was born, which seemed
to indicate that his wife was already preparing herself to say goodbye:

> I still see Gianna, on Easter morning 1962, in the
> maternity section of the Monza Hospital as she picks up
> the baby with great effort, lifts her and kisses her, looking
> with sadness and suffering that prove to me she was aware
> that she was going to leave her an orphan. From that day,
> her sufferings never ceased. She called on her mother

---

[64]   Ibid., 25–26.

to be near and help her, because she could not manage, the pain was so great. It seemed to be a slow, dramatic suffering, which accompanied Christ on the Cross.[65]

When Gianna gazed upon her baby girl, she realized how sacred and fragile life is—not only her child's life, but also her own life. Saying goodbye to our children is one of the most heart-wrenching moments any parent will ever face, realizing that someday we will no longer be physically present to them. Above all, Gianna wanted her daughter to know that she loved her and would love her for all eternity even though she would be gone soon. During the midst of her agony, Gianna said:

> Pietro, I was already over there and you know what I saw? Someday I will tell you. But because we were so happy, we were too comfortable with our marvelous babies, full of health, and grace, with all the blessings of heaven, they sent me down here, to suffer still, because it is not right to come to the Lord without enough suffering.[66]

From all indications, Gianna had a glimpse of Heaven. Perhaps Gianna even saw her parents and her siblings who died, and her two miscarried babies, which was a gift from God to fill her with hope and courage. Gianna's sister, who was then Mother Virginia, came all the way from India to be vigilantly at her side. On a side note, what greater gift can siblings give to their parents outside of loving God and His Church than to truly love and sacrifice for their siblings, especially in their dying moments. The sacredness of life reminds us that our siblings are not here accidentally, even though at times we can wonder how we are related; rather, our siblings were chosen by God from all eternity to lead us to Heaven and for us to do the same. Gianna's fearlessness in the face of death, that is, to sacrifice her life by carrying her baby to full term rather than abort it, was perhaps inspired to some degree by the thought of being reunited with her departed loved ones should God take her life, which He

---

[65] Ibid., 86–87.
[66] Ibid., 87.

did. As she lay dying in her home, Gianna repeated, "Jesus, I love you,"[67] before going to the Lord on April 28, 1962.

While St. Gianna Beretta Molla was canonized on May 16, 2004, by Pope St. John Paul II, God had been preparing this heroic mother's heart long before her birth, when her parents, Alberto and Maria Beretta, entered into the Sacrament of Matrimony on October 12, 1908. By virtue of their holy vows and their desire to love God above everything and to manifest His love to their children, Alberto and Maria truly embraced the sacredness of life, which they passed on so beautifully to their children. They not only welcomed as many children as God wanted to bestow on them, but also surrendered as many children as God would call home. God never promised Alberto and Maria a lifetime of happiness together as we so often wish upon every couple that gets married. Instead, the sacredness of life reminds us that suffering cannot be avoided. Yet God will repay those faithful parents like Alberto and Maria, maybe not in this life, but certainly in the next. And, perhaps, because of their fidelity and openness to life, God may even raise up a saint as He did with Gianna.

Ruggero and Maria Teresa Badano

After praying with her husband for nearly eleven years to conceive, Maria Teresa became pregnant at the age of thirty-seven. Maria Teresa's initial response was one of shock. She said, "I just couldn't believe it. I didn't tell anyone I was pregnant and tried to rest as much as possible, because the doctor had explained that it would be three weeks or so before we would have confirmation. That day Ruggero could not contain his joy and he began to speak about 'our pregnancy.'"[68] In response to Maria Teresa's pregnancy, Ruggero ensured his wife had the most comfortable pregnancy possible. For instance, Ruggero often carried Maria Teresa to their upstairs bed. Ruggero declared, "My love for my wife moved on to another plane for those nine months. But so did my love for the Lord."[69] Clearly,

[67] Ibid., 10.
[68] Zanzucchi, *Chiara Luce: A life lived to the full*, 13.
[69] Ibid.

Ruggero's child in the womb helped him discover the reason for his existence—the call to greatness, which was none other than to love God and lay down his life for his family. Ruggero's actions show that a man only becomes a real man when he gives himself away in love. That is why the sacredness of life beckons each person to the heights of virtue, to self-donation.

When Bl. Chiara was born on October 29, 1971, Maria Teresa was filled not only with great joy, but also some disbelief. She declared, "For twenty-four hours it was like living in a dream. I kept asking myself if my baby really had been born, because they didn't let me see her. . . . Then eventually I saw that little bundle of a baby and my heart was filled with joy. But at the same time as feeling this immense joy, we both realized that, in the first place, that baby was a child of God."[70] Certainly, this holy couple shed many tears of gratitude that blessed day! Since Chiara would be their only child, not by their choice, but God's will, they treasured her as the greatest gift of their marriage before God called their daughter home at eighteen years old.

After his daughter died, Ruggero immediately declared, "God gave her to us and he has taken her back. Blessed be God. I don't know if we will be able to do anything else in this life, but maybe we have made at least one masterpiece."[71] Yes, human life is not only God's greatest masterpiece, but it also became the *magnum opus*—the greatest work—of the parents of the saints. And the greatest masterpieces are not formed in one day; rather, they are the culmination of years of heroic struggle.

From the few accounts above, it is apparent that many of the saints came from large families because their parents took God's word literally when He declared, "Be fruitful and multiply" (Gn 1:28). However, some saints and blesseds, like Pope John Paul II and Chiara Badano, hailed from small families. By today's standards, Pope John Paul II's family, which included three children, would be considered larger than average as many Christian parents are having fewer children. If any conclusions can be drawn, it might be that

---

[70] Ibid., 13–14.
[71] Ibid., 40.

those couples enjoying, or desiring to enjoy, material success tend to
have fewer children. Also, we can't discount the influence of culture
on those living in countries that emphasize material success at the
cost of having more children.

More than any other time period, the parents of the saints offer a
light to our darkened world by reminding parents that bringing one
more soul to Heaven, especially one of our own, is infinitely greater
than our good looks, inconveniences, money, and persecution from
family members and strangers. God always has the final laugh
because, even after giving birth to nine children, St. Zélie Martin
retained her figure and attractiveness according to photographs. She
beautifully sums up this entire chapter with the following words:

> But when we had our children, our ideas changed
> somewhat. We lived only for them. They were all our
> happiness, and we never found any except in them. In
> short, nothing was too difficult, and the world was no
> longer a burden to us. For me, our children were a great
> compensation, so I wanted to have a lot of them in order
> to raise them for Heaven.[72]

And so these parents were not afraid to lay down their lives for
their families as Christ laid down His life for the Church. Whether
it was welcoming twenty-five children, keeping a child rather than
aborting it, even against the doctor's wishes and the risk of death,
raising a child with special needs, praying for eleven years to get
pregnant, or burying several children, these parents knew that the
sacredness of life is at the heart of the Gospel. When these parents
gazed on their child for the first time, they were not simply looking
at their biological DNA, but an immortal soul who was in the mind
of God from all eternity. They were gazing upon God's greatest
masterpiece, and, in a mysterious way, they were gazing upon God
Himself, for each of us is made in His image and likeness. And, for
these reasons, all the sufferings associated with pregnancy and all
the persecutions that came for being pro-life were worth it, for God
blessed them with an opportunity to raise a future saint. At the same

---

[72]   Martin and Martin, *A Call to A Deeper Love,* 289.

time, gratitude coincides with the sacredness of life for every child is a gift from God. Or, as St. Louis Martin once wrote to his Carmelite daughters in 1888, "I want to tell you, my dear children, that I have the urgent desire to thank God and to make you thank God because I feel that our family, though very humble, has the honor of being among the privileged of our adorable Creator."[73]

---

[73] Ibid., 365.

CONCLUSION

With a nature such as my own, had I been reared by parents
without virtue or even if I had been spoiled by the maid,
Louise, as Céline was, I would have become very bad and
perhaps have been lost.[1] —St. Thérèse of Lisieux

At the heart of this book is St. Thérèse's words above, which reveal
that a holy father and mother are irreplaceable because no one is
born a saint. There is no greater mission for parents than to navigate
their children safely to Heaven by leading them to a love affair with
the Blessed Trinity now and for all eternity. At the same time, there
would be no greater tragedy than for us or our children to end up in
Hell, forever deprived of seeing the face of God—our heart's deepest
longing—not to mention the unending torment of demons. It is no
wonder that Céline, Thérèse's best friend and closest surviving sister
in age, echoed similar words:

> I consider the greatest grace of my life was to have had
> Christian parents and to have received from them a
> vigorous education that left no place for petty vanities.
> In our house, nothing was ever sacrificed to human
> respect. The only altar erected was that to God alone,
> and if sometimes the sacrifices seemed austere, the time
> always came when I enjoyed their delightful perfume.[2]

We only need to recall the lives of Margaret Sanger and Dr.
Bernard Nathanson to show how godless parents can make or break
a century and, perhaps, even a civilization, while holy Christian

---

[1]   St. Thérèse of Lisieux, *Story of a Soul*, 24.
[2]   Piat, *Celine*, 18.

parents, such as Sts. Louis and Zélie Martin, can build a civilization of love. And, just as the Holy Family changed history by bringing God's love and God Himself to our fallen world, so too did the devout parents of the saints change history by bringing Our Lord into the hearts of mankind.

Just as an oyster with its hard shell is designed to produce and protect a pearl, the parents of the saints had a similar mission, i.e., to raise saints in the midst of a hostile world, especially toward Catholicism. A seashell, which is frequently used by a priest or deacon to pour water on the baptized person, drives home a deeper point: the lives of the parents of the saints were like a seashell because they were often hidden beneath the surface and then washed ashore when their time had come, while their pearl lives on! Interestingly enough, scientists believe that for every 10,000 oysters, only one pearl is made in a span of a few years.

Unlike a pearl, though, forming and raising a saint takes a lifetime of hard work with God's grace, which could be another reason why so few become canonized. In fact, historians estimate there are over 10,000 canonized saints in the Roman Martyrology. Contrast these numbers with the roughly seven billion people who, according to the US Census Bureau, inhabited the world in 2012, not to mention every single soul who has lived and died since Christ founded the Church some 2,000 years ago, and one ought to believe that becoming and raising a canonized saint is a miracle in itself. And, just as an oyster forms a pearl as a defense mechanism against deadly attackers like parasites, so too must parents form saints with a greater urgency because the forces of evil are greater than at any other period of history. While the mission appears daunting, each parent must never forget that nothing is impossible with God.

Despite the fact that many of the parents of the saints will never have a stained glass window in their honor, or a Church named after them, and will continue to pass forgotten, buried like a seashell on the bottom of the ocean floor, these souls are very dear to God and will shine for all eternity, for without their witness the Church and our world would have been deprived of God's greatest human capital—the saints. And, as Christians are slowly becoming the minority, and Satan's fury is being unleashed like never before, the Church longs for saints from parents.

If you want to know the power of the saints just read what St. Peter Julian Eymard once wrote, "A saint keeps watch over his country and obtains its salvation. His prayers and virtues are more powerful than all the armies in the world."[3] And that is why the legacy of the parents of the saints was the pearl they co-created with God—saints who, in turn, converted millions of souls through their prayers, sacrifice, and even martyrdoms, which now forms the most splendid necklace that adorns Our Lady in Heaven. And, when these parents departed from this life as their children toiled in this valley of tears, the thought of being reunited with their blessed parents became a great consolation to many of the saints in their darkest nights. As Thérèse once wrote:

> When I think of these things, my soul is plunged into infinity, and it seems to me it already touches the eternal shore. I seem to be receiving the embraces of Jesus. I believe I see my heavenly Mother coming to meet me with Papa, Mama, the four little angels. I believe I am enjoying forever a real and eternal family reunion.[4]

Even after the passing of these devout parents, their lessons continued to inspire their saintly children. Louis Martin used to recite a line from a beautiful poem to his children called "Reflection" by Lamartine saying, "Time is your barque, not your home."[5] According to Thérèse, "When very little, these words gave me courage, and even now, in spite of the years which have put to flight so many impressions of childish piety, the image of the barque still charms my soul and helps it put up with its exile."[6] Or, in the beautiful words of Céline, Thérèse's sister, "We and our family have lived leaning out a window opening onto Heaven."[7]

---

[3]   Eymard, *The Real Presence Eucharistic Meditations*, 22.
[4]   St. Thérèse of Lisieux, *Story of a Soul*, 87–88.
[5]   Ibid., 87.
[6]   Ibid.
[7]   Piat, *Celine*, 137.

The parents of saints and their saintly children clearly had one foot on earth and one foot in Heaven for they realized this life is but a blink of an eye compared to Eternity. These holy parents discovered throughout their lives that the key to holiness involves more than spending long hours before the Most Blessed Sacrament, fasting for days, or memorizing copious Scripture verses, all of which are beautiful in themselves; rather, the key to holiness is friendship with God as seen in their love for the sacraments, which poured over to every facet of their lives. At the same time, these parents guarded against viewing themselves as holier than others. They were keenly aware of their need for daily conversion and, therefore, their desire for holiness never waned. As Zélie Martin once wrote her teenage daughters, Marie and Pauline, who were away at boarding school:

> My dear little daughters, I must go to Vespers to pray for the intention of our dear late relatives. There will come a day when you will go there for me, but I have to see to it that I won't have too much need of your prayers. I want to become a saint, and that won't be easy. There's a lot of wood to chop and the wood is as hard as rock. It would have been better if I'd tried earlier, while it was less difficult. Oh well, "better late than never."[8]

And what better way did these parents reveal God's presence to their children than by a rich sacramental life, surrender, sacrificial love, embracing suffering for the love of God, adopting a simplistic lifestyle, seeking to be alone with God in prayer, and living the Gospel of Life generously. Moreover, these seven hallmarks were like proven mile markers, which kept their children on the narrow road, pointing them to the "crown of life" (Jas 1:12)—the imperishable crown that awaits those who love God. By virtue of these hallmarks, their fathers, in particular, revealed God the Father's love for His children, while their mothers revealed, in particular, Our Blessed Mother's love. And, in the process, these devout parents helped unveil in an imperfect way the mystery of God, Who is love (see 1 Jn 4:8).

---

8   Martin and Martin, *A Call to a Deeper Love*, 139.

While Zélie Martin desired to be a saint, she, along with so many of the parents of the saints, cared little whether or not the Church would publicly recognize her as a saint. It was more important that God be praised while they passed obscurely in this life as they sought to love God with every fiber of their being. If the parents of the saints could speak to us from Heaven, they might say: "Forget yourself. Be nailed to the Cross with Our Lord and you will be blessed." Most of all, these godly parents desired that their children become saints, and that they could die peacefully knowing their sons and daughters still practiced the Faith. As St. Monica said to St. Augustine before she died, "One thing there was for which I did desire to stay a little longer in this life, which was that I might see you a Catholic before I died. And my God granted me this more abundantly, in that I see you now despising all worldly happiness, devoted to His service. What have I now to do here?"[9]

Despite our own parent's failures and shortcomings, even our own, it is my hope that we can all become saints and raise our children to become saints. And, while some of us might feel bitterness over the parents God gave us, we must strive to become the parents we have always wanted to be or, if we were blessed to have holy parents like those listed in this book, to imitate their example. No two saints were alike; they hailed from various backgrounds and situations, from holy upbringings to immoral parents. Some saints were abused, abandoned, or belonged to the occult. Some experienced dramatic conversions and great sufferings, while others had every material thing and then lost it. Some saints were healthy, while others were sick. They lived short lives and long lives, were rich and poor, quiet and talkative. No matter their professions, no matter how many siblings or children they had, or whether they were orphans, religious, married, or single, or whether they were well educated or not, may we never forget that God's grace is not wanting, as these parents and their children have unveiled to us.

Mother Angelica said it best about canonization, which can appear intimidating at times:

---

[9] St. Augustine, *The Confessions of St. Augustine*, 254.

Canonization is nothing more than the Church saying publicly that they know for sure the person is in heaven. I mean, there are millions of people in heaven who are not canonized. That's why we have All Saints' Day...

I always thought, personally, that the saints who are canonized may be the very least in the kingdom. We don't know that, but it's a good guess. Some little old washerwoman who had tremendous love for God may be greater than St. Augustine up there. I think we're going to have lots of little surprises when we arrive.[10]

And while these parents did nothing spectacular in the world's view, they did do something far greater in God's eyes, which was to co-create a new human life and form that soul into a saint. The greatest legacy of these holy parents was raising saintly children. One of the biggest surprises in Heaven will be discovering just how incredible these parents' lives truly were. And, while we honor the parents of the saints' collectively, along with all those in Heaven, every November 1, All Saints Day, these devout parents will continue to be forgotten, and they would have had it no other way. May we strive to imitate the example of these heroic parents and above all their seven hallmarks. And when our earthly life ends, and God asks us what we have done, may we respond like them, "I gave you saints with Your grace."

All you holy parents of the saints, canonized and uncanonized, pray for us, and help us, like you, to raise our children to become saints.

---

[10] Mother Angelica, *Mother's Angelica's: Little Book of Life Lessons and Everyday Spirituality* (New York: Doubleday, 2007), 163–164.

A Parent's Prayer to Our Lady of Providence

O Lady of Providence, my Mother and Queen, to thee I confide the children God has entrusted to me. Provide for them safety of body and soul, now in their youth and especially in the years to come when the responsibilities and the temptations of life will be theirs. Then, O Mary, for my sons and daughters continue to be a provident Mother. Above all, O my Queen, be with my children when the angel of death hovers near. In thy maternal arms enfold them and lead them into Eternity, so that forever and ever they may praise the Father, Son, and Holy Spirit. Amen.

Confraternity of Our Lady of Providence, Saint Mary-of-the-Woods, Indiana.

Ecclesiastical approbation, 1967

SAINTLY SAYINGS

"Hear Mass daily; it will prosper the whole day. All your duties will be performed the better for it, and your soul will be stronger to bear its daily cross. The Mass is the most holy act of religion; you can do nothing that will give greater glory to God or be more profitable for your soul than to hear Mass both frequently and devoutly. It is the favorite devotion of the saints."[1]
—St. Peter Julian Eymard

"Disorder in society is the result of disorder in the family."[2]
—St. Angela Merici

"To dissociate the child from love is, for our species, a methodological error: contraception, which is to make love without making a child. Artificial (in vitro) fertilization, which is to make a child without making love; abortion, which is to unmake the child; and pornography, which is to unmake love: all these, to varying degrees, are incompatible with natural law."[3]
—Dr. Jerome Lejeune

"The saints have not been made saints by applause and honor, but by injuries and insults."[4]
—St. Alphonsus de Liguori

---

[1]   St. Peter Eymard, *Holy Communion* (New York: Sentinel Press, 1940), 28.

[2]   "Saint Angelica Merici," CatholicSaints.info, catholicsaints.info/saint-angela-merici/.

[3]   Clara Lejeune-Gaymard, *Life is a Blessing: A Biography of Jerome Lejeune, Geneticist, Doctor, Father* (Philadelphia: National Catholic Bioethics Center, 2010), 31.

[4]   St. Alphonsus de Liguori, *The True Spouse of Jesus Christ*, 339.

*"A married woman must leave God at the altar
to find Him in her domestic cares."*[5]
—St. Frances of Rome

*"Forgotten people are the mothers of saints, and yet, by
their influence over their offspring, they had an immense
influence over the history of the Church."*
—Anonymous Source

*"The saints are like the stars. In his providence Christ conceals
them in a hidden place that they may not shine before others
when they might wish to do so. Yet they are always ready to
exchange the quiet of contemplation for the works of mercy as
soon as they perceive in their heart the invitation of Christ."*[6]
—St. Anthony of Padua

*"In conversations I have had with so many married couples, I tell them
often that while both they and their children are alive, they should
help them to be saints, while being well aware that none of us will be
a saint on earth. All we will do is struggle, struggle, struggle."*[7]
—St. Josemaría Escrivá

---

[5]   Martin and Martin, *A Call to a Deeper Love*, 217.
[6]   "Saint Anthony of Padua," CatholicSaints.info, catholicsaints.info/saint-anthony-of-padua/.
[7]   St. Josemaría Escrivá, *The Way, Furrow, The Forge*, 746.

Bibliography

_____*A Year with the Saints.* Translated by a member of the Order of Mercy. Rockford, IL: TAN Books, 1988.

Ackroyd, Peter. *The Life of Thomas More.* New York: Anchor Books, 1998.

Adams, Stephen. "Twenty-six Babies Aborted for Cleft Lips or Palates." *The Telegraph,* July 4, 2011. telegraph.co.uk/news/health/news/8616978/Twenty-six-babies-aborted-for-cleft-lips-or-palates.html.

Agreda, Venerable Mary. *The Mystical City of God.* Rockford, IL: TAN Books, 1978.

_____. "Alessandro Serenelli: A Miraculous Conversion." Mariagoretti.org. mariagoretti.org/alessandrobio.htm. Accessed November 23, 2015.

Álmeras, Charles. *St. Paul of the Cross: Founder of the Passionists.* Translated by M. Angeline Bouchard. Garden City, New York: Hanover House, 1960.

Andre Marie, Br. "Saint Robert Bellarmine." Catholicism.org. May 12, 2016. catholicism.org/ad-rem-no-269.html.

Apostoli, Andrew. *Fatima for Today: The Urgent Marian Message of Hope.* San Francisco: Ignatius Press, 2010.

Aquinas, St. Thomas. *Summa Theologica,* Volume I. New York: Benziger Brothers, 1947.

Augustine, St. *The Confessions of St. Augustine.* Totowa, NJ: Catholic Book Publishing Corp., 1997.

Ball, Anne. *Modern Saints: Their lives and Faces,* Book One. Rockford, IL: TAN Books, 1983.

Ball, Anne. *Modern Saints: Their lives and Faces,* Book Two. Rockford, IL: TAN Books, 1990.

Ball, Anne. *The Saints' Guide to Joy That Never Fades.* Atlanta: Charis Books, 2001.

Baur, Benedict. *Frequent Confession: Its Place in the Spiritual Life.* New York: Scepter, 1999.

Bergeron, Henri-Paul, CSC. *Brother André, The Wonder Man of Mount Royal.* Translated by Real Boudreau. Montréal: Saint Joseph's Oratory, 2007.

Bosco, St. John, *Life of Dominic Savio: Pupil at the Oratory of St. Francis de Sales.* sdb.org/en/Don_Bosco/Writings/Writings/Life_of_Dominic_Savio__Pupil_at_the_Oratory_of_St_Francis_de. Accessed May 15, 2017.

Bossis, Gabrielle. *He and I.* Translated by Evelyn M. Brown. Boston: Pauline Books, 2013.

Boyton, Neil, SJ. *The Blessed Friend of Youth: Saint John Bosco.* New York: Macmillan Company, 1942.

Breiling, Margaret. "A Saint to Emulate." EWTN.com. ewtn.com/library/MARY/GORETTI.htm. Accessed January 12, 2015.

Budnick, Mary Ann. *Raise Happy Children . . . Teach Them Virtues!* Springfield, IL: R.B. Media, Inc., 2002.

Catechism of the Catholic Church. Rome: Libreria Editrice Vaticana, 1994.

Chaput, Charles J. "What's Next: Catholics, America and a World Made New." CatholicPhilly.com, July 27, 2017. catholicphilly.com/2017/07/think-tank/homilies-speeches/whats-next-catholics-america-and-a-world-made-new/.

Coverdale, John F. *Uncommon Faith: The Early Years of Opus Dei, 1928-1943.* New York: Scepter, 2002.

Cingolani, Gabriele, CP. *Saint Gabriel Possenti, Passionist: "A Young Man in Love."* Translated by S.B. Zak. Staten Island, NY: Alba House, 1997.

Cruz, Joan Carroll. *Secular Saints.* Rockford, IL: TAN Books, 1989.

Czaczkowska, Ewa K. *Faustina: The Mystic and her Message.* Stockbridge, MA: Marian Press, 2014.

da Ripabottoni, Alessandro. *Guide to Padre Pio's Pietrelcina.* Edited by Fr. Gerardo Di Flumeri. San Giovanni Rotondo: Editions: Padre Pio of Pietrelcina, 1987.

de Liguori, St. Alphonsus. *Preparation for Death.* Philadelphia: J.B. Lippincott & Co., 1869.

de Liguori, St. Alphonsus. *The Glories of Mary.* Edited by Rev. Eugene Grimm. Brooklyn: Redemptorist Fathers, 1931.

de Liguori, St. Alphonsus. *The Incarnation Birth and Infancy of Jesus Christ.* Edited by Rev. Eugene Grimm. Brooklyn: Redemptorist Fathers, 1927.

de Liguori, St. Alphonsus. *The True Spouse of Jesus Christ.* Edited by Rev. Eugene Grimm. Brooklyn: Redemptorist Fathers, 1929.

de Lisieux, St. Thérèse. *General Correspondence, Volume I.* Translated by John Clarke, OCD. Washington D.C.: ICS Publications, 1982.

de Lisieux, St. Thérèse. *General Correspondence, Volume II.* Translated by John Clarke, OCD. Washington, D.C.: ICS Publications, Publications, 1988.

de Lisieux, St. Thérèse. *Her Last Conversations.* Translated by John Clarke, OCD. Washington, D.C.: ICS Publications, 1977.

de Lisieux, St. Thérèse. *Story of a Soul.* Translated by John Clark, OCD. Washington, D.C.: ICS Publications, 1996.

de Marchi, John, I.M.C. *Fatima: From the Beginning.* Translated by I.M. Kingsbury Fatima: Edicóes Missóes Consolata, 2006.

de Montfort, St. Louis. *True Devotion to Mary.* Rockford, IL: TAN Publishers, 1985.

de Prada, Andres Vázquez. *The Founder of Opus Dei: The Life of Josemaria Escriva, Volume I: The Early Years.* Princeton, NJ: Scepter, 2001.

de Sales, St. Francis. *Introduction to the Devout Life.* New York: Vintage Books, 2002.

dos Santos, Ven. Lucia. *Fatima in Lucia's Own Words: Sister Lucia's Memoirs, Volume II.* Third ed. Edited by Fr. Louis Kondor, SVD. Translated by Dominican Nuns of Perpetual Rosary and Dominicans of Mosteiro de Santa Maria. Fatima, Portugal: Secretariado dos Pastorinhos, 2004.

Doyle, Kenneth. "Funeral Mass for Non-Baptized. When to Call a Priest?" CatholicHerald.org, February 18, 2016. catholicherald.org/web-extras/question-corner/funeral-mass-for-non-baptized-when-to-call-a-priest. Accessed August 31, 2018.

Dubay, Thomas, SM. *Deep Conversion, Deep Prayer.* San Francisco: Ignatius Press, 2006.

Ertelt, Steven. "Book: Pope John Paul II's Mother Rejected Doctor's Abortion Suggestion." Lifesitenews.com, October 16, 2013. lifenews.com/2013/10/16/report-pope-john-paul-iis-mother-rejected-doctors-abortion-suggestion. Accessed October 4, 2017.

Escrivá, St. Josemaría. *The Way, The Furrow, The Forge.* New York: Scepter, 2013.

Evert, Jason. *Saint John Paul the Great: His Five Loves.* Lakewood, CO: Totus Tuus Press, 2014.

Eymard, St. Peter Julian. *The Real Presence Eucharistic Meditations.* New York: Sentinel Press, 1938.

Eymard, St. Peter Julian. *Holy Communion.* Translated by Clara Rumball. New York: Sentinel Press, 1940.

Farrell Walter, OP, and Martin Healy. *My Way of Life: Pocket Edition of St. Thomas, the Summa Simplified for Everyone.* New York: Confraternity of the Precious Blood, 1952.

Filz, Gretchen. "A Story of Great Mercy: St. Maria Goretti & Alessandro Serenelli," Catholiccompany.com, July 6, 2017.

Fink, Salvator, OFM. "The Doorkeeper," *The Anthonian* 6 (1987).

Frassati, Luciana. *A Man of the Beatitudes: Pier Giorgio Frassati.* San Francisco: Ignatius Press, 2001.

Frossard, Andre. *Be Not Afraid.* New York: St. Martin's Press, 1982.

Garrido, Manuel. *El Beato Josemaría Escrivá y Barbastro.* Barbastro: Ayuntamiento de Barbastro, 1995.

Gaudiose, Dorothy M. *Mary's House. Mary Pyle: Under the Spiritual Guidance of Padre Pio.* New York: Alba House, 1993.

Germanus, Ven. Fr., CP. *The Life of St. Gemma Galgani.* Charlotte, NC: TAN Books, 2012.

Gertrude, St. *The Life and Revelations of St. Gertrude the Great.* Translated by the Poor Clares of Kenmare. Rockford, IL: TAN Books, 2002.

Gladiator. DVD. Universal Pictures, 2000.

Goodier, Alban. *Saints for Sinners.* Manchester, NH: Sophia Institute Press, 2007.

Groeschel, Benedict J. *Why Do We Believe?* Huntington, IN: Our Sunday Visitor, 2005.

Hebblethwaite, *John XIII: Pope of the Century.* New York: Bloomsbury Academic, 2005.

Hrynkiw, Ivana. "Mother Angelica, Founder of EWTN, Dies on Easter Sunday," al.com, March 28, 2016. al.com/news/index.ssf/2016/03/mother_angelica_founder_of_ewt.html.

Hoever, Hugo. *Lives of the Saints Illustrated Part 1.* Totowa, NJ: Catholic Book Publishing, 1999.

Holbock, Ferdinand. *Married Saints and Blesseds Through the Centuries.* Translated by Michael Miller. San Francisco: Ignatius Press, 2002.

The Holy Bible: Revised Standard Version, Second Catholic Edition. San Francisco: Ignatius Press, 2006.

Illanes, Jose Luis. *Dos de Octubre de 1928: Alcance y Significado de una Fecha,* Scripta theologica, 13.2-3 (1981).

John XXIII, Pope St. *Journal of a Soul.* New York: McGraw-Hill, 1964.

John Paul II, Pope St. *Crossing the Threshold of Hope.* Edited by Vittorio Messori. New York: Alfred A. Knopf, Inc., 1994.

John Paul II, Pope St. *Gift and Mystery.* New York: Image Books, 1996.

John Paul II, Pope St. Homily, Puebla de Los Angeles (Mexico), January 28, 1979.

John Paul II, Pope St. Homily for the Beatification of Five Servants of God, October 3, 2004.

John Paul II, Pope St. *Man and Woman He Created Them: A Theology of the Body.* Translated by Michael Waldstein. Boston: Pauline Books and Media, 2006.

John Paul II, Pope St. *Silence Transformed into Life: The Testament of His Final Year.* Hyde Park, NY: New City Press, 2006.

John of the Cross, St. *The Collected Works of St. John of the Cross.* Translated by Kieran Kavanaugh, OCD, and Otilo Rodriguez, OCD. Washington, D.C.: ICS Publications, 1991.

Johnston, Francis W. *The Voice of the Saints.* Rockford, IL: TAN Books, 1986.

Kelley, Fr. Bennett. *The New Saint Joseph Baltimore Catechism, Official Revised Edition, No. 2.* Totowa, New Jersey: Catholic Book Publishing, 2011.

Kowalska, St. Maria Faustina. *Diary: Divine Mercy in My Soul.* Stockbridge, MA: Marian Press, 2011.

Lejeune-Gaymard, Clara. *Life Is a Blessing: A Biography of Jerome Lejeune, Geneticist, Doctor, Father.* Translated by Michael Miller. Philadelphia: National Catholic Bioethics Center, 2010.

Leifeld, W. *Mothers of the Saints.* Ann Arbor, MI: Servant Publications, 1991.

"Lives of the Saints—St. Joseph Moscati," Piercedhearts.org. piercedhearts.org/theology_heart/life_saints/st_joseph_moscati. html. Accessed December 6, 2017.

Love Is a Choice. DVD. Ignatius Press, 2005.

Madrid, Patrick. *Search and Rescue: How to Bring Your Family and Friends Into or Back Into the Catholic Church.* Manchester, NH: Sophia Institute Press, 2001.

"Margaret Sanger." Biography.com. biography.com/people/ margaret-sanger-9471186. Accessed January 20, 2016.

Martin, Céline. *The Father of the Little Flower: Louis Martin, 1823-1894.* Rockford, IL: TAN Books, 2005.

Martin, Céline. *The Mother of the Little Flower: Celine Martin, 1831-1877.* Rockford, IL: TAN Books, 2005.

"Martin Luther." New Advent.org. newadvent.org/ cathen/09438b.htm. Accessed March 23, 2016.

Martin, St. Louis and St. Zélie Martin. *A Call to a Deeper Love.* Edited by Frances Renda and translated by Ann Connors Hess. Staten Island, NY: St. Paul's, 2011.

Massa, Bonaventura. *Mary Pyle: She Lived Doing Good to All*. San Giovanni Rotondo: Our Lady of Grace Capuchin Friary, 1986.

Matthews, V.J., *Saint Philip Neri: Apostle of Rome and Founder of the Congregation of the Oratory*. Rockford, IL: TAN Books, 1984.

McGregor, Augustine, OCSO. *Padre Pio: His Early Years*. Edited by Fr. Alessio Parente. San Giovanni Rotondo, 1981.

Michalenko, Sr. Sophia, CMGT. *The Life of Faustina Kowalska: The Authorized Biography*. Ann Arbor, MI: Servant Publications, 1987.

Molla, Pietro and Elio Guerriero. *Saint Gianna Molla*. Translated by James G. Colbert. San Francisco: Ignatius Press, 2004.

Monti, James. *The King's Good Servant but God's First: The Life and Writings of St. Thomas More*. San Francisco: Ignatius Press, 1997.

Mother Angelica. *Mother Angelica's Little Book of Life Lessons and Everyday Spirituality*. Edited by Raymond Arroyo. New York: Doubleday, 2007.

Muck, Mellis and Anna Keating. *The Catholic Catalogue: A Field Guide to the Daily Acts That Make Up a Catholic Life*. New York: Image Books, 2016.

Nolan, Geraldine. *A View of Padre Pio from Mary's House*. Edited by Fr. Alessio Parente. San Giovanni Rotondo, 1993.

Oben, Freda Mary, Ph.D. *Edith Stein: Scholar, Feminist, Saint*. Staten Island, NY: Alba House, 1988.

Oder, Slawomir with Saverio Gaeta. *Why He Is a Saint*. New York: Rizzoli, 2010.

Piat, Stéphane-Joseph, OFM. *Celine: Sister and Witness of St. Thérèse of the Child Jesus*. San Francisco: Ignatius Press, 1997.

Piat, Stéphane-Joseph, OFM, *Celine: Sister Genevieve of the Holy Face: Sister and Witness of Saint Thérèse of the Child Jesus*. San Francisco: Ignatius Press, 1997.

Piat, Stéphane-Joseph, OFM. *The Story of a Family: The Home of St. Thérèse of Lisieux*. Translated by a Benedictine of Stanbrook Abbey. Rockford, IL: TAN Books, 1994.

Pope Paul VI. *Gaudium et Spes*. Vatican.va, December 7, 1965.

Pope Paul VI. *Humanae Vitae*. Boston: Daughters of St. Paul, July 25, 1968.

Preziuso, Gennaro. *The Life of Padre Pio: Between the Altar and the Confessional.* New York: Alba House, 2002.

Pronechen, Joseph. "Body of St. Maria Goretti Arriving in the U.S." *National Catholic Register,* September 15, 2015. m.ncregister. com/blog/joseph-pronechen/the-body-of-st.-maria-goretti-will-soon-be-brought-to-the-u.s.-part-ii#.WjhfGkFOnYU. Accessed July 6, 2016.

Pumphrey, Louis. "Dr. Bernard Nathanson's Conversion Highlighted in Cleveland Speech 35 Years Ago." Cleveland. com, September 13, 2015. cleveland.com/articles/16929039/ dr_bernardnathansons_conversi.amp. Accessed January 15, 2016.

Ratzinger, Joseph Cardinal. *God and the World: A Conversation with Peter Seewald.* San Francisco: Ignatius Press, 2002.

Rega, Frank. *Padre Pio and America.* Rockford, IL: TAN Books, 2005.

"Richard Pampuri, OH. (1897-1930)," Vatican.va. Accessed July 7, 2017.

"Rite for the Baptism of the Child (1970 Missal)." Catholic Liturgical Library. catholicliturgy.com/index.cfm/FuseAction/ TextContents/Index/4/SubIndex/67/TextIndex/7. Accessed September 5, 2017.

Rytel-Andrianik, Pawel. "Beatification Processes of St. John Paul II's Parents Inaugurated." Zenit.org, May 8, 2020. zenit. org/articles/beatification-processes-of-st-john-paul-iis-parents-inaugurated/. Accessed May 8, 2020.

"Sayings of Saint Paul of the Cross." saintpaulofthecross.com. saintpaulofthecross.com/2009/10/words-quotes-of-st-paul-of-cross.html.

Schadt, Devin. *Joseph's Way: The Call to Fatherly Greatness-Prayer of Faith: 80 Days to Unlocking Your Power as a Father.* San Francisco: Ignatius Press, 2014.

Sheen, Ven. Fulton. *From the Angel's Blackboard: The Best of Fulton J. Sheen, A Centennial Celebration.* Edited by Patricia A. Kossmann. Liguori, MO: Triumph Books, 1995.

Sheen, Ven. Fulton. *Treasure in Clay. The Autobiography of Fulton J. Sheen.* New York: Image Books, 2008.

"Solitude." *Online Etymology Dictionary.* etymonline.com/index. php?term=solitude. Accessed May 5, 2017.

Spink, Kathryn. *Mother Teresa: An Authorized Biography.* New York: Harper One, 2011.

Spencer, Paul Francis, C.P. *As A Seal Upon Your Heart: The Life of St. Paul of the Cross, Founder of the Passionists.* Maynooth: St. Paul's, 1994.

Stein, Edith. *Life in a Jewish Family: Her Unfinished Autobiographical Account.* Edited by L. Gelber and Romaeus Leauven, O.C.D. Translated by Josephine Koeppel, O.C.D. Washington, D.C: ICS Publications, 1986.

Sterlini, Christine. "Meeting the Parents of Blessed Chiara Luce Badano," Diocese of Westminster, August 18, 2014. dowym.com/ voices/meeting-parents-blessed-chiara. Accessed January 20, 2016.

Sullivan, Robert and the editors of *Life. Pope John Paul II: A Tribute of Life.* New York: Time, 1999.

"Teresa Benedict of the Cross—Edith Stein (1891-1942) *nun, Discalced Carmelite, martyr,*" Vatican.va. Accessed August 9, 2016.

Teresa of Ávila, St. "Prayer of Saint Teresa of Avila." EWTN. com. Accessed December 8, 2017.

Teresa of Ávila, St. *The Life of Teresa of Jesus. The Autobiography of St. Teresa of Avila.* Edited and translated by E. Allison Peers. New York: Image Books, 1991.

Teresa of Calcutta, St. *A Simple Path.* New York: Random House, 1995.

Teresa of Calcutta, St., "An Address at the National Prayer Breakfast, February 3, 1994." Washington, DC. Catholic.org.

Teresa of Calcutta, St., *Mother Teresa: Come Be My Light: The Private Wrings of the "Saint of Calcutta."* Edited by Brian Kolodiejchuk, M.C. New York: Image, 2007.

Teresa of Calcutta, St., *No Greater Love.* Novato, California: New World Library, 1997.

Tertullian. "The Apologeticum." tertullian.org/works/ apologeticum.htm. Accessed November 28, 2017.

"The Divine Mercy," Divinemercy.org. Accessed November 15, 2017.

The Liturgy of the Hours, Volume IV. New York: Catholic Book Publishing Co, 1975.

Traub, George. SJ, and Debra Mooney. "St. Ignatius Loyola: Founder of the Jesuits." Xavier University, 2015. xavier.edu/ mission-identity/heritage-tradition/documents/1IgnatiusLoyola-RevisedText-June20151.pdf.

Trochu, Francis. *The Cure D'Ars*. Rockford, IL: TAN Books, 1977.

Weigel, George. *Witness to Hope*. New York: Harper Collins, 1999.

White, Beatrice, ed. *The Vulgaria of John Stanbridge and the Vulgaria of Robert Whittington*. London: Early English Text Society, 1932.

Wollenweber, Leo, OFM, CAP. *Meet Solanus Casey. Spiritual Counselor and Wonder Worker*. Cincinnati, OH: Servant Books, 2002.

Wojtyła, Karl. *Love and Responsibility*. Translated by H.T. Willets. San Francisco: Ignatius Press, 1993.

Wust, Louis and Marjorie Wust. *Louis Martin: An Ideal Father*. Boston: Daughters of St. Paul, 1957.

Wust, Louis and Marjorie Wust. *Zelie Martin: Mother of St. Thérèse*. Boston: Daughters of St. Paul, 1969.

Zani, Lino, and Marilu Simoneschi. *The Secret Life of John Paul II*. Charlotte, NC: Saint Benedict's Press, 2012.

Zanzucchi, Michele. *Chiara Luce : A life lived to the full*. Translated by Frank Johnson. London: New City, 2017.

Zdrojewski, Mary Felicita, CSSF. *To Weave a Garment: The Story of Maria Dabrowska Kolbe, Mother of Saint Maximilian Kolbe*. Enfield, CT: Felician Sisters, 1989.

INDEX

Parents of St. Josemaría Escrivá (*José and Dolores Escrivá*)
Parents of St. Katherine Drexel (*Francis and Emma Drexel*)
Parents of St. Louis de Montfort (*Jean-Baptiste and Jeanne Grignion*)
Parents of St. Louis Martin (*Pierre and Marie-Anne Martin*)
Parents of Servant of God, Sr. Lucia dos Santos (*Antonio and Maria Rosa dos Santos*)
Parents of St. Maria Goretti (*Luigi and Assunta Goretti*)
Parents of St. Martin de Porres (*Don Juan de Porres and Anna Velázquez*)
Parents of St. Maximilian Kolbe (*Julius and Maria Kolbe*)
Parents of St. Nicholas of Tolentino (*Compagnonus and Amata de Guarutti*)
Parents of St. Padre Pio (*Grazio and Maria Forgione*)
Parents of St. Paul of the Cross (*Luca and Anna Maria Danei*)
Parents of St. Philip Neri (*Francesco and Lucrezia Neri*)
Parents of Pope St. Pius X (*Giovanni and Margarita Sarto*)
Parents of St. Riccardo Pampuri (*Innocenzo and Angela Pampuri*)
Parents of St. Robert Bellarmine (*Vincenzo and Cinzia Bellarmine*)
Parents of Bl. Solanus Casey (*Bernard and Ellen Casey*)
Parents of St. Teresa Benedicta of the Cross (*Siegfried and Auguste Stein*)
Parents of St. Teresa of Ávila (*Alonso and Beatriz Sánchez de Cepeda*)
Parents of St. Teresa of Calcutta (*Nikola and Dranafile Bojaxhiu*)
Parents of St. Thérèse of Lisieux (*Sts. Louis and Zélie Martin*)
Parents of St. Thomas More (*John and Agnes More*)
Parents of St. Zélie Martin (*Isidore and Louise-Jeanne Guérin*)